# Beech Aircraft

*Beech Model A36 Bonanza (N8154L) in 1994.* (A J Pelletier collection)

# Beech Aircraft and their Predecessors

A J Pelletier

Naval Institute Press

*'It takes a Beechcraft to beat a Beechcraft'*



First published in Great Britain in 1995 by
Putnam Aeronautical Books,
an imprint of Brassey's (UK) Ltd,
33 John Street,
London WC1N 2 AT

Published and distributed in the United States
of America and Canada by the
Naval Institute Press
118 Maryland Avenue, Annapolis, Maryland 21402-5035

Library of Congress Catalog Card No.
95-69497

ISBN 1-55750-062-2

This edition is authorized for sale only
in the United States, its territories
and possessions, and Canada



Manufactured in Great Britain

# Contents

# Preface and Acknowledgements

'Well, we've got an airplane. Now let's see if we can sell a couple!', Walter H Beech said one day, when considering the brand new Beech 17 Staggerwing his engineers had just designed. As a tremendous salesman, Walter H Beech had only one idea in mind all his life, market and sell the best aircraft in the world. More than sixty years after the Beech Aircraft Company had been established, the least we can say is that the Beech adventure was quite a success. To date, more than 50,000 aircraft have been delivered to countless customers throughout the world, ranging from the elegant Model 17 Staggerwing to the innovative Model 2000 Starship, not to mention the ubiquitous Model 18 and Bonanza. In fact, the aircraft designed by the Wichita-based company not only won the respect of their owners but had became a true reference in the aviation world and today, more than ever, Beechcraft remains deeply committed in the research for perfection.

When I was asked to write this book about Travel Air and Beech aircraft I was simply not aware of the important role this company had played in aviation history, and I underestimated the complexity of the Beech aircraft family. As the book progressed I discovered its richness. This volume is somewhat thicker than I originally expected. As my research continued, I was faced with another problem, had the Travel Air designs to be included in the book? After much discussion with some fellow historians, I decided to do so, aware of the fact that there was absolutely no formal connection between the two companies and from a purely historical standpoint Travel Air and Beech Aircraft were entirely separate entities, despite the fact that both companies used the same facilities and the same people to a great extent. Therefore, this book is divided into two separate parts, one devoted to Travel Air designs and the other to Beech designs. With such a vast subject, there have been limits to the exhaustiveness of detail that can be included, that is why here and there performance and data figures have been intentionally restricted.

* * *

This book is the work of a team of people throughout the world. First of all, I am indebted to several fellow historians for reading and correcting parts of my manuscript, namely Peter M Bowers and Gary L Killion. Many other friends around the world shared their files with me. My special thanks go to André Bréand, Jean Brugaro, Robert L Burns, Dustin W Carter, Juan Arraez Cerda, Michel Cristescu, Jean Delmas, René J Francillon, Joseph G Handelman, Gordon B Inglis, Benjamin Knowles Jr, Keith Palmer, John L Parish, Edward H Phillips, Tom K Rayer, Louis Sampité, Rod W Simpson, Martin R Smith, Carl J Waldenmaier, John Wegg, John Zimmerman, and all those I may have overlooked.

Although this book has not been sponsored by Beech, public affairs managers assisted with photographs and information wherever possible, namely Mike Potts and Pat A Zerbe. My thanks also to Allison Gas Turbine (Jim D Jackson), Colemill Enterprises, Continental Airlines, Excalibur Aviation Co. (Michael M Davis), National Air and Space Museum, Raisbeck Engineering Inc., RAM Aircraft Corp. (Chuck Morrow), Scaled Composites (Kaye LeFebvre), Short Brothers PLC, Sierra Industries Inc (Peter W Conrad), Smithsonian Institution, Tradewind Turbines (Joe C Boyd).

A very special thanks to my San Francisco friend René J Francillon for his very valuable assistance, and my gratitude to the Putnam editorial team as well as to Carl G Ahremark who produced most of the general arrangement drawings.

ALAIN J PELLETIER
Gif, April 1994

# Author's Notes

This book conforms with most other Putnam titles. Only the histories of aircraft have been covered and these are presented in chronological order of first flight year. Where applicable the aeroplanes are identified by both Travel Air and Curtiss-Wright, or Beechcraft and US Forces designation. As far as Beech aircraft are concerned, several types, such as Queen Airs and King Airs, have been spread in different chapters when evolution from one variant to another are salient. The Models, variants and sub-variants have been judged too numerous to include exhaustive technical data for each of them. Nevertheless a selection of comprehensive data and performance have been included for the main types and some significant variants. At the end of the book, numerous appendixes are included and devoted to selected projects, milestones, production details, etc.

## Travel Air Designations

The first Travel Air aeroplane was simply that – the Travel Air. As improved and new models appeared, they were designated Models B and C, and the original model became Model A. In 1927, the model numbers were changed to a consecutive series of 'thousands', starting with Model 2000. Variants of the basic biplane, and new models, got additional thousand designations through 9000, after which the system was changed again. It has been implied that the original Model A Travel Airs became the Model 1000, but this cannot be verified. After Model 9000 was reached, the system was changed to place all Travel Air biplanes under the 4000 designation, with prefix letters used to identify the particular powerplant. The procedure was systematic but inconsistent. The Model A-4000 used the Axelson engine, but the B-4000 had the Wright J-5 engine of the standard Model 4000 and a new outrigger undercarriage. Model C-4000 had the Curtiss Challenger engine, but the D-4000 had shortened Speedwings' for airshow aerobatics and racing. The E-4000 of 1929 had the new Wright J-6-5 Whirlwind engine. Sometimes the prefixes were doubled, as the DW-4000 being a Model 4000 with Speedwings and a Warner Scarab engine. Other prefix letters had double meanings, such as 'S' used either to identify seaplane versions or in other cases to identify a Curtiss OXX-6 engine used in place of an OX-5.

After the merger with Curtiss-Wright in 1929, the designation system was changed again. Models already in production were to be produced under their existing 'thousand' designations, but modifications developed after that received their 'thousand' designations shortened to single digit variations of the basic Model 4000 becoming Model 4, with appropriate prefixes and suffixes. Entirely new models started with Model 10, but true Travel Air designs ended with Model 11. Models 12 to 16, although designed by the same team and built originally in the same Wichita plant, must be regarded as Curtiss-Wright designs and introduced an entirely new serial numbering system.

## Beech Designations

For a long period, Beech Model numbers were allocated in sequential order, variants being given prefix and suffix letters. At a later date, this designation system was used in a different way. Chosen Model numbers were not necessarily given in sequential order, thereby creating gaps.

However, one may wonder why there are model designations such as 35-33, 65-80, 95-55, etc. This was due to a very incorrect policy decision an office of the CAA made. In order for a Type Certificate to be amended to include a new model, the new model was required to have a model designation in the same numerical series as the models already on the Type Certificate. Since the Debonair was the Model 33, Beech was told that Type Certificate 3A15 could not be amended to include the Model 33 in addition to the Model 35 Bonanza series already on it. In order to get around that policy, Beech simply called the Debonair the Model 35-33. Eventually, it was recognised that there was no legal basis for that policy and it was also creating considerable confusion. The Model D33 was, therefore, type certificated as such rather than as the 35D33!

Manufacturer's serial numbers, generally called constructor's numbers or c/n, were allocated within different sequences. Beech c/n sequences begin with a primary prefix and then sometimes a type prefix (both letters) followed by the production sequence number.

The US military designations, where applicable, were given in the traditional way with the usual sequence of type symbol letter, model number, series letter, block number, and letters. For Beech, the manufacturer identification letters were as follows:

BH for Beech Aircraft Corp, Wichita, Kansas.
GF for Globe Aircraft, Fort Worth, Texas.
CCF for Canadian Car and Foundry.

# Origin and Corporate History

The son of Cornelius and Tommie (Hay) Beech, Walter Hershel Beech was born in Pulaski, Tennessee, on 30 January 1891. As a youth he showed mechanical aptitude, performing repair and installation work in sawmills and municipal power plants. The fever of flying caught him quite early and he made his first venture into the field of aeronautics while he was 14-years old. Using his mother's new bed sheets and a wooden frame, he built a glider. While his attempt to fly ended disastrously for the glider, the incident did not lessen his enthusiasm for flying.

After attending public schools and Giles College in his native city, he was employed by an automobile company in Minneapolis, Minnesota. For two years he travelled in Europe as a sales representative for this company. While in Minneapolis, he made his first recorded solo flight in a Curtiss pusher-type biplane which he acquired as a wreck and repaired in a workshop outside. On 11 July 1914 W H Beech, with little instruction from the previous owner, flew the aircraft from a meadow on his first try. From that moment flying became his prime interest.

In 1917 he joined the aviation section of the United States Army Signal Corps, and as a pilot and engine expert, he was assigned to Kelly Field, Texas, where he instructed young pilots and was recognised for taking part in record-setting ferrying operations. At the close of the 1914–18 War, he remained in the Service where, as an instructor, he continued to give student fliers the benefit of his flying and mechanical experience.

He resigned and, for a year, joined in the barnstorming and exhibition flying that focused the attention of much of the nation on aviation. In war-surplus Standard and Curtiss Jenny biplanes, he visited nearly every State. Flying under all kinds of operating conditions, he gained valuable insight into flying techniques and equipment design which were to guide him in his later career.

In 1921, he began his association of nearly thirty years with Wichita, an oil-prosperous booming south central Kansas city. The second of the early aeroplane firms to be established in Wichita had produced

*The Beech Model G17S c/n B-4 (NC80305) was delivered to J W Reid Co of Houston, Texas, on 24 August 1946.* (Beech)

*Swallow biplane (Wright J4 engine) operated by Varney Air Lines in June 1926.* (courtesy of United Airlines)

*Walter H Beech* (left) *and Brice H Goldsborough* (right) *winners of the 1926 Ford Reliability Tour, in Pioneer Instrument equipped Travel Air BW.* (Beech)

the Laird Swallow, a three-seat tandem open-cockpit biplane. The president of the company, Jacob Mollendick, offered W H Beech a position as test pilot and demonstrator, and he promptly accepted. Believing that the best way to sell an aeroplane was to demonstrate what it could do, W H Beech flew the Swallow in airshows throughout the country and, in 1921, he won his first trophies, awarded for his skill in aerobatics contests and races.

In 1923, with the reorganisation of Laird as the Swallow Airplane Manufacturing Company (the aeroplane being called the New Swallow), W H Beech was put in charge of all field work. As his contributions to design and sales rose in importance, he was advanced to vice-president and general manager. Despite the company's success with the Swallow, a dispute arose over the question of whether metal or wood should be used to frame the new Swallow fuselage. W H Beech was one of those favouring metal, in opposition to J Mollendick. Determined to prove the advantage of the metal frame, W H Beech and others decided to resign from Swallow. W H Beech then organised, in 1924, a new aeroplane company in Wichita.

# Travel Air Manufacturing Co

In a space of just 900 square feet, in a leased portion of an old planing mill building, W H Beech and his group went to work to design and produce their new aircraft, which was at first unnamed. At the suggestion of a Wichita businessman the name *Travel Air* was eventually adopted. Early in 1925, the first Travel Air was completed. As a three-seat open-cockpit design powered by a war-surplus Curtiss OX-5 engine, it incorporated many of the design principles which W H Beech had proved in his barnstorming and racing experience.

W H Beech led the Travel Air Manufacturing Company in producing aircraft with the very latest equipment and design advantages.

In 1925, he was instrumental in the company's design of the first United States commercial cabin aircraft with liquid-cooled engine completely faired-in, a concept which was followed on all Travel Airs from that time, and was adopted throughout the industry. W H Beech also took up a personal campaign of promotion by competing in air meetings. Most notable of his many victories in Travel Airs was the sensational winning of the 1926 Ford Commercial Airplane Reliability Tour in a Travel Air equipped with Pioneer instruments, and with Brice Goldsborough as navigator. On this occasion, he demonstrated the practicability of flying blind on instruments, and led the twelve-day tour of fourteen cities over forty entrants to bring home the Edsel Ford Trophy.

W H Beech devoted more and more of his time to the manufacturing end of the business, turning over the racing of Travel Airs to others. It was a design competition, in fact, which sparked the creation of the famous Travel Air Model 5000, the first United States aircraft built to airline specifications. In 1927, after producing more than two hundred biplanes, Travel Air built its first monoplanes. Their success exceeded even that of his biplanes. Two dramatic performances added much to the reputation of the company. The first was the winning of the 1927 Dole Race. Art Goebel, with William Davis as co-pilot, flew the Phillips Petroleum Company's *Woolaroc* Travel Air from Oakland, California, to Wheeler Field, Hawaii, to capture the $25,000 first prize. The second outstanding victory was won in 1929, when the Travel Air Model R, later named the *Mystery Ship* was entered in and won the National Air Races' 50-mile closed course free-for-all (event No.26). This marked the first occasion on which a civilian aircraft defeated a military aircraft in speed competition. Showing their heels to nearly all comers in racing events and setting endurance and altitude records, Travel Air aircraft reaped tremendous popularity. Production boomed, reaching approximately 1,000 units in 1929, to make the Travel Air Company the world's largest producer of both monoplane and biplane commercial aircraft.

*Second location of Travel Air Airplane Mfg Co in West Douglas, Wichita. The text on the window says: Large or small, we lead them all.* (P M Bowers collection)

Late in that same year, Travel Air entered into a new organisational set-up. The Company was merged with the gigantic Curtiss-Wright Corporation. W H Beech became the president of Curtiss-Wright Airplane Company and vice-president in charge of sales of the Curtiss-Wright Corporation.

*Walter H Beech in front of 160hp Curtiss C-6 powered Travel Air B6.* (Beech)

HOME OF TRAVEL AIR

(Circa 1927)

From a 30 x 30 foot space in the rear of an old planning mill, the Travel Air Company had, in only three years time, expanded its facilities to include this new manufacturing hangar located four miles east of Wichita's city limits.

*The Travel Air factory, four miles east of Wichita, in 1928.* (Beech)

In 1930, W H Beech married Olive Ann Mellor, his secretary and office manager at the Travel Air Company who had joined Travel Air in 1925. They eventually had two daughters, Suzanne (Mrs Thomas N Warner), born in 1937, and Mary Lynn (Mrs William L Oliver Jr) born in 1940.

## Beech Aircraft Company is born

W H Beech's duties with Curtiss-Wright took him to New York City, but he did not take to the life of a big city executive. Accustomed to being on the front line of designing and manufacturing, as well as selling, he resigned from Curtiss-Wright in 1932, still moved by his ambition to built the finest aeroplanes in the world. The economic situation in America was critical. In 1932, the entire aviation industry produced only 549 commercial aircraft valued at a little more than two million dollars. In the darkest year of the great depression, when business spirits generally were as low as prices, W H and O A Beech moved back to Wichita. They took with them a handful of employees from Travel Air and, in April 1932 established the Beech Aircraft Company. Walter was the president and Olive Ann was appointed secretary-treasurer and director. One of these employees was Ted Wells, a Princeton University graduate who was recognised as one of the top aeronautical engineers. He was named vice-president and chief engineer.

In small quarters rented in a depression-closed Wichita factory, W H Beech and his staff went to work. Their objective was to design and built a five-seat closed-cabin biplane with the luxury and comfort of a fine sedan, a top speed of 200mph and a nonstop range close to 1,000 miles.

Determination and many hours of creative hard work were rewarded on 4 November 1932 when the first Beechcraft, the Model 17, made its maiden flight. Its silhouette was unique, for W H Beech had taken advantage of the aerodynamic features of a little-employed design, the negative stagger wing. The prototype was eventually sold to Ethyl Corporation and at the Miami Air Races in January 1933 it captured the Texaco Trophy. This was the first of dozens of triumphs which Beechcrafts were to post down through the years.

Early in 1934, Beech Aircraft had become a full aircraft manufacturer and the company was moved back to the familiar surroundings of the former Travel Air Company factory and aerodrome six miles east of downtown Wichita. Closed since 1931, this factory resumed aircraft production on 23 April 1934. With his reputation riding on the wings of his new aircraft, W H Beech decided to enter air racing. In 1936, at the urging of his wife, he arranged for aviatrixes Louise Thaden and Blanche Noyes to fly a Beechcraft Model 17 in the Bendix Transcontinental Speed Dash. Both women not only won the nation's most famous cross-country race, beating their nearest competitor by almost 45min, but they also set a new transcontinental speed record for women and earned a $10,000 cash prize.

More and more records fell to the Beechcraft Model 17 and the slogan *It takes a Beechcraft to beat a Beechcraft* made the rounds of aviation circles. Desiring versatility to please a wide range of customers, the company produced numerous Model 17 variants, ranging in top speed from 150 to 240mph (240 to 390km/h), the latter powered by a 650hp engine. With design and performance features years ahead of its time, the Model 17 became a classic among the world's aircraft. More than 780 commercial and military units were produced until 1948 and more than a hundred are still flying.

Never satisfied, W H Beech set, in 1935, the wheels turning on preliminary engineering for a second design, the twin-engined Model 18 monoplane. The new seven-seat aircraft, to be known for many years as the 'Twin Beech', was rolled from the factory for its maiden flight on 15 January 1935. This aircraft was an immediate success. On 6 January 1940 to boost interest in the Model 18, a standard Model 18, with H C Rankin as pilot and W H Beech as co-pilot, captured one of the most prized of all aviation honours, the Macfadden Trophy. The distance of more than 1,080 miles was covered in 4hr 37min at an average speed of over 234mph (376km/h). Flown throughout the world in every kind of commercial application, the Beechcraft Model 18 became known as the standard of the industry.

From 1937 to 1969, when the last 'Twin Beech' was delivered, more than 1,800 commercial Model 18s and advanced Super 18 versions had been produced. Its 33-year civil and military history constituted the longest continuous production record of any aircraft.

In 1937, John P Gaty joined the management of Beech Aircraft and was appointed vice-president in charge of sales. He would be promoted in 1942 to vice-president-general manager, to help direct the company's rapid and tremendous growth during the Second World War. That same year, the company built 199 aircraft and had 220 employees. They were 273 a year later, and 1938 brought the company's first 'over a million dollar' sales record ($1.141 million exactly).

**Beech Personnel and Sales Data, 1932–38**

| *Fiscal year* | *Government aircraft* | *Civil aircraft* | *Employee average* | *Employee peak* | *Total sales $ millions* | *Net profit $ millions* |
|---|---|---|---|---|---|---|
| 1932 | – | – | 6 | – | – | – |
| 1933 | – | 2 | 10 | – | 17 | – |
| 1934 | – | 11 | 35 | – | 174 | – |
| 1935 | 1 | 32 | 60 | – | 424 | – |
| 1936 | – | 50 | 175 | – | 444 | – |
| 1937 | 1 | 71 | 220 | – | 788 | 14 |
| 1938 | 1 | 67 | 250 | 273 | 1,141 | –2 |

## The War Years

In 1939 as war clouds gathered over the world, Beechcrafts were called upon to perform in new rôles. Late in 1940, military orders began to flood the company and all commercial production was suspended. By the end of 1940, the company had promised to provide the military with aircraft totalling more than $22 million in backlog orders. Model 18s were equipped as bomber and gunnery trainers, and Model 17s were procured as fast personnel transports for the US Army Air Corps and US Navy. The military Model 17s went into accelerated production in a factory of their own of 50,000sq ft (4,645sq m) at the south end of the Beech airport. An avalanche of orders in mid-1941 increased Beechcraft's backlog of commitments to more than $82 million. Employment too, took on a phenomenal increase. Starting from 660 employees in 1939, the company payroll increased to more than 1,990 in 1940, more than doubled the following year (5,763), and doubled again in 1943 (11,321) on its way to hitting a peak of 14,100 early in 1945.

So perfectly did the Model 18 configuration meet military requirements for trainers that more than 90 per cent of all American bombardiers and navigators learned their skills in the different versions of the *Twin Beech*. It is estimated that at least 50 per cent of the Army's multi-engine pilots received their transitional training in Beechcraft AT-10s, a predominately plywood twin-engined aircraft, so constructed to save scarce metal. Besides, in 1943, the rising demands

*Two months after the end of the Second World War, the Beechcraft D18S became the first postwar commercial aircraft to receive a government Type Certificate.* (Beech)

*The Model 26 Wichita in full production in the Beech factory. Production of the AT-10 totalled 1,771 aircraft.* (Beech)

on Douglas Aircraft Company caused that firm to look to the proven capabilities of the Beech team to produce more than 1,600 complete sets of wings for the A-26 Invader twin-engined attack aircraft. In all, during the Second World War, more than 7,400 military Beechcrafts were delivered to the armed Services, and the company received five Army-Navy E awards for production efficiency, an honour that was accorded to only 5 per cent of war contracting firms.

### Beech Personnel and Sales Data, 1939–45

| *Fiscal year* | *Government aircraft* | *Civil aircraft* | *Employee average* | *Employee peak* | *Total sales $ millions* | *Net profit $ millions* |
|---|---|---|---|---|---|---|
| 1939 | 10 | 61 | 660 | 776 | 1,328 | –91 |
| 1940 | 28 | 59 | 780 | 1,990 | 2,345 | 68 |
| 1941 | 148 | 18 | 2,354 | 5,763 | 8,062 | 472 |
| 1942 | 1,283 | 4 | 9,127 | 11,252 | 59,593 | 2,418 |
| 1943 | 2,921 | – | 10,915 | 11,321 | 126,578 | 4,036 |
| 1944 | 2,091 | – | 12,479 | 13,387 | 90,469 | 2,705 |
| 1945 | 945 | – | 9,270 | 14,100 | 123,752 | 3,722 |

## Back to Peace

With the war's end, Beech Aircraft was faced with the difficult assignment of transition from wartime to peacetime production. Employment decreased dramatically to 9,270 in 1945, and to 3,961 the following year. To put the company in a strong position for postwar business, Walter H Beech focused production refinements on the Model 17 and Model 18, and pushed design efforts on a new single-engine aircraft. Just two months after the surrender of Japan, an eight-seat deluxe variant of the Model 18 was introduced. It was the first United States postwar commercial aircraft to be licensed. Also, a new and advanced version of the reliable Model 17, the G17S, joined the civil fleet. But the company made its biggest postwar news with the introduction of the third design to bear the name Beechcraft, the all-metal, four-seat Model 35 Bonanza, easily distinguishable by its butterfly tail. Popularity of this aircraft was immediately found in the more than 500 orders placed before any detailed information had been released on its performance, and nearly 1,000 were delivered during an eight-month period in 1947. To enhance its success, two headline-making flights in 1949 helped to put the Bonanza in the spotlights. Bill Odom, flying the now-famous *Waikiki Beech*, smashed nonstop records for aircraft in the Bonanza category when he surpassed an 11-year-old record by flying from Honolulu, Hawaii, to Oakland, California in just over 22 hours. Three months later in the same year, Odom broke his own record, flying the *Waikiki Beech* from Honolulu to Teterboro, New Jersey, setting a new world record for all light aircraft.

In 1949 and 1950, as a sharp curtailment of business volume was felt throughout the nation, aircraft sales slowed down (385 aircraft sold in 1949 and 427 in 1950, against

*The Beechcraft trademark as seen on a preserved Model 17.*

*Walter H Beech.* (Beech)

**Beech Personnel and Sales Data, 1946–50**

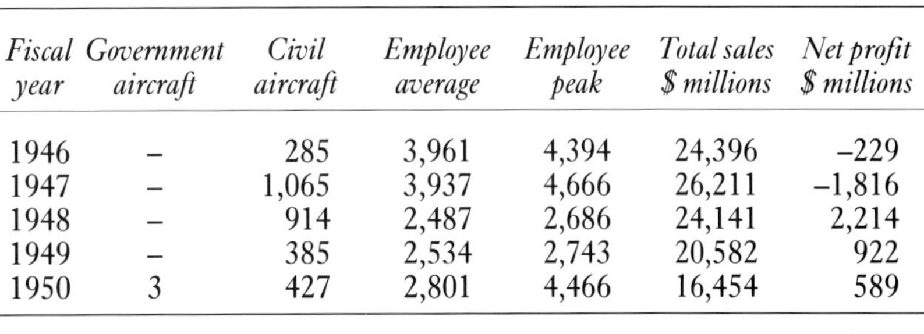

| *Fiscal year* | *Government aircraft* | *Civil aircraft* | *Employee average* | *Employee peak* | *Total sales $ millions* | *Net profit $ millions* |
|---|---|---|---|---|---|---|
| 1946 | – | 285 | 3,961 | 4,394 | 24,396 | –229 |
| 1947 | – | 1,065 | 3,937 | 4,666 | 26,211 | –1,816 |
| 1948 | – | 914 | 2,487 | 2,686 | 24,141 | 2,214 |
| 1949 | – | 385 | 2,534 | 2,743 | 20,582 | 922 |
| 1950 | 3 | 427 | 2,801 | 4,466 | 16,454 | 589 |

914 sold in 1947). Employment at Beech Aircraft plummeted to 2,200 and the company turned to non-aircraft production of corn harvesters, and a variety of aluminium assemblies for customer items to help retain a nucleus of experienced employees. Even in these troubled times, W H Beech put two new aircraft on the drawing boards. One was the Model 45 Mentor, a single-engine trainer, first flown on 2 December 1948. The second was the Model 50 Twin Bonanza, announced in July 1949. The two-seat tandem Mentor was to be ordered into production for the US Navy and the US Air Force, and produced under licence agreements in Argentina, Canada and Japan. It was also chosen by several foreign nations as a primary trainer. For its own part, the dependable Model 50 Twin Bonanza became a popular aircraft for industry. Adopted by the US Army as the L-23 (later U-8), the rugged Beechcraft saw service in Korea and became the backbone of the Army Aviation utility aircraft fleet.

In 1950, with commercial Beechcraft production slightly looking up, with two new aircraft drawing acclaim during testing and demonstration, and with a backlog of $50 million for military production on the company's books, W H Beech's success-crowned career came to an end. Active to his last day, he was stricken with a heart attack and died suddenly on the evening of 29 November 1950. The reigns of Beech Aircraft were then taken up by his widow, Olive Ann Beech, who had worked closely at his side as secretary-treasurer and director for eighteen years. That year, Beech Aircraft produced 515 aircraft, 480 of which were Bonanzas, but the company also built hundreds of jettisonable fuel tanks for US Air Force fighters such as the F-80, F-86, F-84E and F-94.

## Towards More Diversification

In 1951, Beech leased facilities at Liberal, Kansas, to enlarge manufacturing space. A seventeen-year association with Lockheed was begun that year, on a project to produce more than 6,200 wings for the Air Force T-33 and US Navy T2V-1 trainers, wings for the F-94C all-weather fighter, fuselages for the F-104 interceptor and bonded panels for the C-130 transport. Beechcraft also produced major assemblies for the Convair F-102 and F-106 century-fighters as well as for the B-58 Hustler. Another long-term team operation was begun with McDonnell Aircraft in 1953 when Beechcraft began deliveries of nose major assemblies for the F-101A/RF-101A Voodoo. Under a sub-contract agreement in 1953, Beechcraft supplied flaps and ailerons for the Republic F-84F.

In 1955, in a forward-looking move, Beech Aircraft opened its Boulder Division (Colorado) to pursue a diversified programme of Research and Development, and production of rocket, missile and space vehicle systems, such as the feasibility of liquid hydrogen storage systems, verification of components for Boeing's Dyna-Soar, the Minuteman missile, the Centaur booster

*Aerial view of Beech aircraft Corp plant. Travel Air buildings can still be seen.* (P M Bowers collection)

and the Saturn V moon rocket. For North American Rockwell's Space Division, Beech developed a highly sophisticated cryogenic gas storage system for the Apollo spacecraft. In 1956 a new model was added to the company's growing line. It was the twin-engined Model 95 Travel Air. In the same year, Beech Aircraft established a wholly-owned subsidiary, Beech Acceptance Corporation, and entered the field of missile targets with the production of the KDB-1 for the US Navy. Over the same period, Beechcraft produced thousands of C-26 (1951), MD-3 (1954) and MA-3 (1956) multipurpose, self-propelled ground power units to support USAF aircraft such as the B-47 and B-52.

During the three successive years, three new Models were added to the production line: the Model 65 Queen Air in 1958, the Model 33 Debonair in 1959 and the Model 55 Baron in 1960. The year 1961 saw the introduction of the single-engine Model 23 Musketeer and the twin-engined Model 80 Queen Air, both certificated by FAA on the same day, 20 February 1962. In 1962, the US Navy awarded Beech Air an initial contract for the production of AQM-37A (KD2B-1) target missiles and, a year later, the German Federal Republic was the first NATO country to order Model 1001 missile targets. Then in 1963, production of the Musketeer was assigned to Liberal. The same year, production was initiated on major assemblies for the McDonnell F4B/RF-4B and F-4C/RF-4C Phantom II, and late that year, the company announced its most sophisticated model to date, the King Air, a fast, pressurised, turbine-powered corporate transport.

In 1965 total available models were increased to 15. The new models introduced were the pressurised Queen Air 88 and the turbocharged V35TC Bonanza. Milestones reached during 1965 included deliveries of the 8,000th Bonanza, of the 1,000th Debonair and the first delivery of the Queen Airliner to Commuter Airlines of Chicago. The company was also called upon to produce bomb dispensers and containers for the US Army. Commercial product activity continued its accelerated pace during 1966 with the first flight of the Model 56TC Turbo Baron, the delivery of the 1,000th Baron, the delivery of the 25,000th Beechcraft (a King Air A90 to Westinghouse Corporation), the first flights of the Model 60 Duke and Model 99 Airliner.

In 1967 the 35th anniversary year of the founding of Beech Aircraft, production lines were expanded through the introduction of the Models E33 and E33A Bonanzas, the E95 Travel Air, the D55 Baron and the B90 King Air. In 1966 and 1967, for exceptional quality production of metal-bonded panels for the Bell UH-1D, Beech Aircraft received the Bell Gold Rotor Award, but the largest sub-contract for helicopter production was announced in March 1968, calling for production and delivery of more than 4,000 complete airframes, under a five-year $75 million award, for Bell's Model 206 JetRanger commercial and army observation helicopters. Production of these airframes was assigned to Wichita Plant III and initial deliveries to Fort Worth began in October 1968.

*Beechcraft Model V35B Bonanza.* (Beech)

# An Historic Turn

On 18 January 1968, O A Beech announced an historic move in turning over the presidency of Beech Aircraft Corporation to her nephew Frank E Hedrick, executive vice-president since 1960. Mrs Beech, after nearly two decades of service as president, continued as chairman of the Board and chief executive officer. New Beechcrafts making their debuts that year were the aerobatic Musketeer Sport and Custom, the Bonanza E33B and E33C and the Bonanza 36. The same year, the International Exposition of Flight honoured Beech Aircraft with its Industry Award, and the last ten Super H18s were ordered by Japan. This transaction extended production of the Model 18 into 1969.

After a production slowdown in 1971 with only 544 aircraft produced, 1972 saw the first flight of the Model 200 Super King Air. Production increased steadily over the following years (785 aircraft built in 1972, 998 in 1973 and 1,262 in 1974). In 1974, Beech was awarded a sub-contract to produce the power reactant storage assembly for the Space Shuttle Orbiter. In September 1975, Beech Aircraft and Hawker Siddeley Aviation Ltd, terminated by mutual consent a five-year agreement under which Beech Hawker Corp marketed the Hawker 125-400 and -600 in North America. Between 1970 and 1975, 64 Hs 125s had been delivered through this subsidiary.

In 1976 2,214 aircraft were built and Beech announced receipt of a $9.6 million follow-on contract for continued production of airframes for the Bell JetRanger II. A year later, Beech Aircraft observed 30 years of V-tail Bonanza production by sponsoring a nation-wide tour of the 10,000th Bonanza Model 35, and delivered its 40,000th aircraft, a Model 58TC. Production marked a peak in 1979 with 1,657 aircraft produced, and similar levels were achieved the two following years (1,446 in 1980 and 1,336 in 1981). At the end of 1979, Beech, which was the last of the prewar aviation companies in America to remain under the direction of the founding family, agreed to merge with Raytheon Co. This merger received the approval of the stockholders on 8 February 1980. Unfortunately, shortly after the deal was finalised, the general aviation market entered an eight-year depression. The 1981 performance was down, cut by a half in 1982 with only 772 aircraft built, and slowed once again in 1983 with 466 civil aircraft leaving the production lines. The worst was still to come as only 232 aircraft were built in 1986.

*The Beechcraft Model C90 King Air was introduced in 1971.* (Beech)

In 1983, Linden S Blue became vice-president and the company announced the Model 2000 Starship, an advanced revolutionary business aircraft making use of composite materials, and a 19-seat regional transport, the Model 1900 which entered service in late 1983. A year later, Linden S Blue was replaced at the head of the company by James S Walsh who, in turn, was replaced by Max E Bleck in May 1987. Meanwhile, the flagship of the company, namely the Starship, had accomplished its first flight on 15 February 1986 and a few weeks before Beech had acquired from Mitsubishi the Diamond II programme, enabling the Wichita company to enter the business jet market. Known as the Model 400, it was followed in 1989 by the Model 400A improved version and, in 1991, by the T-1A Jayhawk, the winning entry of the USAF's JPTAS competition. That year too, on 1 March, Jack Braly, former vice-president-operations, responsible for manufacturing the company's full line of aircraft, replaced Max E Bleck as president.

The early 1990s saw more company expansion with the introduction of the larger Model 1900D. By mid-1991, Beech Plant IV had to be extended for the Jayhawk production, and, in 1992, Beech opened an office in Munich, to enhance its sales and support operation for the regional airline market in Europe.

*Olive Ann Beech.*

*The innovative Beechcraft Model 2000 Starship received FAA certification in June 1988.* (Beech)

# Beech Today

Beech today is a company with annual sales in excess of $1 billion, and about a half of the annual revenue is generated from the manufacture and sale of new commercial aircraft. The remainder comes primarily from military aircraft, target missiles sales, and the activities of its two major subsidiaries, Beech Holding Inc and Beech Aerospace Services Inc (BASI) of Madison, Mississipi, as well as sub-contract manufacturing for such firms as Boeing (Boeing 737 control surfaces) and McDonnell-Douglas (winglets and composite undercarriage doors for C-17 Globemaster III). Beech Holdings operates a network of 19 fixed base operations (FBOs) across the United States. Other subsidiaries are Beech Acceptance Corporation Inc and Travel Air Insurance Company Ltd.

Beech aircraft has about 10,900 employees worldwide and occupies 4,000,000sq ft (371,612sq m) of plant area at its two major facilities in Wichita and Salina, Kansas. The magical number of 50,000 aircraft produced was reached during 1992, and total production had reached 50,342 at the start of 1993, a quite honourable score for a little company founded in April 1932 by a handful of individuals. But time had flown, and sadly, on 6 July 1993 Olive Ann Beech died at her home in Wichita. An important part of Beech history was now over.

# Travel Air

## Travel Air No.1 and Model A

The formation of the Travel Air Manufacturing Co was announced on 26 January 1925 by Walter P Innes Jr, president and treasurer, as well as the construction of a three-seat, Curtiss OX-5 powered biplane. At the time, William 'Bill' Snook acted as the factory manager, Clyde Vernon Cessna was vice-president, Walter H Beech was secretary and Lloyd C Stearman was chief engineer. As the new born company had no factory, the Breitwieser brothers (Fred, Bert and Ernest) put their Kansas Planing Mill Co as well as some tooling at their disposal.

The first Travel Air aeroplane, commonly known as No.1, was designed by Stearman. It was rather classical and retained a straightforward construction, with a welded chrome-moly steel-tube fuselage and spruce/plywood wings braced with steel wires. For the wings, Stearman selected a British Fage and Collins aerofoil section and chose as the engine the reliable and ubiquitous 90hp Curtiss OX-5. On 13 March 1925 the disassembled aeroplane was trucked to the California Section, south of Wichita, were she was re-assembled and readied for her maiden flight. This was accomplished on the same day by Irl Beach, and load carrying tests were made under the control of the National Aeronautic Association representative, L S Seymour. All these preliminary tests proved to be successful and the Travel Air team prepared to start production. In due course, W H Beech started demonstration flights and pamphlets were distributed to prospective customers. The first sale occurred when W H Beech sold the No.1 to O E Scott.

During March and April 1925, six OX-5 engined aircraft were built and more orders were coming in every week. Three more aircraft were delivered to customers in Tulsa, Oklahoma, two to customers in Moline and O E Scott purchased five more machines for use in St Louis. Even a detective agency, the International Automotive Protection Association of Ponca City, Oklahoma, ordered an aircraft. This aeroplane was similar in every respect to the standard Travel Air but it had a special storage compartment in the fuselage for dogs and guns.

*Travel Air Model No.1 near Wichita with Walter H Beech at the controls.* (Beech)

*The Travel Air Model A was powered by a war-surplus 90hp Curtiss OX-5 engine and had 'elephant ear' ailerons.* (P M Bowers collection)

As a matter of fact, at first, none of these aeroplanes had a specific designation, they were simply called Travel Airs or, as the advertisements said, 'Travel Air 3-place OX-5 powered commercial aeroplanes'. By May 1925, some 15 aircraft were on order and the workspace of the company reached a limit, that is why 80 acres were purchased at the East Central flying field. Unfortunately, the actual number of aircraft built could not be determined precisely up to now.

### Travel Air No.1

One 90hp Curtiss OX-5.

Span 33ft (10.06m); length 23ft 6in (7.16m); height 8ft 6in (2.59m); wing area 300sq ft (27.87sq m).

Empty weight 1,300lb (589kg); gross weight 2,050lb (928kg); wing loading 6.83lb/sq ft (33.29kg/sq m); power loading 22.78lb/hp (10.3kg/hp).

Maximum speed 96.5mph (155km/h) at sea level.

## Model B and B6C Special

The Travel Air Model B was a refinement of the Model A. The plain Model B featured a divided-axle undercarriage while retaining the surplus Curtiss OX-5 engine. Besides, three variants using different powerplants were also produced: the BH, BW and B6C models. Unfortunately, the exact number of Model Bs which were built remains unknown to date. However, it is known that, by 31 December 1927 Travel Air had built and delivered 162 Model Bs, 16 Model BWs and 5 Model BHs.

### Model BH

This variant was powered by a 150hp V-8 Wright-Hispano A, better known as the Hisso engine (in the BH designation, H stood for Hisso) and had a 2,100lb (951kg) gross weight. Few were produced and some of them were later registered as Model 3000s.

### Model BW

The Model BWs (W standing for Wright) had a 200hp Wright J-4 Whirlwind radial engine installed. One of these was completed for the Pioneer Instrument Co with new flight and engine instruments installed. This aircraft, which featured a slightly larger fuselage and wheel brakes, was finished at the end of July 1926 and entered the Ford Reliability Tour with W H Beech

*The Model BH was powered by a 150hp Wright A engine. All Travel Air Model Bs had the forward flying wires attached to the fuselage at the rear of the engine cowling.* (P M Bowers collection)

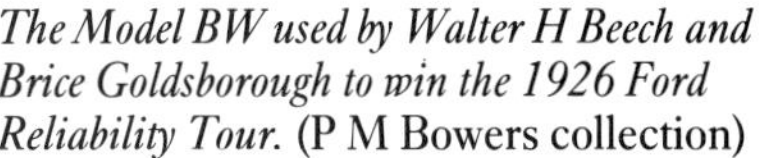
*The Model BW used by Walter H Beech and Brice Goldsborough to win the 1926 Ford Reliability Tour.* (P M Bowers collection)

and Brice Goldsborough as crew members. Thanks to outstanding navigation, the two men won the Tour, as well as the Edsel Ford Trophy. This particular aircraft then participated in the Sesqui Air Meet which was held in Philadelphia in September 1926 where it was sold. Most Model BWs eventually appeared on the US civil register as Model 4000s (which see).

## Model B6C Special

In 1925, Lloyd Stearman and Mac Short, who had just graduated from MIT, designed a racing aeroplane powered with a six-cylinder Curtiss C-6A developing 160hp at 1,750rpm. It was expected to fly at 120mph (190km/h) and was known as the Travel Air Special. This aircraft had shorter wingspan, a shorter fuselage and a small aerofoil was placed over the cross bar between the V-type undercarriage. Another special feature was the radiator which could be partially raised in flight to minimise the drag. These modifications had a bad influence on the gross weight which increased by 150lb (68kg). Construction of the Model B6C began at the end of July 1925, and a month or so later, on 30 August, the black and gold painted biplane accomplished her maiden flight with W H Beech at the controls, just in time to enter the Tulsa Air Meet. Flying OX-5 Travel Airs, C Cessna, M Short and L Stearman were also present. W H Beech won the 30-mile air race in 15min 29sec; Stearman won the On-to-Tulsa race for heaviest load carried and Mac Short won the On-to-Tulsa race for stock aeroplanes.

In the first Ford tour, held from 28 September to 4 October 1925, three Travel Airs were also entered: an OX-5 engined aeroplane piloted by E 'Rusty' Campbell (race No.0), an OXX-6 powered aircraft piloted by Francis 'Chief' Bowhan (race No.2) and the Special piloted by W H Beech (race No.4), and these three aircraft were among the eleven machines which finished the Ford Reliability Tour. After sale to the West Coast Travel Air dealer, the

*The Travel B6C, also known as the 'Special', was fitted with a 160hp Curtiss engine and a mechanically raised or lowered radiator. This aircraft finished the Ford Reliability Tour with a perfect score, carrying a 201 per cent overload.* (D W Carter collection)

Special was purchased by Pacific Air Transport in December 1926. It was then fitted with a 200hp Wright J-4 Whirlwind radial engine and converted to a mailplane, but eventually crashed at Shasta Springs, California, on 22 January 1928.

* * *

The wreck of the Travel Air B c/n 150 (registered C100) which had been badly damaged at Glovesville, New York, on 14 May 1927 was delivered to Sikorsky which converted it as a 43ft (13.11m) wingspan parasol monoplane.

### Model B6C

One 160hp Curtiss C-6A.
Span, upper 31ft 6in (9.6m), span, lower 25ft 2in (7.67m); length 24ft 1in (7.34m).
Gross weight 2,542lb (1,151kg); power loading 15.89lb/hp (7.19kg/hp).
Maximum speed 125mph (201km/h).

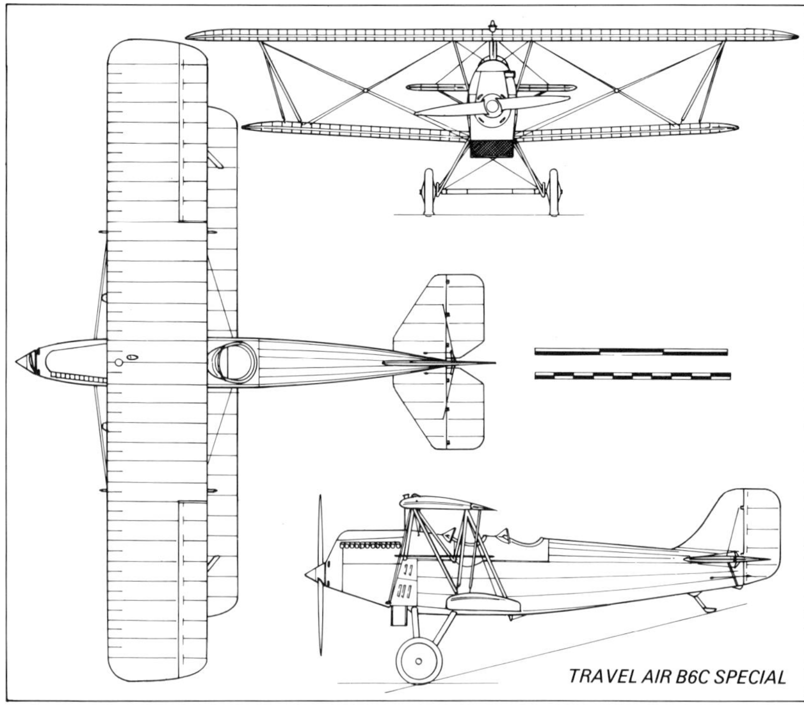

TRAVEL AIR B6C SPECIAL

## Model C/ Model 7000

Introduced in 1926, the Model C was larger than the Model As and Bs with a span of 42ft (12.8m) and a gross weight of 3,000lb (1,360kg). It had wings using a Clark Y aerofoil section, and accommodation for four passengers in a cabin between the wings, while the pilot was located in an open cockpit behind the wings. Only four aircraft of the C model are known to have been built in 1926/27, and in 1927, the existing Model Cs became collectively known as Model 7000s. Two variants were developed.

### Model CH

Introduced in July 1926, this variant was powered by a 180hp V-8 Wright-Hispano A (or Hisso I) engine and therefore designated Model CH. It was eventually sold to a private owner.

### Model CW

The Model CW appeared in 1927, powered either with a 200hp Wright J-4 Whirlwind or a 220hp Wright J-5. Three Model CWs were built among which one (c/n 134, registered C-194) was operated by AAT Inc, in Anchorage, Alaska, either on skis or on floats. This particular aircraft, powered by a 200hp Wright J-4B Whirlwind en-

*Only four Travel Air Model Cs were built.* (P M Bowers collection)

gine, was destroyed in a crash on 16 September 1929.

### Model CW

One 220hp Wright J-5C.

Span 42ft (12.80m); length 26ft 5in (8.05m); height 8ft 11in (2.72m); wing area 383sq ft (35.58sq m).

Empty weight 2,140lb (969kg); maximum take-off weight 3,719lb (1,685kg); wing loading 9.7lb/sq ft (47.35kg/sq m); power loading 18.59lb/hp (8.42kg/hp).

Maximum speed 107mph (172km/h) at sea level; cruising speed 90mph (145km/h); range 375 miles (603km).

# Model 5000

In October 1926 National Air Transport (NAT) sent out a request for bids for a transport aircraft for mail and passengers to be powered by a single Wright Whirlwind engine. The new transport was to have at least 100cu ft of cargo space and be capable of carrying a 1,000lb (453kg) load at 105mph (170km/h). NAT also specified that a demonstrator had to be available for flight evaluation within two months. The Travel Air Co board decided to bid on the NAT programme even though the response time was fairly short. In 38 days, the team led by Walter Beech and Clyde Cessna designed, constructed and delivered the prototype Travel Air Model 5000 to NAT for evaluation.

The Model 5000 broke with the biplane tradition. It was a high-wing monoplane with a 51ft 7in (15.72m) wing span. The single Wright J-5-C Whirlwind radial engine provided 230hp and its mounting had been designed to allow an engine change within 20 minutes. The pilot sat well above the passenger cabin in a heated cockpit under a fully enclosed jettisonable canopy. Travel Air designed the cabin to make the passengers as comfortable as possible. The heated cabin was soundproofed and had large windows for good visibility. Some of the other advanced features of the Model 5000 were a self-starter, wheel brakes and retractable landing lights.

*Travel Air Model CH operated by Gerbracht Aeronautic Corporation and nicknamed* Pegasus, *in September 1926.* (P M Bowers collection)

Walter Beech delivered the first aircraft to Kansas City on 18 December 1926 and, after evaluating the prototype, NAT bought eight Model 5000s to be delivered within 120 days, to bolster service on its Chicago to Dallas route (including a stop at Wichita). The first NAT aircraft was ready on schedule and was first flown by Beech with several passengers on board among which were E P Lott of NAT, Marcellus Murdock and Jack Turner. It was delivered on 28 April 1926 and the second aircraft was ready in May but NAT did not need it so soon and released it for sale. This aeroplane was eventually bought by Pacific Air Transport, in California. The prototype Model 5000 was sold to Pacific Air Transport who operated it for several months on West Coast routes and then sold it to some private individuals.

NAT's 5000s were first used to carry only mail but began carrying passengers in the autumn of 1927 by special arrangements. By early 1928, they were carrying passengers regularly between Chicago and Kansas City at $62.50 one way. Only one Model 5000 was lost while in service. On 20 January 1929, aircraft c/n 177A piloted by John B Story, crashed at Davenport, Iowa.

The eight Model 5000s were:

*The first Model 5000 taking off on the first civil flight from Oakland, California, to Hawaii, manned by Ernest Smith and Emery Bronte, in July 1927.* (P M Bowers collection)

| c/n | reg'n | del. to NAT | fate |
|---|---|---|---|
| 171 | 2614 | May 1927 | scrapped December 1929 |
| 172 | 3002 | May 1927 | released March 1931 |
| 173A | 2906 | June 1927 | scrapped December 1929 |
| 174A | 2908 | June 1927 | scrapped August 1929 |
| 175A | 2907 | June 1927 | sold September 1929 |
| 176A | 769 | July 1927 | sold September 1929 |
| 177A | 770 | July 1927 | scrapped November 1929 |
| 178A | 771 | July 1927 | scrapped September 1929 |

## *Woolaroc* and *Oklahoma*

On 14 July 1927 Ernest Smith and Emery Bronte flew the prototype Model 5000 from Oakland, California, to Hawaii, becoming the first commercial aircraft to fly to Hawaii, but the aircraft was damaged on landing. Two months earlier, on 25 May 1927 James D Dole had offered a $25,000 first prize and a $10,000 second prize to the winners of a race from Oakland, California, to Wheeler Field, Honolulu, Hawaii, to be held during the summer. As a result fourteen aeroplanes were built or prepared for the race, which was to start on 12 August but actually began on the 16th. Travel Air's board of directors authorized the construction of two machines for this race. The aircraft were modified Model 5000s specially prepared for long-distance flight by Horace E Weihmiller, Herb Rawdon, Walter Burnham and C B Bennett. One aircraft, nicknamed *Oklahoma* (registered N-X-911), was completed on 29 July, 1927 and its crew consisted of Bennett H Griffin of Tulsa, Oklahoma, and Al Henley. During the race, *Oklahoma* was the first to take off at noon. However, it returned some 45 minutes later with a burned out engine. The second aircraft, named *Woolaroc* (registered NX869), was completed on 2 August, 1927. It was very similar to the *Oklahoma* but it was heavier due to the installation of equipment in the cockpit. This Wright J-5 powered aeroplane was sponsored by Frank E Phillips, manager of Phillips Petroleum Co, and flown by 31-year old Arthur C Goebel Jr with Lt William V Davis Jr of San Diego as navigator. It was painted blue and yellow, and its tanks could carry 425 US gallons (1,608 litres) of fuel. *Woolaroc* took off at 12:36 on 16 August. Twenty-six hours, 17 minutes and 33 seconds later, it landed at Wheeler Field, Hawaii, to win the Dole Race. The *Woolaroc* is the only surviving Travel Air 5000. It has been on display at the Frank Phillips Woolaroc Museum at Bartlesville, Oklahoma, since August 1929.

### Model 5000

One 230hp Wright J-5-C Whirlwind.

Span 51ft 7in (15.72m); length 30ft 5in (9.27m); height 8ft 9in (2.67m); wing area 312sq ft (28.98sq m).

Empty weight 2,160lb (978kg); gross weight 3,600lb (1,630kg); wing loading 11.54lb/sq ft (56.24kg/sq m); power loading 15.65lb/hp (7.09kg/hp).

Maximum speed 123mph (198km/h) at sea level; cruising speed 108mph (174km/h); rate of climb 750ft/min (228m/min) at sea level; service ceiling 13,600ft (4,145m).

### Travel Air *Woolaroc*

One 230hp Wright J-5-C Whirlwind.

Span 50ft 4½in (15.35m); length 31ft 2in (9.5m); height 7ft 3½in (2.22m); wing area 309sq ft (28.7sq m).

Empty weight 2,200lb (997kg); gross weight 5,300lb (2,400kg); wing loading 17.14lb/sq ft (83.62kg/sq m); power loading 23.04lb/hp (10.43kg/hp).

Maximum speed 125mph (201km/h) at sea level; cruising speed 95mph (152km/h).

*Travel Air Model 5000 c/n 177A was delivered to NAT in July 1927. It was sold in September 1929.* (United Airlines)

*Walter H Beech and Art Goebel with the Travel Air* Woolaroc. *The narrow cockpit enclosure is well shown.* (Beech)

*The* Woolaroc *as it appeared after it has been re-engined with a 400hp Pratt & Whitney. Other modifications included removal of the front cockpit and installation of large windows.* (Beech)

## Model 8000

The Model 8000 appeared in 1927. It was originally the Model B c/n 275, registered 3562, which had been refitted with the unique new 120hp four-cylinder Fairchild-Caminez radial engine. This peculiar engine, designed by Harold Caminez, had a new system of connecting the pistons to the crankshaft and thus obtained a power stroke from each cylinder in one engine revolution instead of the customary two. This geared the engine down two-to-one and required a very large, slow turning propeller. Registered as a Model 4000-CAM, the aircraft was also known as the Model 8000. It was shipped to the Travel Air dealer in Albany, New York, on 30 December 1927 who resold it to the Fairchild-Caminez Engine Corp on 9 February 1928. The Cam engine was very rough running and troublesome, with a tendency to split propellers due to vibration, and the manufacturer encountered difficulties getting its engine to meet the requirements for an engine ATC. It was finally awarded Powerplant ATC No.1 on 1 June 1928. To complete the 6,304-mile 1928 Ford Reliability Tour, the aircraft needed several spare engines and was placed 14th out of 25. The Caminez engine was

*The Travel Air blue painted* Woolaroc *receives a push as it takes off with Art Goebel at the controls.* (P M Bowers collection)

*The Travel Air Model 8000, fitted with the unique 120hp four-cylinder Fairchild-Caminez radial engine, was originally a Model B.* (P M Bowers collection)

eventually withdrawn from the market and the aircraft was reconverted to a plain Model 2000 in March 1929. It should be mentioned that two other so-called Model 8000s were registered (one being c/n 459) but no details are available about them.

### Model 8000

One 135hp Fairchild-Caminez.

Span, upper 34ft 8in (10.56m); span, lower 28ft 8in (8.73m); length 24ft 2in (7.36m); height 8ft 9in (2.67m); wing area 296sq ft (27.5sq m).

Empty weight 1,475lb (668kg); gross weight 2,300lb (1,042kg); wing loading 7.77lb/sq ft (37.89kg/sq m); power loading 17.04lb/hp (7.72kg/hp).

Maximum speed 110mph (177km/h) at sea level; cruising speed 92mph (150km/h); initial rate of climb 700ft/min (213m/min); service ceiling 12,000ft (3,660m); range 450-500 miles (725-805km).

## Model 9000

Various types of engines were adapted to the standard and well established Travel Air biplanes. The four Model 9000s which were built made use of the new 125hp nine-cylinder Siemens-Halske SH-14 imported from Germany by T Claude Ryan and marketed as the Ryan-Siemens. The prototype Model 9000 was converted from Model 4000 c/n 302 and registered X-3791. The three other aircraft were another Model 4000 (c/n 380, registered NC4420) and a pair of Model 3000s (c/n 420, registered C-4836 and c/n 421, registered C-4837). The prototype received a temporary licence on 16 December 1927 but did not receive its Type Certificate until the following April. It was eventually sold to a Texan, who resold it. The new owner then installed an extra 40-US gallon fuel tank and it was used by Viola Gentry to set a new endurance record for women. After several resales, the last licence for c/n 302 expired 1 March 1938. For a brief period, Model 9000 c/n 380 was fitted with a 120hp French Anzani six-cylinder twin-row radial engine, and nicknamed the Smith Incubator, but it was refitted with a Siemens SH-14 engine in May 1931.

### Model 9000

One 125hp Siemens-Halske (Ryan) R-517.

Span, upper 34ft 8in (10.56m); span, lower 28ft 8in (8.73m); length 24ft 4in (7.41m); height 9ft (2.74m); wing area 296sq ft (27.5sq m).

Empty weight 1,475lb (668kg); gross weight 2,300lb (1,042kg); wing loading 7.77lb/sq ft (37.89kg/sq m); power loading 18.4lb/hp (8.33kg/hp).

Maximum speed 112mph (180km/h) at sea level; cruising speed 93mph (150km/h); rate of climb 700ft/min (213m/min) at sea level; service ceiling 12,000ft (3,657m); range 450 miles (724 km).

*Built in 1927, the Model 9000 was powered by a German 125hp Siemens-Halske radial engine.* (P M Bowers)

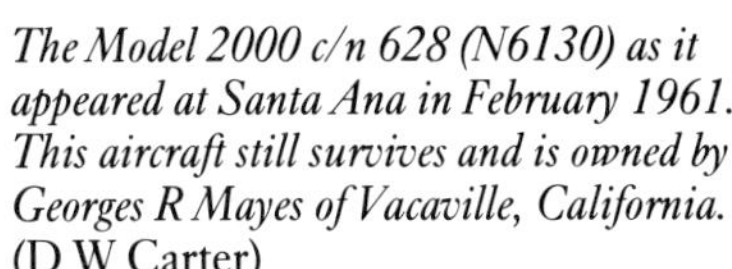
*The Model 2000 c/n 628 (N6130) as it appeared at Santa Ana in February 1961. This aircraft still survives and is owned by Georges R Mayes of Vacaville, California.* (D W Carter)

# Model 2000

## Model 2000

Introduced in 1927, the Model 2000 was the improved version of the OX-5 powered Model B. It was also the first Travel Air aircraft to receive type certification (ATC A-30 for both the Model 2000 and the Model S-2000 were granted on 22 March, 1928). The fuselage framework was built up of welded chrome-moly steel tubes, faired to shape with wood fairing strips and fabric covered. The wing had spruce spars, and spruce and plywood ribs. There were minor refinements to the Model 2000, including an increase of fuel capacity to 43 US gallons (163 litres) and a gross weight of 2,180lb (987kg). The distinguishing external detail from the Model B was relocation of the forward flying wire from c/n 312 on. Most of the older Model Bs and a few Model As were registered as Model 2000s, that is why the total of Model 2000s built is not exactly known, but it is estimated to be 600. Prices for Model 2000s ranged from $2,950 to over $3,700 depending on year and optional equipment.

## Model B-2000

The use of this designation remains obscure and is not official. It would indicate either the use of a later outrigger undercarriage, or that the aircraft were originally built as Model Bs.

## Model D-2000

The Model D-2000 was a special OX-5 powered racer (c/n 794, registered X-6473) which was completed early in October 1928. It had the short-span 'Speedwings' incorporating a centre section fuel tank, had its fuselage five inches narrower than standard and new vertical tail surfaces similar to the later Model 11. It was known in the house as 'The Bug' and later became the first Model 11 with the same fuselage but entirely different wings, a full NACA cowling and a cleaned-up undercarriage. After a relatively short racing career, flown sometimes by Arthur Goebel who named it *Chaparral*, the D-2000 was rebuilt as a radial engined Model 11 racer that was once again known as 'The Bug'.

## Model S-2000

Although unofficial, this designation identifies a Model 2000 fitted with twin floats, though this designation appears also to indicate a Model 2000 fitted with the 100hp Curtiss OXX-6 engine, a twin-ignition version of the OX-5.

## Model SC-2000

At least three Model SC-2000s were built or converted, all as landplanes with the outrigger undercarriage of the B-4000 and 160hp Curtiss C-6 six-cylinder inline water-cooled engine. They were externally distinguishable by their left-side mounted exhaust manifold. Two Model SC-2000s were c/n 157, registered NC7574 and c/n 882, registered NC8110. A third aircraft was the C-6 powered Travel Air c/n 137.

## Model SD-2000

This single aircraft (c/n 757, registered X-6416) was powered with a 150hp water-cooled V-8 Aeromarine B engine. It was completed on 19 March 1928 and sold to the Douglas Davis Flying Service. Service with the Aeromarine was short, and it was converted to a Model 4000 in February 1929.

## Model 2000-T

The Model 2000-T was a variant powered by a 115hp air-cooled Milwaukee-Tank engine, a conversion of the OX-5. This model was distinguishable by the absence of the belly radiator and the addition of a

*Curtiss OX-5 engined Travel Air Model 2000 NC9072 displaying a Sioux insignia.* (A R Krieger via J Wegg)

*Travel Air 2000 c/n 707 (N6268) was modified to look like a German First World War Fokker D VII. Elephant-ear ailerons are well shown.* (A R Krieger via J Wegg)

large air intake at the front of the cowling. Production totalled 15, and some Model 2000-Ts were among the five or six Travel Airs which were used along with a single Fokker D VII in the 1938 film, *Men With Wings*.

## A Rare Modification

Besides the handful of aircraft which were converted to crop dusters, it must be known that Travel Air 2000 c/n 359 (registered X-4259) was fitted by the Boeing School of Aeronautics, on behalf of Besler brothers, of Doble Steam Motors Corp, with a 150hp two-cylinder compound double-acting steam engine. This aircraft flew for the first time as such on 12 April 1933 at Oakland, piloted by William Besler, and was later reconverted to a standard 2000.

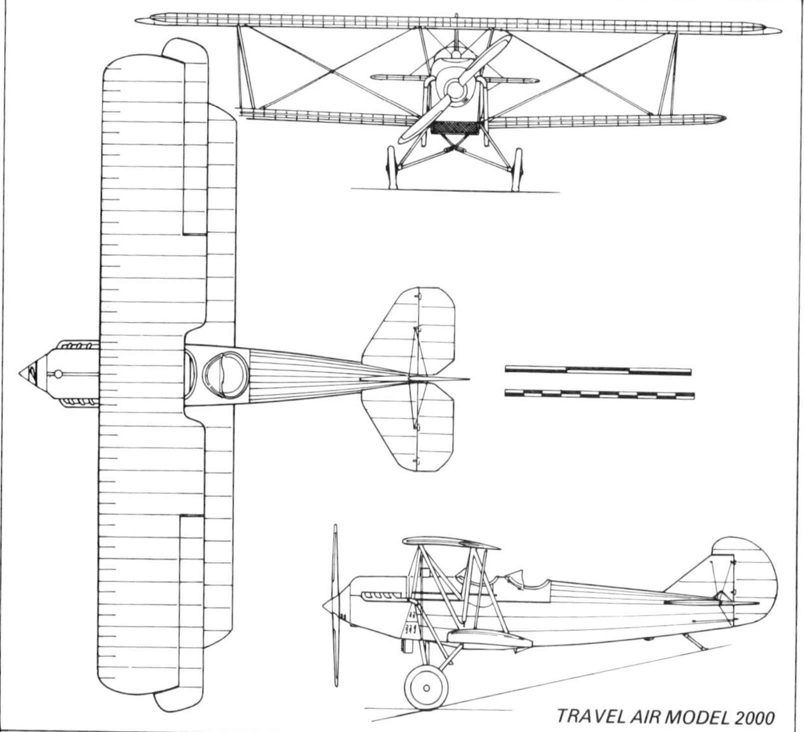


## Model 2000

One 90hp Curtiss OX-5.

Span, upper 34ft 8in (10.56m); span, lower 28ft 8in (8.73m); length 24ft 2in (7.36m); height 8ft 9in (2.67m); wing area 296sq ft (27.5sq m).

Empty weight 1,335lb (605kg); gross weight 2,180lb (987kg); wing loading 7.36lb/sq ft (35.89kg/sq m); power loading 24.2lb/hp (10.96kg/hp).

Maximum speed 100mph (160km/h) at sea level; cruising speed 85mph (137km/h); initial rate of climb 550ft/min (168m/min); service ceiling 10,000ft (3,050m); range 400-420 miles (645-675km).

## Model SC-2000

One 160hp Curtiss C-6A.

Span, upper 34ft 8in (10.56m); span, lower 28ft 8in (8.73m); length 24ft 2in (7.36m); height 9ft 2in (2.79m); wing area 296sq ft (27.5sq m).

Empty weight 1,659lb (751kg); gross weight 2,600lb (1,178kg); wing loading 8.78lb/sq ft (42.84kg/sq m); power loading 16.25lb/hp (7.36kg/hp).

Maximum speed 120mph (193km/h) at sea level; cruising speed 102mph (164km/h); rate of climb 850ft/min (259m/min) at sea level; service ceiling 15,000ft (4,572m); range 400-575 miles (645-925km).

*This Travel Air 2000-T was modified as a Fokker D VII and appeared in the 1938* Men With Wings *movie, directed by William A Wellman.* (P M Bowers collection)

*William 'Bill' Besler poses in front of his steam-powered Travel Air, at Oakland Airport, on 12 April 1933.* (Owen A Darcey collection)

# Model 3000

The Model 3000 was an improved version of the earlier BH. Its most distinguishable feature was the relocation of the forward flying wire from c/n 320 on. Generally referred to as the Hisso-Travel Air, it was powered with either the 150hp Hisso A or the 180hp Hisso I V-8 engines. While some Model 3000s had contoured upper engine cowlings over the cylinder banks, others had a much simpler form that was flat, and flyers used to call them the 'Flat Nose 3000s'. Production of the Model 3000 is estimated to have been 51, mostly built as such, but a few were converted from other models.

On 7 December 1928 Louise Thaden, flying the 180hp Hisso I powered Model 3000 c/n 515 (registered 5426) set the first officially recorded woman's altitude record with 20,260ft (6,175m). Some Model 3000s were among the Travel Air biplanes which were used in the making of the 1938 film, *Men With Wings*.

*Travel Air Model 2000 c/n 423 (NC4839) was converted to Model 4-U with a Comet seven-cylinder radial engine.* (P M Bowers collection)

*A 180hp Hisso I powered Model 3000 (c/n 1174, NC606H) fitted with 33ft-span 'standard' wings.* (G S Williams)

## Model D-3000

The Model D-3000 was fitted with 'Speedwings'. Some were used for cross-country and pylon racing in their particular horsepower categories.

### Model 3000

One 150hp Hisso Model A.

Span, upper 34ft 8in (10.56m); span, lower 28ft 8in (8.73m); length 24ft 2in (7.36m); height 8ft 9in (2.67m); wing area 296sq ft (27.5sq m).

Empty weight 1,664lb (754kg); gross weight 2,590lb (1,173kg); wing loading 8.75lb/sq ft (42.65kg/sq m).

Maximum speed 112mph (180km/h) at sea level; cruising speed 100mph (160km/h); rate of climb 800ft/min (245m/min); service ceiling 15,000ft (4,570m); range 425miles (685km).

*The Model 3000 registered C3823 had 'elephant ear' ailerons and a 180hp Hisso I engine.* (A R Krieger via J Wegg)

# Model 4000 and Model 4 Series

Introduced early in 1926, the Model 4000 was a three-seat open cockpit biplane typical of Travel Air biplanes with the fuselage made of welded steel tubing and the wings built up of spruce spars with plywood ribs. The engine was the 220hp nine-cylinder Wright J-5 Whirlwind that had been introduced over a year earlier, but the older J-4 was also offered. This model was externally distinguishable by a slightly longer nose, and the relocation of the forward flying wire. Model 4000s built as such were delivered only with Type A 'Elephant Ear' wings. The Model 4000 was priced $9,800 and approximately a hundred aircraft were registered. Two of them which started as Model 2000s were completed as special Model 4000 dusters for Huff-Daland and powered with J-4 engines. Later in 1928, all Travel biplanes with radial engines other than the Wright J-4 and J-5 were put into the Model 4000 series with prefix letters to identify the different engines.

The Travel Airs used different sets of wings. The Type 'A' wings featured balanced ailerons and had

*A genuine Fokker D VII modified with Hisso engine* (left) *and a modified Model 3000* (right) *flown by Paul Mantz in the film* Men with Wings. *The Fokker was painted red overall with black trim.* (P M Bowers collection)

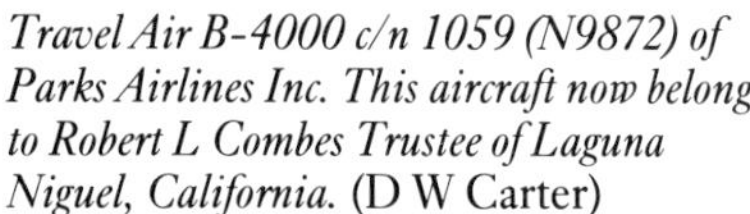
*Travel Air B-4000 c/n 1059 (N9872) of Parks Airlines Inc. This aircraft now belongs to Robert L Combes Trustee of Laguna Niguel, California.* (D W Carter)

*The Model B-4000 had a new outrigger undercarriage with vertically aligned shock absorbers. The engine was a Wright Whirlwind J-5-C and the wings were of the B type. Note the landing light installed in the wing struts.* (Beech)

no wing tanks. The Type 'B' wings had Frise ailerons and centre section fuel tank. The Type 'E' wings had Frise ailerons and no wing tank. The Speedwings were strenghtened wings.

## Model A-4000

The Model A-4000 was powered by the 115-120hp seven-cylinder Floco engine that was also known as the Axelson (hence the A-prefix) which changed the behaviour of the aircraft but offered good performance. The A-4000 used A-type wings and carried 60 US gallons (227 litres) of fuel. The Model A-4000 was priced $6,240 and Edo P-3300 floats were approved. The prototype became a Model 4000, and nine aircraft were built (c/ns 818, 979, 1006, 1019, 1123, 1164, 1236, 1344 and 1370).

## Model B-4000

The Model B-4000 was a three-seat open-cockpit biplane but numerous noticeable changes were introduced. The 'Elephant ear' wings were discarded and the aerofoil section of the upper wing was changed. A new outrigger undercarriage was installed, and the wing (E or B-Type) had 4° of dihedral on top. The main fuel tank was mounted high in the fuselage and an extra fuel tank was mounted in the centre section of the upper wing. Fuel capacity was 68 US gallons (257 litres) and the gross weight was 2,900lb. The Model B-4000 was priced $8,600 and some 25 were registered initially (c/ns 897, 1000, 1011, 1014, 1042, 1064/1065, 1168/1172, 1176/1178, 1242, 1261/1262 and 1365).

## Model C-4000

The C-4000 had the unique 165-185hp six-cylinder twin-row Curtiss Challenger engine but it was not a Travel Air development. In October 1928, a D4000 (c/n 754, registered X6413) was modified and tested by Curtiss as the C-4000 (the C stood for Curtiss). This Model became quite popular, with 22 registered initially (c/ns 754, 971/972, 1013, 1015, 1044/1045, 1110, 1301/1302, 1306, 1309/1312, 1315, 1318, 1335 and 1350). Later, seven Model 2000s and two E-4000s were converted to C-4000. Price was $6,275.

## Model BC-4000

A single BC-4000 (c/n 1041, registered C9821) was built. It was a B-wing C-4000 using the outrigger undercarriage of the B-4000. It was later mounted on Edo twin-floats as the Model SBC-4000. Price was $6,500.

## Model SBC-4000

This Model was the BC-4000 fitted with Edo P-3300 floats.

## Model SC-4000

This Model could be a Model 4000 airframe fitted with a 160hp Curtiss C-6 engine or a BC-4000 on floats.

## Model D-4000

This Model had Speedwings and J-5 engine, however, the first D-4000 was the special racer built for Ted Wells in July 1928 (c/n 626, registered NR6128). Some of the D-4000s were built as single seaters but most of them were three-seaters. In August 1929, the first Women's Air Derby was flown between Santa Monica and Cleveland. Among the 20 entrants, seven were Travel Airs (piloted by Florence 'Pancho' Barnes, Claire Fahy, Opal Kunz, Marvel Crosson, Mary von Mack, Blanche Noyes, and Louise Thaden). Louise

*The outrigger undercarriage of the B-4000 is shown to advantage on aircraft c/n 1011 (NC8888). Note the engine enclosed in a Townend Ring.* (P M Bowers collection)

Thaden, flying a Travel Air D-4000 (registered R671H) won first place; Kunz was placed 8th. At the 1929 National Air Races, held from 24 August till 2 September, Louise Thaden was placed 2nd in the Ladies DW Class Race, and 2nd in the Australian Pursuit Race for Women. Several D-4000s were used in Hollywood films such as *Hell's Angels*, *Young Eagles* and *Dawn Patrol* where they represented Nieuports.

### Model E-4000

Introduced in 1929, the Model E-4000 became the most popular of the series. It was powered with the new 165hp Wright J-6-5 engine. Aircraft c/n 1060 (registered C-9874) served as production version prototype, and some 59 E-4000s were registered initially. The 1929 price was $6,425, reduced to $5,850 in 1930.

### Model BE-4000

The Model BE-4000 was possibly an E-4000 using the B-4000 outrigger undercarriage. A total of 12 Model BE-4000s were registered.

*Travel Air 4000 NC9831 seen in 1987. Note cowled engine, faired-in undercarriage struts and airwheels.* (J Wegg)

### Model J4-4000

There were at least six J4-4000s (c/ns 318, 372, 381, 735, 868 and 1339) using J-4 engines. They could be distinguished from the BW by the attachment of the forward flying wire to the fuselage right at the forward undercarriage strut.

*Travel Air B-4000 (NC8883) with outrigger undercarriage but without spinner.* (A R Krieger via J Wegg)

*The Travel Air E-4000 (c/n 849, N9048) illustrated was powered by a J-6-5 engine.* (J Wegg)

## Model L-4000

The Model L-4000 was created by Parks Air College in 1941 in order to upgrade its Travel Air 4000s with the new 225hp nine-cylinder radial Lycoming R-680-B4. The Parks L-4000s were dual-control trainers with folding blind flying hoods over the rear cockpit. After the Second World War various Travel Airs were fitted with Lycoming engines and used as duster/sprayers.

## Model BM-4000

The BM-4000 was a single-seat open cockpit biplane with front cockpit replaced by two mail compartments (the M prefix stood for mailplane). The BM-4000 was powered with a Wright J-5C engine and had A-type 'Elephant Ear' wings. The three wing tanks had a total capacity of 67 gallons. The vertical tail was entirely different and fitted with an unbalanced rudder. At least seven Model BM-4000s are known to have been built, or at least converted to BM-4000s at the factory (c/ns 180, 524, 525, 553, 800, 1368 and 1370).

*Travel Air E-4000 c/n 869 (N9088) was modified as a crop duster and operated by Moore Aviation from Buckeye, Arizona, where it is seen in March 1958.* (D W Carter)

*The E-4000 registered N648H (c/n 1224) belongs to EAA Museum at Oshkosh, Wisconsin.* (A R Krieger via J Wegg)

## Model K-4000

This Model was powered with the 100hp Kinner K-5 engine (hence the K in the designation). Edo M-2665 floats were approved, and price was approximately $5,000. Six Model K-4000s were manufactured (c/ns 1005, 1161/1163, 1359 and 1373). A seventh K-4000 (c/n 1005) had Speedwings and was designated DK-4000.

## Model B9-4000

This variant was powered with the 300hp Wright J-6-9 engine, and seven machines of this Model were built or converted from other models. They featured standard 'small' rudders, 4° of dihedral on the top wing, and outrigger undercarriage. Later, some, were fitted with full NACA cowlings. The seven B9-4000s were c/ns 1001, 1010, 1102/1103, 1307, 1396/1397.

## Model D9-4000

Airshow pilot Arthur Goebel had D-4000 c/n 1396 modified for airshow work. This particular aircraft was a single seater, with chemical smoke tank in the former front cockpit, a 300hp J-6-9 engine, and either 'Speedwings' or clipped wings. At a later date, a BM-4000 vertical tail was added.

## Model U-4000

Alternate designation for Model 4U (which see).

*Travel Air 4000 c/n 374 (N4321) has been re-engined with a 300hp Lycoming R-680 engine with constant speed propeller. This aircraft is still in the airshow business.* (P M Bowers)

*The Model 4000-T was a stock Model 4-D which was fitted with Curtiss Tanager floating ailerons and a Curtiss-designed undercarriage.* (P M Bowers collection)

*Travel Air Model 4-D c/n 1354 (NC480N) fitted with wheel pants in order to boost speed.* (N Benner via J Wegg)

## Model W-4000

The Model W-4000 was quite successful and 27 were registered. It was powered with a 110hp Warner Scarab seven-cylinder radial engine, and priced $5,646. The prototype W-4000 (c/n 708 registered X-6269) was flown to 3rd place by William H Emery Jr in the 1928 Transcontinental Air Derby (Class A).

## Model DW-4000

This was the prototype Model W-4000 fitted with 'Speedwings'.

*The Model 4-P was powered by an ACE LA-1 radial engine enclosed in a NACA cowling. This one is c/n 1332 (NC-419N).* (B Wildprett via J Wegg)

## Model 4000-CAM

Alternative designation for the Caminez-powered Model 8000.

## Model 4000-SH

Alternate designation for the Ryan-Siemens powered Model 9000.

## Model 4000-T

The 4000-T was a stock model Model 4-D (c/n 1400, registered X165V) which was sent to Curtiss for conversion. This was a Curtiss experiment. Curtiss built new wings with shorter span, automatic leading-edge slats on both wings, almost full-span flaps on both and the unique Curtiss Tanager floating ailerons on the lower panels. An entirely new high impact undercarriage was designed and installed. This aircraft was eventually returned to the factory for reconversion to a D-4-D.

## Model 4-D

The 4-D was a direct development of the J-5 powered Model B-4000 designed especially for sportsman-pilots. It featured the same outrigger undercarriage and B-wing with four degrees of dihedral, and a 67-US gallon fuel capacity. The engine was the boosted 240hp version of the Wright J-6-7 Whirlwind (R-760). Altogether, 19 4-Ds were registered (c/ns 898, 1102, 1160, 1166, 1263/1265, 1270, 1320, 1322, 1327, 1329, 1360/1364, 1366/1367). Edo P-3300 floats could be used, and wheel pants and Townend rings were later additions by owners. Two 4-Ds are known to have been converted from BE-4000s (c/ns 1160 and 1367) and another (c/n 1102) was later converted to B9-4000.

## Model 4-P

The Model 4-P was one of the rarest Travel Air variants. It used the new seven-cylinder 140hp ACE LA-1 engine (later known as the Jacobs) enclosed in a NACA low-drag cowling, and was fitted with E-wings.

## Model 4-PT

Alternate designation for the 4-P.

*The Model D-4-D was essentially a D-4000 powered by a Wright J-6-7 engine. This aircraft (NC606K) was converted from a Model 2000. It is seen at Franklin, Wisconsin, in May 1972.* (A R Krieger via J Wegg)

*This D-4000 (C-6239) was modified for racing, with smaller cockpit openings. It was owned and piloted by Paul R Braniff.* (D W Carter collection)

## Model 4-S

In December 1929, Model 4000 c/n 1383 (registered X469N) was used as a testbed for the experimental Powell Power engine, and used this unofficial designation.

## Model 4-U

The Model 4-Us were all conversions of early models using the 130-165hp Comet seven-cylinder radial engine. These conversions were made by Otto Timm of Van Nuys, California and concerned 16 aircraft (c/ns 242, 268, 322, 418, 423, 551, 611, 735, 763, 767, 788, 818, 871, 1004, 1016 and 1162).

## Model D-4-D

The Model D-4-D was a considerably different aeroplane, with shorter wings, shock-cord type undercarriage and gross weight reduced to 2,650lb (1,200kg). Five Model D-4-Ds were originally registered (c/ns 1340, 1372, 1374, 1376 and 1391). Later, six more were converted from other models (c/ns 515, 1208, 1282, 1373, 1391). Note that in the designation the first D identified 'Speedwings' and the second identified J-6-7 engine.

## Model W-4-B

This aeroplane was a special racing model designed by Ted Wells. It had a J-5 engine under a NACA cowling, a wingspan of only 23ft 8in, the shock absorbers were inside the fuselage to reduce drag and the wings were connected by I-struts. This aircraft was destroyed during a demonstration flight on 10 September 1930.

## Model Z-4-D

The first Z-4-D was specifically for crop dusting. It was powered with the J-6-9 engine. At 3,053lb (1,383kg) gross weight with 600lb (272kg) of dust, the Z-4-D was the heaviest of all the Travel Air biplanes. Only two, the prototype and a former Model 4000 (c/n 1339) were registered. After the war, many Travel Airs were modified as dusters/sprayers and were equipped with war-surplus engines such as the 220hp Continental R-670, the 220hp Lycoming R-680,. 225hp Jacobs R-755, 245hp Wright R-760,

*This Model D-4-D began its life as Model 3000 c/n 515. It was modified to D-4000 configuration in 1936, and in 1941 was fitted with a Wright J-6-7 to become a D-4-D.* (J Wegg)

420hp Wright R-975 and 450hp Pratt & Whitney R-985 Wasp Jr.

## Model 4000

One 220hp Wright Whirlwind J-5C.
Span, upper 34ft 8in (10.56m); span, lower 28ft 8in (8.73m); length 24ft 2in (7.36m); height 8ft 9in (2.67m); wing area 296sq ft (27.5sq m).
Empty weight 1,485lb (673kg); gross weight 2,400lb (1,087kg); wing loading 8.11lb/sq ft (39.53kg/sq m); power loading 12lb/hp (5.43kg/hp).
Maximum speed 130mph (209km/h) at sea level; cruising speed 110mph (177km/h); rate of climb 1,200ft/min (366m/min) at sea level; service ceiling 20,000ft (6,100m); range 500-550miles (805-885km).

## Model A-4000

One 150hp Axelson.
Dimensions as for Model 4000 except span, lower 28ft 10in (8.79m); length 24ft 8in (7.52m).
Empty weight 1,600lb (725kg); gross weight 2,600lb (1,178kg); wing loading 8.78lb/sq ft (42.84kg/sq m); power loading 17.33lb/hp (7.85kg/hp).
Maximum speed 110mph (177km/h) at sea level; cruising speed 95mph (153km/h); rate of climb 525ft/min (160m/min) at sea level; service ceiling 10,000ft (3,050m); range 400-420miles (645-675km).

## Model B-4000

One 220hp Wright Whirlwind J-5-C.
Dimensions as for A-4000 except wing area 289sq ft (26.85sq m).
Empty weight 1,885lb (854kg); gross weight 2,900lb (1,314kg); wing loading 10.03lb/sq ft (48.94kg/sq m); power loading 14.5lb/hp (6.57kg/hp).
Maximum speed 125-130mph (201-209km/h) at sea level; cruising speed 110mph (177km/h); rate of climb 900ft/min (274m/min) at sea level; service ceiling 14,000ft (4,270m); range 500-550miles (805-885km).

## Model C-4000

One 170hp Curtiss Challenger.
Span, upper 34ft 8in (10.56m); span, lower 28ft 10in (8.79m); length 24ft 6in (7.47m); height 8ft 9in (2.67m); wing area 296sq ft (27.5sq m).
Empty weight 1,600lb (725kg); gross weight 2,600lb (1,178kg); wing loading 8.78lb/sq ft (42.83kg/sq m); power loading 15.29lb/hp (6.92kg/hp).
Maximum speed 130mph (209km/h) at sea level; cruising speed 105mph (169km/h); rate of climb 800ft/min (244m/min) at sea level; service ceiling 14,000ft (4,267m); range 550-660miles (885-1,060km).

## Model BC-4000

One 170hp Curtiss Challenger.
Span, upper 33ft (10.06m); span, lower 28ft 10in (8.79m); length 24ft 6in (7.47m); height 9ft 1in (3.3m); wing area 289sq ft (26.85sq m).
Empty weight 1,793lb (812kg); gross weight 2,800lb (1,268kg); wing loading 9.68lb/sq ft (47.22kg/sq m); power loading 16.47lb/hp (7.46kg/hp).
Maximum speed 122mph (196km/h) at sea level; cruising speed 104mph (167km/h); rate of climb 720ft/min (220m/min) at sea level; service ceiling 12,500ft (3,810m); range 600 miles (965km).

## Model E-4000

One 165hp Wright Whirlwind J-6-5.
Dimensions as for BC-4000 except length 24ft 1in (7.34m); height 8ft 11in (2.73m).
Empty weight 1,640lb (743kg); gross weight 2,700lb (1,223kg); wing loading 9.34lb/sq ft (45.55kg/sq m); power loading 16.36lb/hp (7.41kg/hp).
Maximum speed 122mph (196km/h) at sea level; cruising speed 103mph (165km/h); rate of climb 700ft/min (213m/min) at sea level; service ceiling 13,000ft (3,960m); range 690miles (1,110km).

## Model K-4000

One 100hp Kinner.
Span, upper 34ft 8in (10.56m); span, lower 28ft 10in (8.79m); length 24ft 8in (7.52m); height 8ft 9in (2.67m); wing area 296sq ft (27.5sq m).
Empty weight 1,400lb (634kg); gross weight 2,300lb (1,042kg); wing loading 7.77lb/sq ft (37.89kg/sq m); power loading 23lb/hp (10.42kg/hp).
Maximum speed 105mph (169km/h) at sea level; cruising speed 90mph (145km/h); rate of climb 500ft/min (152m/min) at sea level; service ceiling 10,000ft (3,050m); range 400-420 miles (645-675km).

## Model BM-4000

One 220hp Wright J-5.
Dimensions as for BC-4000.
Empty weight 1,928lb (873kg); gross weight 3,000lb (1,359kg); wing loading 10.38lb/sq ft (50.61kg/sq m); power loading 13.63lb/hp (6.18kg/hp).
Maximum speed 130mph (209km/h); cruising speed 112mph (180km/h); rate of climb 900ft/min (274m/min) at sea level; service ceiling 13,500ft (4,115m); range 550 miles (885km).

## Model B9-4000

One 300hp Wright Whirlwind J-6-9.
Span 33ft (10.06m); length 23ft 2½in (7.07m); height 8ft 9in (2.67m); wing area 289sq ft (26.85sq m).
Empty weight 1,885lb (854kg); gross weight 2,800lb (1,268kg); wing loading 9.69lb/sq ft (47.22kg/sq m); power loading 9.33lb/hp (4.23kg/hp).
Maximum speed 135mph (217km/h) at sea level; cruising speed 115mph (185km/h); rate of climb 1,500ft/min (457m/min) at sea level; service ceiling 18,000ft (5,490m).

## Model W-4000

One 110hp Warner-Scarab.
Span, upper 34ft 8in (10.56m); span, lower 28ft 8in (8.73m); length 24ft 7in (7.49m); height 8ft 9in (2.67m); wing area 296sq ft (27.5sq m).

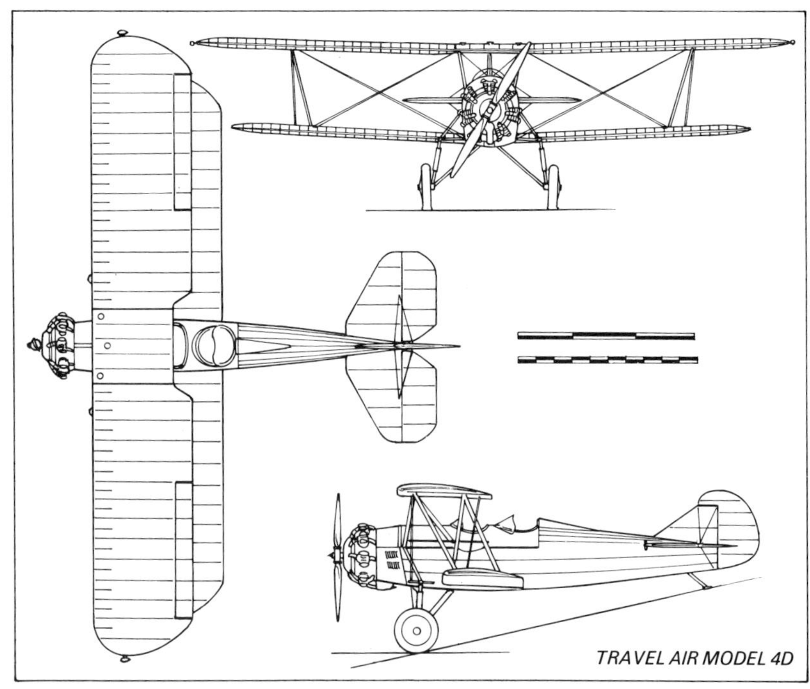
TRAVEL AIR MODEL 4D

*Travel Air Model 6000 prototype (X4765) flew for the first time on 15 April 1928.*
(P M Bowers collection)

Empty weight 1,400lb (634kg); gross weight 2,300lb (1,042kg); wing loading 7.77lb/sq ft (37.89kg/sq m); power loading 20.9lb/hp (9.47kg/hp).

Maximum speed 108mph (174km/h) at sea level; cruising speed 93mph (150km/h); rate of climb 560ft/min (170m/min) at sea level; service ceiling 11,000ft (3,350m); range 400-420 miles (645-675km).

## Model 4-D

One 225hp or 240hp Wright J-6-7.

Dimensions as for BC-4000 except length 23ft 4in (7.11m).

Empty weight 1,837lb (832kg); gross weight 2,880lb (1,305kg); wing loading 9.96lb/sq ft (48.6kg/sq m); power loading 12.8lb/hp (5.8kg/hp).

Maximum speed 130mph (209km/h) at sea level; cruising speed 110mph (177km/h); rate of climb 980ft/min (299m/min) at sea level; service ceiling 14,000ft (4,270m); range 520 miles (837km).

## Model 4-P

One 140hp ACE LA.1.

Dimensions as for BC-4000 except length 24ft 6in (7.47m); height 8ft 11in (2.72m).

Empty weight 1,531lb (693kg); gross weight 2,388lb (1,082kg); wing loading 8.26lb/sq ft (40.3kg/sq m); power loading 17.06lb/hp (7.73kg/hp).

Maximum speed 115mph (185km/h) at sea level; cruising speed 97mph (156km/h); rate of climb 700ft/min (213m/min) at sea level; service ceiling 12,000ft (3,660m); range 485 miles (780km).

# Model 6000 and Model 6

## Model 6000

Designed by Horace E Weihmiller, the prototype Model 6000 (registered X4765) was rolled-out and flown for the first time, by Clarence Clark, on 15 April 1928. This monoplane transport aircraft was powered with a 200hp Wright J-5C Whirlwind engine. It had accommodation for six in a heated cabin fitted with roll-down windows. The fuselage framework was made of welded chrome-moly steel tubing. The semi-cantilever wings had a Göttingen 398 aerofoil section. The structure was of spruce box-type spars with plywood ribs and fabric covered. Fuel capacity totalled 65 US gallons (246 litres) and the ailerons were of the Frise balanced-hinge type. The wide-track undercarriage was of the outrigger type fitted with Aerol shock absorber struts. During June 1928, W H Beech organised a demonstration tour and got 14 firm orders for production aircraft.

*The Model 6000-B (NC9810) as operated by Camel City Flying Service.*
(R Patterson)

### Model A-6000-A

Basically the same as the six-seat Model 6000, the A-6000-A was developed in answer to the urgent demands from various airlines for a single-engine cabin monoplane with high performance. The engine was a 425hp Pratt & Whitney R-1340 Wasp driving a two-blade metal propeller. The Model A-6000-A was slightly larger than the basic Model 6000. The cabin was soundproofed and offered confortable accommodation for six passengers, but seats were easily removable to provide space for bulky cargo. Altogether, 25 aircraft of this type were built among which nine were seven-seaters. Price at the factory averaged $18,000.

### Model SA-6000-A

Seaplane variant of the A-6000-A with twin Edo JF-1 floats and featuring removable seats for hauling cargo. Only a small number of this model were built, one of which found its way to Canada as CF-AFK.

### Model 6000-B

The Model 6000-B, also referred to as the B-6000 was similar in most respects to the Model A-6000-A but it was powered with a 300hp nine-cylinder Wright J-6-9.

### Model S-6000-B

Twin-float variant of the Model 6000-B fitted with Edo floats.

*The Model 6000-B (N9084) as operated by Kachemak Air Service Inc. of Homer, Alaska. The aircraft had a blue fuselage and orange wings.* (J Wegg)

### Model A-6-A Travel Air Sedan

The Model A-6-A was basically a Travel Air 6000-series monoplane but it was immediately distinguishable from the latter by its bulge-type pilot's cabin enclosure. The larger interior dimensions (112x52x36) allowed an eight-seat accommodation and toilet facilities. It was powered with a 420hp nine-cylinder Pratt & Whitney Wasp C1 radial engine. A single example was built by the Travel Air Division of Curtiss-Wright (c/n 2009, registered NC469W).

### Model 6-B Travel Air Sedan

Introduced in 1930, the Model 6-B was a derivative of the earlier Model 6000-B featuring numerous improvements including a bulged pilot's cabin for more visibility. Retaining a 300hp Wright J-6-9 (R-975) engine, its overall performance deteriorated due to the 200-lb increase in the gross weight. At least four examples of the Model 6-B were manufactured (c/ns 2037/2040) by the Travel Air Division of Curtiss-Wright. Four additional aircraft (c/ns 2041/2044) were assembled by the Airtech Flying Service of San Diego, California, according to factory drawings after Travel Air closed down.

*One Travel Air Model 6-B operated as a floatplane on Edo floats. It had c/n 2037 and was registered NC452N.* (G S Williams)

### Service History

On 1 February 1928 National Air Transport (NAT) opened a daily passenger service between Chicago and Kansas City, using Travel Air Model 6000s. In 1928, retaining the corporate identity, the Robertson Aircraft Corp was awarded the mail contract CAM28 for the St Louis–Kansas City–Omaha route. Travel Airs were used among other types. Universal next acquired Continental Airlines which had started mail and passenger service on the Cleveland-Louisville route (CAM16) on 1 August 1928 using three Model 6000s, with an eastward extension to Akron on 15 November 1928. Next was Braniff Airways, formerly Paul R Braniff Inc, organized in May 1928. On 17 June, 1929, Delta Air Service opened the Dallas (Texas)–Jackson (Mississippi) route with a Travel Air piloted by John Howe. This line was later extended from Fort Worth (Texas) to Birmingham (Alabama). From July till September 1929 Ludington Flying Service was responsible for the Cape Cod Airways, linking Philadelphia with resort areas in New England, including Newport, Rhode Island and Woods Hole (Massachusetts) using two Model 6000s. From August 1929 until January 1930, Canadian American Airlines linked St Paul to Winnipeg using Travel Air 6000s. In the early 1930s, Northwest Airlines used model A-6000-As between Minneapolis, St Paul, Chicago, Fargo and Bismark. On 10 April 1932 Woodley Airways, founded by Arthur Woodley, began operations southwest of Anchorage, Alaska, using a small fleet of Travel Air 6000s.

During service, several Model 6000s were victims of accidents: on 12 July 1929 a Texas Air Transport (TAT) Model B-6000 (c/n 997) was destroyed in a hangar fire at Meacham Field, Fort Worth. On 30 December 1929 a TAT Model B-6000, piloted by Lt Robert H Gray, crashed at Amarillo, Texas, killing five. On 27 January 1930 a Universal Model A-6000-A (c/n 963), piloted by Dyke Lauderman, crashed at Fairfax Airport, killing five. On 25 November 1932 a Hunter Airways Model S-6000-B, piloted by Kenneth E Yoder, crashed 12 miles northeast of Marianna, Arkansas, killing two.

Known Model 6000s:

| c/n | type | reg'n | owner |
|---|---|---|---|
| 779 | A-6000-B | C6458 | Braniff, to Universal |
| 790 | 6000 | NC6469 | Wilbur D May |
| 815 | A-6000-A | C9014 | Braniff |
| 816 | A-6000-A | NC9015 | Wallace Beery |
| 865 | 6000-B | NC9084 | Phillips Petroleum Co |
| 884 | 6000 | NC8112 | Arkansas Aviation Historical Society |
| 892 | 6000 | | TACA |
| 962 | 6000-B | NR8139 | Wadlow Bros |
| 963 | A-6000-A | C8178 | Central Air Lines |
| 967 | 6000 | NC8159 | Alaska Aviation Heritage Museum |
| 986 | 6000-A | NC8865 | Staggerwing Museum |
| 987 | 6000-B | | Hobi Airways |
| 988 | S-6000-B | C8878 | Fox FS, to Delta Air Service, to Southern Air Fast Express |
| 997 | B-6000 | | Texas Air Transport |
| 999 | S-6000-B | NC8885 | Robert S Fogg |
| 1040 | SA-6000-A | CF-AEJ | Starratt Airways |
| 1072 | S-6000-B | C9905 | Fox FS, to Delta Air Service, to Southern Air Fast Express |
| 1081 | S-6000-B | C9930 | Delta Air Service, to Southern Air Fast Express |
| 1084 | A-6000-A | NC9933 | Northwest Airways (Fleet No.46) |
| 1097 | A-6000-A | NC9976 | Long and Harman Airlines |
| 2003 | A-6000-A | NC377M | Arkansas Air Museum |

### Model 6000

One 220hp Wright Whirlwind J-5C.

Span 48ft 8in (14.83m); length 30ft 6in (9.3m); height 9ft (2.74m); wing area 282sq ft (26.2sq m).

Empty weight 2,350lb (1,064kg); gross weight 4,000lb (1,812kg); wing loading 14.18lb/sq ft (69.16kg/sq m); power loading 20lb/hp (9.06kg/hp).

Maximum speed 120mph (193km/h) at sea level; cruising speed 105mph (169km/h); rate of climb 700ft/min (213m/min) at sea level; service ceiling 10,000ft (3,050m); range 725 miles (1,165km).

### Model A-6000-A

One 425hp Pratt & Whitney R-1340 Wasp.

Span 54ft 5in (16.58m); length 31ft 2in (9.5m); height 9ft 3in (2.82m); wing area 340sq ft (31.59sq m).

Empty weight 3,225lb (1,460kg); gross weight 5,250lb (2,378kg); wing loading 15.44lb/sq ft (75.27kg/sq m); power loading 12.35lb/hp (5.59kg/hp).

Maximum speed 140mph (225km/h) at sea level; cruising speed 120mph (193km/h); rate of climb 1,000ft/min (305m/min) at sea level; service ceiling 18,000ft (5,490m); range 680 miles (1,095km).

### Model 6000-B

One 300hp Wright Whirlwind J-6-9.

Span 48ft 6½in (14.79m); length 31ft 2in (9.5m); height 9ft 0½in (2.75m); wing area 282sq ft (26.2sq m).

Empty weight 2,700lb (1,223kg); gross weight 4,230lb (1,916kg); wing loading 15lb/sq ft (73.13kg/sq m); power loading 14.1lb/hp (6.39kg/hp).

Maximum speed 130mph (209km/h) at sea level; cruising speed 110mph (177km/h); rate of climb 800ft/min (244m/min) at sea level; service ceiling 16,000ft (4,880m); range 550 miles (885km).

# Model 10

Introduced in March 1929, the Model 10 was in appearance very similar to the larger Model 6000. It had been especially designed as a fast air-taxi and charter service monoplane. It displayed fairly high performance, and was offered with various engines ranging from 185hp to 300hp, but due to the depressed market, the offer was soon reduced to the single Model 10-D variant. The fuselage framework was built up mainly of welded steel tubing and fabric covered. It had accomodation for four people and had a 125lb baggage compartment. The wing, which retained a Göttingen 593

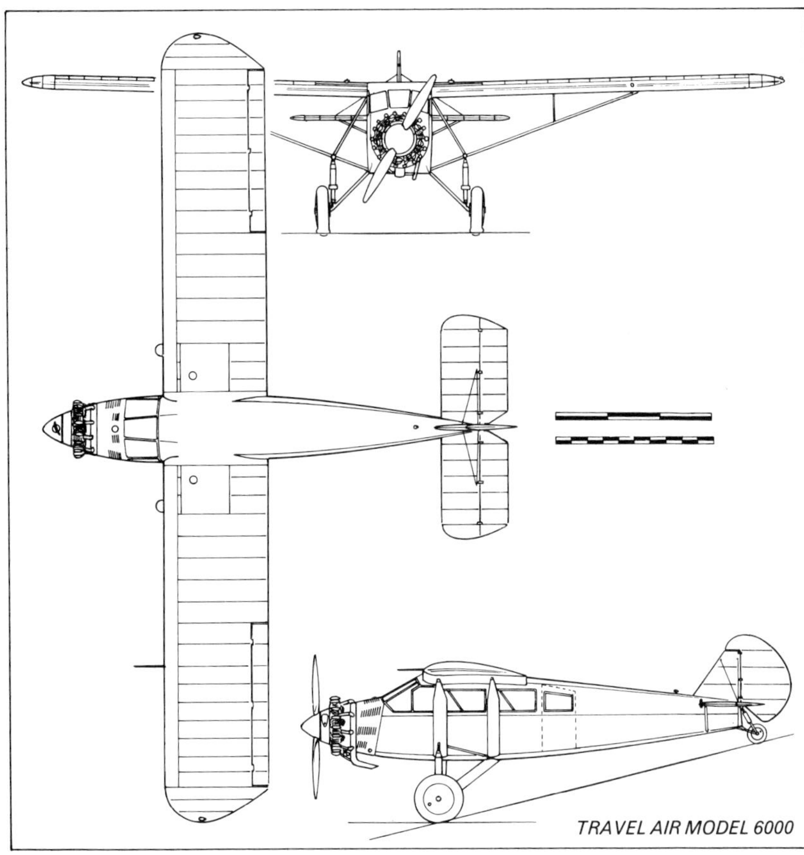


aerofoil section was made of spruce spar beams with spruce and plywood ribs. The leading edge was covered with dural sheet. Airlerons were of the Frise balanced-hinge type.

The prototype Model 10 (c/n 1008, registered C8844) was initially powered with a Wright J-6-9, but it was later fitted with a 185hp Curtiss Challenger for certification purposes, and at a later date with a Wright J-6-7.

## Model 10-B

This variant was the initial version and was powered with a 300 hp Wright J-6-9.

## Model 10-D

This was the production variant powered by a 225hp seven-cylinder Wright J-6-7 (R-760) radial engine. It introduced several innovations such as a bulge-type pilot's cabin enclosure for better visibility. Some eleven examples (c/ns 2001/2011) of this model were manufactured by Travel Air. The Model 10-D was priced at the factory $11,250, but this was lowered to $8,495 in 1930.

### Model 10-B

One 300hp Wright Whirlwind J-6-9.

Span 43ft 6in (13.26m); length 27ft 4½in (8.34m); height 8ft 8in (2.64m); wing area 239sq ft (22.2sq m).

Empty weight 2,255lb (1,021kg); gross weight 3,400lb (1,540kg); wing loading 14.22lb/sq ft (69.37kg/sq m) power loading 11.33lb/hp (5.13kg/hp).

Maximum speed 140-145mph (225-233km/h) at sea level; cruising speed 115mph (185km/h); rate of climb 1,140ft/min (347m/min) at sea level; service ceiling 17,000ft (5,180m).

### Model 10-D

One 225hp Wright Whirlwind J-6.

Dimensions as for Model 10-B except length 26ft 10in (8.18m).

Empty weight 2,130lb (967kg); gross weight 3,400lb (1,540kg); wing loading 14.22lb/sq ft (69.37kg/sq m) power loading 15.11lb/hp (6.84kg/hp).

Maximum speed 126mph (203km/h) at sea level; cruising speed 106mph (170km/h); rate of climb 675ft/min (205m/min) at sea level; service ceiling 13,000ft (3,960m); range 550 miles (885km).

*The prototype Travel Air Model 10 was fitted at a later date with a Wright J-6-7 radial engine.* (P M Bowers collection)

*The prototype Travel Air Model 10 (c/n 1008, C8844) in its original form with a 300hp Wright J-6-9 installed.*
(P M Bowers collection)

*In its original form, the travel Air B-11-D was known as 'The Bug'. Flown by W H Emery Jr, this aircraft was placed fourth in the 1929 Portland-to-Cleveland race.*
(P M Bowers collection)

## Model 11/11000

The final design of what can be considered the basic Travel Air biplane was the Model 11000 or Model 11. It is believed that two aircraft of this model were actually built. The first was most certainly the rebuilt Model D-2000 c/n 794, which was fitted with different wings using a thicker aerofoil section as well as different strut and aileron control arrangement, a different undercarriage, and a 240hp Wright J-6-7 engine under a full NACA cowling. It was flown by Marvel Crosson in the women's Los Angeles–Cleveland event of the 1929 National Air Races, on a restricted licence (registered R6473). Test flights showed that it was the fastest entry in the women's race, and so was given race number 12, but Miss Crosson crashed fatally near Wellton, Arizona.

### Model B-11-D

Completed in August 1929, the Model B-11-D (c/n 1267, registered NR612K) was a special two-seat cross-country racer. Apparently, it had a shortened and narrowed Model 4-D fuselage and modified undercarriage, but retained the short-span wings and vertical tail of the original 'Bug'. The engine was a 240hp Wright J-6-7 housed under a narrow-chord Townend ring that was eventually replaced by a full NACA cowling. As the Model B-11-D, and piloted by W H Emery Jr, this aircraft won fourth place in the Portland-to-Cleveland race of the 1929 National Air Races. At Cleveland, Ira M McConaughey flew it to fourth place in the 'Australian Pursuit' race at an average speed of 145.22mph. The Model B-11-D was eventually extensively modified for further racing. Refinements included a new forward fuselage adapted to the new NACA cowling, installation of a new low-drag undercarriage, and fitting of a rear turtledeck to fair in the closed rear cockpit canopy. At a later date, wingspan and wing area were reduced.

# Model R Mystery Ship

At the end of the 1928 air racing season, Herb Rawdon persuaded W H Beech to build an aircraft for the 1929 season that would defeat every aircraft in its category. In great secrecy, with the help of Walter Burnham, Rawdon designed a sleek monoplane with fixed undercarriage, and a 425hp Wright radial air-cooled engine as no inline engine was available in the desired power range. The externally braced low-wing made use of a RAF 34 aerofoil section, retained a two-spar construction and was covered with a layer of plywood. The fuselage was made of welded steel-tube, covered with plywood aft of the cockpit while sheet metal covered the area between the cockpit and cowling. The wheels were fully enclosed, and hydraulically-operated shock absorbers and wheel brakes were fitted. Construction of what was known as the Model R-100 (later as the Model R) began in June 1929. As this was a hush-hush project, no journalist was admitted in its vicinity, and the aircraft became rapidly known as the Mystery Ship. The maiden flight of the Model R took place on 18 August 1929 with Clarence Clark in the cockpit. The Model R (c/n R-2001, registered R613K, race No.31) was completed just in time to be entered in the National Air Races at Cleveland. Flown by Douglas Davis, the Mystery Ship startled the aviation world by outclassing all other contestants, military and commercial, in the free-for-all contest. Davis piloted the red-and-black Mystery Ship over the 50-mile course at an average speed of 194.96mph (313.69km/h), a remarkable performance for its day. This was the first occasion in which a civil aircraft had defeated military types in speed competitions (a Curtiss Hawk P-3A was placed second), and greatly boosted the monoplane as a speed competitor. NR613K was eventually damaged during 1930 while piloted by Lt Leroy McGrady. It was then bought by Walter Hunter and repaired to flying condition at Parks Air College. In 1931, during a test flight, the aircraft crashed and was totally destroyed.

Mystery Ship NR613K appeared in two films, *Tailspin Tommy* produced by Universal in 1934, and *International Squadron* produced by

*The Mystery Ship before leaving for Cleveland. The aircraft was painted bright red overall with black trim.* (D W Carter collection)

*In the Mystery Ship the Wright engine was carefully mated to the fuselage in order to reduce drag.* (D W Carter collection)

*After the Cleveland races, R613K was fitted with a Wright J-6-7 engine and sold to Florence 'Pancho' Barnes in May 1930.* (D W Carter collection)

Warner Bros in 1942. In the latter, the aircraft played the role of a RAF fighter.

A second Model R was entered at the National Air Races in 1929: a 175hp six-cylinder inline Chevrolair powered aircraft (c/n R-2002, registered R614K, race No.32), flown by Doug Davis, who won the experimental ship race at a speed of 113.38mph (182.428km/h). After the races, the Chevrolair engine was replaced by a Wright J-6-7, and the aircraft was sold to Florence Lowe 'Pancho' Barnes, then to Paul Mantz. Several years later, when the Paul Mantz collection was sold, the Model R was re-bought by Pancho Barnes and her son Bill Barnes.

A third Model R (c/n R-2003, registered NR482N) was delivered in April 1930 to the Shell Oil Co. The aircraft was piloted by James Haizlip who won the Illinois Air Races, at Glenview, and was placed second at the 1930 Thompson Trophy Race. In 1932, the aircraft was modified at Parks Air College and fitted with a 550hp Pratt & Whitney R-985 engine but it was destroyed during a test flight while piloted by Jimmie Doolittle.

*The third Model R to be built (c/n R-2003) was delivered to Shell Oil Co and piloted by James Haizlip and Jimmy Doolittle. The aircraft was painted yellow overall with red trim.*

*NR1313 as it appeared in 1931. Piloted by Frank Monroe Hawks, this aircraft set some 200 records.*

*The fifth and last Model R to be built was accepted by Commander Paulo Sbernadori for the Italian Government in 1931, but nothing is known of its career or its fate.* (D W Carter collection)

In June 1930, Travel Air began construction of their fourth Model R at the request of Capt Frank Monroe Hawks. The aircraft (c/n R-2004, registered NR1313), painted cream and vermilion was rolled out in July and named *Texaco 13*. After several city-to-city records had been set, the aircraft underwent modification for the coming Thompson Trophy Race. It was fitted with a 27ft 8in (8.43m) span wing. Unfortunately, Hawks was forced to pull off the course on the third lap. But during 1930-32, Hawks established more than 200 new city-to-city speed records in America and Europe, and earned the Ligue Internationale des Aviateurs medal as the world's outstanding airman. The *Texaco 13* career came to an end when it made a rough landing near Worcester, Massachusetts, on 22 September 1932. It was eventually donated to the Museum of Science & Industry in Chicago.

A fifth and last Model R (c/n R-2005) was built and sold to the Italian Government in July 1931. This aircraft was identical to *Texaco 13* in every respect. Its career and ultimate fate remain unknown to date.

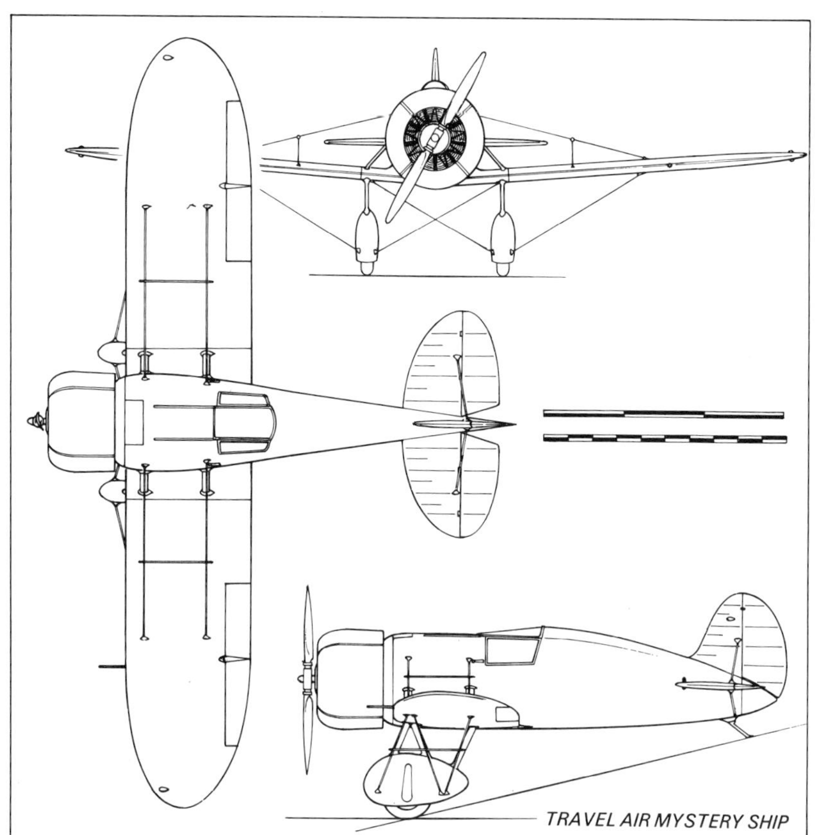


## Model R

One 425hp Wright J-6-9.

Span 29ft 2in (8.89m); length 20ft 2in (6.15m); height 7ft 9in (2.36m); wing area 125sq ft (11.61sq m).

Empty weight 1,485lb (672kg); gross weight 1,950lb (883kg); wing loading 15.6lb/sq ft (76.05kg/sq m); power loading 4.59lb/hp (2.08kg/hp).

Maximum speed 230mph (370km/h) at sea level; cruising speed 185mph (297km/h); rate of climb 3,200ft/min (975m/min) at sea level.

# Curtiss-Wright CW-12 Sport Trainer

During 1930, after the merging of Travel Air with the huge Curtiss-Wright Corporation, former Travel Air engineers Ted A Wells and Herbert Rawdon designed a new series of two-seat light biplanes to be powered by a variety of engines. Designed and built in Wichita with the designation CW-12, and often referred to as Curtiss-Wright Travel Airs, these aircraft retained a fuselage made of welded chrome-moly steel tubing faired to shape with wooden formers and spruce/plywood wing panels with dural metal covered leading edges. These aeroplanes were made available in three versions.

## Model 12Q

Introduced at the 1931 Detroit Air Show, this model powered by the 90hp four-cylinder, air-cooled Wright L-320 Gipsy inline engine, was developed specifically for sporting flying. Its wings had a Clark Y-15 aerofoil section and the prototype (c/n 2001, registered X-430W) first flew with Curtiss-Wright test pilot Lloyd Child at the controls. Price was $3,500 and production totalled 26 (c/ns 2001, 2004/2010, 2022/2039).

## Model 12K

This variant, powered with a 125hp five-cylinder radial Kinner B-5, was introduced soon after the Model 12 and displayed better overall performance. Priced $788 higher than the Model 12Q, the Model 12K did not sell well and only two were built (c/ns 2003 and 2011).

## Model 12W

Using a 110hp seven-cylinder radial Warner Scarab faired in a NACA low-drag cowling, the Model 12W was a deluxe variant featuring additional accessories. It was priced at $4,455 and 12 machines were built (c/ns 2002, 2012/2020, 2041/2042). Some Model 12Qs were eventually modified to 12W standards.

*The Model 12Q (here c/n 2030, N417W) was powered by a Wright Gipsy in-line engine. Optional equipment included an electric engine starter, metal propeller and weatherproof engine cover. This aircraft is owned by Dolph D Overton of Orlando, Florida.* (A R Krieger via J Wegg)

## Model 12Q

One 90hp Curtiss-Wright Gipsy.

Span upper 28ft 10in (8.78m); span lower 26ft 4in (8.02m); length 21ft 5in (6.52m); height 8ft 10in (2.69m); wing area 206.4sq ft (19.18sq m).

Empty weight 1,071lb (486kg); gross weight 1,725lb (782kg); wing loading 8.43lb/sq ft (40.77kg/sq m); power loading 19.17lb/hp (8.69kg/hp).

Maximum speed 105mph (169km/h); cruising speed 88mph (141km/h); rate of climb 600ft/min (183m/min) at sea level; service ceiling 12,000ft (3,660m); range 480 miles (772km).

## Model 12K

One 125hp Kinner B-5.

Dimensions as for Model 12Q except length 20ft 7in (6.27m).

Empty weight 1,164lb (527kg); gross weight 1,800lb (815kg); wing loading 8.72lb/sq ft (42.51kg/sq m); power loading 14.4lb/hp (6.52kg/hp).

Maximum cruising speed 112mph (180km/h); economic cruising speed 88mph (141km/h); initial rate of climb 800ft/min (244m/min) at sea level; service ceiling 14,000ft (4,270m); range 420 miles (675km).

## Model 12W

One 110hp Warner Scarab.

Dimensions as for Model 12Q except length 20ft 10in (6.34m).

*Model 12W c/n 2017, seen at Van Nuys in July 1964. Today, this aircraft is the property of James E Smith of Fortine, Montana.* (D W Carter)

*Model A-14D Sportsman c/n 2009 (NC12329). Only five A-14Ds were built.* (J Juptner via M P Bowers)

Empty weight 1,186lb (538kg); gross weight 1,800lb (816kg); wing loading 8.72lb/sq ft (42.51kg/sq m); power loading 16.36lb/hp (7.42kg/hp).

Maximum speed 117mph (188km/h); cruising speed 99mph (160km/h); rate of climb 780ft/min (237m/min) at sea level; service ceiling 15,000ft (4,570m); range 480 miles (772km).

# Curtiss-Wright CW-14 Sportsman, Speedwing and Osprey

A development of the Travel Air Model 4000 series, the Curtiss-Wright CW-14 was designed by Fred Landgraf in both three-seat civil and two-seat military versions. The wings had a NACA N-9 aerofoil section and a 23-US gallon (87 litres) fuel tank was mounted in the centre-section of the upper wing. A 43-US gallon (163 litres) fuel tank was installed in the fuselage ahead of the front cockpit. The undercarriage had Hydra-Flex shock absorbing struts.

## Model A14D Sportsman

This variant had the 240hp Wright R-760E (J-6-7) Whirlwind engine and five examples were built.

## Model B14B Speedwing Deluxe

Introduced at the 1932 Detroit Air Show, this Model was a high-performance aircraft. It was powered with the 300hp Wright R-975E (J-6-9). The Model B14B was priced $13,500, and only two examples were built, one (c/n 2010) operated by Curtiss-Wright Flying Service, the other (c/n 2011) by the Bureau of Air Commerce.

## Model B14R Special Speedwing Deluxe

Only one aircraft was built, for 'Casey' Lambert. It was powered by a 420hp Wright SR-975E radial engine and fitted as a single-seater.

## Model 14C

This military model prototype was fitted with a 185hp Curtiss Challenger engine and was eventually sold to the Argentine Government.

## Model C14B Osprey

This 300hp Wright R-975E powered variant was offered as a cheap fighter-bomber to small foreign countries. It was armed with two machine-guns and had provision for light bombs under the wings.

## Model C14R

This variant had a Wright J-6-9 Whirlwind engine installed, was armed with two machine-guns, and had provision for light bombs under the wings.

## Model A14D

One 240hp Wright J-6-7.

Span 31ft (9.44m); length 23ft 6½in (7.17m); height 9ft 1½in (2.78m); wing area 248sq ft (23.03sq m).

Empty weight 1,772lb (804kg); gross weight 2,870lb (1,302kg); wing loading 11.57lb/sq ft (56.53kg/sq m); power loading 11.96lb/hp (5.42kg/hp).

Maximum speed 155mph (250km/h); rate of climb 1,000ft/min (305m/min) at sea level; service ceiling 16,000ft (4,880m); range 600 miles (966km).

## Model C14R

One 420hp Wright R-975E.

Dimensions as for Model A14D.

Empty weight 2,186lb (992kg); gross weight 3,250lb (1,474kg); wing loading 13.1lb/sq ft (64kg/sq m); power loading 7.74lb/hp (3.51kg/hp).

Maximum speed 174mph (280km/h); cruising speed 157mph (253km/h); rate of climb 1,700ft/min (520m/min) at sea level; service ceiling 18,500ft (5,640m); range 580 miles (933km); armament one fixed and one flexible machine-gun, 500lb (227kg) bombs.

## Model 14C

One 185hp Curtiss Challenger.

Span 36ft (10.97m); length 23ft 10in (7.26m); height 9ft 7½in (2.93m); wing area 266.8sq ft (24.78sq m).

Empty weight 1,569lb (712kg); gross weight 2,600lb (1,179kg); wing loading 9.74lb/sq ft (47.58kg/sq m); power loading 14.05lb/hp (6.37kg/hp).

Maximum speed 120mph (193km/h); rate of climb 740ft/min (225m/min) at sea level; service ceiling 14,500ft (4,420m); range 600 miles (966km).

*The Model C14R Osprey was the armed export version of the Model 14. Machine-gun and bomb racks are clearly visible.* (P M Bowers collection)

*Only three Model 15Ds were built. These were powered by Wright J-6-7 engines. Seen here is Model 15D NC10928 in September 1935.* (P M Bowers)

## Curtiss-Wright CW-15 Sedan

In 1930 the former Travel Air engineer Walter Burnham designed a four-seat monoplane known as the Curtiss-Wright CW-15. Several versions of this type were offered. The CW-15C powered by a 185hp Curtiss Challenger radial, the prototype of which flew in 1931, was followed by eight production machines. The CW-15D was a more capable aeroplane with a 240hp Wright J-6-7 radial engine (three machines built), and the CW-15N was powered with a 210hp Kinner C-5 radial engine (three built).

### Model 15C

One 185hp Curtiss Challenger.

Span 43ft 5in (13.23m); length 30ft 5in (9.27m); height 8ft 10in (2.69m); wing area 240sq ft (22.29sq m).

Empty weight 2,083lb (945kg); gross weight 3,281lb (1,488kg); wing loading 13.67lb/sq ft (66.75kg/sq m); power loading 17.73lb/hp (8.04kg/hp).

Maximum speed 115mph (185km/h); cruising speed 97mph (156km/h); rate of climb 600ft/min (180m/min) at sea level; service ceiling 12,000ft (3,658m); range 525 miles (845km).

*The prototype Model 15 (X436W) first flew in 1931.* (P M Bowers collection)

### Model 15N

One 210hp Kinner C-5.

Dimensions as for CW-15C.

Empty weight 2,081lb (944kg); gross weight 3,279lb (1,487kg); wing loading 13.66lb/sq ft (66.71kg/sq m); power loading 15.61lb/hp (7.08kg/hp).

Maximum speed 125mph (201km/h); cruising speed 105mph (169km/h); rate of climb 700ft/min (210m/min) at sea level; service ceiling 13,000ft (3,962m); range 475 miles (764km).

# Curtiss-Wright CW-16 Light Sport

Introduced in 1932, the Curtiss-Wright CW-16 Light Sport was a three-seat version of the earlier CW-12. Only ten examples of the 165hp Wright J-6-5 radial engine powered CW-16E were built, followed by eleven CW-16Ks powered with a 125hp Kinner B-5 radial engine and a single 110hp Warner Scarab engined CW-16W. In 1935, the Forçà Aerea Brasileira bought fifteen 125hp Warner Scarab series 30 powered CW-16s which were used as primary trainers until 1940 (these aircraft were serialled K-175 to K-189).

### Model 16E

One 165hp Wright R-540E (J-6-5).

Span 28ft 10in (8.78m); length 21ft 1in (6.42m); height 8ft 10in (2.69m); wing area 206sq ft (19.13sq m).

Empty weight 1,320lb (599kg); gross weight 1,950lb (885kg); wing loading 9.46lb/sq ft (46.26kg/sq m); power loading 11.82lb/hp (5.36kg/hp).

Maximum speed 131mph (211km/h); cruising speed 111mph (179km/h); service ceiling 18,900ft (5,760m); range 336 miles (540km).

*The Model 16K c/n 2004 (N422W) survives today and is owned by Arthur L Lowe Jr of Lynchburg, Virginia* (G S Williams)

*The Model 16E illustrated (NC12380) was powered by a 165hp Wright R-540E radial.* (A R Krieger)

*Eleven Model 16Ks were built and fitted with Kinner B-5 radial engines.* (A R Krieger via J Wegg)

# Beech

## Model 17 Staggerwing, GB, JB, UC-43 Traveler

At the beginning of the thirties, Walter Beech foresaw a market for a fast enclosed-cabin biplane for executives. He visualised this aircraft having a top speed of 200mph (322km/h) and able to carry four or five passengers in luxury and comfort on long distances up to 1,000 miles (1,610km). When designing the Travel Air Model R, Ted Wells, Herb Rawdon and Walter Burnham had gained experience in high-speed flight. So, Ted Wells began designing a biplane the unique feature of which was the negative-stagger wing layout which procured good stall and recovery characteristics as well as good visibility for the crew. Unfortunately, the project did not draw the interest of the board at Curtiss-Wright. But, when Walter Beech formed his own company in 1932, he decided to complete the design which became the first Beechcraft aircraft, the Model 17.

The reliable 420hp Wright R-975-E2 Whirlwind radial engine was chosen as powerplant, which was to be enclosed in a NACA-type cowling and drove a two-blade Lycoming-Smith controllable-pitch propeller. A Navy N-9 aerofoil section was retained for the wings for low drag and a split rudder was fitted in order to reduce substantially the landing speed. This innovative rudder was activated by means of a lever in the cockpit. The structure of the fuselage was made of steel-tubes with wood and metal formers and wooden stringers. The wings were made of steel-tubes, had I struts and were fabric covered. The wheels of the fixed undercarriage could be partly retracted into their trouser fairings after take-off.

After a full-scale mock-up had been built with the help of Theodore and William Cochrane, in the old Cessna hangar, construction of the prototype was completed on 2 November 1932. Painted brilliant vermilion overall with brown trim and registered 499N, the first Beechcraft biplane took off from the Wichita Municipal Airport, built on the California Section grounds southeast of Wichita, for its uneventfull maiden flight at 12:30pm on 4 November 1932 with Pete Hill at the controls. Speed tests were begun on 9 November and showed a top speed of 199.5mph (321km/h). In later tests, top speed was increased to 201.2mph (324km/h). These tests also showed, a cruising speed of 180mph (290km/h), a landing speed of 60mph (96km/h), a take-off time of 12 seconds, a rate of climb of 1,600ft/min (487m/min), and a ceiling of 21,500ft (6,555m). The aircraft received its Type Certificate (No.496) on 20 December 1932 and Beechcraft c/n 1 was eventually sold to Ethyl Corporation. It was entered in the Miami Air Races held in January 1933, and, with Eric H Wood at the controls, it won the Texaco Trophy.

Although the prototype showed outstanding performance, W H Beech was not satisfied and asked for improvements. The engineers spent a year improving the aircraft and this resulted in better streamlining and a fast-acting fully retractable undercarriage. A new engine, a 225hp Jacobs R-775 radial, was installed. Flight tests of the new Beechcraft Model B17L (c/n 3, NC270Y) began on 2 February 1934

*The prototype Model 17 with its non-retractable faired undercarriage.* (P M Bowers collection)

and proved that these improvements were sound. Tooling for production was set up and three basic models were offered for sale: the Model B17L, the Model B17R and a high powered variant, the Model A17F with a 650hp Wright R-1820-F11 Cyclone.

Though the Cyclone-powered Beechcraft could fly faster than the Army Air Corps pursuit aircraft, there were few buyers. That is why most of the 18 aircraft built during 1934 were Model B17Ls. Happily for the young manufacturer, business climbed in 1935 and production doubled. The B17B, powered by a 285hp Jacobs L-5, was introduced in late 1934, and two new models were introduced in 1935: the Model B17E powered by a 285hp Wright R-760-E1 and the Model B17R fitted with a 420hp Wright R-975, while the Model A17F was abandoned. That year, a successful flight around the world by a Model B17R enhanced the fame of Beech. The trip was undertaken by Capt H L Farquhar, first secretary of the British legation at Mexico City, with Fritz Beiler as his navigator. The aircraft flew from North Beach, New York, to Heston, England, via Canada, Alaska, Siberia, China, India, and North Africa.

In 1936, more important improvements were introduced in the Model 17. The wing flaps were relocated, and the undercarriage legs shortened, resulting in better landing, take-off, and taxi-ing qualities. Minor changes were also incorporated. These improved biplanes were designated Models C17L, C17B, C17R. Permanent improvements led to seven new versions introduced on the production lines between February 1937 and April 1939 (D, E and F Models).

Throughout the war years, Beechcraft Aircraft Corp produced 105 Model 17s for the US Army and 320 for the US Navy. After cessation of war, production was resumed on a new version, the Model G17S, on a low scale. Not for long however for, in 1948, production was discontinued. A very last Staggerwing, a G17S, was assembled from parts on hand at the factory in 1949 (c/n B-20, registered N80321, sold by Henry Seale Aviation Supply of Dallas, Texas). In all, 781 Model 17s had been built of which 356 had been sold on the civil market.

*The prototype Model 17 was further modified to have a wider-track undercarriage. This aircraft, which crashed near Nunda, New York, on 10 December, 1935, is now on display at the Staggerwing Museum Foundation, in Tullahoma, Tennessee.* (Beech)

## Production History

### Model 17R

Introduced in 1934 and powered by a 420hp Wright R-975-E2 Whirlwind radial engine driving a 9ft (2.74m) diameter Hamilton Standard adjustable-pitch two-blade propeller, this variant had a non-retractable faired main undercarriage with electric motors that partially retracted the wheels in flight. It also had an electrically-operated pitch trim system that pivoted the entire empennage. Two aircraft were built: c/n 1 (499N, later NC499N) which flew on 4 November 1932 and c/n 2 (NC58Y) which was delivered on 11 July 1933 to Loffland Brothers Company of Tulsa, Oklahoma. Aircraft c/n 1 was eventually modified with narrow-chord flaps, wider track main undercarriage and fully-swivelling tailwheel before delivery to Ethyl Corporation on 19 April 1934. It was eventually destroyed in an accident at Nunda (New York) on 11 December 1935 during an abortive flight to Buffalo from New York. Pilot Dewey L Noyes and Ethyl assistant sales manager Edford M Walter were killed in the accident. In 1983, Steve Pfister recovered the remains of the aircraft and began a painstaking seven-year rebuilding. The Model 17R was priced at $19,000.

## Model A17F

Introduced in 1934 and designed to fly at 240mph (386km/h), the Model A17F had a 690hp Wright R-1820-F11 Cyclone radial engine driving a 9ft 6in (2.89m) diameter Hamilton Standard controllable-pitch two-blade propeller. It had narrow-chord flaps on the upper wings, a wider track undercarriage and a swivelling tailwheel; gross weight was 5,200lb (2,355kg). In the cabin, the rear seat was fitted with shock absorbers to reduce fatigue. Only one aircraft of this type was built (c/n 5, NC12583) for the Goodall Wortsted Company and Sanford Mills of Sanford, Maine, which took delivery of it on 30 May 1934. This aircraft was sold to Howard Hughes in November of the same year and eventually entered in the 1937 and 1938 Bendix races with Bob Perlick as its pilot. It was eventually used by the Curtiss-Wright Technical Institute and destroyed in a hangar fire in April 1944. Model A17F was priced at $24,500.

## Model A17FS

This model was a variant of the A17F powered by a 710hp Wright SR-1820-F3 radial engine; gross weight was 6,000lb (2,718kg). A single example (c/n 11, NC12569) was built in June 1934 for Louise Thaden and Frank Hawks to enter the Mac.Robertson Air Race. It was withdrawn before the race and eventually delivered to the Bureau of Air Commerce in Washington (with registration NS68) but its fate is not known. The Model A17FS was priced at $30,000.

*Beech Model A17F c/n 5 (NX12583) was delivered to Goodall Worsted Co of Sanford, Minnesota. It was eventually destroyed in a hangar fire in April 1944.* (A W Schmidt via P M Bowers).

## Model B17B

Introduced in late 1934, the Model B17 series had a retractable undercarriage as well as a Clark CYH aerofoil section and drag flaps. The Model B17B was powered by a 285 hp seven-cylinder Jacobs L-5 (R-830) radial engine driving an 8ft 3in (2.51m) diameter, laminated wood, black micarta, fixed-pitch metal or Hamilton Standard adjustable-pitch two-blade propeller. A single B17B was built in December 1934 (c/n 20, registered NC14408), which was delivered to F & W Martin and Co of Tulsa, Oklahoma. Its fate remains unknown. The Model B17B was priced at $9,000.

## Model B17E

Introduced in 1935, and powered by a 285hp seven-cylinder Wright

*Walter Beech poses with Model B17L c/n 15 (NC12598), which was delivered to Richard Archbold in November 1934.* (Beech)

*Model C17B c/n 130 (NC17072) was delivered to Wilcox Oil and Gas of Tulsa, Oklahoma, in May 1937.* (A R Krieger via J Wegg)

R-760-E1 radial engine driving an 8ft 3in (2.51m) diameter, laminated wood, black micarta, fixed-pitch metal or Hamilton Standard adjustable-pitch two-blade propeller, the Model 17E had drag flaps on the upper wings, shortened undercarriage legs and redesigned wingtip shape. Four of them were built and priced at $12,980.

### Model B17L

Introduced in 1934, with a 225hp seven-cylinder Jacobs L-4 (R-775) radial engine driving an 8ft (2.44m) diameter laminated wood, black micarta, fixed-pitch metal or Hamilton Standard adjustable-pitch two-blade propeller, the Model B17L cruised at 152mph (245km/h) and had a top speed of 166mph (267km/h). The first example (c/n 3, NC270Y) was first flown on 2 February, 1934 and received its Type Certificate on 4 December, 1934. Production totalled 48 examples priced at $8,000.

### Model SB17L

One Model B17L (c/n 40, NC15402) was built on 452lb Edo 38-3430 floats in September 1935 and delivered to Thomson Airways of Baltimore, Maryland. This aircraft, which was used in 1938 in a feature film entitled *Too hot to handle* with Clark Gable, Walter Pidgeon and Myrna Loy, was destroyed when it crashed into the Gulf of Mexico on 3 March 1943.

### Model B17R

Introduced in 1935, this variant was powered by a 420hp nine-cylinder Wright R-975-E2/E3 engine driving an 8ft 6in (2.59m) diameter Hamilton Standard adjustable- or controllable-pitch two-blade propeller, and was the first to be fitted with blind-flying instruments. Production totalled 16 aircraft, priced at $14,500.

### Model C17B

Introduced in February 1936, the C17 series replaced the B17 series. The Model C17B was powered by a 285hp seven-cylinder Jacobs L-5 (R-830) radial engine driving an 8ft 3in (2.51m) diameter laminated wood, black micarta, fixed-pitch metal or Hamilton Standard adjustable-pitch two-blade propeller. It featured drag flaps on the lower wings and the angle of incidence of the tailplane was changed. An additional fuel tank could be fitted as an option and increased total capacity to 166 US gal (628 litres). Forty Model C17Bs were built, priced at $9,250.

### Model SC17B

Only one example of this amphibian variant of the Model C17B was built in 1936 (c/n 99, NC16440), and was delivered to E O McDonnell of New York. Later impressed as an UC-43G, it was written off on 4 December 1942.

### Model C17E

Introduced in 1937, the Model C17E was powered by a 285hp seven-cylinder Wright R-760-E1 radial engine driving an 8ft 3in (2.51m) diameter laminated wood, black micarta, fixed-pitch metal or Hamilton Standard adjustable-pitch two-blade propeller. This variant had upper wing drag flaps and a 98-US gal (371 litres) lower wing fuel tank. In 1936 Nihon Koku Yuso KK (Japan Air Transport Company Ltd) imported one Model C-17E which was assembled in Japan and first flown there on 29 September 1936. In addition, Tachikawa purchased the manufacturing rights from Beechcraft and received a second aircraft in dismantled form and eventually produced 20 additional aircraft which were delivered to Dai Nihon Koku KK. Manshu, Chuka Koku and agencies such as the provincial police headquarters. The Model C17E was priced at $13,450.

*The sole Model SC17B floatplane (c/n 99, NC16640) was later impressed as a UC-43G and was wrecked at Bridgeport, Connecticut, on 25 September 1942.* (P M Bowers)

*J-ACHE was one of the twenty Model C17Es which were built under licence by Nihon Koku Yuso KK of Tokyo in 1936.* (P M Bowers)

## Model C17L

Introduced in 1936, the Model C17L was powered by a 225hp seven-cylinder Jacobs L-4 (R-775) radial engine driving an 8ft (2.44m) diameter laminated wood, black micarta, fixed-pitch metal or Hamilton Standard adjustable-pitch two-blade propeller. Having a top speed of 166mph (267km/h), only six C17Ls were built and priced at $8,550.

## Model C17R

This variant was introduced in 1936, and had a 420hp nine-cylinder Wright R-975-E2/E3 radial engine driving a 8ft 6in (2.59m) diameter Hamilton Standard adjustable- or controllable-pitch two-blade propeller. The C17R had upper wing drag flaps and a 98-US gal (371 litres) lower wing fuel tank. Production totalled 16. The Model C17R was priced at $14,500.

*Model D17A c/n 305 (NC19453) was delivered to S J Coughran in September 1939, and was later impressed as a UC-43F. This variant had a lengthened fuselage and a fully cantilevered tailplane.* (Beech)

## Model SC17R

With skis replacing wheels, the sole Model SC-17R (c/n 113, CF-BBB) was the first Model 17 to find its way to Canada, where it was flown by Mackenzie Air Service Ltd and several other operators. It was destroyed in a crash on 21 October 1955.

## Model D17A

Introduced in 1937, the D17 series had major changes including NACA 23012 aerofoil section plywood outboard wing panels, full-length flaps mounted on the trailing edge of the lower wing, relocation of the ailerons on the upper wing, redesigned tail unit providing full cantilever type tailplane and fin structure of greater cleanness and higher control efficiency, new shock absorbers and three fuel tanks with capacity totalling 102 US gal (386 litres). The fuselage was lengthened by 13⅜in and rib spacing was reduced to 6½in. The Model D17A, introduced in 1939, had a 350hp seven-cylinder Wright R-760-E2 Whirlwind radial engine driving an 8ft 6in (2.59m) diameter fixed-pitch metal or Hamilton Standard adjustable-pitch two-blade propeller. Ten Model 17As were built and priced at $16,350.

## Model D17R

The Model D17R was introduced in 1937. It was powered by a 420hp nine-cylinder Wright R-975-E3

*Model D17S c/n 396 (NC129M) was delivered to General Tire and Rubber Co in February 1940, and operated as* Miss Streamline III. *It was later impressed as a UC-34B.* (A R Krieger via J Wegg)

*Model D17S c/n 147 (NC18028) as operated by Aero Service Corp of Philadelphia, Pennsylvania.* (P M Bowers)

Whirlwind radial engine driving an 8ft 3in (2.51m) diameter Hamilton Standard adjustable- or controllable-pitch two-blade propeller. The Model D17R was priced at $18,370 and production totalled 27.

## Model D17S

Introduced in 1937, the Model D17S had a 450hp nine-cylinder Pratt & Whitney R-985-SB Wasp Junior radial engine driving an 8ft 3in (2.51m) diameter Hamilton Standard controllable-pitch two-blade propeller. Gross weight was 4,250lb (1,925kg) and 53 were built. The Model D17S was priced at $18,870.

## Model SD17S

The Model SD17S was a floatplane variant of the D17S fitted with Edo WA-4665 floats. A single aircraft was built (c/n 168, NC18566) and delivered to G A Hobart of Paterson, New York, in August 1937. Impressed in the US Navy as a GB-1 in 1942, it was struck off charge in July 1945.

## Model D17W

Introduced in 1937, the first Model D17W (c/n 136, NX17081) was built to the order of Frank Hawks. This variant had a 600hp supercharged and geared Pratt & Whitney R-985-SC-G Wasp Junior radial engine, but it was later re-engined with a 420hp Wright R-975 and delivered as a D17R in October 1936. A second D17W was built (c/n 164, R18562) and delivered in January 1937 to Jacqueline Cochran, who set with it several speed and altitude records. The Model D17W was priced at $20,600.

## Model E17B

The E17 series was introduced in 1937. This series retained the longer fuselage of the Model D17 but had a semi-cantilever tailplane, It also had long-span flaps on the trailing edge of the lower wing, and relocation of the ailerons on the upper wing. The Model E17B was powered by a 285hp seven-cylinder Jacobs L-5MB (R-830) radial driving an 8ft 6in (2.59m) diameter fixed-pitch metal or Hamilton Standard adjustable-pitch two-blade propeller. Gross weight was 3,390lb (1,535kg). Production totalled 50 aircraft and the Model E17B was priced at $10,490.

## Model SE17B

The Model SE17B was the amphibian variant of the E17B. Four of them were built (c/n 150, NC18039; c/n 210, NC18561; c/n 227, CF-BKQ and c/n 280, NC18778).

## Model E17L

Introduced in 1937, the Model E17L was powered by a 225hp seven-cylinder Jacobs L-4 (R-775) radial engine driving an 8ft 6in (2.59m) diameter laminated wood, fixed-pitch metal or Hamilton Standard adjustable-pitch two-blade propeller. Only one aircraft was built (c/n 161). It went to Argentina, being successively registered LV-AAK, LV-JEA, LV-AAK and LV-FBY. The Model E17L was priced at $9,690.

## Model F17D

Introduced in 1938, the F17D had upper wing ailerons, a lengthened fuselage and was powered by a 330hp seven-cylinder Jacobs L-6 (R-915) radial engine driving an 8ft 3in (2.51m) diameter Hamilton Standard adjustable or controllable pitch two-blade propeller. Production totalled 61 and this Model was priced at $13,980.

## Model SF17D

Only one SF-17D was built (c/n 414, NC21931) and delivered in

*GB-2 BuNo.01624 was accepted by the US Navy on 10 July 1941. It entered the civil market in 1947. Successively registered NC74584 and CF-GPO, it was mounted on floats and operated by Queen Charlotte Airlines.* (E M Sommerich)

April 1934 to the Maine Forest District. It was eventually scrapped in 1972 to help the rebuilding of another Model 17.

## Model G17S

Introduced in 1946, the Model G17S had a new type of engine mounting, a drag-reducing cowling, a redesigned windshield, a new exhaust system, larger control areas on the tailplane for easier and more positive control at all speeds, a new instrument panel, and many other refinements. This model, powered by a 450hp nine-cylinder Pratt & Whitney R-985-AN4 Wasp Junior radial engine driving an 8ft 3in (2.51m) diameter Hamilton Standard controllable-pitch two-blade propeller, had a top speed of 212mph (341km/h), a cruising speed of 201mph (323km/h), and a range of 1,000 miles (1,600km). Production totalled 20, of which 16 were built by Beech and four assembled from components procured from Henry Seale Aviation Supply Co. in Dallas, Texas. The last Model 17, delivered on 17 June 1949, was the Model G17S c/n B-20 (registered N80321). The Model G17S was priced at $29,000.

## GB-1

US Navy designation for ten Model D17Ss powered by the 400hp Pratt & Whitney R-985-48 and eight impressed Model D17s. In 1939 the Navy purchased its first seven GB-1s (BuNos. 1589/1595), followed in 1940 by three additional aircraft (BuNos. 1898/1900).

## GB-2

US Navy designation for 342 aircraft powered by the 450hp Pratt & Whitney R-985-AN1 radial engine. Deliveries were as follows: 23 aircraft in 1941, 44 in 1942, 85 in 1943, and 158 in 1944. These, named Traveller, were procured both for the Navy and for Lend-Lease delivery to Great Britain (75 aircraft). Brazil also received 14 GB-2s.

## JB-1

The first example of the Beech Model 17 to serve with the US Navy was purchased in 1937 and was a

*Model D17S c/n 404 (CF-DTF) was originally delivered to the Canadian Department of Transport in March 1940. It was destroyed in a crash in May 1960.* (P M Bowers)

*Model D17S c/n 424 (NC21934) was the last D17S produced. It was improved by Beech as the G17S. The new engine cowling and windscreen are noticeable.* (Beech)

civil C-17R. Designated JB-1 (c/n 115, BuNo. 0801), it flew as a staff transport for two years.

## YC-43

In November 1938, evaluation competitions were held by the US Army Air Corps to select a single-engine aircraft for use by military and naval attachés. The Beech Model 17 was selected for evaluation. Three examples of the commercial D17S were purchased with the designation YC-43, and were allocated to the United States Air Attachés in London (c/n 295), Paris (c/n 296) and Rome (c/n 297). These had Pratt & Whitney R-985-17 radial engines and with civil-type interior weighed 4,700lb. Aircraft c/n 295 was eventually impressed in to the Royal Air Force as DR628 and is still flying (it is owned by M J S Corvettes Inc of El Dorado, Kansas, and registered N295BS).

*The Model F17D was introduced in 1938 and was powered by a 330hp Jacob L-6 radial engine. This one (c/n 230, NC19466) is still flying but has been re-engined with a 300hp Jacob L-6MB.* (B Yeager)

## UC-43-BH

The results of the evaluation competitions were excellent, and work was started in 1939 on the US Government contracts. Beechcraft delivered to the Air Corps standard commercial aircraft with only slight modifications. Production totalled 270 aircraft of which 111 were transferred from the US Navy (of which two were eventually re-transferred to the US Navy), 63 went to the US Navy and 35 were delivered to the RAF as Traveller Is. These aircraft had landing lights under the lower wings and an ADF sensing loop antenna under the forward fuselage.

## UC-43A-BH

Designation given to 13 impressed Model D17Rs.

**UC-43B-BH**
Designation given to 13 impressed Model D17Ss.

**UC-43C-BH**
Designation given to 38 impressed Model F17Ds.

**UC-43D-BH**
Designation given to 23 impressed Model E17Bs.

**UC-43E-BH**
Designation given to 5 impressed Model C17Rs.

**UC-43F-BH**
Designation given to 1 impressed Model D17A.

**UC-43G-BH**
Designation given to 10 impressed Model C17Bs.

**UC-43H-BH**
Designation given to 3 impressed Model B17Rs.

**UC-43J-BH**
Designation given to 3 impressed Model C17Ls.

**UC-43K-BH**
Designation given to 1 impressed Model D17W.

**Traveller I**
British designation for the UC-43-BH; 106 delivered.

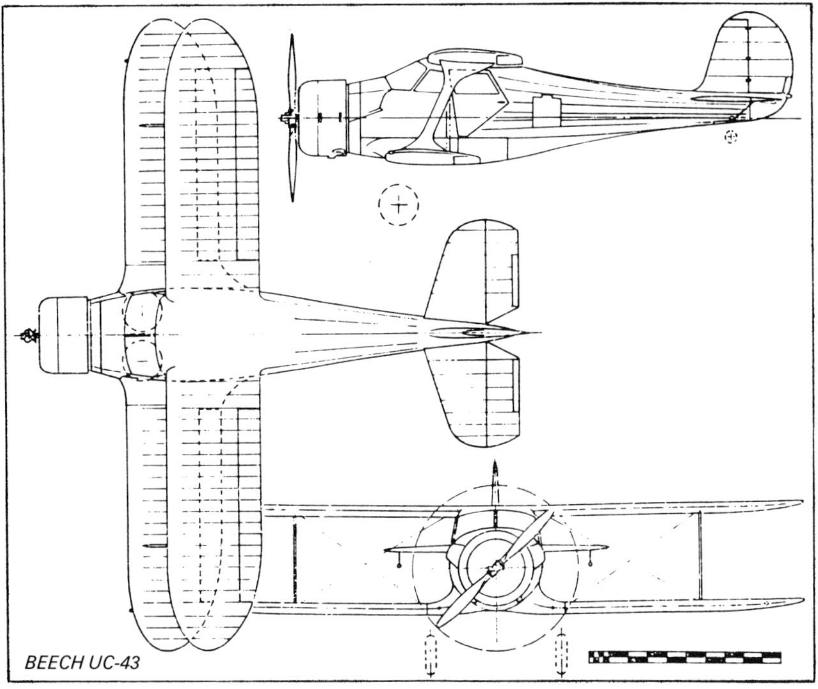

*NC80302 was the first production Model G17S (c/n B-1). It wears a temporary colour scheme with oversized US flags before delivery to the West Indies Sugar Corp in the Dominican Republic.* (Beech)

*Beech GB-1 BuNo, 1593 (c/n 302) was delivered to the US Navy on 26 June 1939 and operated by the Naval Attaché in Spain and Portugal. It is seen here in Barcelona in 1940.* (J A Cerdá collection)

## Service History

From the beginning, the Beechcraft Model 17 distinguished itself as an outstanding aircraft. Just a few weeks after its maiden flight, the prototype was entered in the Texaco Trophy held in Miami during January 1933. The aircraft, piloted by Eric H Wood, won first place at the average speed of 163mph (262km/h). In December 1934, one of the first Model B17Ls (c/n 18, ZS-BBC) went to the Danish consul-general at Johannesburg, Capt Otto Thaning. With it, Thaning broke almost every existing cross-country record in that part of the world. In 1936, the Mile-High Air Races at Denver, Colorado, held on 4 and 5 July, featured the Frank E Phillips Trophy. Like the Thompson Trophy Race, this race was a 50-mile run over a 5-mile (8km) closed course. Of the five aircraft which finished, three were Beechcrafts. First place was taken by a Model C17R flown by Bill Ong at an average speed of 191.971mph (308.881km/h). Second and fourth places also went to Beechcrafts. Then, in September 1936, Walter H Beech entered the Bendix Transcontinental Speed Dash, in the National Air Races from New Jersey to Los Angeles. The aircraft used was the same C17R (c/n 77, NC15835, race number 62) that had done so well in the Denver coast-to-coast race. In addition Olive Ann Beech persuaded her husband that the demonstration of the Beechcraft's outstanding performance would be even more convincing if a woman flew it. The selected woman pilot was Louise Thaden, who had broken altitude and endurance records in 1929 and 1932, and won several races flying Travel Air aircraft. As her navigator, Mrs Thaden chose Blanche Noyes. Vincent Bendix offered a special $2,500 prize to the first women to finish the race. To begin with, Louise Thaden set a national speed record for women on 29 May at St Louis, Missouri, flying the Model C17R at 197.958mph (318.514km/h) for a distance of 100km. Then, taking off early in the morning of 4 September, she flew to Los Angeles in exactly 14h 55min 1sec, almost 45 minutes ahead of her nearest competitor. Doing so, she had set a new transcontinental speed record for women pilots. She earned $7,000 in prize money, and received the Harmon Trophy, awarded by the Ligue Internationale des Aviateurs, as '*the outstanding woman pilot in the United States in 1936*'. Finally, Walter Beech offered Louise Thaden a job at the factory as a demonstration pilot. Far less sensational than the Bendix Trophy, but more important as a demonstration of the aircraft's safety features, was a special exhibition staged daily at the National Air Races. This consisted of a voluntary belly landing performed by Bill Ong aboard a Model C17B (c/n 110, NC15838). After each demonstration the aircraft was hoisted, the undercarriage was extended, and it taxied away. To close 1936 Beech victories, a C-17B won the Colonel E H R Green Trophy at 185mph (297km/h), in the Miami All-American Races.

During 1937, four modernised variants were introduced: Models E17B, D17R, D17S and D17W, but just a few examples of the last were sold. However, one of those Model D17Ws (c/n 164, NX18562) established a record when flown by its owner, Jacqueline Cochran. She set a new US women's speed record of 203.895mph (328.067km/h) over a course of 1,000km (621 miles) on 26 July 1937. Two days later, piloting the same aircraft, she set another speed record with 200.712mph (322.945km/h) over a 100-km (62-mile) course. This performance was so encouraging that Jacqueline Cochran entered her aircraft in the 1937 Bendix Race. A single-seat pursuit (Seversky SEV-S2) and a single-seat racer (Marcoux-Bromberg), each with 1,200hp engines, won first and second places, and Cochran took third place at the average speed of 194.740mph (313.337km/h). With a 600hp powered aircraft, this was a real accomplishment, both for Jacqueline Cochran and Walter Beech.

On 7 January 1938 the same Model D17W, with Max Constant at the controls, won first place in the 1,120-mile (1,800km) cross-country MacFadden Race between Floyd Bennett Field, New York, and Miami at the average speed of 204.277mph (328.681km/h). In the 1938 Bendix Race, Max Constant competed with Jacqueline Cochran who, for the occasion, flew a fighter (Seversky SEV-S2) and won first place. Second place went to another SEV-S2 aircraft; third place to a commercial monoplane (Lockheed Orion); fourth place to Max Constant at the average speed of 199.330mph (320.722km/h) and fifth place to a Model D17S flown by Ross Hadley.

On 7 January 1939 the D17W again proved its ability, winning the New York to Miami Sports record with Max Constant as pilot, flying 1,195 miles (1,922km) in 5h 43min. The same year, on 24 March, the

*GB-2 BuNo. 23689 (c/n 6701) was delivered to Britain under Lend-Lease agreement, where it served with the Royal Navy as FT475. It became G-BRVE with Early Birds Ltd in March 1990. It is seen at North Weald in May 1992.* (A J Pelletier)

indefatigable Jacqueline Cochran, flying a Model D17W, set a national women's altitude record at Palm Springs, California, climbing to 30,052.43ft (9,160m).

A few Staggerwings served in South-America on airline service. Aeronaves de Mexico operated a single B17R in 1938 (c/n 52, registered XA-BEV). In 1939, two of them (C-17D c/n 271, C-48 and C-17B c/n 135, C-49) were used in Colombia by ARCO (Aerovìas Ramales Colombianas). On 3 January 1940 in Argentina, TARSA (Transportes Aéreos Ranqueles) opened a service between Córdoba and Huinca Renancó using Model 17s, and, in 1941 D17S c/n 314 (PP-NAC) served with NAB (Navegação Aérea Brasileira) on the Rio de Janeiro–Recife route.

## Military Operators

**United States**: an initial contract for 27 production Model UC-43s was placed, these being similar to the Service test aircraft apart from having the R-985-AN-1 engine and some equipment changes which put the gross weight up to 4,800lb (2,175kg). Further contracts brought the total procurement of UC-43s to 207. Immediately after the entry of the US into the Second World War, considerable numbers of Model 17s were impressed for military service with UC-43 designations.

On 31 December 1941, 27 GB-1/GB-2s were on the US Navy inventory and used as Naval Stations' liaison aircraft: ten GB-1s were stationed at GINA New York, NAS Norfolk, NAS Pensacola, NAS Corpus Christi, NAS San Diego, NAS New York, NAF Air Detachment, and with Naval Attachés in Madrid and Mexico City; six GB-2s were stationed at NAS Anacostia, GINA Wright Field, NAD Pensacola and NAS New York; eleven GB-2s served on Naval Reserve Air Base Anacostia, Detroit, New Orleans, Boston, Long Beach, New York, Chicago, Kansas City, Seattle, Oakland and Atlanta.

**Australia**: three aircraft were impressed into the RAAF where they served as fast transports (c/n 108, 248 and 357, respectively serialled A39-3, A39-1 and A39-2).

**Bolivia**: a single Model 17R received the Fuerza Aérea Boliviana colours (most probably c/n 184) but its fate is not known to date.

**Brazil**: four D-17As were bought from Beechcraft and designated D1Be (serialled D1Be-205/208). They served with the Brazilian Navy in 1940/41, and three were eventually transferred to Fuerza Aérea Brasileira in 1941. A total of 51 Beechcraft D-17S/GB-2s (serialled FAB-01/51, later FAB-2736/2786) were operated by the FAB from 1942 till 1960 under UC-43 designation and were most commonly known as the Beech Mono.

**China**: in 1938, a fleet of eleven D17Rs fitted out with ambulance equipment was built for the Chinese Government commited in the undeclared war with Japan (c/ns 181/182, 217, 235/237, 239, 325/326, 328/329). A later batch of ten UC-43s was delivered under Lend-Lease agreement (c/ns 3116, 3189/3197).

**Cuba**: after the war, a single Model 17 was operated by the Fuerza Aerea Ejercito de Cuba. Its identity remains unknown.

**Finland**: Two aircraft were operated by the Ilmavoimat, C17L c/n 124 with BC-1 serial and D17 c/n 6885 with BC-2 serial.

**Germany**: in October 1936, the Model B17R c/n 66 (F-APFD) was sold to René Drouillet of Paris, sometime adviser to the Emperor Haïlé Selassié of Ethiopia. The purchase and use of the aircraft involved a plot to kidnap the Emperor which was financed by the Italians but became unnecessary when the government in Abyssinia collapsed. The aircraft was sold, re-sold and, in July 1937, became *The Negus* of the Spanish-subsidised French airline Air Pyrénées. Flown by Georges Lebeau, it was used to search for Abel Guidez's aircraft, shot down near Bilbao. This aircraft was captured by the German Army and eventually displayed at the Beutepark der Luftwaffe 5 at Paris-Nanterre along with other captured aircraft, in order to provide Luftwaffe personnel with a knowledge of Allied equipment. It was flown by the Germans and crashed on take-off, killing its crew. The wreck of this Staggerwing was discovered at the end of the war by Robert Louis, who salvaged the constructor's number plate and sent it back to W H Beech.

**Great Britain**: two civil Beech 17s (DR628 and DS180) were impressed for the Royal Air Force in May 1941, and in June two more aircraft (EN279/280) were purchased for the use of the British Purchasing Commission in Washington. A total of 95 additional aircraft were purchased under Lend-Lease agreement. The type was widely used by the Royal Navy and some went to the RAF. With the Fleet Air Arm, the Travellers were mainly used in communications units such as No.701 Squadron at Heathrow, No.712 Squadron at Hatston, No.725

*The first YC-43 (c/n 295, s/n 39-139) served with the USAAC and RAF before being sold on the commercial market as NC91397 in 1947. It then became G-AMBY and later VP-YIV to be operated by Commercial Air Service of Kumalo, Southern Rhodesia. It still flies as N295BS.* (John Wegg collection)

Squadron at Eglinton, No.730 Squadron at Ayr, No.740 Squadron at Machrihanish, No.781 Squadron at Lee-on-Solent and No.782 Squadron at Donibristle. Others were spread among various units, and stations, as hacks. Various RAF communications flights flew Travellers in the Middle East and a few were assigned as personal transports.

**Honduras**: two Model 17s were delivered to the Escuela Militar de Aviacion (B17L c/n 9 serialled 11, and D17R c/n 77 also serialled 11).

**Netherlands**: one D17S (c/n 420, serialled PB1) was delivered to the Netherlands Purchasing Commission in 1941 and flown in the United Kingdom. It is reported to have been destroyed at Antwerp on 1 January 1945.

**New Zealand**: in September 1939, Model C17L c/n 107 (registered ZK-AEU) was impressed by the RNZAF and received the serial NZ573. It was re-registered in March 1946 as ZK-AJS.

**Peru**: the Fuerza Aérea del Peru received five aircraft (two surplus UC-43s and three GB-2s, serialled FAP428/432). They were withdrawn from use at the end of the fifties.

**Spain**: the Model B17L bought by F Fernandez in 1935 (c/n 33, registered EC-BEB) was impressed in 1937 into the Republican Air Force. It was used as a reconnaissance aircraft, and even once as a bomber on the Aragon front line. It was completely destroyed by a storm together with a Potez 43 at Sarinena. Another Model 17 is also known to have served with Republican forces.

**Uruguay**: one UC-43 (c/n 4939, serialled S-501) was delivered in 1943 and operated by Escuela Militar de Aeronautica at Aerodromo Militar General Artigas, in Pando.

## Preserved Aircraft

More than 220 Staggerwings survive today, most of which are in the United States. At the time of writing some 210 could be found on the US civil register (one B17E, nine B17Ls, two B17Rs, five C17Bs, four C17Ls, three C17Rs, one D17A, two D17Rs, 147 D17Ss, six E17Bs, seven E17Ls, 21 F17Ds, one G17S and one SE17B) and several other machines are preserved in Museums. The Staggerwing Museum in Tullahoma, Tennessee, has Model 17R NC499N miraculously unearthed from a ravine in which it was buried after its crash in 1935, B17L c/n 58, D17S c/n 395, E17B c/n 231, F17D c/n 333 and G17S c/n B-3. The Lone Star Flight Museum in Houston, Texas, has D17S c/n 6737. The Planes of Fame East in Eden Prairie, Minnesota, has D17S c/n 6897. The USAF Museum in Dayton, Ohio, has D17S c/n 6913. The Yankee Air Corps in Chino, California, has D17S c/n 4890. The US Naval Aviation Museum in Pensacola, Florida, has D17s c/ns 6700 and 6917. The Wedell Williams Memorial Aviation Museum in Patterson, Louisiana, has D17S c/n 264. The Museum of Flight in Seattle, Washington, has D17S c/n 295. The National Air and Space Museum in Washington, DC, has C17L c/n 93 and the Colonial Flying Corps Museum in Toughkenamon, Pennsylvania, has an unidentified D17S.

### Model 17R

One 420hp Wright R-975-E2 Whirlwind.

Span 34ft 4in (10.46m); length 24ft 3in (7.39m); height 8ft 8in (2.64m); wing area 323sq ft (30sq m).

Empty weight 2,700lb (1,223kg); gross weight 4,500lb (2,038kg); wing loading 13.93lb/sq ft (67.95kg/sq m); power loading 10.71lb/hp (4.85kg/hp)

Maximum speed 201 mph (323km/h); cruising speed 170mph (273km/h); rate of climb 1,500ft/min (457m/min); service ceiling 20,000ft (6,100m).

### Model B17L

One 225hp Jacobs L-4 (R-775-D).

Span 32ft 0in (9.75m); length 24ft 5in (7.44m); height 8ft 6in (2.59m); wing area 273sq ft (25.36sq m).

Empty weight 1,650lb (747kg); gross weight 3,165lb (1,433kg); wing loading 11.53lb/sq ft (56.50kg/sq m); power loading 14.07lb/hp (6.37kg/hp).

Maximum speed 175mph (281km/h) at sea level; cruising speed 162mph (260km/h) at

*A GB-1 taken over by the USAAF and sent to China under Lend-Lease agreement.* (Beech via E Phillips)

5,000ft (1,525m); rate of climb 1,000ft/min (305m/min); service ceiling 15,000ft (4,570m).

### Model C17B

One 285hp Jacobs L-5/5M/5MB (R-830-1).
Dimensions as for Model B17L except height 8ft 2in (2.49m).
Gross weight 3,165lb (1,433kg); wing loading 11.53lb/sq ft (56.50kg/sq m); power loading 11.10lb/hp (5.03kg/hp).
Cruising speed 177mph (285km/h) at 7,200ft (2,195m); rate of climb 1,100ft/min (335m/min) at sea level.

### Model D17R

One 450hp Wright R-975-E3 (R-975-11).
Span 32ft (9.75m); length 26ft 11in (8.2m); height 8ft (2.44m); wing area 296sq ft (27.5sq m).
Empty weight 2,460lb (1,114kg); gross weight 4,250lb (1,925kg); wing loading 14.36lb/sq ft (70.01kg/sq m); power loading 9.44lb/hp (4.28kg/hp).
Maximum speed 211mph (339km/h) at sea level; cruising speed 202mph (325km/h) at 9,700ft (2,955m); rate of climb 1,400ft/min (426m/min) at sea level; service ceiling 24,000ft (7,315m).

### Model E17B

One 285hp Jacobs L-5 (R-830-1).
Dimensions as for Model D17R except length 25ft 11in (7.9m).
Empty weight 2,080lb (942kg); gross weight 3,390lb (1,535kg); wing loading 11.32lb/sq ft (55.84kg/sq m); power loading 11.89lb/hp (5.38kg/hp).
Maximum speed 185mph (297km/h) at sea level; cruising speed 177mph (284km/h) at 7,200ft (2,195m); rate of climb 1,200ft/min (365m/min) at sea level; service ceiling 18,000ft (5,485m).

### Model F17D

One 330hp Jacobs L-6/6M/6MB (R-915-A3).
Dimensions as for Model E17B.
Gross weight 3,590lb (1,626kg); wing loading 12.13lb/sq ft (59.13kg/sq m); power loading 10.88lb/hp (4.93kg/hp).
Cruising speed 182mph (293km/h); rate of climb 1,300ft/min (396m/min).

### Model G17S

One 450hp Pratt & Whitney R-985-AN-1.
Dimensions as for Model D17R except length 26ft 9in (8.15m).
Empty weight 2,800lb (1,268kg); gross weight 4,250lb (1,925kg); wing loading 14.35lb/sq ft (70.01kg/sq m); power loading 9.44lb/hp (4.28kg/hp).
Maximum speed 212mph (341km/h) at 5,500ft (1,675m); cruising speed 201mph (323km/h) at 10,000ft (3,050m); rate of climb 1,250ft/min (381m/min) at sea level; service ceiling 20,000ft (6,100m).

## Model 18 C-45 and JRB Expeditor, AT-7 and SNB Navigator, AT-11 Kansan

With the intention of not relying on a single aircraft design, Walter H Beech and Ted A Wells thought of a new aircraft able to fulfil customers' needs. From a survey of the potential customers, they drew a set of specifications and put them out to a small team of engineers including Dean Burleigh, Virgil Adamson, W B Woody, W R Blakley, Jack Wassail and others. This team, led by Ted Wells, spent a full year deciding on the general layout of the future aircraft. The new Beech model would combine low operating cost, cabin comfort and safety comparable to that found on airliners, the ability to operate from small airfields, a high degree of reliability and ease of repair. Work on the Model 18, as it was now known, began in December 1935, approximately 14 months ahead of its first flight. The Model 18 was radically different in construction and design to the now familiar Model 17. In order to combine maximum strength with light weight, the airframe had a truss-type centre section built by welding together high-strength chrome steel tubing into a one-piece structure. However, precise hand crafting was necessary for this kind of structure and Beech had no experience in this field. The wing retained a NACA 23000 series aerofoil section (NACA 23018 at the root, and NACA 23012 outboard of the nacelles to the tip). This kind of aerofoil had been chosen for its handling and

*The prototype Beech 18. It was powered by two 320hp R-760-E2 radials.*

*The prototype Model 18 postwar, after it had been modified to Model 18B configuration. The aircraft is nicknamed* Son of Beech. (E M Sommerich)

speed characteristics (the same general aerofoil section was to be used on many future Beech designs). A twisting of the wing was also employed to control stall characteristics. Control surfaces, including ailerons, rudder and elevators, had an all-metal structure but were fabric covered. As powerplants, two 320hp Wright R-760-E2 seven-cylinder air-cooled radial engines had been selected. The electrically operated classic undercarriage retracted backwards into the engine nacelles.

The aircraft was rolled out in early January 1937. For the maiden flight, a pilot from Trans World Airlines, James N Payton, was selected because he was familiar with twin-engine aircraft. H C 'Ding' Rankin, Beech test pilot, acted as co-pilot for the flight, and R E Williams of Wright Aeronautical Corporation flew as an observer. On Friday afternoon 15 January 1937 Payton took the new Twin Beech, (c/n 62, registered NC15810) as it was known in-house, aloft. An intensive test programme including static load tests was followed by an uneventful first flight, and further test flights were made by the TWA pilot Capt Jack Thornburg. After 23 hours 20 minutes had been logged, the government type certification was granted on 4 March 1937. The Model 18 offered a cruising speed of 196mph (315km/h) at a gross weight of 6,700lb (3,035kg), a range in excess of 1,000 miles (1,610km), and was priced approximately at $30,000.

The prototype was the first to be sold (for $32,752.80), and was sold on 23 June 1937 to Ethyl Gasoline Corp which sold it to W C Talbot on 5 April 1938, who in turn sold it back to Beech on 23 August 1939. It was sold to the Department of Munitions and Supply, offered for sale to the British Commonwealth Air Training Plan in Canada and taken on charge by the RCAF on 16 September 1941 with serial 8650. This historic aircraft eventually found its way to the Smithsonian Institution, where it is in storage.

Despite the survey carried out by Beech and Wells in 1935, sales were limited. The Beech could not compete with the Lockheed Electra

*Two months after the end of the Second World War, the Model D18S became the first postwar commercial aircraft to receive a government Type Certificate.* (Beech)

*Model D18S N4711V of Angeles Flying Service was fitted with an extra-large door.* (P M Bowers)

Junior because it was seriously underpowered. However, through the late 1930s, improvements were made to the Model 18 resulting in Wright, Jacobs and Pratt & Whitney-powered variants in five series with gross weight increased to 7,200lb (3,261kg) and cruising speeds to 225mph (362km/h). Then, in August 1938, Ted Wells and Dean E Burleigh started the design of a more powerful variant, the Model 18S. Powered by 450hp Pratt & Whitney Wasp Junior radial engines, the prototype, in January 1940, won the famous MacFadden Trophy. With Rankin at the controls and W Beech serving as co-pilot, the aircraft flew 1,084 miles (1,744km) nonstop from St Louis, Missouri, to Miami at an average speed of 234mph (376km/h).

Beechcraft Model 18 sales reached a total of 39 units by the formal start of the war, including a order by the Chinese Government. (Three Model 18As, one Model S18A, three Model 18Bs, one Model S18B, nine Model 18Ds, three Model S18Ds, one Model 18R, twelve Model 18Ss and six Model M18Rs). After the war and the huge military orders, Beech Aircraft lost no time in returning to civilian production. Only two months after the Japanese surrendered, the first postwar commercial Beechcraft, an eight-seat deluxe executive version of the military C-45, was ready for flight tests. This new model, known as the D18S, had a 20 per cent increase in gross weight, as well as increased range and payload. Aerodynamic drag had been reduced with the introduction of flush riveting. Model 18 production continued into 1957, with a total of 6,326 aircraft delivered since 1937, 499 of which had been exported. Super 18 deliveries totalled 762, from 1954 to 1969, with exports accounting for 117. Continued attention to the almost limitless variety of missions of the Model 18 had resulted in a total of 207 improvements to the basic design from January 1954 to August 1958. In 1959, modification kits were made available to update all C-45G, C-45H, TC-45G, and D-18S series to the newer Super 18 configuration. The world's longest continuous air-

*One of the last Model 18s to be delivered was this Super H18 (JA5000) ordered by Japan Air Lines.* (Beech)

*The Model E18S was introduced in 1954. It had increased cabin area, square wingtip extensions and a 9,300lb gross weight. This one is registered N3460B.* (Beech)

craft production record came to an end on 26 November 1969, when the last three Super H18s were delivered to Japan Air Lines, making a total of 13 Super H18s for that company.

## Production History

### Model 18A and S18A

First production model powered by two 320hp Wright R-760-E2 engines driving two-blade constant-speed propellers. The Model S18A was capable of operating on floats or skis. Production totalled four aircraft (c/n 62, NC15810, went to Ethyl Gasoline Corp, c/n 172/CF-BGY went to Staratt Airways and Transportation, c/n 291/CF-BQG and c/n 318/CF-BQH went to Canadian Airways).

### Model 18B and S18B

This variant was offered in 1938, with 285hp Jacobs L-5 engines, and was capable of operating on floats or skis. Production totalled four aircraft (c/n 170/NC18583 went to O J Whitney, c/n 171/NC18567 to E W Wiggins, c/n 173/NC18569 to Aerovias de Puerto Rico and c/n 174/NC1284 was used for the McFadden Trophy, bearing race number 11).

### Model 18D and S18D

This production variant was introduced in 1938. It had two 330hp Jacobs L-6 engines, and the Model S18D was capable of operating either on floats or skis. The first production Model 18D was built in May 1938 and production totalled 12 aircraft (c/n 169/NC19578, 175/NC18571, 176/NC18572, 177/CF-BKN, 178/CF-BKO, 220, 221/NC20775, 223, 224/CF-BMI, 265/NC3250, 267/CF-BMU and 268/NPC-54).

### Model 18R

Only one Model 18R was built (c/n 321) and it was equipped as a flying hospital and taken on charge by the Swedish Air Force on 9 April 1940. It had Wright R-975 engines.

### Model M18R

Six Wright R-975 engined aircraft were delivered to the National Chinese Government in September 1940.

### Model 18S

This Model was a more powerful variant equipped with two 450hp Pratt & Whitney Wasp Junior radial engines and had a larger vertical fin and rudder and increased gross weight due to the engine installation. Twelve aircraft were built: c/n 222/NC19452 went to Olson Drilling Co, c/n 266/NC2814 went to Belfair Co Inc, c/n 269/NC77V went to Lawrence H Hughes, c/n 290/CF-BQQ went to Canadian Airways, c/n 292/NC20756 went to E W Wiggins, c/n 294/NC20757 went to W C Talbot, c/n 316/NC2500 went to Continental Can Co, c/n 430/PP-NAA and 431/PP-NAB went to NAB, c/n 432/NC21927, c/n 433/NC21925 went to Electric Auto-Lite and c/n 434/NC1040 went to Evening News Publishing Co).

### Model B18S

This model differed from the Model 18S only in having interior changes. According to Aircraft Specification A757, aircraft c/ns 430/434 were originally B18S aeroplanes. The military F-2s, C-45s, C-45As and C-45Cs were also B18Ss.

### Model C18S

In late 1944, Beech produced a small quantity of this variant for the civil market, but all of the Second World War military models, except for AT-11/SNB-1, were C18Ss. The prototype C18S was the C-45B c/n 5862. Engines were 450hp Pratt & Whitney R-985s. It was soon replaced by the Model D18S. After the war, all Second World War military models (except AT-11/SNB-1) became eligible for civil certification as C18Ss.

### Model D18S

Introduced in 1947, the Model D18S was a six- to nine-seat deluxe executive version with 20 per cent increase in gross weight and increased range and payload. Flush riveting was employed on wing leading edges, nose section and in other areas to reduce aerodynamic drag. The top of the engine nacelle fairings were extended further aft on the wing for the same reason. This first postwar commercial aircraft received its government type certificate on 26 April 1946. The Model 18S was the first Beech aircraft to be concerned with the new constructor's number system which assigned a separate c/n for each model. The Model D18S was thus designated by the prefix letter A followed by the c/n. The Model D18S was priced at approximately $63,000.

### Model D18C

This variant of the D18S was introduced during 1947 for feeder airlines. It had twin 525hp Continental R-9A radial engines, which were a development of the 450hp Wright R-975 Whirlwind. Seating ten, the

*A C-45F-BH in prewar yellow and blue colour scheme.* (P M Bowers)

Model D18C had a 9,000lb (4,077kg) gross weight and a 231mph (371km/h) cruising speed. The D18C was priced at $64,250 and production totalled 13 aircraft. Most surviving D18Cs and D18C-Ts were eventually converted to D18Ss because of problems with the Continental engines.

## Model D18C-T

Introduced in 1946, this variant was designed to seat 8-9 passengers and to be used as a small airliner. It was powered by two 525hp Continental R-9A engines driving fully-feathering propellers. Three aeroplanes (NC80010, NC80011 and NC80363) went into mail pickup service with All American Aviation. Other operators included Empire Airlines, Florida Airways, Hawaiian Airlines, Texas Airlines, Challenger Airlines and Inland Airways. Production totalled 16 aircraft. The Model D18C-T was priced at $64,887.

## Model E18S and E18S-9700

Early in 1954, the redesigned Super 18 (Model E18S) was introduced. It had greater cabin area through an increase in fuselage height (6in). The cabin windows and the door were enlarged and the pilot's compartment had a new layout. Added wing area was provided by new wingtips, and improved cooling of the power plant installation increased rate of climb, single-engine service ceiling and cruising speed, to 215mph (346km/h). A 550lb (249kg) increase in gross weight made possible the provision of an 80-US gallon (302 litre) nose fuel tank. The Model E18S was produced until January 1960 when it was replaced by the Model G18S. A variant was the Model E18S-9700 which was equipped with three-blade Hartzell propellers and had a gross weight of 9,700lb (4,394kg). Production totalled 403 E18Ss and 57 E18S-9700s.

## Model G18S

This improved variant of the E18S was introduced in December 1959. Identical to the E18S-9700, it had a new two-piece windshield and a large centre cabin window. Production totalled 156 aircraft delivered between 1959 and 1963.

*The Model G18S was the first Twin-Beech to have three-blade propellers. A new windshield and large centre cabin windows were other features of this variant.* (Beech)

*A tricycle undercarriage and extended nose section were offered as factory installed optional items on the Model H18 series.* (Beech)

### Model H18

This was the final version of the Twin Beech. The H18 was powered by two 450hp Pratt & Whitney R-985-AN14B Wasp Junior radial engines driving three-blade lightweight Hamilton Standard fully-feathering propellers. It seated from six to ten people and had, among several other improvements, new half-fork undercarriage struts, smaller wheels and electric cowl flaps. Air conditionning was also made available and main fuel tank capacity was increased to 99 US gallons (375 litres). From 1963, the Volpar-designed tricycle undercarriage installation was made available and installed at the Beech factory. Production totalled 149 aircraft. A standard-equipped Model H18 was priced at $179,500.

## Military Models

### C-45-BH

This six-seat transport model, similar in all respects to the commercial model, was powered by two 450hp R-985-17 radial engines. Eleven examples were purchased by USAAC with the first aircraft delivered on 29 February 1940; became UC-45-BH.

### C-45A-BH

Second military variant with eight-seat interior, DF loops on the rear fuselage and two 420hp R-985-AN1 radial engines for use as general duty light transports. Twenty delivered between March and August 1940; became UC-45A-BH.

### RC-45A-BH

Designation given in June 1948 to surviving F-2As and F-2Bs.

### UC-45A-BH

ex-C-45A-BH.

### C-45B-BH

Variant similar to C-45A but with revised interior, higher gross weight. Production totalled 222 plus one AT-7-BH completed as C-45B-BH.

### UC-45B-BH

ex-C-45-BH.

### UC-45C-BH

Designation given to two commercial six-seat Model B18S transports impressed for war service.

### UC-45D-BH

Two aircraft from an AT-7-BH contract which were completed as five-seat communications aircraft, with two 450hp Pratt & Whitney R-985-AN-1 engines.

### UC-45E-BH

Six aircraft from an AT-7B-BH contract which were completed as five-seat communications aircraft, with two 450hp Pratt & Whitney R-985-AN-3 engines.

### DC-45F-BH

Designation given in June 1948 to surviving CQ-3-BHs.

### RC-45F-BH

At least, one aircraft (s/n 43-35937) converted for photographic survey work.

### UC-45F-BH

Final production model with seven seats, two 450hp Pratt & Whitney R-985-AN-1 engines and a slightly lengthened nose. Production totalled 1,522 of which 42 were completed as F-2B-BH and 343 were diverted to the US Navy as JRB-3 and JRB-4.

### C-45G-BH

In 1951, the continuing value of the C-45 led to a major programme of 'rejuvenation' for most of the existing C-45Fs, RC-45As, AT-7s and AT-11s. After re-manufacture by Beech in its Herington modification centre with 450hp Pratt & Whitney R-985-AN-3 engines and a

*Beech C-45F-BH (s/n 44-87183) after the war, displaying buzz-number TC-183.* (A J Pelletier collection)

Jack and Heinz A-3A autopilot, these aircraft were redesignated C-45G and new constructor's numbers and serial numbers were allocated. Other modifications included a heavier wing centre section truss structure, new undercarriage struts, wheels and brakes, new instrument panel and Aeroproducts constant-speed, fully-feathering propellers. Production totalled 372 aircraft.

### Model TC-45G-BH

Ninety-six aircraft which were rebuilt as navigational trainers with accommodation for two crew and three students.

### C-45-BH

Rebuilt aircraft similar to C-45G-BH but powered by 450hp Pratt & Whitney R-985-AN-14B engines driving fully-feathering Hamilton Standard Hydromatic propellers, and no auto-pilot. Production totalled 432 machines.

### RC-45H-BH

Photographic survey conversion of the C-45H-BH.

### TC-45H-BH

Navigation training conversion of the C-45H-BH with accommodation for three students and instructor. Became UC-45J.

### C-45J

Designation given to two UC-45Js which went to the Army (BuNos. 23822 and 51312).

### NC-45J

Designation given to two TC-45Js (BuNos. 23829 and 39829) used as flying test beds.

### RC-45J-BH

Designation given in 1962 to surviving SNB-5Ps.

### TC-45J-BH

Designation given in 1962 to surviving SNB-5s.

### UC-45J-BH

New designation given to TC-45Js when primary mission changed from training to utility transport.

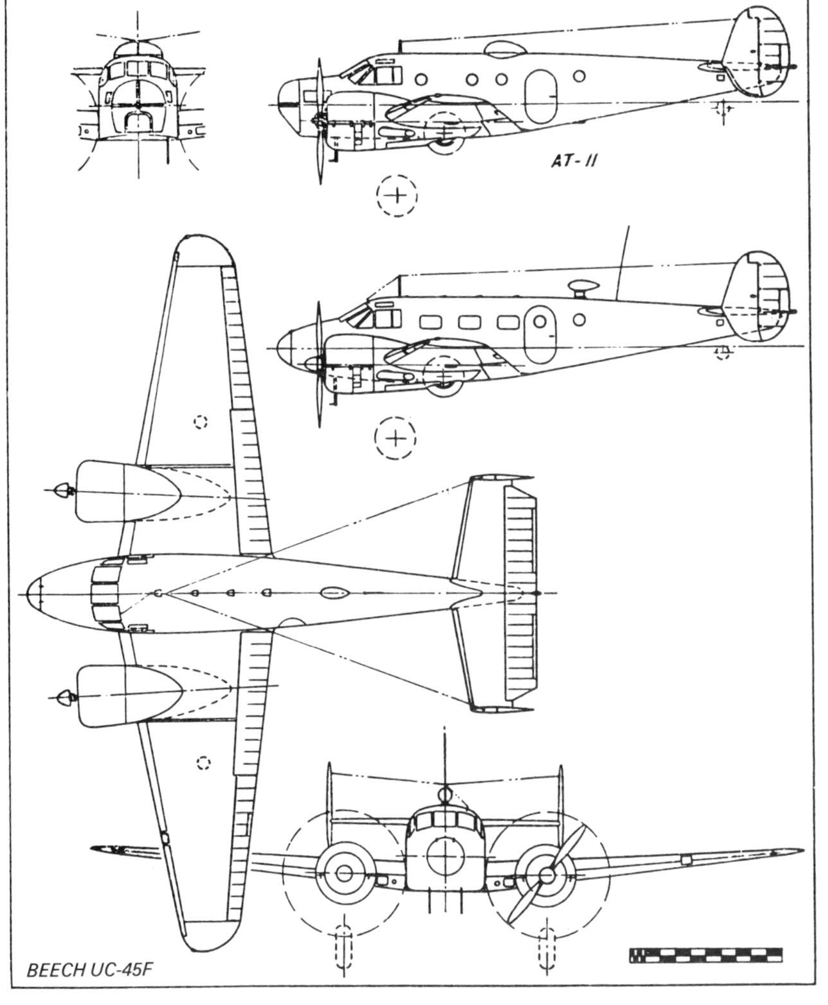

*The remanufactured C-45G-BH (s/n 51-11495 illustrated) had a new wing centre section, extended nacelles and other alterations.* (Beech)

*Beech C-45H-BH s/n 52-10864 was the support aircraft of the Wyoming Air National Guard during the 1953–61 period.* (R J Francillon collection)

*One of the two Beech NC-45Js which were operated by the US Army. This one (BuNo. 23829) is seen at MASDC, Davis Monthan, Arizona, in July 1974.* (B Knowles)

## VC-45J

Designation given to one aircraft used as staff transport by the US Army (BuNo. 23783).

## C-45-T

Unofficial designation of those aircraft converted with a tricycle undercarriage.

## AT-7-BH

This variant was first ordered in 1941 as a version of the C-45 specially equipped as a navigation trainer with individual chart tables and instruments for three students. A rotatable astrodrome on the fuselage just behind the cockpit was an external distinguishing feature. Powered by two 450hp Pratt & Whitney R-985-25 radial engines. Production totalled 577 and they later became T-7-BH. Unofficial name for AT-7 was Navigator.

## AT-7A-BH

Powered by two 450hp Pratt & Whitney R-985-AN-1 engines, this floatplane variant had a large ventral fin added to compensate for the added side area of the Edo floats; provision was made for alternative installation of skis. Seven aircraft were procured.

## AT-7B-BH

Winterized variant of the AT-7-BH; nine aircraft were built of which five were diverted to the Royal Navy.

## AT-7C-BH

Known as the Navigator, 549 aircraft of this variant were procured. They had two Pratt & Whitney R-985-AN-3 engines and more complex avionics; gross weight was increased to 8,060lb (3,651kg). Some of these aircraft were diverted to the US Navy as SNB-2Cs.

## T-7-BH

Designation given in June 1948 to surviving AT-7s.

## T-7C-BH

Designation given in June 1948 to surviving AT-7Cs.

## AT-11-BH

Version evolved from the Chinese M18R, for bombing and gunnery training. A bomb bay for 1,000lb (450kg) of bombs was provided in the fuselage in place of the special navigation equipment. The nose was remodelled with a bomb-aiming position equipped with a Norden bombsight, and flexibly-mounted nose and dorsal 0.3-in machine-guns were fitted. The AT-11, readily recognisable by its large Plexiglas nose, had two Pratt & Whitney R-985-AN-1 radials. Deliveries began in December 1941, and production totalled 1,582 aircraft and 24 more, ordered by the Dutch, were repossessed. Some 36 aircraft were converted to AT-11A-BH and many were rebuilt as C-45G and C-45H. Unoffical name was Kansan.

## AT-11A-BH

Thirty-six AT-11-BHs modified for navigational training and aerial photography missions with Pratt & Whitney R-985-AN-3 engines.

## T-11-BH

Designation given in June 1948 to surviving AT-11s.

*The AT-7A-BH had Edo floats and a large ventral fin.* (P M Bowers)

### T-11B-BH

Designation given to a number of AT-11-BHs rebuilt in the early 1950s to approximate C-45H standards.

### F-2-BH

This variant was the first specialised high-altitude photographic reconnaissance type used operationally by the USAAC. The F-2 had two 450hp Pratt & Whitney R-985-19 engines, two multiple-lens mapping cameras mounted in tandem in the cabin, and a piped oxygen system for the crew. A special device was installed in the entry door permitting side-view or oblique-angle photography. In 1940, 14 commercial Model 18s were ordered as F-2s (c/ns 340/353). The first aircraft was delivered to the USAAC on 21 December 1939 and the last one in July 1940.

*After the war T-7-BH s/n 42-56710 was operated by the USAF 1st Air Force. Note the buzz-number on the fuselage.*

### F-2A-BH

During 1942/43 thirteen UC-45A-BHs and UC-45B-BHs were modified as F-2As with four fuselage cameras mounted in the belly of the fuselage and Pratt & Whitney R-985-AN-3 engines. They became RC-45A-BH in 1948.

### F-2B-BH

Variant of the UC-45F with a trimetrogen camera system, and camera ports in each side of the fuselage as well as the floor. Engines were Pratt & Whitney R-985-AN-1s. Production totalled 42 aircraft which became RC-45A-BH in 1948.

### PCQ-3

A small number of UC-45Fs which were used in the late stages of the war in the role of drone-directors for radio-controlled targets. They became DC-45F-BH in 1948. They were easily recognisable by the array of aerials mounted on their fuselages.

*The Beech AT-11 was designed to train bombardier and gunnery students.* (Beech)

*Beech AT-11-BH Kansan s/n 42-37162.* (P M Bowers)

Crocker-Wheeler dorsal turret equipped with two 0.30-in machine-guns, bomb racks in the lower fuselage for 100lb (45kg) bombs and a modified nose with a bomb-aimer's station, and was used to train crews for Naval patrol aircraft. The first production batch was built in August 1942 and production totalled 320 aircraft.

### JRB-1

Intended primarily for directing radio-controlled target aircraft, the JRB-1 used by the Navy and Marine Corps had a distinctive fairing over the cockpit to enable the radio operator to see in all directions. JRB-1s were powered by two 450hp Pratt & Whitney R-985-AN-4 or -50 engines. Beech modified the first Model 18S for experimental flight testing, and eleven were built (all delivered by late 1940) plus one impressed machine without the cabin fairing.

### JRB-2

Designation given to 15 aircraft ordered by the US Navy for use as light transports with six seats and two 450hp Pratt & Whitney R-985-50 or -AN-4 engines. Five of them were transferred from the USAAF.

### JRB-3

Designation given to twenty UC-45B-BHs transferred from the USAAF and fitted with photographic survey equipment.

### JRB-4

Designation given to 328 ex-USAAF UC-45F-BHs. Several of them were later transferred to US Coast Guards, Japanese and French navies, and many were rebuilt as SNB-5s.

### JRB-5

Proposed transport version of the SNB-5.

### JRB-6

Modernised aircraft, but not fully to C-45G-BH standards. In particular, they lacked the D18S main and tail undercarriage.

### SNB-1

Variant equivalent to the AT-11 (450hp Pratt & Whitney R-985-AN-3 engines) acquired by the US Navy in 1942. The SNB-1 had an electrically-operated Beech and

### SNB-2

This variant, ordered in 1942 by the US Navy, was similar to the JRB-2 and equivalent to AT-7. It was used primarily as a navigation trainer and general purpose transport and was

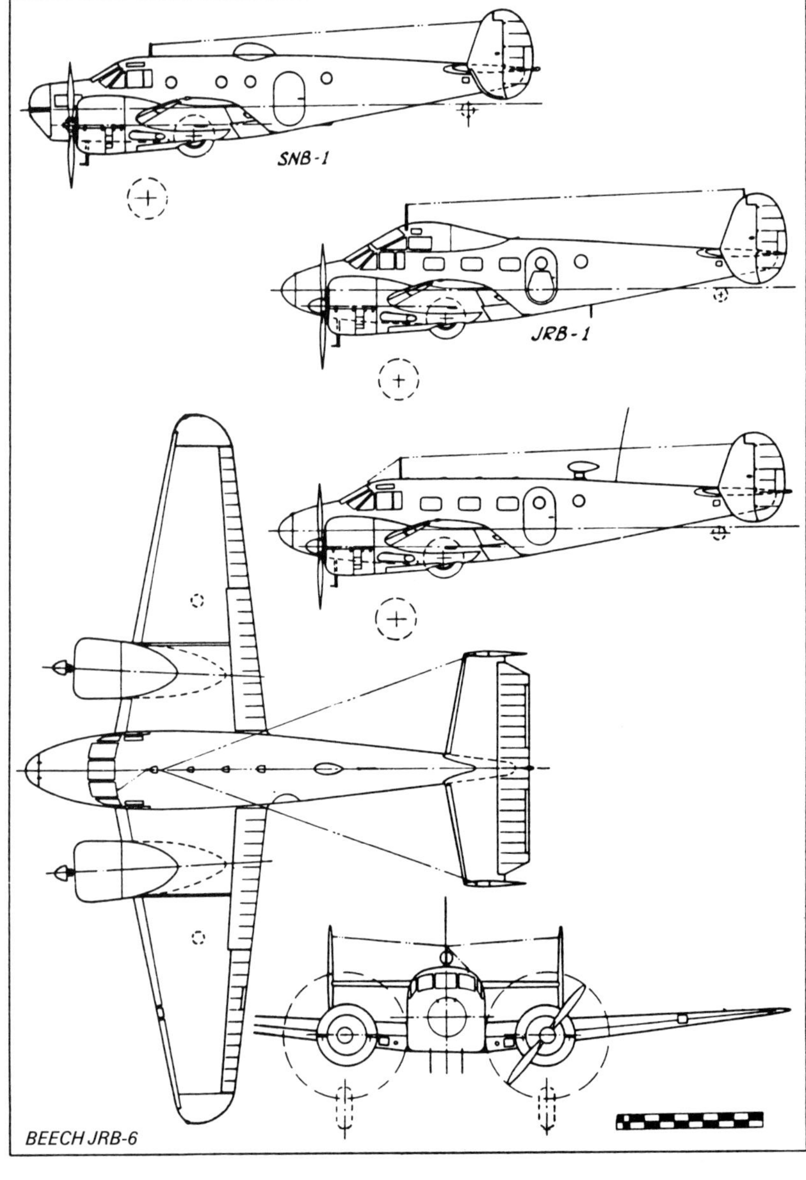

*The Beech F-2-BH was the high-altitude photographic variant of the ubiquitous C-45.* (P M Bowers)

powered by 450hp Pratt & Whitney R-985-25 engines. Production totalled 509 aircraft.

## SNB-2C

Variant similar to AT-7C of which 376 were built.

## SNB-2H

SNB-2s modified for ambulance duties.

## SNB-2P

Photographic reconnaissance conversion of the SNB-2.

## SNB-3Q

Designation given to at least one aircraft (BuNo. 55167) which was modified as a flying classroom to train aircrews in electronic countermeasures missions.

## SNB-4

Designation given to 117 SNB-1s returned to Beech factory in 1947 for rebuilding and modification.

## SNB-5

Designation given to SNB-2s remanufactured in 1951 to approximate C-45G standards. They were redesignated TC-45J in 1962 and later UC-45J.

*Orange-and-white Beech SNB-5 BuNo. 67185, operated by the US Marines from MCAS El Toro, California.* (P M Bowers)

## SNB-5P

Remanufactured SNB-2Ps; became RC-45J in 1962.

## Expeditor Mk.3N, 3NM and 3TM

These aircraft, similar to the D18S, were purchased directly from Beech by Canada, and had no other military model designations.

*Beech SNB-5 BuNo. 67220 on its delivery flight.* (Beech)

*American Turbine 600R No.22 (N432U) was modified in January 1967 from Model E18S c/n BA-161. It is seen at Reading, Pennsylvania, in June 1967.* (P M Bowers)

From the late 1950s a number of companies offered modified Beech 18s for the executive, cargo, and commuter markets.

### Airlines Training Inc:

this company, headed by William F Conrad, produced two increased gross-weight conversions, the Conrad 9800D (9,800lb or 4,440kg) and the Conrad 10200 (10,200lb or 4,620kg). The Conrad 10200 had a nosewheel undercarriage, one-piece windshield, oval cabin windows, redesigned wingtips. Known Conrad 9800Ds are c/ns A-32, A-57, A-88, A-166, A-813 and A-843; Conrad 10200s are c/ns A-11, A-26, A-20, A-57, A-843, and s/ns 43-35637 and 43-47188.

### American Turbine Aircraft Corp:

Edward West Jr was one of the major modifiers of Model 18 aircraft. He is best known for his kits to convert military C-45Gs and C-45Hs to the civil configuration, and for his later installation of PT6A engines.

*The prototype Dumod Liner (c/n AF-152 N445DM) in 1964 with the normal twin fin and rudder layout.* (P M Bowers)

### Avco:

this company installed horizontally opposed Lycoming TIGO-541-B1A engines in Model 18 c/n A-260. This modification was eventually approved by the FAA at reduced maximum weights, but the aeroplane was too underpowered to be commercially viable.

### Dee Howard Co:

this company, in conjunction with Aircraft Industries of Canada Ltd, modified some aircraft with PT6A-20 engines. One identified aircraft is the Expeditor Mk.3N c/n CA-43 (CF-RSY).

### Dumod:

in the early 1960s, Dumod Corporation of Opa Locka, Florida, produced a Volpar nosewheel-equipped piston-powered conversion known at first as the Infinité I and later as the Dumod I. Among other refinements, it featured a panoramic windscreen, large double-glazed cabin windows, modified high-performance wingtips and glass-fibre control surfaces. A total of 37 conversions is reported to have been completed by 1966. These were followed by the stretched 15-seat Infinité II/Dumod Liner which included a 6ft 3in (1.90m) forward fuselage extension and a third, central fin and rudder. The prototype was completed in 1964 and received certification on 12 April 1966. About ten Dumod Liners are known to have been produced. Further projected developments included installation of R-1340, PT6A, TPE-331 and Astazou engines. Known aircraft are c/ns A-89, AF-152*, -225, -298, -401, -488, -573, -690*, -696, 804* (aircraft marked with an asterisk are Dumod Liners).

### Hamilton:

in 1959, Hamilton Aviation of Tucson, Arizona, offered the Little Liner, a considerably improved conversion of the Model D18S. Modifications included fully-enclosing main undercarriage doors, a longer fully-retractable tailwheel unit which improved take-off performance by placing the aircraft in a more favourable attitude, redesigned engine cowlings, a streamlined nose cone, a two-piece wrap-around windscreen, wing root fairings, extended wingtips, etc. Total fuel capacity was increased and a cargo door was fitted. In all, more than 400 conversions are reported to have been made. In 1970, Hamilton acquired the company of Mr West which had produced some 22 conversions of the Westwind (a PT6 powered conversion of the Model 18). Production continued with 42 more aircraft under designation Westwind III. The Westwind III had PT6A-20, - 27 or -34 engines as well as an extended nose and an optional cargo door. Known examples are c/ns AF-209, BA-20, -77, -105, -155, -157, -232, -236, -321, -368, -385, -414, -454, -559, -713, CA-99, -179, -257 and BuNo. 51028. A new variant, the Westwind IISTD, was introduced in 1975. It had a fuselage stretch which enabled the number of passenger to be increased from eight to seventeen, but only one aircraft (BuNo. 23835) is believed to have been modified.

### Pacific Airmotive:

using the Volpar nosewheel kit,

Pacific Airmotive Corporation of Burbank, California, produced its own conversion which had a single swept fin and rudder (made with half of the tailplane and elevator from a scrapped Model 18), panoramic windscreen, redesigned cowlings and wingtips, all-metal control surfaces, updated avionics and increased tankage. First flight of the prototype was on 13 July 1962 and certification was granted on 25 March 1963. More than 22 Model 18s are believed to have been converted as Tradewinds. The Turbo-Tradewind was introduced in 1964 and had PT6A propeller-turbines. It flew for the first time on 3 November 1964. Known aircraft are c/ns AF-208, -399, -511, -523, -588, -640, -816, -831, BA-15 -154 and CA-176.

*Hamilton Westwind III N149R was converted from Beech E18S c/n BA-414. It is seen here as operated by S M B Stage Lines.* (K Krämer)

### Rausch:

this company produced a tricycle undercarriage conversion known as the Star 250 which had main undercarriage legs from a North American P-51D Mustang, and a T-28 Trojan nosewheel. The fuselage had a 3ft (76cm) nose extension, a 4ft (1.27m) stretch, a higher roof and panoramic windows. Only one aircraft is known to have been converted, c/n AF-101, which was never certificated by FAA.

### Remmert-Werner:

this company offered executive conversions comprising luxurious interiors with larger cabin windows.

### SFERMA:

in collaboration with Beech, a Turboméca Bastan-powered conversion was made in France by SFERMA in the late 1960s. The project was initiated late in 1957 and the first flight of the prototype (registered F-ZWVO) took place on 19 September 1958. Other specific features of this aircraft included deeper vertical tail surfaces, an extended tailwheel, full enclosure wheel-well doors, etc. The project was not proceeded with, although conversion of a second aircraft is believed to have started.

### Volpar Inc:

this company was formed in 1959 by Frank Nixon and Richard W Hanson, who were the presidents of the Volitan Aircraft and Paragon Tool and Die Co, to market conversion kits for a variant of the Model 18 fitted with a nosewheel unit retracting into a new streamlined nose which lengthened the fuselage by some 28in (71cm) and could house a 12in weather radar dish. Subsequently, the main undercarriage was mounted 48in (122cm) aft and retracted forward. These modifications, designed by Thorp Engineering, improved ground handling. Well over 400 kits had been sold by the end of 1970 and, from September 1963, the installation was offered by Beech as an option on the

*The most distinctive features of the Tradewind produced by Pacific Air Motive are its single fin and rudder and the Volpar nosewheel kit.* (J Wegg)

*The Rausch Star 250 used undercarriage units from North American T-28s and P-51s. N18186H was modified from C-45H c/n AF-101.* (P M Bowers)

new Model H18. It must be noted that the Volpar conversion kit also featured as part of conversions offered by other companies. In 1964 a refinement was introduced with the installation of 575shp Garrett TPE-331-25 propeller-turbines and wing leading-edge extensions which increased internal tankage by 90 US gallons. These new engines increased the cruising speed to 265mph (426km/h). The prototype of the Volpar Turbo 18 (c/n BA-65, registered N340V), as it was known, flew for the first time in the spring of 1965 and received FAA supplemental Type Certification on 17 February 1966. In all, conversion by Volpar totalled 25 aircraft with TPE-331-25, -47 and -101 engines. Known examples are c/ns BA-65, AF-65, -171, -186, -236, -280, -320, -350, -357, -409, -458, -487, -509, -704 and -884.

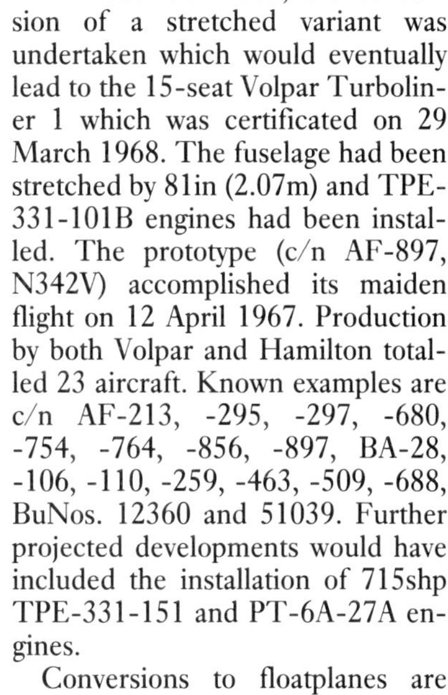

In December 1966, the conversion of a stretched variant was undertaken which would eventually lead to the 15-seat Volpar Turboliner 1 which was certificated on 29 March 1968. The fuselage had been stretched by 81in (2.07m) and TPE-331-101B engines had been installed. The prototype (c/n AF-897, N342V) accomplished its maiden flight on 12 April 1967. Production by both Volpar and Hamilton totalled 23 aircraft. Known examples are c/n AF-213, -295, -297, -680, -754, -764, -856, -897, BA-28, -106, -110, -259, -463, -509, -688, BuNos. 12360 and 51039. Further projected developments would have included the installation of 715shp TPE-331-151 and PT-6A-27A engines.

Conversions to floatplanes are also worth a mention. Joe G Marrs first obtained FAA approval to convert Model C18Ss to floatplanes. Later, Bristol Aerospace Ltd, of Canada, received both FAA and Transport Canada approval to install Edo 56-7850A floats on Model D18S, C-45G and H, Expeditor Mk.3NM and 3TM aircraft.

Besides these conversions, a number of Beech 18s have been modified into one-off test-beds, such as United Aircraft of Canada's PT-6 testbed (registered CF-ZWY-X) and FANASA's variable-incidence wing test-bed (registered OB-E-939).

## Service History

There was little interest among airlines in the United States for the Twin Beech in the late 1930s. However, in Canada, feeder lines regularly served territories located off the main air routes. That is why the first foreign order for the Model 18 came from Starratt Airways and Transportation Ltd of Hudson, Ontario. On 8 December 1937 this company took delivery of Model S18A c/n 172 (CF-BGY) equipped for interchangeable operation from skis or floats. This aircraft eventually

*In France, a Turboméca Bastan-powered conversion of the Beech 18 was produced by SFERMA. Note the nose probe used during flight tests.* (P M Bowers)

*The prototype Volpar (c/n BA-65, N340V) when in use with Ransome Airlines. The fuselage lengthening is quite apparent.* (J L Sherlock)

crashed on 7 January 1941. Prairie Airways Ltd of Edmonton, Alberta, purchased the first fleet of Model 18s in 1938. Two S18Ds (c/ns 177/178, CF-BKN/BKO) were taken in charge on 7 and 16 July 1938. Another early Model S18B (c/n 173, NC18569) was delivered to Aerovias de Puerto Rico, where, operating with floats, it was required to alight on the open sea as it provided inter-island passenger services. Two additional Model 18As were purchased by Canadian Airways (c/n 291, CF-BQG and c/n 318, CF-BQH, delivered respectively on 29 April and 1 May 1940). Nevertheless, a few aircraft found their way to United States customers such as Michigan Carbon Paper Company (Model 18D, c/n 176, NC18572) and Olson Drilling Company (Model 18S, c/n 222, NC19452).

After the war, a number of Beech Model 18/AT-11s were operated by South American airlines such as TACA de Venezuela (c/ns 171 and 177), Navegação Aérea Brasileira (two aircraft, c/ns 430 and 431), Cruzeiro do Sul (six AT-11s, c/ns 1247, 3059, 3090, 3304, 3546 and 3698), Transportes Aéreos Salvador (one AT-11, c/n 3530), Aerolíneas Argentinas (c/n 4542) and ALFA (c/ns 4542 and 4958). War surplus made dozens of aircraft available and the Model 18 became more widely used. Soon there were few airports in the world without one or two Twin Beeches parked on the ramp. A very particular operator was Air America. The Model 18 and the Volpar Turboliners were used quite extensively by this company owned by the Central Intelligence Agency, for its operations in Southeast Asia (identified aircraft are c/ns AF-57/N5269V, AF-65/N3728G, AF-97/N9573Z, AF-171/N9664C, AF-186/N9838Z, AF-280/N9671C, AF-179/N9577Z, AF-320/N7770B, AF-350/N9518C, AF-352/N7950C, AF-357/N7695C, AF-458/N91295, AF-509/N6154U, AF-674/N9542Z, AF-689/N3674G, AF-704/N9956Z and AF-884/N9157Z.

*Volpar Turboliner c/n 008 was converted from C-45H c/n AF-754 and first flew as N353V. It is seen here before delivery to National Air Charter of Indonesia as PK-WWD.* (J Wegg)

## Military Service

The Beech Model 18 was succesfully involved in a USAAC evaluation competition which took place at Wright Field in 1939. Experience gained in development of the M18R for China brought an order for 150 similar units from General H H

*One C-45 conversion floatplane was C-FSFH of Selkink Air of Selkink, Manitoba.* (J G Handelman)

*C-45H c/n AF-817 operated by NASA had the Volpar trigear conversion. This aircraft remained in service until April 1982.* (H B Adams/AAHS)

*A Beech SNB-1 (N6665C) modified for crop dusting, at Fort Lauderdale in August 1971.* (M Cristescu)

1952 through 1961. The rebuild was so extensive that the airframes were zero-timed and reserialled. The last Air Force C-45s were phased out in November 1963 and the US Navy retired its last SNB-5 in July 1972. However, the Army, in 1976, continued to operate five Model 18s in utility and liaison personnel transport configurations.

Arnold, commanding general of the Air Forces, following an inspection tour of the Beech Aircraft plant in 1941. This contract was the first of several and the Wichita based company produced more than 5,257 aircraft for training pilots, gunners, bombardiers and navigators, and transporting priority military cargo as well as officials throughout the war. It is estimated that over 90 per cent of American bombardiers and navigators who saw service in the Second World War trained in military versions of the Twin Beech.

The US Navy was concerned as well. On 31 December 1941 this Service had 26 JRB-1/-2s on inventory: 11 JRB-1s flying with VJ-3 Base Force (four aircraft), VJ-5 in Cape May (five aircraft) and two aircraft at the Naval Aircraft Factory; and 15 JRB-2s flown by Navairdet in Corpus Christi, Miami and Jacksonville, Naval Attachés in Bogota and Lima, NAS Norfolk, Wing Headquarters in Quantico, BAD-2 in San Diego, Commander Aircraft Scouting Force, Naval Research Laboratory in Anacostia and the Naval Aircraft Factory. For its own part, on 31 August 1943, the US Marine Corps had 8 JRB/SNBs on inventory flying with Headquarters Squadron No.1 (First marine Air Wing), No.2 (Second Marine Air Wing), No.15 (Marine Air Group 15), No.24 (Marine Air Group 24) and BAD in MCAS Cherry Point and El Toro.

Many of these aircraft underwent one or more rebuilding and updating programmes. Under a government programme, a total of 2,263 were refurbished by Beech Aircraft from

## Foreign Military Operators

Some thirty countries outside the United States operated the ubiquitous Beechcraft Model 18:

**Argentina**: 30 AT-11s (serialled E-101/130) were operated by the Escuela de Aviación Militar, some of which were later modified with an unglazed nose. One was transferred to the Navy and the type was withdrawn from use in 1967/68. The Fuerza Aerea Argentina also operated a single C-45H (serialled T-78). The Comando de Aviación Naval received at least 28 C-45/SNBs of which two were presented to the Uruguayan Navy in 1979. For its own part, the Army had a handful C-45s which went to Instituto Geográphico Militar (serialled in the AE-250 range).

**Bolivia**: the Fuerza Aerea Boliviana operated a single C-45G (c/n AF-

*A South African Beech H18 operated by Letaba Airways, at Wonderboom in October 1975.* (B Parkinson)

*Beech C-45H s/n 52-10883 of the North Carolina Air National Guard.* (R J Francillon collection)

366, serialled 809) which was written off on 20 September 1959.

**Brazil**: the Fuerza Aerea Brasileira operated a large number Twin Beeches (known by the Brazilians as Beech Bi). Some 22 AT-11s are believed to have been delivered (serialled 1363/1372, 1520/1529 and 1819/1820) and operated until 1975. Over the 1942-1976 period, at least 42 AT-7s were operated (serialled 1348/1362, 1437/1446, 1507, 1510/1519 and 1593/1598), several of them being eventually converted to C-45 standard (aircraft serialled 1349/1350, 1354/1355, 1437/1438, 1444, 1446, 1513, 1519, 1594 and 1597/1598). But the most numerous were the C-45/ Model 18s, with some 70 aircraft of different variants: 22 C18Ss (known as UC-45F 2787/2794, 2862/2865 and 2867/2875), 28 D18Ss (known as UC-45F 2820/2822, 2824/2830, 2833/2842, 2848/2851 and 2853/ 2856), 7 E18Ss (2876/2880 and 2882/2883) 16 H18Ss (known as TC-45T 2885/2887 and 2889/ 2897 and 2898/2899 and 2908/ 2909).

**Canada**: in addition to six civil models already in service and the 55 British-serialled aircraft taken on strength, the RCAF was to acquire, between March 1944 and March 1953, an additionnal 327 Model 18s, making a grand total of 388 machines. All Expeditor 3s in the RCAF were powered by Pratt & Whitney Wasp R-985-AN-14B engines. They were mainly used as multi-engine pilot, navigator and radio operator trainers, transport, liaison, search-and-rescue and VIP aircraft. Variants were Expeditor Mk. 3N (navigational trainer), Mk. 3NM (navigational trainer/ transport), Mk.3T (crew trainer) and Mk. 3TM (crew trainer/transport). In addition, during the fifties, two armed aircraft (D18Ss c/ns A-141/ 142, CF-MPH and CF-MPI) were on strength with the Royal Canadian Mounted Police. These aircraft had two 0.50-in Browning machine-guns mounted in the nose. One peculiar Mk.3T (s/n HB109) was used by Pratt & Whitney Canada Inc in 1960 as a testbed for the PT6A propeller-turbines.

**China**: in February 1940, a $750,000 contract was finalised for six aircraft (c/ns 375 to 380) to be used as advanced pilot trainers and light tactical bombers. Initial work began in Wichita to fit five aircraft with a clear nose, an upper-fuselage gun turret, a machine-gun installation in the rear floor and internal bomb racks for 25lb bombs. These aircraft were designated Beechcraft M18Rs and the first (tested as NX25474) was delivered on 30 September 1940.

Twenty Model D18Ss (probably in the A-483/505 range) were delivered to the Chinese Air Force in Taiwan in 1949.

**Colombia**: the Fuerza Aerea Colombiana recieved two AT-7Cs (in use from 1943 till 1964), five AT-

*A Twin Beech operated in Argentina by Transportes Aereos Buenos Aires, at Jorge Newberry Airport.* (J A Cerdá)

*The Força Aérea Brasileira operated twenty-two AT-11s, known as T-11s, from 1943 until 1975.* (D L de Camargo)

11s (serialled 900/904, withdrawn from use in 1956) and at least ten C-45s of various versions (serialled in the 500 range).

**Costa Rica**: the air section of the Public Security Ministry of the Republic of Costa Rica operated a single Beech C-45F (registered TI-505SP).

**Dominican Republic**: possibly two AT-11s were operated by the Escuela de Aviación Militar along with T-6Gs, T-41Ds and T-33As.

**Ecuador**: the Fuerza Aérea Ecuatoriana took delivery of some ten C-45s.

**France**: during the Autmun of 1944, the Armée de l'Air received 26 C-45Fs. These aircraft were used at first by transport group GT 2/15 and, at a later date, by GT 4/15 Poitou. During the early fifties some ten more C-45s (among them ex-RAF aircraft HB226, KJ500, KJ524, KN121, KN129 and KN147) were delivered and five others were loaned by the USAF. In 1955, the Armée de l'Air took delivery of four Beech Super 18s. In 1959, the Canadian Government offered two batches (19 plus 10) of C-45s. By January 1970, 41 aircraft were still flying with various squadrons (GTLA 2/60, ELA 41, 43, 44, EARS 99 and EAA 601) and the last flying examples were withdrawn from use in May 1972. Most of them ended their career on fire dumps.

The French Navy took delivery of more than twenty JRB-4/SNB-5s which were used by Escadrilles 55S and 56S. The remaining aircraft were withdrawn from use in 1972 and some of them found their way on to the US civil register. When flying for the French Navy, the Twin Beech were identified by the last digits of the BuNo. (8, 12, 15, 25, 29, 32, 38, 53/54, 62 104, 558, 676, 702, 706, 709, 711/714 and 717)

**Great Britain**: from April 1944, Great Britain received 430 Navigators and Expeditors, the latter in two variants: the Expeditor Is were C-45Bs, and the Expeditor IIs were C-45Fs. These aircraft were delivered to both the Royal Air Force and the Fleet Air Arm. With the RAF, the aircraft served in India, Burma, the Middle East and British Air Forces South-East Asia (BAFSEA) with Group Communication Flights (such as Nos.216, 221, 224, 225, 231 and 238). Most of these aircraft were returned to the United States in 1946.

**Guatemala**: the Fuerza Aérea Guatemalteca operated two AT-11s.

**Honduras**: the Fuerza Aérea Hondureña took delivery of a dozen C-45s.

**Indonesia**: the army aviation had one Model H18 in use in 1982 (serialled A-8037). The Indonesian NAF-Police had a single Model H18 (serialled P-2022).

**Italy**: acquired by the Italian Air Force as an interim aircraft in 1949 with a projected active life of two or three years, the C-45 remained in

*HB148 was one of the fifty-five British-serialled Expeditor Is operated by the Royal Canadian Air Force.* (W Larkins/AAHS)

*Expeditor 3N s/n 1460 was delivered to the French Armée de l'Air on 12 May 1959. It was subsequently operated by GTLA 2/60 and ELA 43 Squadrons before being withdrawn from use on 18 May 1972. It is seen here at Châteaudun in June 1971.* (A J Pelletier)

use until the early eighties. In all, some 125 C-45s were operated by AMI, of which 59 were delivered under MDAP. Deliveries began in March 1949 to the 46th Stormo and the C-45s eventually served with most of the liaison units. These aircraft were serialled in the MM61640/61831 range, although no USAF s/n-MM serial tie-ups are known. A few of them were transfered to the Somali Air Force.

**Ivory Coast**: one UC-45 was delivered in 1964 (c/n AF-14) which became registered TU-TAB and at a later date TU-TXO.

**Mexico**: the Fuerza Aeréa Mexicana received some 24 AT-11s under lend-lease agreement (serialled in the BHB-1500 range and operated by Escuadrón Aéreo 101 and Escuadrón Aéreo de Reconocimiento Fotográfico) and ten C-45s (serialled in the TEB-5500 range). The Mexican Navy was equipped with six C-45s (serialled MP-80/85) which were flown by the Tercer Escuadrón Aeronaval (3rd Naval Aviation Squadron), formed in Oaxaca province on 2 June 1961.

**Netherlands**: in 1941, 24 AT-11s were ordered for use in the Netherlands East Indies but these aircraft were confiscated by the USAAF before delivery and allocated to the Royal Netherlands Military Flying School, in Mississippi. In addition six AT-11s were loaned by the USAAF to the RNMFS. After the war was over, 28 AT-7s were delivered to the Dutch Air Force in 1951/52 and used until the last ones were struck off charge on 26 June 1959. The Dutch Navy used six SNB-5s which were delivered by the US Navy in 1953/54. These were flown by No.5 Squadron stationed in Valkenburg until the squadron was disbanded in early 1974. In addition the Dutch Rijksluchvaartschool received a number of Model D18Ss in 1946.

**Nicaragua**: in 1947-48, the Fuerza Aeréa de Nicaragua took delivery of at least seven C-45s, four of which were still in use in 1978. All are now withdrawn from use.

**Niger**: a single Model E18S was delivered in 1965 (c/n BA-184, registered 5U-MAW, ex-F-OAXQ) and eventually sold back to France as F-BUOP in 1973.

**Peru**: the Fuerza Aeréa del Peru received two AT-7Cs (s/ns 43-33478 and 43-33531), five AT-11s (four of which were serialled 441, 442, 494 and 495) and some 30 C-45G/Hs (serialled in the 700 range).

**Philippines**: the Philippine Army Air Corps was the first foreign military customer. In September 1938, it took delivery of a first Model 18D (c/n 220) followed by a second aircraft (c/n 223) in April 1939. Both aircraft were equipped for aerial photography.

*This C-45 was transferred to the Italian Air Force as s/n MM61685, but its USAAF serial remains unkown. Its subsequent codes were RM-50, RM-57 and RR-02 of the 2°RTA.* (J Wegg collection)

*The only known UC-45 operated by the Ivory Coast Air Force, seen at Abidjan in November 1967.* (R Caratini via J Delmas)

*TC-45Js were operated by the Netherlands naval air arm for twenty years. This one (s/n 085, BuNo.134697) was delivered on 18 January 1945 and struck off charge on 1 March 1974. It is now preserved at Deelen.* (R Flinzner)

**Portugal**: both the Air Force and the Navy operated AT-11s (serialled 2506/2507), Beech D18S/UC-45s (2509/2520) and Expeditor Mk.3T (2521/2525).
**San Salvador**: the Fuerza Aeréa Salvadoreña operated at least three AT-11s.
**Somali**: two aircraft transferred from Italian Air Force (ex MM61724 and MM61750).
**Sri Lanka**: one ex-Canadian Super H18 (serialled CS450) was operated by the No.2 Training Wing at Ratmalana.
**Sweden**: in 1940, a Model 18R (c/n 321) was supplied to the Swedish Air Force as an ambulance aircraft. This aircraft was accepted at Wichita on 9 April 1940. Known as Tp4 by Flygrapnet, it was operated by F4 Wing at Froson, and later by F21 Wing at Kallax. Between 18 October 1951 and 25 August 1952 it was operated as SE-BTX in the Antarctic. It finished its career when it crashed into mountains on New Year's Day 1953.

*This Twin Beech operated by Turkish State Airports as TC-KON is most certainly an ex-Turkish Air Force aircraft.*

**Turkey**: the Turkish Air Force received a number of AT-11s and D18Ss but details are not known.
**Uruguay**: the Fuerza Aeréa Uruguaya received ten AT-11s (serialled 100/109) and eight UC-45/C-45Fs. The Navy had three SNB-5s

*The Swedish Air Force operated a single Model 18R, under the designation Tp4, with F4 Wing stationed at Froson.* (Beech via E Phillips)

(A-210/212) plus three ex-Argentine navy TC-45Js (A-215/217).
**Venezuela**: the Fuerza Aeréa Venezolana had about ten C-45/D18Ss, three AT-7Cs and six AT-11s.
**Zaïre**: three Model E18S were operated (9T-JEA, -JEB and PRS) and withdrawn from use circa 1982.

### Model D18S

Two 450hp Pratt & Whitney R-985-AN14B Wasp Junior.

Span 47ft 7in (14.5m); length 33ft 11½in (10.4m); height 9ft 2½in (2.8m).

Empty weight 5,615lb (2,546kg); loaded weight 8,750lb (3,980kg); power loading 9.72lb/hp (4.42kg/hp).

Maximum speed 230mph (368km/h) at 5,000ft (1,525m); cruising speed 212mph (339km/h) at 10,000ft (3,050m); rate of climb 1,190ft/min (363m/min) at sea level; service ceiling 20,500ft (6,250m); range 750 miles (1,200km).

### Model H18

Two 450hp Pratt & Whitney R-985-AN-14B Wasp Junior.

Span 49ft 8in (15.14m); length 35ft 11 11/16in (10.7m); height 9ft 4in (2.84m); wing area 360.7sq ft (33.54sq m).

Empty weight 5,680lb (2,576kg); maximum take-off weight 9,900lb (4,490kg); wing loading 27.5lb/sq ft (134.2kg/sq m); power loading 11lb/hp (4.99kg/hp).

Maximum speed 234mph (374km/h) at 3,300ft (1,512m); cruising speed 207mph (331km/h) at 5,000ft (1,525m); rate of climb 1,490ft/min (450m/min) at sea level; service ceiling 23,300ft (7,106m); range 1,626 miles (2,616km).

### Dumod Liner

Two 450 hp Pratt & Whitney R-985.

Span 47ft 7in (14.5m); length 43ft 5in (13.23m); height 9ft 9in (2.97m); wing area 349sq ft (32.42sq m).

Empty weight 6,400lb (2,900kg); maximum take-off weight 10,200lb (4,625kg); wing loading 29.22lb/sq ft (142.6kg/sq m); power loading 11.33lb/hp (5.14kg/hp).

Cruising speed (60% power) 220mph (354km/h) at 10,000ft (3,000m); rate of climb 1,325ft/min (405m/min) at sea level; service ceiling 16,500ft (5,030m); range 1,000 miles (1,600km).

### Volpar Turboliner

Two 705shp Garrett AiResearch TPE 331-1-101B.

Span 46ft (14.02m); length 44ft 2½in (13.47m); height 9ft 7in (2.92m); wing area 374sq ft (34.75sq m).

Empty weight 5,660lb (2,567kg); maximum take-off weight 10,286lb (4,666kg); wing loading 27.51lb/sq ft (134.3kg/sq m); power loading 8.5lb/hp (3.85kg/hp).

Maximum speed 266mph (428km/h) at 10,000ft (3,050m); cruising speed 256mph (412km/h) at 10,000ft (3,050m); rate of climb 1,700ft/min (518m/min) at sea level; service ceiling 25,000ft (7,620m); range 1,500miles (2,415km).

### PAC Tradewind

Two 450hp Pratt & Whitney R-985-AN-4 or 14B Wasp Junior.

Span 47ft 3in (14.4m); length 37ft 9in (11.51m); height 13ft 8in (4.16m); wing area 349sq ft (32.43sq m).

Maximum take-off weight 10,200lb (4,627kg); wing loading 29.2lb/sq ft (142.6kg/sq m); power loading 11.3lb/hp (5.14kg/hp).

Maximum speed 240mph (386km/h) at sea level; maximum cruising speed 230mph (370km/h) at 10,000ft (3,050m); rate of climb 1,200ft/min (365m/sec) at sea level; service ceiling 17,000ft (5,180m); range with 45min reserves 1,100miles (1,770km).

### Hamilton Westwind III

Two 579ehp Pratt & Whitney Canada PT6A-20.

Span 46ft (14.02m); length 35ft 7¼in (10.85m); height 4ft (1.22m); wing area 326.4sq ft (30.32sq m).

Empty weight 5,500lb (2,495kg); maximum take-off weight 11,230lb (5,094kg); wing loading 34.4lb/sq ft (167.9kg/sq m); power loading 9.69lb/hp (4.39kg/hp).

Maximum speed 270mph (435km/h) at 12,000ft (3,660m); cruising speed 250mph (402km/h) at 12,000ft (3,660m); rate of climb 1,800ft/min (549m/min) at sea level; service ceiling 24,000ft (7,315m); range 3,731 miles (6,004km).

# Model 25/26 AT-10 Wichita

In 1941, at the request of Air Corps officials, Beech engineers designed an entirely new type of advanced twin-engine trainer, the airframe of which comprised mainly non-strategic material, namely wood, in order to conserve metals for combat aircraft. Another prime aspect of the specification was ease and speed of manufacture on a large scale. The Model 25 had a similar layout to the Model 18, but was an entirely new aircraft. It was powered by the same 295hp Lycoming R-680-9 radial engines, driving two-blade Hamilton Standard propellers as used in the Cessna AT-8 and Curtiss AT-9. The wing, which had 6° dihedral and 3°43′35″ incidence at the roots, retained a NACA 23019 Mod aerofoil section at the root. The airframe was built entirely of plywood except for the cowlings and cockpit enclosure, which was fitted with a sliding canopy. Production totalled 1,771 aircraft, most of which were produced by Globe Aircraft Corporation.

During the war, the AT-10 was mostly used in the advanced training schools, and it is estimated that about half the Army's multi-engine pilots received their transitional training flying AT-10s. After the war a few AT-10s went on to the civil market, but because of the wooden structure most did not oper-

*During the course of the Second World War, the Wichita was made standard equipment of advanced training schools.* (E Phillips collection)

*AT-10 s/n 42-2272 was fitted with a V-tail to get engineering data from flight characteristics.* (Beech via E Phillips)

### Model 25/26

Two 295hp Lycoming R-680-9.

Span 44ft (13.41m); length 34ft 4in (10.46m); height 10ft 4in (3.15m); wing area 297.86sq ft (27.67sq m).

Empty weight 4,757lb (2,155kg); gross weight 6,465lb (2,928kg); wing loading 21.70lb/sq ft (105kg/sq m); power loading 10.95lb/hp (4.96kg/hp).

Maximum speed 200mph (320km/h) at 4,900ft (1,500m); cruising speed at 75% power 168mph (270km/h); rate of climb 1,1150ft/min (350m/min) at sea level; service ceiling 19,700ft (6,000m); range 770 miles (1,240km).

ate very long. In December 1945, one aircraft (AT-10-BH s/n 42-2272) was fitted with a V-tail arrangement in order to get engineering data from flight characteristics. The experiment confirmed that the arrangement weighed much less than a conventional tail unit and had a lot less aerodynamic drag, all without appreciable drop-off in handling characteristics.

Only two AT-10-GFs are known to have survived and they are owned by the US Air Force Museum, in Dayton, Ohio (s/ns 42-35143 and 42-35180).

BEECH AT-10

## Model 28 XA-38 Grizzly

Intended to meet a US Army Air Force requirement for a two-seat attack bomber, two prototypes of the Beech Model 28 were ordered on 2 December 1942 under contract AC33348. The aircraft were designated XA-38-BH and were assigned s/ns 43-14406 and 43-14407. Beechcraft's Model 28 was designed as an aircraft capable of delivering knock-out blows to fortified gun emplacements, armoured vehicles and coastal surface vessels. It was designed to be highly manoeuvrable and could absorb heavy battle damage.

Development of the Model 28, known to Beech as the Destroyer, and later named Grizzly after the largest predator of North America, began in 1943 with a team led by Bill Cassidy. Other Wichita engineers involved in the project were Jess Vint and Alex Odevseff for the armament, Gus Ericson for the wing, Bill Irig for the flight controls, Mervin Meyers for hydraulics, Noel Naidenoff for the powerplant and Ralph Harmon worked on the undercarriage.

*With the end of the war, the Wichitas were rapidly withdrawn from use and lay derelict on airfields. This one (s/n 41-9332) displays national insignia crudely painted over.* (E M Sommerich via Bowers)

The Model 28 was certainly not a modified Model 18 but it benefited from the experience gained by Beech with this model. The Grizzly was a two-seat, twin-engined monoplane retaining an all-metal semi-monocoque structure with full cantilever wings. Flush riveting and butted skin joints were employed everywhere and gave the aircraft a perfect, shiny finish. The wing retained a NACA 23000 series aerofoil section for both good high speed performance and slow landing speed. Aspect ratio was 7.19 and positive wing dihedral was 5 degrees. Ailerons were conventional, with balance tabs and an in-flight adjustable trim tab on the port aileron. Flaps were of the slotted type and could be extended to 45 degrees. The vertical fins followed traditional Beech construction methods and were similar to those of the Model 18. The undercarriage was also conventional, with oleo-pneumatic shock absorbers and hydraulic brakes, for suitability for rough field work.

The Beech Model 28 was powered by two 2,300hp Wright Duplex Cyclone GR-3350-43 eighteen-cylinder, twin-row radial engines, fitted with Chandler-Evans Model 58 CPB 4 Hydro-metering carburators, two-speed superchargers and driving 170in diameter (4.32m) three-blade Hamilton-Standard 33E60 constant-speed propellers. These powerful engines were enclosed by NACA cowlings made of aluminium alloy and stainless steel, and oil coolers were located in the wings. The fuel system comprised four self-sealing tanks installed in the wings with a total capacity of 640 US gallons (2,422 litres) and two self-sealing fuel tanks located behind the pilot's cockpit containing an additional 185 US gallons (681 litres). All of these tanks were designed to be easily removed and repaired. Pumps and connections were mounted on top of the tanks so that damage would cause fuel flow to stop from the damaged tank. Four auxiliary fuel tanks could be carried under the wing if desired.

But the heart of the XA-38 Grizzly was its armament, the masterpiece of which was the large nose-mounted 75mm Type T15E1 fitted with a Type T-13 automatic feed mechanism cannon with 20 rounds. Aiming this cannon was fairly simple: it consisted of pointing the whole aircraft at the target and firing, but this crude procedure was somehow aided by a Type N-6 reflector sight. When the pilot pressed the button, the entire magazine would automatically fire at 1.2sec intervals. For easy maintenance, the entire nose fairing was hinged and could be opened. Six 0.50in (12.7mm) machine guns complemented the cannon's firepower. Two of them were mounted forward in the nose section, just under the cannon. The four others were located in pairs under General Electric remote-controlled turrets. Each gun was fed with 500 rounds. A

*The XA-38 was conceived to attack enemy bombers using its stunning firepower.* (Beech)

*The only two Grizzly destroyer aircraft during flight tests. Unfortunately Wright Duplex Cyclone engines were in short supply and the B-29 programme was given top priority.* (Beech)

*In this view of the Grizzly, the gunner's entry hatch is visible just behind lower turret, as are the underwing bomb racks.* (Beech)

gunner, seated in the rear fuselage, controlled the turrets by means of a periscope arrangement, but the pilot could fire the lower turret and the nose guns plus the cannon simultaneously if desired. A special device was incorporated so that the guns would cease fire whenever any part of the aircraft came under fire. In addition, the XA-38 could carry a variety of underwing stores such as bombs, chemical tanks for laying smoke screens, depth charges for ASM warfare, napalm, auxiliary fuel tanks and even torpedoes.

## Production History

The first aeroplane (s/n 43-14406) flew at Beech Field, Wichita, on 7 May 1944 with Vern L Carstens at the controls. This uneventful flight ended with an involuntary touch-an-go because landing such a big aeroplane was not familiar to Carstens. During the following test flights, performance of the aircraft proved impressive. During one of these flights a speed of 376.5mph (604km/h) was attained at an altitude of 3,100ft (945m). During another, the factory-fresh P-51B Mustang used as a chase plane was just unable to follow the Grizzly. The aircraft was delivered to the USAAF at Wright Field on 7 July

1945 where flight tests were resumed. Capt Jack W Williams conducted 38 flight tests for the Army from 13 to 24 October 1944 with the first Grizzly, on which the turrets had been deleted and replaced with dummies. Overall controllability of the XA-38 was considered 'good for all normal conditions of flight'. It was very manoeuvrable for an aircraft of its size and easy to fly through most aerobatic manoeuvres.

The second prototype (s/n 4314407) accomplished its maiden flight with Carstens on 22 September 1945. Unlike aircraft number one, number two had the turrets and armament fully installed and accordingly was used for the armament tests. The cannon was fired successfully for the first time on 1 July 1944, at Great Bend Army gunnery range, and after more tests the aircraft went to Eglin Field, Florida, where it logged 38 flight hours with Army pilots.

Unfortunately for Beech, the war was nearing its end and the R-3350 engines were not made available at the time, all being required for Boeing B-29 production. The Grizzly was thus never ordered into production. In 1948, one of these beautiful aeroplanes went to Davis-Monthan AFB, Arizona, but its fate remains unknown, and the other was most certainly scrapped.

*The second XA-38 was delivered to the US Air Force on 3 July 1945. The compactness and sleek lines of the aircraft are shown to advantage.* (Beech)

### Model 28

Two 2,300hp Wright GR-3350-43 Duplex Cyclone.

Span 67ft 4in (20.52m); length 51ft 9in (15.77 m); height 15ft 6in (4.72m); wing area 626sq ft (58.15sq m).

Empty weight 22,480lb (10,197kg); loaded weight 29,900lb (13,563kg); maximum take-off weight 35,265lb (15,996kg); wing loading 56.3lb/sq ft (275.1kg/sq m); power loading 7.67lb/hp (3.48kg/hp).

Maximum speed 330mph (531km/h) at sea level, 348mph (560km/h) at 5,000ft (1,525m), 370mph (595km/h) at 17,000ft (5,180m); cruising speed (75% power) 289mph at sea level, 350mph (563km/h) at 16,000 ft (4,875m); rate of climb 2,600ft/min (792m/min) at sea level; service ceiling 29,000ft (8,840m); range 1,625miles (2,615km) at 225mph (362km/h), 745miles (1,200km) at 289mph (465km/h).

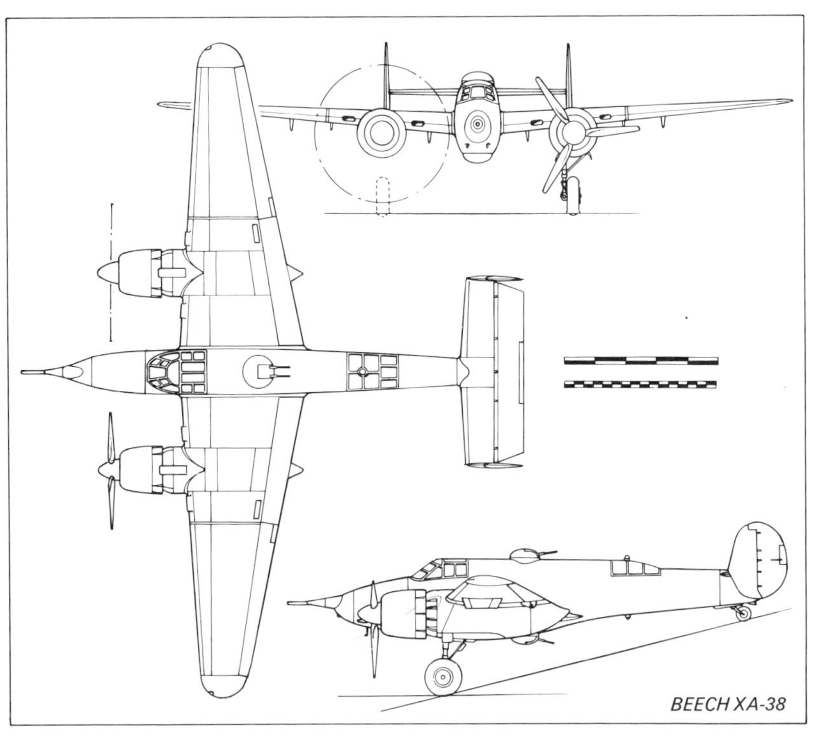


# Model 35 Bonanza

Beech Aircraft's biggest post-war news was the introduction of the third design to bear the name Beechcraft, the Model 35 Bonanza. This aircraft was designed to meet W H Beech's demand for an aircraft that would carry four people and their baggage in car-like comfort at 180mph (290km/h). Five engineers were assigned by Ted Wells to design the Model 35: Ralph Harmon led a team composed of Noel Naidenoff, Alex Odevseff, Jerry Gordon and Wilson Erhart (all but Erhart had worked previously on the XA-38 Grizzly). Five prototypes were built (c/ns 1 to 5): c/ns 1 and 2 were used for fatigue testing; c/n 3 (NX80150) was fitted with a Lycoming GO-290-A engine and a laminar wing, c/n 4 (NX80040) was fitted with a 165hp Continental engine and NACA 23000 wing, and c/n 5 was another fatigue test airframe. The Bonanza c/n 3 flew for the first time on 22 December 1945 with Vern L Carstens at the controls, and certification was granted on 25 March 1947.

*The prototype Bonanza.* (Beech)

The Bonanza was a four-seat all-metal cabin monoplane. The cantilever low-wing had a Beech-modified NACA 23000 series aerofoil section, and NACA slotted flaps between the ailerons and fuselage. The butterfly type tail-unit consisted of tailplane and elevators set at 33° dihedral angle. Balanced elevators, with a controllable trim-tab in each, also acted as rudders. The powerplant was a Continental E-185-11 six-cylinder horizontally-opposed air-cooled engine rated at 185hp at 2,300rpm at sea level and with 205hp at 2,600rpm available for take-off, driving a Beech B-215 two-blade electrically-controlled continuously variable-pitch propeller, 7ft 4in (2.23m) diameter.

The Bonanza was an immediate success, with 500 orders placed before any detailed information had been released on its performance. Production started in 1947 and 1,196 were built that year. The 7,000th production machine was delivered in July 1962, and the 9,000th V-tail Bonanza appeared in June 1969. Beech completed the 10,000th Model 35 (c/n D-10000), on 9 February 1977 and the aircraft was flown on a nationwide tour. Production of the V-tail Bonanza ceased with the Model V35B c/n D-10403, delivered to Beech production flight test department on 11 November 1982.

## Model 35

The Model 35 was the first production version, of which 1,500 were built, more than any other Bonanza model. It was powered by a 165hp Continental E-165 and had a range of 750 miles (1,200km) on 40 US gallons of fuel (151 litres). Later production Model 35s had Continental E-185-1 engines developing 185hp for one minute at 2,300rpm, and 165hp continuous. Flying Model 35 c/n D-4 *Waikiki Beech* (N80040), Capt William Odom accomplished two famous record trans-oceanic flights: on 13 January 1949 he set a new distance record for light aircraft, flying the 2,407.383 miles (3,873.479km) from Honolulu to Oakland in 22hr 6min. On the following 7 and 8 March, he made a nonstop flight of 4,957.24 miles (7,976km) between Hickam Field, Hawaii, and Teterboro Airport, New Jersey, in 36hr 2min. His aircraft is now on display at the National Air and Space Museum in Washington, DC.

## Model A35

Introduced in 1949, the Model A35 was the first to incorporate a box-type, sheet metal spar carry through that replaced the tubular design used in the 1947-48 aircraft. It was also the first Bonanza to be licenced in the Utility category at full gross weight of 2,650lb (1,200kg). Other features were a steerable nosewheel, useful load increased to 1,070lb (485kg), an undercarriage lowered speed increased from 105mph to 125mph, and a flap extended speed increased to 105mph. A total of 701 A35s were built, all produced in 1949.

## Model B35

The Model B35 was introduced in 1950. It was similar to the Model A35 in every respect, but had a 196hp Continental E-185-8 engine. Some minor improvements included front and rear cabin armrests and chart pockets, and flap extension increased from 20 to 30 degrees. Production totalled 480 aircraft, all produced during 1950, which were priced at $11,975.

## Model C35

The Model C35 was introduced in late 1950. It had a more powerful 185hp Continental E-185-11, and the chord of the butterfly tail was increased 20 per cent while the dihedral was increased to 33 degrees. In all, 719 C35s were manufactured: 410 in 1950/51 priced at $12,990, and 309 in 1952 priced at $18,990.

## Model D35

Introduced in 1953, the Model D35 was distinguishable by its new exterior paint scheme. Production totalled 298, which were priced at $18,990.

*The prototype Bonanza, (c/n 4, N80040), was fitted with wingtip tanks for postwar record breaking with Capt Bill Odom at the controls.* (P M Bowers)

*A Bonanza B35 (N2955V) in manufacturer's standard colour scheme.* (W Larkins/AAHS)

## Model E35

Introduced in 1954, the Model E35 was available with two engines: a 185hp E-185-11 or a 225hp Continental E-225-8. Production totalled 301 aircraft which were respectively priced at $18,990 (E-185 engine) and $19,990 (E-225 engine).

## Model F35

The Model F35, which appeared in 1955, was externally distinguishable by its third cabin window. It also had heavier gauge aluminium skin on the wing leading edges and strengthened butterfly-tail spar cap. Two engines were available: the E-185-11 or E-225-8 Continental, but customers preferred the higher power rated E-225-8. A total of 392 Model F35s were built in 1955.

*An early Bonanza registered in Mexico (XB-HAT).* (M Mayborn/AAHS)

## Model G35

The Model G35, which was introduced in 1956, had an E-225-8 as standard powerplant. The windshield was thicker, and undercarriage extension speed was increased to 140mph (225km/h). In all, 476 G35s were manufactured in 1956, and priced at $21,990.

## Model H35

Introduced in 1957, the Model H35 had the new 240hp Continental O-470-G engine. It also had Model 50 Twin Bonanza wing spar caps, and butterfly-tail spar caps and elevators were strengthened. The leading edge skin thickness was reduced. Production totalled 464 aircraft.

## Model J35

In 1958, the Model J35 introduced a major improvement. It had a fuel-injected Continental IO-470-C engine rated at 250hp at 2,660rpm, driving a Beech Series 278 aluminium-alloy-blade hydraulically-controlled continuously variable-pitch propeller of 6ft 10in (2.08m) diameter. Production totalled 396 aircraft which were priced at $24,300.

## Model K35

The Model K35, which was introduced in 1959, was the first to have 50-US gallon (190 litres) fuel capacity, and an optional fifth seat. With such improvements gross weight increased to 2,950lb (1,336kg). A total of 436 Model K35s were produced in 1959, and priced at $25,300.

## Model M35

The 1960 Model M35 was identical in most respects to the Model K35. Production totalled 400.

## Model N35

Introduced in 1961, the Model N35 had a new, larger, third cabin window, and a 260hp Continental IO-470-N engine. Production totalled 280 aircraft.

## Model O35

A single Model O35, with laminar flow wing, was manufactured in 1961.

## Model P35

The 1962 Model P35 was powered by a 260hp Continental IO-470-N engine driving a Beech Series 278 propeller. It also had optional wing tanks which gave a total usable capacity of 78 US gallons (295 litres), and a completely redesigned instrument panel. A total of 467 Model P35s were built (225 in 1962, and 242 in 1963).

## Model S35

Introduced in 1964, the Model S35 had its fuselage length increased by 19in (48cm) to allow six passengers to be seated in the cabin. It was powered by a 285hp Continental IO-520-B engine fitted in a redesigned cradle to reduce rudder forces during take-off and climb. A total of 667 Model S35s were built (331 in 1964, 327 in 1965, and 9 in 1966).

## Model V35

Introduced in 1966, the Model V35 was powered by a 285hp Continental IO-520-B. Among other improvements, the most salient was the introduction of a one-piece windshield. Production totalled 622 (325 in 1966, and 297 in 1967), including 79 V35TC turbo-charged models.

*Introduced in 1957, the Model H35 (N5403D shown) had the new 240hp Continental O-470-G engine.* (Beech)

### Model V35TC

The turbocharged Model V35TC was developed in 1966. Retaining the 285hp TSIO-520-D, the V35TC could maintain full rated power up to 19,000ft (5,790m). Optional extras included the Beech-designed *Magic Hand* introduced in May 1965, designed to eliminate the possibility of wheels-up landing or inadvertent retraction of the undercarriage on the ground. Production totalled 79 aircraft.

### Model V35A

Introduced in 1968, the Model V35A was powered by a 285hp Continental IO-520-B, driving a McCauley two-blade metal constant-speed propeller (the three-blade Hartzell propeller was available optionally), and had the new Speed-Sweep windshield. A total of 470 V35As were built (273 in 1968, and 197 in 1969) including 46 V35ATC turbo-charged models. The Model V35A was priced at $36,850.

### Model V35A-TC

The Model V35A-TC was generally similar to the Model V35A, but it was fitted with a Continental TSIO-520-D turbo-charged engine and oxygen system as standard equipment. A total of 46 were built which were priced at $42,750.

### Model V35B

The Model V35B was introduced in 1970, and only minor changes were introduced, such as three undercarriage-down check lights, anti-slosh fuel bladder cells and new interior styling. The 1972 Model V35B had a major interior redesign that required structural changes. The Bonanzas for 1976 were equipped

*Production of Model P35 Bonanzas totalled 467. This one (c/n D-7077, F-BASF, previously F-OBSF and N9548Y) is seen in 1970 when owned by M. Violette.*

with a dual-duct fresh air system and safety features which included a three-light strobe system and single diagonal strap shoulder harness. In 1978, the V35B received a 24-volt electrical system and a 4-second undercarriage retraction/extension time. The Model V35B was powered by a 285hp Lycoming IO-520-BA, and total usable fuel capacity was 44 US gallons (166.5 litres). Optionally, these tanks could be replaced by tanks with total usable capacity of 74 US gallons (280 litres). Production totalled 1,335 aircraft manufactured between 1970 and 1982, and including seven V35B-TC turbo-charged models. Production breakdown by year was as follows: 141 in 1970, 77 in 1971, 104 in 1972, 147 in 1973, 149 in 1974, 129 in 1975, 132 in 1976, 121 in 1977, 110 in 1978, 124 in 1979, 51 in 1980, 29 in 1981, and 21 in 1982.

On 17 February 1977 Beech released the 10,000th Bonanza, a Model V35B registered N35VB. This aircraft was eventually engaged in a presentation tour throughout the United States.

## Model V35B-TC

Introduced in 1970, only seven Model V35B-TC were built. This Model had a 285hp TSIO-520-D turbo-charged engine.

* * *

In 1948, a Model 35 was modified by Beech as the Model 40. This aircraft was powered by two 180hp Franklin installed in an over-under arrangement in a single-nose cowling and geared to drive a single propeller. This project was abandoned after FAA requirement for a firewall between the engines led to impossible servicing.

Colemill Enterprises Inc of Nashville, Tennessee, offered conversion of Models S35, V35A and V35B with new 300hp Teledyne Continental IO-550-B engines, driving Hartzell Sabre Blade four-blade Q-tip propellers and Zip Tip winglets. Such modified aircraft, known as Colemill Starfire Bonanzas, had a cruising speed of 203mph (326km/h) and a maximum rate of climb of 1,210ft/min (369m/min).

R/STOL Systems of Raleigh, North Carolina, modified a Model V35B with a full-span trailing-edge flap system and a full-span distributed-camber leading-edge as well as vortex generators to improve low-speed performance and to permit safe STOL landings and take-offs. With these modifications the take-off run was reduced to 785ft (239m)

*A Model V35B of the 1978 Model Year (N9135S). This variant, which was introduced in 1970, had only minor changes.* (Beech)

*One of the Bonanzas re-engined by Colemill Enterprises with a 300hp Teledyne Continental IO-550-B driving a four-blade Hartzell propeller.* (Colemill Enterprises Inc)

*One of the few Fleet Super-V twin-engined conversions of the Bonanza built in Canada.* (P M Bowers)

and landing run was reduced to 478ft (146m).

Mike Smith Aero Series modified Bonanzas to straight tail configuration. One aircraft is known to have been so modified (c/n D-8249, N111MS).

A far more interesting variant was the Fleet Super-V, which was a light twin-engined monoplane produced by modification of the single-engined Bonanza. The design was initiated by David Peterson of Tulsa, Oklahoma. The structure retained a strengthened Bonanza airframe fitted with two 180hp Lycoming O-360-A1D engines. The original Super-V was first flown in 1956, and the modifications were so extensive that the FAA Type Certificate, issued on 17 June 1960, authorised manufacture of the Super-V as a new aeroplane. Production of the Super-V was undertaken originally by Oakland Airmotive Company (later renamed Bay Aviation Services Co) of San Francisco. On 21 September 1962, the type Certificate was re-issued to Pine Air Ltd (later known as Fleet Aircraft Co. Ltd), and the first production model was flown in January 1963. To help sales, a Pan Am pilot, 'Chuck' Banfe, flew a Super-V round the world, covering some 21,000 miles (33,800km) in 212 hours. This aircraft (originally c/n SV101) was later rebuilt by Fleet as SV116 and became the company's demonstrator. Only five Super-Vs were built: c/ns SV112 (ex-D-1243), SV-113 (ex-D-1569), SV114 (ex-D-1388), SV114 (ex-D-422) and SV115 (ex-D-1474).

A lesser known contribution of the Bonanza to aeronautical research occurred in 1955, when a set of wings were incorporated in the Bell Model 68 (X-14) VTOL research aircraft.

## Military Operators

**Argentina**: one aircraft (unidentified) was operated in 1967.
**Brazil**: five Model A35s were operated by the Forçà Aérea Brasileira from 1950 until 1960 (serialled UC-35-2857/2861).
**Nicaragua**: a single Model A35 was operated by Fuerza Aérea de Nicaragua (c/n D-1674, ex N673B, serialled 1017).

### Model A35

One 165hp Continental E-185-1.
Span 32ft 10in (10m); length 25ft 2in (7.67m); height 6ft 6½in (2 m); wing area 177.6sq ft (16.49sq m).

Empty weight 1,580lb (717kg); maximum take-off weight 2,650lb (1,203kg); wing loading 14.92lb/sq ft (72.8kg/sq m); power loading 16.06lb/hp (7.29kg/hp).

Maximum speed 184mph (296km/h) at sea level; cruising speed 170mph (272km/h) at 8,000ft (2,440m); rate of climb 890ft/min (271m/min) at sea level; service ceiling 17,100ft (5,485m); maximum range at 160mph (256km/h) 750 miles (1,207km).

### Model C35

One 185hp Continental E-185-11.
Dimensions as for Model A35.

Empty weight 1,625lb (738kg); loaded weight 2,700lb (1,226kg); wing loading 15.17 lb/sq ft (74.03kg/sq m); power loading 14.59lb/hp (6.62kg/hp).

Maximum speed 190mph (304km/h) at sea level; cruising speed 175mph (282km/h) at 8,000ft (2,440m); rate of climb 1,110ft/min (335m/min) at sea level; service ceiling 18,000ft (5,490m); maximum range at 160mph (256km/h) at 10,000ft (3,050m) 775 miles (1,240km).

### Model J35

One 250hp Continental IO-470-C.
Dimensions as for A35.

Empty weight 1,820lb (826kg); loaded weight 2,900lb (1,315kg); wing loading 16.3lb/sq ft (79.6kg/sq m); power loading 11.6lb/hp (5.26kg/hp).

Maximum speed 210mph (338km/h) at sea level; maximum cruising speed (75% power) 200mph (322km/h) at 7,000ft (2,135m); economic cruising speed (65% power) 195mph (314km/h) at 10,000ft (3,050m); rate of climb 1,250ft/min (380m/min) at sea level; service ceiling 21,300ft (6,490m);

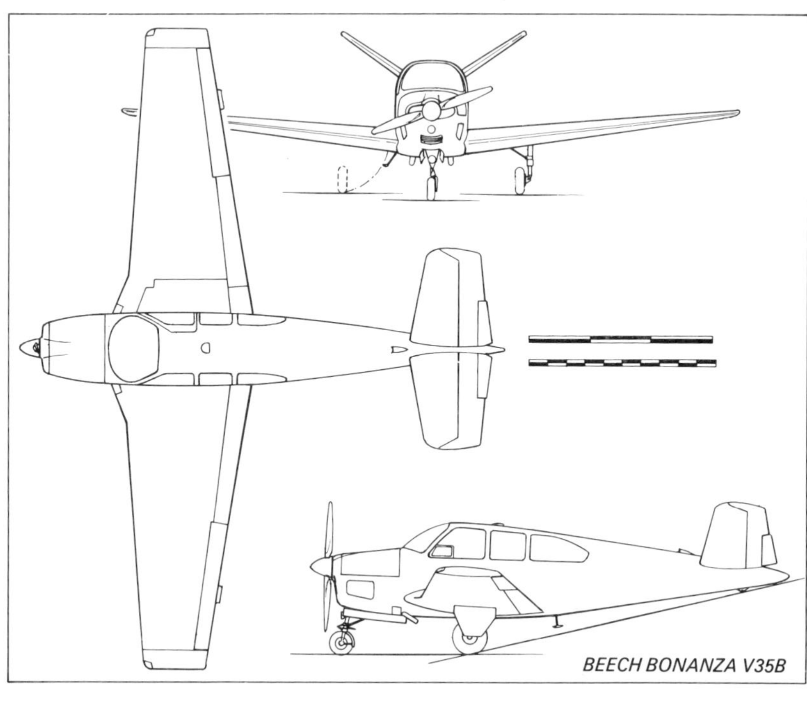

BEECH BONANZA V35B

maximum range at 180mph (290km/h) at 10,000ft (3,050m) 725 miles (1,168km).

## Model P35

One 260hp Lycoming IO-470-N.

Span 33ft 5½in (10.2m); length 25ft 1⅕in (7.67m); height 6ft 6½in (2m); wing area 181sq ft (16.8sq m).

Empty weight 1,855lb (841kg); maximum take-off weight 3,125lb (1,417kg); wing loading 17.3lb/sq ft (84.5kg/sq m); power loading 12.01lb/hp (5.45kg/hp).

Maximum speed 205mph (330km/h); maximum cruising speed (75% power) 195mph (314km/h) at 7,000ft (2,135m); rate of climb 1,150ft/min (350m/min) at sea level; service ceiling 19,200ft (5,850m); maximum range (45% power) 1,215 miles (1,955km) at 10,000ft (3,050m).

## Model V35TC

One 285hp Continental IO-520-B.

Span 33ft 5½in (10.2m); length 26ft 4½in (8.04m); height 7ft 7in (2.31m); wing area 181sq ft (16.8sq m).

Empty weight 2,000lb (907kg); maximum take-off weight 3,400lb (1,542kg); wing loading 18.78lb/sq ft (91.7kg/sq m); power loading 11.93lb/hp (5.41kg/hp).

Maximum speed 240mph (386km/h) at 16,000ft (4,875m); maximum cruising speed (75% power) 224mph (360km/h) at 21,000ft (6,400m); rate of climb 1,225ft/min (373m/min) at sea level; service ceiling 26,600ft (8,100m); maximum range 1,060 miles (1,706km).

## Model V35B

One 285hp Continental IO-520-BA.

Dimensions as for Model V35TC.

Empty weight 2,051lb (930kg); maximum take-off weight 3,400lb (1,542kg); wing loading 18.80lb/sq ft (91.8kg/sq m); power loading 11.93lb/hp (5.41kg/hp).

Maximum speed 210mph (336km/h) at sea level; maximum cruising speed (75% power) 203mph (327km/h) at 6,500ft (1,980m); rate of climb 1,136ft/min (346m/min) at sea level; service ceiling 17,500ft (5,335m); maximum range (45% power) with 45min reserves 1,007 miles (1,620km).

## Fleet Super-V

Two 180hp Lycoming O-360-A1D.

Dimensions as for Model C35.

Empty weight 2,200lb (998kg); maximum take-off weight 3,400lb (1,542kg); wing loading 19.14lb/sq ft (93.51kg/sq m); power loading 9.44lb/hp (4.28kg/hp).

Maximum speed 210mph (338km/h); maximum cruising speed 190mph (306km/h); rate of climb 1,550ft/min (473m/min) at sea level; service ceiling 20,000ft (6,100m); maximum range (50% power) 1,200 miles (1,930km).

# Model 34 Twin-Quad

Early in 1945, after cessation of hostilities, the commercial feeder line market was expected to develop, and Beech Aircraft Corp started development of an all-metal 20-seat high-wing monoplane for economical transport of passengers and mail from unimproved airfields. The aircraft, known as the Model 34 Twin-Quad and designed by Beech engineers Alex Odevseff, W A Day, J W Massey and W O Stephens, displayed several unusual features. The most unusual one concerned the powerplant: it used two engines, housed inside relatively short and narrow cowlings, with individual clutch assemblies, in each wing driving a single propeller through a common gearbox. These engines were four, surplus, eight-cylinder Lycoming geared, supercharged horizontally-opposed GSO-580s developing 375hp each at 3,300rpm, and driving Hamilton Standard constant-speed, fully-feathering propellers. Structurally, the Model 34 was an all-metal high-wing monoplane with a butterfly tail and an electrically-operated tricycle undercarriage with quite long legs. The cabin was designed to carry twenty passengers and their baggage, plus approximately 1,000lb (454kg) of mail or freight. The Model 34 Twin-Quad could carry 1,000lb (453kg) of express cargo and had a range of 1,400 miles (2,250km). A specially designed interior arrangement feature allowed the load to be varied in proportion. In addition to a large cargo space between the passenger compartment and the cockpit, the forward section of the main compartment, normally seating six passengers, could be converted for additional cargo. A movable bulkhead complete with entrance door was provided so that the cargo compartment could be isolated from the passenger compartment. The prototype, registered NX90521, made its first flight on 1 October 1947 from Beech Field. Although

*The powerplant of the Beech Twin Quad consisted of four paired 375hp Lycoming S-580s.* (Beech)

*The prototye Twin Quad in flight. This innovative aircraft had a fuselage keel which could sustain wheels-up landing loads.* (Beech)

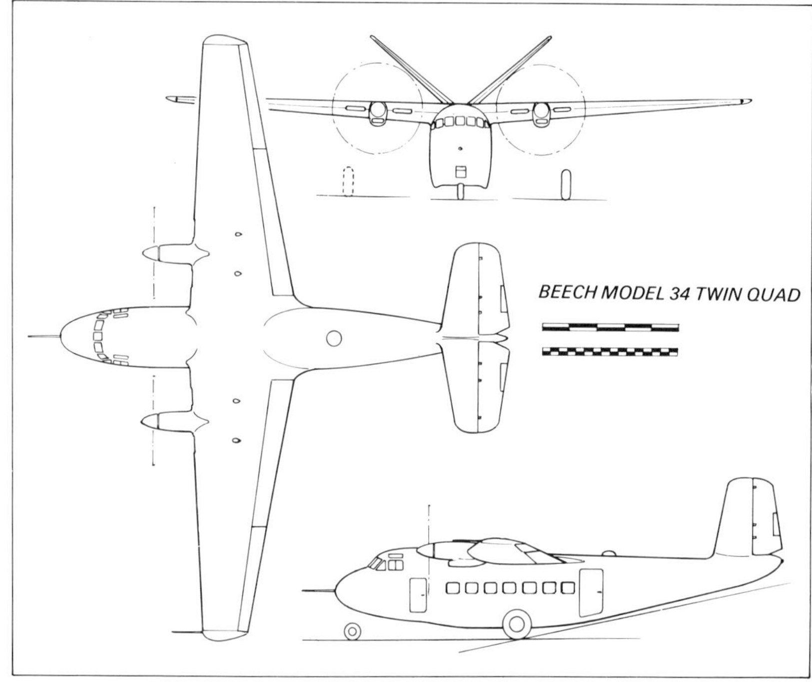


the aircraft was designed for a maximum speed of 300mph (480km/h), that figure was never attained during the two hundred hours of extensive flight testing accomplished from October 1947 to January 1949. The fuselage keel had been designed to withstand wheels-up landing loads and one unintentional landing incident demonstrated that the Twin-Quad could sustain such an accident with minimal damage. Unfortunately, on 17 January 1949 the prototype made a forced landing shortly after take-off. Two crew members were killed and the prototype was damaged beyond repair. Work was started at once on a second similar aircraft, but it quickly became quite obvious that customers were scarce and the project was withdrawn.

### Model 34

Four paired 375hp Lycoming GSO-580.

Span 70ft (21.35m); length 53ft (16.16m); height 17ft (5.18m); wing area 650sq ft (60.38sq m).

Maximum take-off weight 19,500lb (8,853kg); wing loading 30lb/sq ft (146.4kg/sq m); power loading 12.19lb/hp (5.53kg/hp).

Maximum speed 230mph (368km/h) at 8,000ft (2,440m); stalling speed 70mph (112km/h); rate of climb 1,000ft/min (305m/min) at sea level; service ceiling 23,000ft (7,015m); maximum range with 45min reserves 1,450 miles (2,320km).

*(Estimated figures)*

# Model 45 T-34 Mentor and Turbo Mentor

The Model 45 Mentor originated as a private venture by Beech Aircraft Corporation to 'offer the military services a high-performance trainer that would incorporate all the controls and characteristics of heavier, more advanced combat craft'. The Mentor was inexpensively developed from the commercial Model 35. Major departures from the Model 35 were a conventional empennage (Beech also considered a butterfly tail for the Model 45), a narrow fuselage, and a full-vision continuous transparent canopy with sections over each seat which could be independently opened. The airframe was strenghtened to sustain 10 positive and 4.5 negative g, and the Model 45 could perform all aerobatic manoeuvres taught by most military Services around the world. The wings had ailerons and electrically-operated flaps made of magnesium, and metal structure with flush-riveted skin. There was a retractable tricycle undercarriage, Two fuel tanks, capacity 50 US gallons (225 litres), were housed in the wings. An attractive and money saving point was that almost 80 per cent of the tooling for the Bonanza could be used for the production model.

Powered by a 205hp Continental E-185-8, the prototype (with civil registration N8591A) was first flown at Wichita on 2 December 1948 by Beech test pilot Vern L Carstens. It was followed by two other prototypes, the last of which was powered by a 225hp Continental E-225-8.

## Production History

### YT-34

In 1950, the USAF decided to evaluate the Fairchild XT-31, the Temco YT-35 and the Beech YT-34, but this evaluation was not completed. The first YT-34 flew in May 1950, followed in due course by the other two in June and July. Another evaluation programme was initiated in August 1951 with the YT-34 and YT-35, which was won by Beech, and the type was ordered into production by the US Air Force. The YT-34 differed from the prototype only in detail. It retained the Continental E-225-8 engine but was slightly heavier due to equipment. The first YT-34 (s/n 50-735) was eventually used for an Army evaluation of armed trainers suitable for light ground support duties. For these trials the aircraft was fitted with two 0.30-inch machine guns, and six rockets or two 150lb bombs under the wings. One YT-34 (No.50-735) is preserved at Castle Air Museum, California.

### T-34A

In 1953, satisfied with every aspect of the Model 45, the US Air Force ordered an initial production batch of aircraft, designated T-34A. The T-34 was powered by a 225hp Continental E-225-8 (military designation O-470-13), six-cylinder horizontally-opposed, air-cooled engine and had a Beech Model 215-207 all-metal constant-speed airscrew 7ft 4in (2.23m) in diameter. The first two aircraft were accepted in September 1953 and, by September 1954, a total of 88 had been delivered. Production totalled 353 before it ended in October 1956. After obtaining a

*The Model 45 Mentor was first flown on 2 December 1947, by Beech test pilot Vern L Carstens.*

*The prototype Mentor (N8591A) was powered by a 205hp Continental, while the two following prototypes were fitted with 225hp engines.* (P M Bowers)

*This USAF T-34A (s/n 55-5261) had just been civil registered. It still displays its buzz-number TD-261.* (W Steeneck/AAHS)

manufacturing licence from Beech in 1954, the Canadian Car and Foundry Co Ltd delivered 100 Mentors to the US Air Force, and 25 to the RCAF.

### T-34B

On 17 June 1954, after exhaustive operational evaluation, the Mentor was named winner of a US Navy competition in which Temco and Ryan designs had also been involved. Designated T-34B, the Navy variant was powered by the same 225hp Continental O-470-13 engine and had additional equipment. The US Navy started taking delivery of its T-34Bs on 17 December 1954. A total of 423 T-34Bs were produced between October 1954 and October 1957, when the last 12 aeroplanes were delivered. The Navy continued using the T-34B until the late 70s when the turbine-powered T-34C began to replace the earlier models.

### Model B45

The Model B45 was the export version of the Model 45, and Beech granted production licences to Japan in 1953 and Argentina in 1956. Exports totalled 318 Model B45s.

### T-34C

In 1973, with the initiation of a Long Range Pilot Training Syllabus (LRPTS), Beech received a US Navy R&D contract to modify two T-34Bs to determine whether the tough and reliable Mentor could be upgraded for a continuing training role (thus replacing both the T-34B and T-28B/C). The modification involved the installation of a 715shp Pratt & Whitney PT6A-25 (military designation T74) propeller-turbine, torque limited to 400shp and driving a Hartzell three-blade propeller, and the latest avionics (UHF, Omni, DME, LF/DF, transponder, Intercom, etc.). Fuel capacity was increased to a total of 125 US gal. (473 litres). It also included an armament system similar to that of the Beech Model PD-249 Pave Coin Bonanza. Design work was initiated in March 1973, and conversion of two T34B airframes (BuNos 140784 and 140861) started in May 1973. The improved Mentor had a 1,000lb (454kg) increase in gross weight, which required structural strengthening of the fuselage and tail unit. Additional strength for other assemblies and components was achieved by adopting off-the-shelf parts from other Beech aircraft.

Designated YT-34C, the first of these aircraft made its maiden flight on 21 September 1973 and the test programme continued throughout 1974. By February 1976, the two prototypes had flown more than 800 test hours, including nearly 300 hours of evaluation by the US Navy. This programme was concluded by an OPEVAL (Operational Evaluation) at NAS Pensacola. Beech then received $89.5-million contracts for the 184 production T-34Cs and the provision of engineering services and support. Deliveries to NATC (Training Air Wing 5) at NAS Whiting Field, Milton, Florida, began in November 1977 and were completed in June 1981. Deliveries of a further 150-aircraft batch were completed in April 1984. In May 1987, the US Navy ordered a last batch of 19 T-34Cs for delivery between June 1989 and April 1990.

*Beech T-34B (BuNo.144043) operated by NRD Los Angeles, at NAS Moffett Field in July 1975. Colour scheme is night blue and white, with red trim.* (J Whitehead)

### T-34C-1

The T-34C-1 was an armament systems trainer variant also able to undertake forward air control (FAC) and tactical strike training missions. This version had a CA-513 fixed-reticle reflector gunsight and four underwing hardpoints for external stores. The inboard stations were rated at 600lb (272kg) each, the outboard stations at 300lb (136kg) each, with a maximum load of 1,200lb (544kg) total. Weapons which could be carried on MA-4 racks included AF/B37K-1 bomb containers with pratice bombs or flares, LAU-32 or LAU-59 rocket pods, Mk 81 bombs, SUU-11 Minigun pods, BLU-10/B incendiary

*T-34B (BuNo.140725) in orange and white finish at NAS Willow Grove in August 1962.* (R Besecker)

*In 1977, the T-34C N23789 made a nonstop transatlantic flight from Gander, Newfoundland, to Shannon, Ireland, on its way to a five-week demonstration tour in Europe, with Ben Keel as pilot.* (Beech)

bombs, AGM-22A wire guided anti-tank missiles and TA8X towed target equipment.

* * *

In the mid-eighties, a Beech T-34C (c/n GL-108, registered N510NA) was modified by NASA for research on viscous drag reduction. A 7ft 8in (2.34m) chord glove was arranged around the port wing using a NASA natural laminar flow NLF(1)-0215F aerofoil section. Using this test-bed, the researchers at Langley validated the extent of laminar flow predicted by both analysis and wind-tunnel tests.

Allison Gas Turbine Division GMC developed a propeller-turbine conversion of the Model 45 which involved replacement of the classic Continental piston engine with a 420shp Allison 250B-17D propeller-turbine. Other modifications included strengthening of the wing to withstand a maximum load of 6g, additional fuel tanks which increased standard capacity to 80 US gallons (303 litres) and optional 20-US gallon (76-litres) wingtip tanks. Known as the AT-34 Allison Turbine Mentor (registered N4CN), the prototype made its public debut at the Paris Air Show in June 1987, and was demonstrated subsequently to a number of potential military operators.

A far less known contribution of the Mentor to aviation occurred in 1955 when the tail section of a T-34 was used in the construction of the low-cost developed Bell Model 68 (X-14) VTOL research aircraft.

*The AT-34 Allison Turbo Mentor was a conversion developed by Allison Gas Turbine Division GMC.* (Allison)

## Service History

Deliveries of the T-34A to Air Training Command began in 1954, and the type progressively replaced T-6s and other types for primary training. The type equipped training schools at such bases as Moore AFB, Texas, Bainbridge AFB, Georgia, Spence AFB, Georgia, Graham AFB, Florida, Bartow AFB, Florida, and Malden AFB, Missouri. With the introduction of the more powerful T-28 Trojan, they were used to give 30 hours of *ab initio* training to all trainees before they progressed to the T-28, and then to the T-37. In 1960/61, with the introduction of all-through jet training, the T-34As became redundant and were withdrawn from use. Numbers were then assigned to other nations through MAP.

In the US Navy, the T-34B served initially with the Training

*T-34B BuNo.144064 belonging to the Navy Recruiting Office at Ogden MAP, Utah, in February 1974.* (B Knowles)

Squadron VT-1 at NAS Saufley Field, which had a fleet of 135 aircraft by 1959. Subsequently, VT-5 Squadron also flew the T-34B at the same base, whilst others served with more specialised training units. Other Navy units operating T-34Cs were: VT-2 'Doer Birds' at Whiting Field, Florida, VT-3 'Red Knights' at Whiting Field, Florida, VT-4 'Rubber Ducks' at Pensacola, Florida, VT-6 at Whiting Field, Florida, VT-10 'Cosmic Cats' at Pensacola, Florida, and VT-27 'Boomers' at Corpus Christi, Texas.

Six T-34Cs transferred from Navy stocks were used as chase and photographic aircraft by the US Army's Airborne Special Operations Test Board at Pope AFB, North Carolina.

After their retirement, numerous T-34A/Bs went on to the civil market. Several were operated by the Civil Air Patrol and by the US Forest Service (BG-145/N157Z, BG-154/N122Z, BG-163/N121Z, BG-168/N183Z, BG-176/N123Z, BG-417/N124Z, BG-419/N126Z, and BG-?/N102Z).

## Foreign Military Operators

More than twenty foreign countries have taken delivery of and operated Mentors, as follows:

**Algeria**: six T-34C-1s were delivered in March/April 1979 and were in service at the Algerian national pilot training school at Tafaraoui. These bear c/ns GP-1/6 and were registered 7T-WPD, -WPE, -WPF, -WPH, -WPJ, and -WPK.

**Argentina**: in 1956, Beech granted a production licence to Argentina. This involved the supply of 15 complete aircraft, followed by the dismantled components for approximately 75 more, to be assembled in the Argentine government factory (FMA) at Cordoba. All of these aircraft were able to carry the optional armament for weapons training. Beechcraft-built aircraft were serialled E-001/015, while FMA-built aircraft were serialled E-016/090 (c/ns GC-180/199 and CG-224/278). These were operated by the Escuela de Aviacion Militar and some of them by I Grupo de Attaque of the VII Brigata Aérea. In 1980 fifteen T-34C-1s were delivered to Comando de Aviación Naval Argentina (CANA) with serials 0719/0733 and codes 1-A-401/415 and are used by the Escuela de Aviación Naval. During the Falklands conflict, four T-34Cs (1-A-401, 408, 411 and 412) were destroyed by the British commandos at Puerto Calderón. A fifth example (No.0729) was captured, and is now displayed at the Fleet Air Arm Museum at RNAS Yeovilton, Somerset.

**Canada**: in January 1953, the US

*A sharkmouthed T-34C (BuNo.160524) of TAW-5 at NAS Moffett Field, California, in May 1980.* (J Whitehead)

*One of the six T-34Cs which were transferred to the US Army to be operated by USAABNSOTBD (US Army's Airborne Special Operations Test Board) from Pope AFB, North Carolina. This sharkmouthed example bore BuNo.162263.* (N Taylor)

Air Force contracted Canadian Car and Foundry to build 34 T-34As. This was followed by a RCAF contract for 25 more and a second USAF contract for 66. The Canadian prototype was flown in early May 1954 and deliveries began later that month. However, the aircraft of the RCAF contract (T-34A-CCF c/n 34-1/25) did not enter service and 23 of them were turned over to Turkey as part of MAP and one (RCAF 24223) went to Greece.

*A T-34A operated by Department of Agriculture, US Forest Service.* (P M Bowers)

**Chile**: from 1953, Fuerza Aérea de Chile took delivery of sixty-six aircraft (serialled 101/166) which were in use with Escuela de Aviación Capitán Avalos, based at El Bosque, Santiago. Six of them were later transferred to the Navy (two in 1966, and four in 1968) and the surviving aircraft were presented to the Uruguyan Navy (serialled 201/206) and replaced by Pilatus PC-7 Turbo-Trainers.

**Colombia**: forty-two T-34As were delivered (serialled 301/342) complemented by six ex-US Navy T-34Bs in 1978 (with serial/BuNo. tie-up as follows: 301A/140685, 302A/140728, 306A/140753, 308A/140763, 309A/140801 and 312A/144021). They equip the Escuadrón Básico 612 based at Base Aérea Marco Fidel Suárez de Cali.

**Dominicana**: the Air Force took delivery of 12 ex-US Navy aircraft (BuNos. 140677, 140687, 140717, 140727, 140741, 140743, 140796, 140802, 140824, 140886, 144066 and 144103).

**Ecuador**: in 1979, the Air Force took delivery of 14 T-34As and an additonal batch of nine aircraft was taken on charge in 1978. In addition, 20 T-34C-1s (serialled 0014, 0018/0030) were ordered in 1978. They equip the Escuadron Entrenamiento Aérea stationed at Salinas. For its own part, the Navy accepted three T-34C-1s in April 1980 (ANE-223/225).

**France**: in November 1977, the Armée de l'Air evaluated a single T-34C (c/n GM-14) under the military registration F-SEXE. To deliver the aircraft, the ferry pilot Ben Keel accomplished the first transatlantic flight of a Mentor in 8hr 50min. The Armée de l'Air eventually gave preference to the French-built Aérospatiale Epsilon.

**Gabon**: on 22 February 1982, the Presidential Guard took delivery of four T-34C-1s (c/n GM-85/88; registered TR-KFS, TR-KFT, TR-KFU and TR-KFV).

**Greece**: one Canadian-built aircraft (ex RCAF 24223) was delivered.

**Indonesia**: from April 1978, the Indonesian National Armed Forces-Air Forces (TNI-AU) accepted, under a $9 million contract negotiated through Hawker de Havilland Australia Pty Ltd, 16 T-34C-1s to equip its No.2 Training Squadron at Jokjakarta. At first, these were serialled B401/B416 (with c/ns

*One of the Beech Mentors used to train Lufthansa pilots at Goodyear, Arizona, in March 1992. The aircraft is painted yellow overall with dark blue trim.* (J G Handelman)

*An Argentine FMA-built T-34A (E-055, c/n CG-243) operated by the Escuela de Aviación Militar, at Buenos Aires Aeroparque.* (J A Cerdá)

GM-45/48, GM-53/64 respectively) but they were re-serialled at a later date LD-3401/3416. A further nine aircraft were delivered in 1984.

**Japan**: after a licence and technical assistance agreement had been concluded with Beech Aircraft Corp in 1953, Fuji Jukogyo Kabushiki Kaisha (Fuji Heavy Industries Ltd) built the Mentor at the Utsonomiya plant. Deliveries began in August 1954, and Fuji supplied a total of 140 Mentors to the Japanese Government and a further 36, with spares, to the Philippine Air Force. A modified version of the Mentor with both military and civil uses was developped as the LM-1 Nikko, and 27 of these aircraft are in service as the standard multi-purpose liaison aircraft of the JGSDF. The prototype of a more powerful version (340hp Lycoming GSO-480-B1A6), designated KM, flew in December 1958, and the first production model was delivered to the Transportation Ministry in March 1959. On 9 December 1959 the prototype KM set an international Class C-1c height record of 32,536ft (9,917m). A further development of the Mentor series was announced in 1960. Known as the KM-2, this two-seat primary trainer (powered by a 340hp Lycoming IGSO-480-A1F6) was delivered to the Japanese Navy (JMSDF) from September 1962 and deliveries were completed in May 1965. A propeller-turbine version of the KM-2 was the SM. The SM was powered by a 578shp United Aircraft of Canada PT6A-6. Capable of all-weather operation, it accommodated a pilot and five passengers and was intended for military reconnaissance duties and SAR. Another variant was the KM-2B, which combined the airframe and power plant of the KM-2 with the two-seat installation of the T-34A. The first KM-2B (registered JA3725) was flown for the first time on 26 September 1974 and was selected to replace the JASDF's T-34As.

Japanese T-34As were: c/n KD-1/49 (serialled 41-0311/0326; 51-0327/0360); c/ns FM-1/75 (serialled 51-0361/0387; 61-0388/0413; 71-0414/0435).

**Mexico**: three T-34Bs (ME-011/013) were acquired in 1958 to be operated by the Escuela de Aviación Naval (EAN).

**Morocco**: a contract valued at $5.5 million for the supply of twelve T-34C-1s to the Forces Royales Air (FRA) was received during 1975. These aircraft are registered CN-

*A JASDF T-34A (s/n 71-0432, c/n FM-72) of the 11th Flight Training Wing at Shizuhama.* (T Toda)

*The Fuji KM-2 is one of the several Japanese developments of the Mentor. It has a four-seat cabin and is powered by a 340hp Lycoming. This example belongs to the JMSDF.* (J Wegg collection)

ATA-01/CN-ATL-12, and based at Marrakech.

**Peru**: The Air Force operated at least six T-34As with the Academia del Aire, while the Navy has two T-34As (AI-501 and AI-504) and seven T-34C-1s (serialled AI-510/516).

**Philippines**: the 105th Combat Crew Training Squadron of the 5th Fighter Wing, stationed in Basa, operated 36 Fuji-built machines along with T-33As.

**Portugal**: the Portuguese Government's Directorate General of Civil Aeronautics (Direcção General da Aeronáutica Civil) operated three T-34Bs (c/ns BG-307, BG-312 and BG-317, registered CS-DGB, -DGC and -DGD) which are now stored.

**El Salvador**: at least six T-34As were delivered to be operated by the Escuela de Aviación Militar.

**Spain**: twenty-five T-34As, known as E.17s in the Spanish Air Force system, have been delivered to equip the Escuadrón 791 of the Academia General del Aire. These aircraft, serialled E.17-1/25 with codes 791-1/25, were withdrawn from use in 1989.

**Taiwan**: forty T-34Cs have been taken in charge by the Chinese Air Force.

*One of the three T-34Bs which were operated by the Mexican Navy. The aircraft is painted yellow overall.* (J A Cerdá collection)

**Turkey**: twenty-four ex-RCAF aircraft were received to equip the 123 Filo stationed at Cumaovasi. These were ex-RCAF 24201/24219 and 24221/24225 and were re-serialled OK-01/19 and OK-21/25.

**Uruguay**: the Air Force received more than 40 T-34A/Bs of which 25 were ex-US Navy T-34Bs delivered in 1977/1978 (BuNos. 140684, 140694, 140704, 140710, 140714, 140732, 140735, 140748, 140750, 140754, 140756, 140760, 140761, 140769, 140790, 140806, 140808, 140815, 140832, 140847, 140878, 140888, 140889, 140890 and 144017 respectively). The Aviación Naval Uruguaya received six T-34As from the Chilean Air Force

*Formation flight depicting three of the several T-34C operators. Nearest to the camera is a Peruvian Navy aircraft (T-34C-1 No.510), followed by a Moroccan example (CN-ATH), and an Ecudorian aircraft.* (Beech via E Phillips)

*Beech T-34A (E17-17) operated by Escuadrón 791 of the Ejercito Del Aire from San Javier air base.* (J A Cerdá)

and three T-34C-1s (A-270/272) were added to the inventory in May 1981. In 1991, Spain sold to Uruguay 23 of its T-34As for a 'symbolic price' and these aircraft are now operated by the pilot training school at Pando, near Montevideo.
**Venezuela**: forty-one T-34As have been delivered to be operated by the Escuela de Aviación Militar and six other aircraft are in use with the Escuela de Aviación Civil (c/ns GC-286/287 and GC-296/299 serialled MR-25/30).

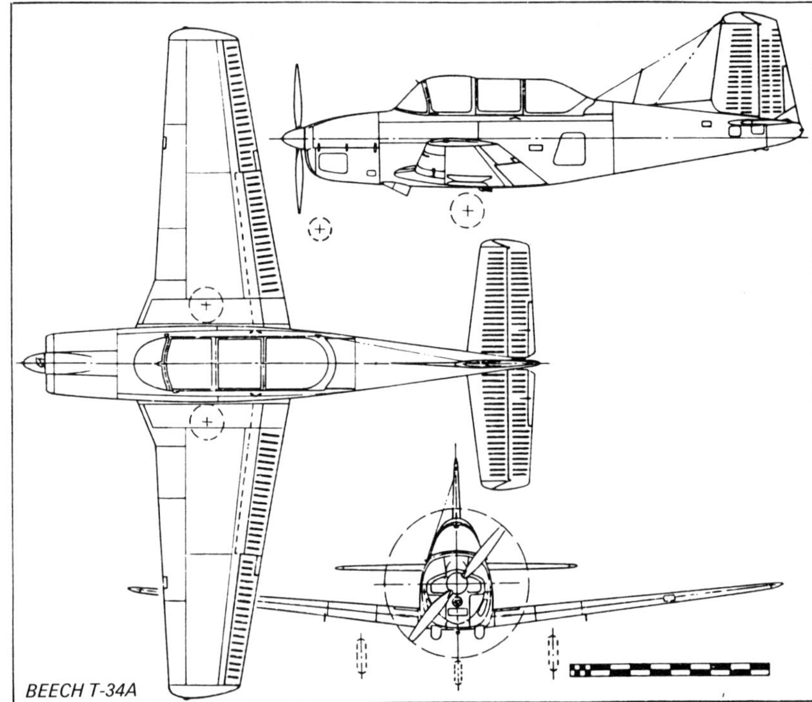


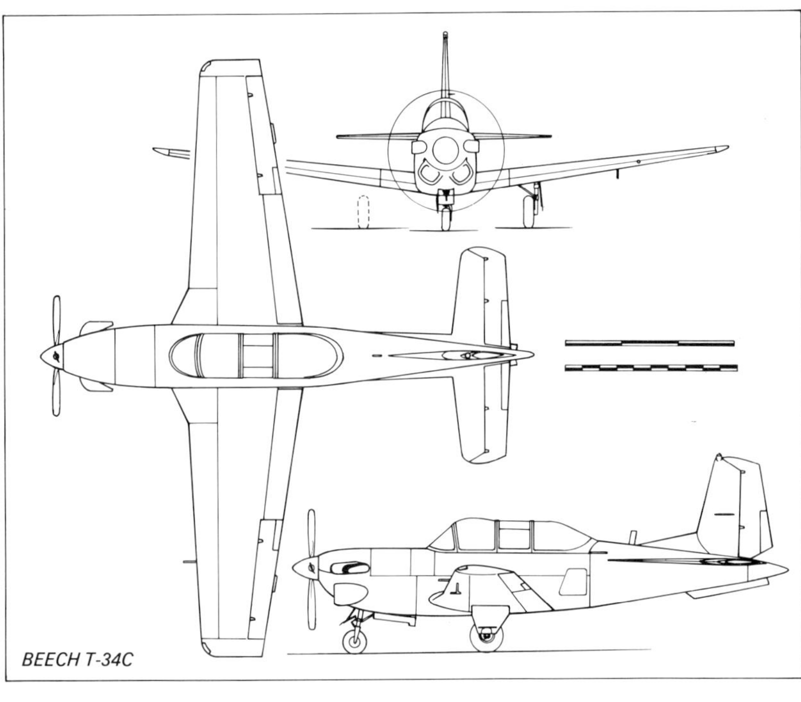


## T-34A

One 225hp Continental O-470-13.
Span 32ft 10in (10m); length 25ft 10in (7.8m); height 9ft 7in (2.92m); wing area 177.6sq ft (16.49sq m).
Empty weight 2,156lb (978kg); loaded weight 2,950lb (1,338kg); wing loading 16.3lb/sq ft (79.54 kg/sq m); power loading 13.11lb/hp (5.94kg/hp).
Maximum speed 189mph (304km/h) at sea level; cruising speed 173mph (277km/h) at 10,000ft (3,050m); rate of climb 1,230ft/min (375m/min) at sea level; service ceiling 20,000ft (6,100m); maximum cruising range 737miles (1,186km).

## T-34B

Engine and dimensions as for T-34A.
Empty weight 2,254lb (1,022kg); loaded weight 2,985lb (1,354kg); wing loading 16.75lb/sq ft (81.78kg/sq m); power loading 13.27lb/hp (6.02kg/hp).
Maximum speed 188mph (302km/h) at sea level; cruising speed 170mph (274km/h); rate of climb 1,160ft/min (354m/min) at sea level; service ceiling 19,500ft (5,945m); range with maximum payload 728 miles (1,171km).

## T-34C

One 715shp Pratt & Whitney (UACL) PT6A-25, torque limited to 400shp.
Span 33ft 3⅞in (10.16m); length 28ft 8½in (8.75m); height 9ft 10⅞in (3.02m); wing area 179.9sq ft (16.71sq m).
Empty weight 2,630lb (1,193kg); maximum take-off weight 4,274lb (1,938kg); wing loading 22.2lb/sq ft (108.3kg/sq m); power loading 5.98lb/hp (2.71kg/hp).
Maximum level speed 257mph (414km/h) at 17,500ft (5,335m); maximum cruising speed 247mph (397km/h) at 17,500ft (5,335m); rate of climb 1,275ft/min (388m/min) at 10,000ft (3,050m); service ceiling 30,000ft (9,145m); range 749 miles (1,205km) at 20,000ft (6,100m).

### Fuji KM

One 340hp Lycoming GSO-480-B1A6.
Dimensions as for T-34A, except length 26ft ¾in (7.94m).
Empty weight 2,400lb (1,090kg); maximum take-off weight 3,860lb (1,750kg); wing loading 21.73lb/sq ft (106.12kg/sq m); power loading 11.35lb/hp (5.15kg/hp).
Maximum speed 220mph (355km/h) at 8,000ft (2,440m); rate of climb 1,000ft/min (306m/min) at sea level; range (50% power) 960 miles (1,545km).

### Fuji KM-2

One 340hp Lycoming IGSO-480-A1F6.
Dimensions as for Fuji KM.
Empty weight 2,500lb (1,134kg); maximum take-off weight 3,860lb (1,750kg); wing loading 21.73lb/sq ft (106.12kg/sq m); power loading 11.35lb/hp (5.15kg/hp).
Maximum speed 230mph (370km/h) at 16,000ft (4,880m); cruising speed 182mph (293km/h) at 10,000ft (3,050m); rate of climb 1,160ft/min (354m/min) at sea level; service ceiling 24,000ft (7,310m); maximum range 570 miles (915km).

### Allison Turbine Mentor

One 420shp Allison 250B-17D Turbine Pac.
Span 32ft 9⅞in (10m); length 28ft 1in (8.56m); height 9ft 7in (2.92m); wing area 177.6sq ft (16.5sq m).
Empty weight 2,020lb (916kg); maximum take-off weight 3,400lb (1,542kg); wing loading 19.1lb/sq ft (93.4kg/sq m); power loading 8.09lb/hp (3.67kg/hp).
Maximum cruising speed 242mph (389km/h) at 10,000ft (3,050m); rate of climb 2,100ft/min (640m/min) at sea level; service ceiling 25,000ft (7,620m); range 1,244 miles (2,000km).

# Model 50 Twin Bonanza L-23 Seminole

In 1949, the Beech Company introduced the first postwar twin business aircraft, which was intended to complement the Model 18 already in production. The prototype Model 50, named Twin Bonanza, accomplished its first flight on 15 November 1949. It was a six-seat all-metal, low-wing cantilever monoplane. A NACA 23014.1 wing section had been retained at the root, and a NACA 23012 at the tips; aspect ratio was 7.51, and dihedral 7 degrees. The wings had NACA slotted flaps, with metal structure and flush-riveted skin. There was a retractable nosewheel undercarriage and it was powered by two 260hp Lycoming GO-435-C2 six-cylinder horizontally-opposed air-cooled engines each driving a Beech Model B200-116 constant-speed, or Model 214-101 fully-feathering propeller.

By 20 September 1950 over 200 hours of flight testing had been completed, and Beech announced that the aircraft was to make a tour of US Air Force bases for Service appraisal. By 1 May 1951 the prototype Twin Bonanza had logged more than 500 hours on flight testing and had been approved by the CAA type certification board.

### Model 50/L-23A Seminole

A pre-production batch of 11 airframes was completed in 1952 which went to both civil and military customers: two were exported to Brazil and Mexico, and the last four were taken on charge by the US Army for, in 1951, the US Army had evaluated the Model 50 at Fort Bragg, North Carolina, and ordered four machines as general and staff personnel transports (under designation YL-23). A second batch of 55 production aircraft (designated L-23A) was ordered for deployment in Korea. The first of these was taken on charge in February 1953 and all had been delivered by September of the same year. The second YL-23 was eventually brought up to L-23A configuration. In 1957, the US Army returned most of its L-23As to Beech for complete rebuild. These aircraft, fitted with 340hp Lycoming GSO-480-B1B6 engines and six-seat accommodation, were re-designated L-23D and eventually in 1962, U-8D.

### Model B50/L-23 Seminole/U-8D

Introduced in 1953, the Model B50 brought in major improvements

*The prototype Twin Bonanza (N3992N) was flown for the first time on 15 November 1949.* (Beech)

*The YL-23s (No.A21803 seen in May 1952) were followed by a first batch of fifty-five 23As for deployment in Korea.* (P M Bowers)

*The L-23A-BH s/n 52-6168 (c/n LH-6) in US Army olive drab livery.* (A R Krieger via J Wegg)

*An impressive shot depicting an L-23A clearing a 25ft-high barrier in 1956.* (P M Bowers)

such as increased gross weight, payload and speed. The Model B50 entered commercial production in December 1952 and totalled 99 aircraft (all built in 1953), of which a few found their way to Australia, Mexico, South Africa and Switzerland. The L-23Bs which were delivered to the US Army were basically similar. A first batch of five aircraft was accepted in September 1953. A total of 40 L-23Bs were delivered to the Army by April 1954, when production terminated. In 1958, many L-23Bs were returned to Beech for rebuilding to L-23D configuration. These aircraft were redesignated U-8D in 1962. Several aircraft were later converted to U-8G standards (55-3465, 56-4039, -4040, -4044, 57-3092, -6089, 58-1339, -1357, 1363, -1364, -3055, -3056, -3061, 59-2537, -2538, -4990).

## Model C50/XL-23C/L23-D Seminole/U-8D

To compete with the Aero Commander 560, Beech introduced its Model C50 in 1955. In order to improve performance, the C50 was fitted with new 275hp Lycoming GO-480-F6 engines which increased maximum speed to 210mph. Production totalled 250 aircraft (25 produced in 1954, 216 in 1955, and 9 in 1956). A single C50 was built for the US Army (c/n CH-123) and designated XL-23C (redesignated U-8G in 1962). This aircraft was followed by 85 L-23Ds, of which two (57-6046 and 58-3060) were converted to RL-23D. All versions of the Twin Bonanza could be adapted to carry an Aerojet-General Model 15NS-250 JATO rocket in each nacelle, to improve take-off performance and provide standby power.

## Model D50

The D50 was introduced in 1956 and 158 were built (147 in 1956 and 11 in 1957) before production switched to the Model D50A. This model had 295hp Lycoming GO-480-G2F6 engines driving three-blade Hartzell propellers, as well as minor airframe and systems refinements.

## Model D50A/L-23E Seminole/U-8E

The Model D50A benefited from two 285hp Lycoming GO-480-G2D6 engines and a fuel capacity of 180 US gallons (681 litres) in two 44

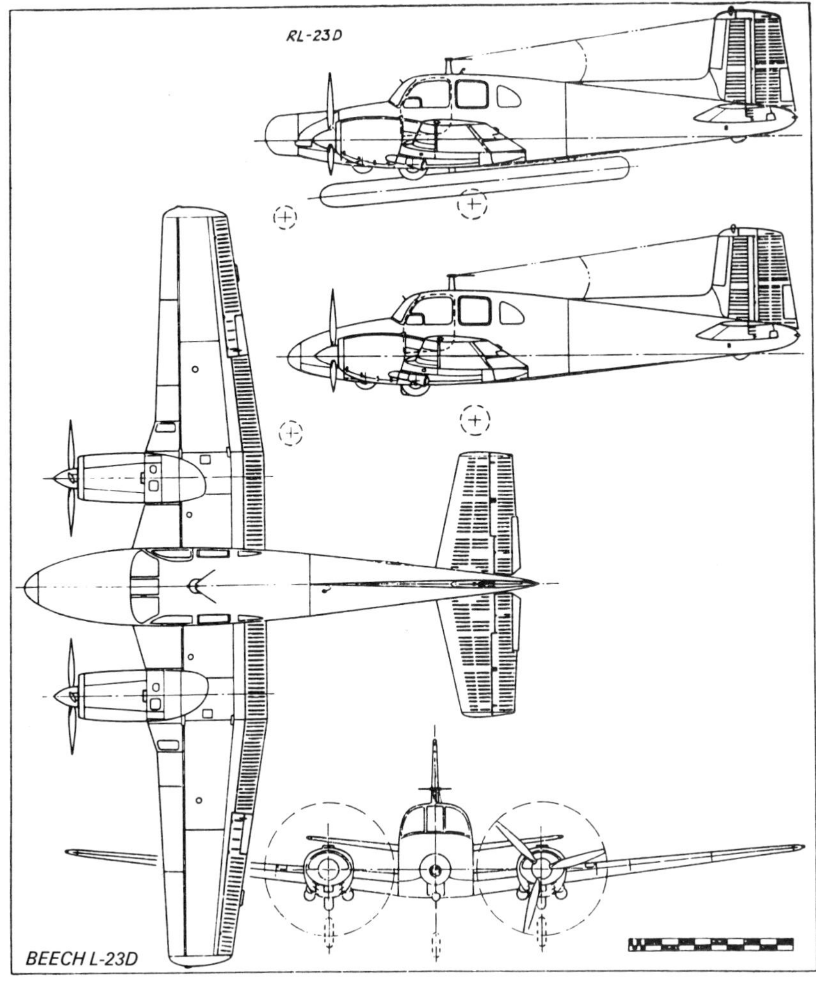


US gallon (166 litres) inboard wing tanks, two 23 gallon (87 litres) outboard wing tanks and two optional 23 gallon (87 litres) auxiliary wing tanks. An RCA weather-avoidance radar was offered as optional equipment with 3in (7.6cm) or 5in (12.7cm) scope. Six aircraft were delivered to the Army as L-23Es and became U-8Es in 1962. Two of them (56-4041 and 4044) were eventually converted to U-8G-BHs.

## Model D50E

Available from 1961, the Model D50E was fitted with two Lycoming GO-480-G2F6 engines, with 295hp at 3,400rpm available for take-off and a normal rating of 285hp at 3,100rpm. A total of 47 aircraft were produced in 1961-63 (25 in 1961, 8 in 1962, and 14 in 1963).

## Model E50/L-23D Seminole/U-8D

The Model E50 of 1957 had 340hp Lycoming GSO-480-A1A6 supercharged engines. The military variant, L-23D, was delivered from January 1957. Two aircraft (48-1348 and 49-2537) were equipped with belly Project Michigan AN/UPD-1 radar. In 1959, the US Army equipped several of its L-23Ds with the advanced AN/APS-85 or AN/APQ-86 SLAR designed to provide all-weather surveillance of the battleground/combat arena for intelligence purposes. These aircraft were known as RL-23Ds (later RU-8Ds). Some had a nose-mounted AN/AVQ-50 or similar weather radar. One aircraft (58-1363) was converted to U-8G-BH configuration.

## Model F50

A total of 25 Model F50s were produced in 1958. These were powered by two 320hp Lycoming GSO-480-B1B6 supercharged engines for improved performance. These were replaced on production lines by the Model G50.

## Model G50

Produced in 1959 (24 aircraft built), the Model G50 introduced minor refinements but still used Lycoming GSO-480-B1B6 engines. Production switched to the Model H50 in 1960.

## Model H50

The Model H50, introduced in 1960, was powered by the same Lycoming GSO-480-B1B6 engines mounted in F50 and G50 models. This Model had a few improvements such as airstair doors and redesigned wingtips to improve single-engine rate of climb. Production totalled 50 Model H50s.

## Model J50

Introduced in 1961, the Model J50 was externally recognisable by its longer and more pointed nose. It was powered by two 320hp Lycoming

*Several Model B50s were exported such as this one registered in Hong Kong as VR-ABB. Note built-in steps.* (C Trask/AAHS)

*Beech L-23D-BH s/n 56/3708 was similar in every respect to the civil Model C50.* (P M Bowers)

IGSO-480-A1B6 geared and supercharged engines with Simmonds Type 570 continuous-flow fuel injection. This installation gave greater speed, higher service ceiling, extended range and increased useful load. Fuel capacity totalled 230 US gallons (872 litres) in two 44-gallon (166 litre) inboard wing tanks, two 46-gallon (174 litre) outboard wing tanks and two optional 25-gallon (96 litre) auxiliary wing tanks. A total of 27 J50s were produced (12 in 1961, 9 in 1962 and 6 in 1963).

### Modifications

Swearingen Aircraft, led by Edward J Swearingen, of San Antonio, Texas, designed the Excalibur modification for all Twin Bonanzas except the Model B50 and C50. This modification consisted of the installation of new 380hp Lycoming IGSO-540-A1A or 400hp Lycoming IO-720-A1A fuel-injection engines driving fully-feathering Hartzell propellers of 7ft 6in (2.29m) diameter, in place of the original GO-480s. The new engines were housed in low-drag glass-fibre cowlings and had revised exhaust systems. Many additional and optional improvements were offered by Swearingen to bring the aircraft to full Excalibur 800 standard, such as fairings to enclose the main undercarriage when retracted, an increase in total fuel capacity to 230 US gallons (870 litres) and several refinements to the interior and exterior trim. A more drastic modification of the Beech Model 50 was undertaken by Swearingen Aircraft with the Merlin II, which used Queen Air wings and Twin Bonanza undercarriage mated to a completely new fuselage.

## Service History

The Model 50 Twin Bonanza saw limited airline service. At least four were used by Windward Island Airways and also in the same area a similar number by Leeward Islands Air Transport. They were also operated with Connellan Airways in Australia, and with Air Cape in South Africa. The largest commercial fleet was that of Carco Air Services of Albuquerque, New Mexico, which operated third-level and other services on behalf of the US Atomic Energy Commission. Lufthansa owned two which were employed for crew training.

*Beech U-8D Seminole s/n 57-3097 belonging to the Mississippi Army National Guard, at Fresno, California, in August 1976.* (A J Pelletier)

*Beech D50 Twin Bonanza (N9654R) operated by John W Waites Associates, at Louisville in March 1969.* (D Musikoff/ AAHS)

*This U-8G-BH (s/n 59-2537) is fitted with a belly mounted 'Project Michigan' AN/UPD-1 airborne radar.* (E M Sommerich)

*Beechcraft RL-23D (s/n 58-1364) featuring the AN/APS-85 side-looking airborne radar. This aircraft was written off on 5 November 1977.* (E M Sommerich via P M Bowers)

*The Model J50 is recognisable by its pointed and longer nose.* (Beech via R J Francillon)

## Foreign Military Operators

**Chile**: five Model C50s (c/ns CH-355/ 359) and six Model D50s (serialled FAC916/917 and FAC991/ 994) are known to have been delivered to Fuerza Area de Chile. These were operated by the Escuela de Especialidades.

**Colombia**: one Model D50 (c/n DH-72) was delivered in 1956 and operated by Escuadrón de Transporte 412, of Grupo 41, based at Barranquilla.

**Jordan**: one Model F50 (c/n FH-80) was delivered and served as B104.

**Pakistan**: one unidentified aircraft was delivered.

**Switzerland**: the Troupe d'Aviation Helvétique took delivery of three Model E50s serialled A-711/713 (c/n EH-56/58).

### Model 50

Two 260hp Lycoming GO-435-C2.

Span 45ft 3⅜in (13.81m); length 31ft 6½in (9.61m); height 11ft 4in (3.46m); wing area 277sq ft (25.83sq m).

Empty weight 3,800lb (1,700kg); loaded weight 5,500lb (2,500kg); wing loading 19.87lb/sq ft (96.96kg/sq m); power loading 10.57lb/hp (4.81kg/hp).

Maximum speed 202.5mph (324km/h) at 2,500ft (760m); cruising speed 190mph (304km/h) at 10,000ft (3,050m); rate of climb 1,500ft/min (456m/min) at sea level; service ceiling 19,000ft (2,745m); maximum range (60% power) at 10,000ft (3,050m) 1,080miles (1,728km).

*The Excalibur modification is powered by new 380hp Lycoming engines driving fully-feathering propellers. This one (N100AV) is seen at Columbia in May 1987.* (J Wegg)

## Model D50A

Two 285hp Lycoming GO-480-G2D6.
Dimensions as for Model 50.

Empty weight 4,090lb (1,855kg); loaded weight 6,300lb (2,858kg); wing loading 22.74lb/sq ft (111kg/sq m); power loading 11.05lb/hp (5.01kg/hp).

Maximum speed 214mph (344km/h) at 2,500ft (760m); cruising speed (70% power) 203mph (327km/h) at 7,000ft (2,135m); rate of climb 1,450ft/min (442m/min) at sea level; service ceiling 20,000ft (6,100m); maximum range at 10,000ft (3,050m) 1,650 miles (2,655km).

## Model F50

Two 320hp Lycoming GSO-480-B1B6.
Dimensions as for Model 50.

Empty weight 4,460lb (2,023kg); loaded weight 7,000lb (3,175kg); wing loading 25.2lb/sq ft (123.03kg/sq m); power loading 10.93lb/hp (4.96kg/hp).

Maximum speed 240mph (386km/h) at 9,000ft (2,750m); cruising speed (70% power) 228mph (367km/h) at 13,300ft (4,050m); rate of climb 1,620ft/min (495m/min) at sea level; service ceiling 24,800ft (7,560m); maximum range 1,650 miles (2,655km) at 169mph (272km/h) at 10,000ft (3,050m).

## Model J50

Two 320hp Lycoming IGSO-480-A1B6.
Dimensions as for Model 50.

Empty weight 4,460lb (2,023kg); maximum take-off weight 7,300lb (3,310kg); wing loading 26.4lb/sq ft (128.9kg/sq m); power loading 11.41lb/hp (5.17kg/hp).

Maximum speed 235mph (378km/h) at 12,000ft (3,660m); cruising speed (70% power) 223mph (359km/h) at 15,200ft (4,630m); rate of climb 1,270ft/min (387m/min) at sea level; service ceiling 29,150ft (8,885m); maximum range 1,650 miles (2,655km) at 172mph (277km/h) at 15,200ft (4,630m).

## Swearingen Excalibur 800

Two 400hp Lycoming IO-720-A1A.

Span 45ft 11⅜in (14m); length 31ft 6½in (9.61m); height 11ft 4in (3.45m).

Maximum take-off weight 7,600lb (3,447kg); power loading 9.5lb/hp (4.3kg/hp).

Maximum cruising speed (75% power) 245mph (394km/h) at 8,300ft (2,530m); rate of climb 1,870ft/min (570m/min) at sea level; service ceiling 22,200ft (6,760m); range at economic cruising speed 1,290 miles (2,075km).

*This Lybian registered Twin Bonanza is seen at Locarno in October 1970.* (J Wegg)

# T-36A

During the summer of 1950, the Secretary of Defence approved a plan proposed by the US Air Force for a design competition for a new twin-engine high-performance transport-trainer aircraft intended to replace the C-45s operated by the Air Training Command. On 11 July 1951, the US Air Force announced that Beechcraft had been selected and would soon receive a contract for development and production, including the construction of an engineering mock-up, a static test airframe and two prototypes. This new aircraft, designated T-36A, was an all-metal low-wing monoplane capable of flying faster than 300mph. It was designed to accommodate three students and an instructor, or 12 passengers and a crew of two when used as a light transport.

It was intended to be powered by two eighteen-cylinder, 2,300hp Pratt & Whitney R-2800-52Ws driving three-blade Hamilton-Standard propellers. On 29 November 1951 members of the Air Force Inspection Board inspected the full-scale mock-up presented by Beech. On 2 June 1952, at Wichita, Beech started the erection of a new building for the production of the T-36, and in January 1953 the last details were fixed in order to start full-scale production as soon as possible with a first batch of 195 aircraft. Unfortunately, on 10 June 1953, the DoD informed Beech Aircraft and its main sub-contractor, Canadair Ltd of Montreal, that the contract had been cancelled and that all operations were to cease immediately. At that time the maiden flight of the prototype was a matter of hours away and the static test airframe was complete. Both aircraft were to be scrapped. The announcement was a blow for Beech, which saw the disappearance of half of its backlog.

### T-36A

Two 2,300hp Pratt & Whitney R-2800-52W (R-2800-57 on production aircraft).

Span 70ft (21.33m); length 52ft 2in (15.9m).

Maximum take-off weight 25,000lb (11,325kg); power loading 5.43lb/hp (2.46kg/hp).

Maximum speed over 300mph (483km/h).

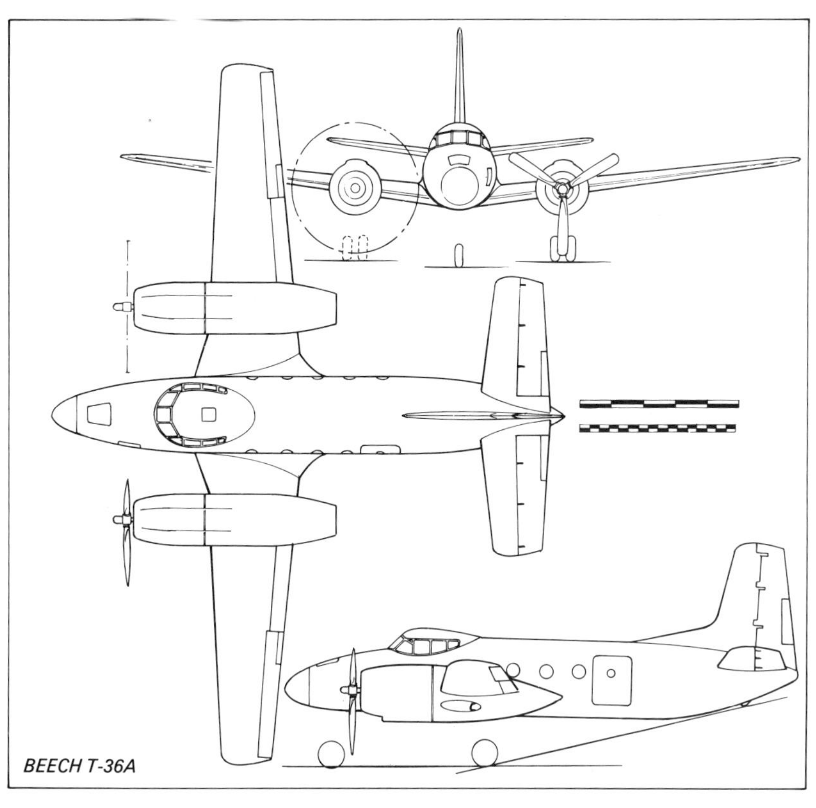
BEECH T-36A

# Model 73 Jet Mentor

During 1954, Beech Aircraft Corp. began the development of a tandem two-seat jet trainer – the first of its kind – as the conditions seemed to indicate that the US Navy was going to need a primary jet trainer. However, although it was intended to meet military specifications, the new Beech aircraft was built as a private venture.

The Model 73 Jet Mentor, as it was known, was designed as a low-cost, economical, high-performance jet trainer, based on the T-34 Mentor airframe and using as many as possible of its components. For its power plant the aircraft retained a single 920lb st (417kg st) Continental J69-T-9 turbojet, the same as its competitor, the Temco Model 51 (developed by Temco Aircraft Corporation of Dallas, Texas, also as a private venture). It was a low-wing cantilever monoplane, basically the same as the Mentor, with 6.05 aspect ratio, 7 degree dihedral and 4 degree incidence. Fuel was housed in two wing tanks with a total capacity of 180 US gallons (681 litres). The wing was equipped with simple flap-type ailerons, single-slotted flaps and dive brakes. The airframe was an all-metal semi-monocoque structure, with bulkheads, centre-section spars, stringers, and aluminium alloy skin. An electrically-retractable tricycle undercarriage with Beech air-oil struts was fitted. The cockpit accommodation included two tandem seats under a power-operated clamshell-type jettisonable canopy, dual instrumentation, a nav/com package specified for military training aircraft, cockpit air conditioning and ejection seats as an option.

The prototype Jet Mentor (N134B) was first flown on 18 December 1955 with test pilot Tom Gillespie at the controls. In the first 30 days the aircraft logged some 45 test and demonstration flights, and these indicated that calculated performance and characteristics would be met. During May and June 1956, Navy pilots evaluated the Jet Mentor

*The jet Mentor during its maiden flight on 18 December, 1955. Test pilot Tom Gillespie is in the cockpit.* (Beech)

*The Model 73 Jet Mentor in a vertical climb. Only one aircraft was built.* (Beech)

and liked it, but the US Navy eventually ordered the competing Temco jet primarily on the basis of price (14 units being eventually built as TT-1s). Only one Model 73 was built and the airframe was still in existence in 1987 at a Wichita vocational-technical school. In fact, the Temco TT-1 never entered service and the Navy went back to using the well proven Beech T-34 Mentor in the primary phase of training.

### Model 73 Jet Mentor

One 920lb st (417kg st) Continental J69-T-9 turbojet.

Span 32ft 9in (9.98m); length 31ft 9½in (9.68m); height 9ft 10½in (3.02m); wing area 177.6sq ft (16.49sq m).

Empty weight 2,854lb (1,295kg); loaded weight 4,450lb (2,018kg); wing loading 25.05lb/sq ft (122.3kg/sq m); power loading 4.84lb/lb st (4.84kg/kg st).

Maximum speed 288mph (463km/h); cruising speed 250mph (402km/h); diving speed 500mph (805km/h); stalling speed 70mph (112km/h); service ceiling 26,600ft (8,105m); rate of climb 1,440ft/min (440m/min) at sea level; maximum range 500 miles (805km).

## Model 95 Travel Air

Bearing the name carried by the reliable biplanes built by the company that made Walter H. Beech's fame, the Model 95 was designed to fill the gap that existed between the single-engined Model 35 Bonanza and the much larger Model 50 Twin Bonanza. This Model was conceived as a four-seat executive aircraft having a cabin with generous window area, and powered by two 180hp four-cylinder horizontally-opposed air-cooled Lycoming O-360-A1A engines, each driving a Hartzell Type 8447-12 propeller. The Model 95 was a low-wing cantilever monoplane with NACA 23000 series wing section, a 7.38 aspect ratio and a 6 degree dihedral. Each wing incorporated a two-cell semi-monocoque box beam of aluminium alloy construction fitted with aluminium alloy single-slotted flaps. It had an electrically operated tricycle undercarriage with Beech air-oil shock absorbers and a combustion heater provided cabin heat. The prototype was first flown on 6 August 1956 and it received its CAA Type Certificate on 18 June of the following year.

### Model 95

Originally named Badger, the Model

*Model 95 Travel Air N2784Y.* (A Swanberg/AAHS)

95 had its name changed to Travel Air to avoid conflict with the US Air Force, who had already assigned the code-name Badger to the Russian Tupolev Tu-16 bomber. Altogether, 301 Model 95s were produced in 1958/1959 (173 in 1958 128 in 1959) before an improved variant was introduced.

## Model B95

In 1960 the Model 95 was followed on Beech production lines by the new Model B95. On this variant, the cabin was lengthened by 19in (48cm), the elevators and tailplane were given increased area for better pitch control and the fin incorporated a dorsal fairing that changed the aircraft silhouette. The Model 95 was proposed during only one year and production totalled 150 aircraft. In 1960 a Model B95 was priced at $51,500.

## Model B95A

The improved Model B95A Travel Air appeared on the civil market in 1961 and had two fuel-injected 180hp Lycoming IO-360-B1A engines, procuring a higher maximum speed. This Model was produced for two years (39 in 1961 and 42 in 1962) and was priced at $49,500.

## Model D95A

The following variant lasted a little longer. Introduced in 1963, the Model D95A had a redesigned and larger (19cu ft) forward luggage compartment in a more tapered nose section, housing virtually all the radio equipment. The aft cabin baggage limit was increased to 400lb (181kg) and an improved interior styling was proposed to customers. Engines were now two 180hp Lycoming IO-360-B1B, driving 6ft-diameter (1.83m) Hartzell Type 8447-12 propellers, and improvements were made to the wheels, brakes and engine fuel injection system. Fuel was housed in four wing tanks with total capacity of 112 US gallons (424 litres). Standard avionics equipment included a Mark 12A nav/com, with VOA-4 VOR/LOC conv/ind and a Beechcraft B-11 antenna. Another distinctive external feature was the introduction of the same larger curved third cabin window that was standard on the Model A55/B55 Baron. A total of 174 Model D95As were built over a period of five years (19 in 1963, 40 in 1964, 48 in 1965, 33 in 1966 and 34 in 1967) before production switched to the E95.

*Beech B95 VH-TKD (c/n TD-356) in Qantas markings. This aircraft was previously registered N8549M.* (J L Sherlock/AAHS)

*The Model 95 Travel Air was originally named Badger.* (P M Bowers)

### Model E95

The last variant of the Beech Travel Air
was the Model E95, only 14 units of which were produced in 1968. This variant included minor refinements to the interior, a redesigned paint scheme, a new one-piece windshield and pointed propeller spinners. Unfortunately, customer demand for the more powerful, affordable Model B55 rapidly brought the Model E95's career to an end and production of the Travel Air was halted in 1968 when the last Model 95 (c/n TD-721) was delivered.

### Model 95

Engines: two 180hp Lycoming O-360-A1A.

Span 37ft 10in (11.53m); length 25ft 4in (7.72m); height 10ft 1½in (3.09m); wing area 193.8sq ft (18sq m).

Loaded weight 4,000lb (1,815kg); wing loading 20.64lb/sq ft (100.8kg/sq m); power loading 11.11lb/hp (5.04kg/hp).

Maximum speed 209mph (336km/h) at sea level; maximum cruising speed 200mph (322km/h) at 7,500ft (2,290m); rate of climb 1,360ft/min (415m/min) at sea level; service ceiling 19,300ft (5,885m); maximum range 1,410 miles (2,270km).

### Model D95A

Engines: two 180hp Lycoming IO-360-B1B.

Span 37ft 10in (11.53m); length 25ft 11in (7.9m); height 9ft 6in (2.9m); wing area 199.2sq ft (18.5sq m).

Empty weight 2,555lb (1,159kg); maximum take-off weight 4,200lb (1,905kg); wing loading 21.1lb/sq ft (103kg/sq m); power loading 11.67lb/hp (5.29kg/hp).

Maximum speed 210mph (338km/h) at sea level; maximum cruising speed (75% power) 200mph (322km/h) at 7,500ft (2,290m); rate of climb 1,250ft/min (381m/min) at sea level; service ceiling 18,100ft (5,500m); maximum range 1,035 miles (1,665km).

## Model 65 and 70 Queen Air, L-23, U-8 Seminole, U-21 Ute

In order to answer an ever increasing demand for twin-engined business aircraft, Beech Aircraft evolved from the L-23F a new 7/9-seat model incorporating the features of a modern airliner. Known as the Model 65 Queen Air, this aircraft was a direct development of the successful Model 50 Twin Bonanza, having a cantilever low-wing with NACA 23018 modified wing section at the roots and NACA 23012 at the tips. This wing was a two-spar all-metal structure of aluminium alloy, had 7.51 aspect ratio, 7 degree dihedral, and single-slotted flaps. The fuselage was made of aluminium alloy and had a semi-monocoque structure. Powerplant was two 340hp Lycoming IGSO-480-A1B6, six-cylinder geared and supercharged engines, with fuel injection, driving Hartzell three-blade fully-feathering constant-speed propellers. Fuel was contained in two 44-US gallon (166-litre) main tanks and two 71-US gallon (269-litre) auxiliary tanks in the wings. The Model 65 was instrumented for all-weather operation and was designed to accommodate the latest electronic equipment. Optional equipment included ARC, Bendix or Collins radar and radio packages, Bendix or RCA weather avoidance radar, oxygen equipment, Junior JATO standby rocket motors, autopilot and additional soundproofing. The Model 65 was so designed to be operated also as a cargo aircraft by removal of bulkheads and passenger seating, procuring 266cu ft (7.53 cu m) of cargo space.The Queen Air first flew in prototype form (c/n L-1; N821B) on 28 August 1958, only four months after its design was started, and received FAA Type Approval on 1 February 1959. Deliveries began in late 1959 (1960 model year) and 56 were built the first year. Among other accomplishments, on 8 February 1960 company test pilot James D Webber took off from Beech Field in a standard production Model 65 (N110Q) and climbed to an altitude of 34,862ft (10,626m), setting a new world record in the C.1.d category.

Production of the straight Model 65 totalled 316 aircraft which were built over the 1959-1967 period. In addition to commercial deliveries, Beech produced Queen Airs for the US Army under the designation U-8F and for the Japanese Maritime Self Defence Force.

### Model A65

The Model A65, which was introduced in 1967, was basically identical to its predecessor, but it differed externally in having a swept tail with dorsal fairing. Engines were two 340hp Lycoming IGSO-480-A1E6s driving Hartzell three-blade fully-feathering constant-speed propellers. Fuel was contained in two

*Queen Air 65 c/n LC-170 (VH-CFI) when operated by Civil Flying Services Ltd of Perth, Australia, in 1971. This aircraft was previously N5867S.* (M W Prime)

*One of the very first Model 65 Queen Airs (c/n LC-10, N810Q). This model retained the tail assembly of the Twin Bonanza.* (Beech)

44-US gallon (166-litre) inboard tanks and two 46-US gallon (174-litre) outboard tanks in the wings. Provision was made for optional auxiliary wing tanks to bring total capacity to 264 US gallons (1,000 litres). As with the Model 65, the A65 was instrumented for all-weather operation and could accommodate the latest avionics. In 1968-69, Beech offered the sub-Model A65-8200 Queen Airliner (initially developed as the Model 79) which had a 8,200lb (3,714kg) gross weight. Production totalled 96 machines (29 in 1967, 38 in 1968, 23 in 1969, and six in 1970).

## Model 65-80

First flown on 25 August 1961 (prototype: c/n LD-1, N841Q), this variant was officially announced in March 1962. It had a new swept tail replacing the straight tail unit of the Model 65, as well as more powerful 380hp Lycoming IGSO-540-A1A, fuel injected, supercharged engines, but it retained the shorter wingspan of the Model 65. It received its FAA Type Certificate on 20 February 1962 and was intended to supplement rather than replace the Model 65, which continued in production. The first production model flew on 26 February 1962 and production totalled 148 aircraft (53 in 1962, and 95 in 1963). The third and fifth aircraft (D-IMPO and D-ILLE) were delivered to Europe in time for the Hanover Show in May 1962. The first British aircraft, G-ASDA, was delivered to Shorts as a British demonstrator in late 1962, and aircraft LD-116 followed later for delivery to the Forte catering group as G-ASKM. The prototype Model 80 was eventually used as the aerodynamic prototype for the Models 99 and 100. In order to fulfil a US Army requirement for a utility and staff transport, Model 65-80 c/n LD-75 was eventually fitted with two United Aircraft of Canada PT6 propeller-turbines and, so modified, flew for the first time on 15 May 1963. Known as the L-23G (NU-8F from 1962), this test-bed acted as a proof-of-concept prototype for the forthcoming Beechcraft King Air.

*Beech Model A65 Queen Air (c/n LC-277, VH-DRV) operated by Hicks of Australia. It had been previously registered N7056N.* (M W Prime)

*A Beech Queen Air 65 (N141) operated by the Federal Aviation Administration.* (R W Simpson)

*The Model 65-80 was officially announced in March 1962. It featured a new swept tail.* (A Swanberg/AAHS)

*The Queen Air 80 (c/n LD-49, N9NA) was operated by NASA at Marshall Space Flight Centre until November 1982.* (R W Simpson)

## Model 65-A80

The Model 65-A80, commonly named Queen Air 80, was introduced in January 1964. This new variant retained the same powerplant (380hp Lycoming IGSO-540-A1Ds driving three-blade Hartzell propellers), and the main differences from the Model 65-80 were wingspan increased to 50ft 3in (15.31m), a strengthened airframe structure to stand a higher gross weight, fuel capacity increased by 34 US gallons (128 litres), and a redesigned nose compartment. Beech also proposed the Model 65-A80-8800 (initially designated Model 89) with 8,800lb (3,986kg) gross weight and a specific airliner interior. A total of 121 aircraft were manufactured over a three-year period (45 in 1964, 56 in 1965, and 20 in 1966). The A80 was followed in turn by the improved B80.

## Model 65-B80

In 1966, production switched to the Model 65-B80 which was powered by 380hp Lycoming IGSO-540-A1A engines driving three-blade propellers, and having the increased wingspan of the Model 80. Production totalled 242 aircraft, including Model 65-B80A (*see below*) and lasted until 1977.

## Model 65-B80A

In 1968, Beech offered the Model 65-B80A equipped with 360hp Lycoming IGSO-540-A1D engines, but few of these aircraft were sold. By 1971, only the Model 65-B80 remained in production.

## Model 65-85

Projected pressurised version of the Queen Air 65-80.

## Model 70 Queen Air and Queen Airliner

The Model 70 (N7458N), which received its Type Certificate on 27 November 1968, combined the 340hp engines of the Model A65 with wide-span wings of the Model 80 in order to increase useful load while having an operating cost comparable with that of the Model A65. The Model 70 was built for commuter airline operators under the designation Queen Airliner, seating nine passengers in a high-density configuration. An optional cargo pod installed under the fuselage held 500lb (226kg) of baggage/cargo and a large cargo door could be fitted to make loading/unloading of bulky

*Beech Model 65-A80 (c/n LD-171, F-BNAP), at Le Bourget in December 1970. This variant was introduced by Beech in January 1964.* (A J Pelletier)

objects easier. Air conditioning could be added for maximum comfort. Only 35 Model 70s were built (20 in 1969, 14 in 1970, and a single one in 1971) before production ended. One of the first orders was for eleven aircraft for Société de Travail Aérien in Algeria, and the last aircraft (c/n LB-35) was delivered to Morgan Crucible Ltd, as G-AYPC.

### Model 65-88

First flown on 2 July 1965, the Model 65-88 was basically a piston-engined variant of the Model 90 King Air, offered to customers as a less expensive alternative, as it was powered by two 380hp Lycoming IGSO-540-A1D engines.. Successively known as the Model 85, then Model 85D, the Model 65-88 was a pressurised Queen Air which could cruise at 221mph (356km/h). Necessary structural changes were introduced to cater for pressurisation, including the use of circular windows. The pressurisation system provided a cabin altitude of 8,000ft (2,440m) at 16,500ft (5,030m). Deliveries began in 1965, and 45 machines were eventually built. After four had been built in 1965, and 36 in 1966, production dropped to a few units in the following years. The last aircraft was delivered in 1969. This was due to an increasing demand for propeller-turbine powered aircraft.

### Model 65-A88

A single Model 65-88 (c/n LP-27) was tested with 400hp Lycoming engines. This aircraft accomplished its maiden flight on 28 March 1966 with test pilot Bob Hagan. Although performance increases were promising, Beech gave up this programme and the prototype was converted to A90 King Air configuration.

## Military Variants

### L-23F/U-8F Seminole

In 1958, the US Army wanted a follow-on design to its U-8 Seminoles. Beech engineers modified the basic Model 50 by increasing the cabin height, width and length, completely redesigning the interior and adding three large cabin windows. The new Model was designated L-23F. Powered by 340hp Lycoming IGSO-480-A1A6s, -A1B6s or

*The Model 65-B80 had 380hp Lycoming engines and increased wingspan.* (Beech)

*The Beech Model 70 combined the engines of the Model A65 and the wings of the Model 80. Illustrated here is c/n LB-19 (VH-ILK, previously N3170A) of AMA.* (M W Prime)

-A1E6s, the L-23F had a maximum cruising speed of 214mph (344km/h). Accommodation was provided for ten people or seven combat-ready troops with equipment. A total of 71 were delivered to the US Army from 1960 to 1963. The designation was changed to U-8F in 1962.

### NU-8F

Designation given to a Queen Air airframe that was fitted with PT6A-6 engines (Model 87 c/n LG-1) and delivered to Fort Rucker, Alabama, in March 1964, after some ten months of flight testing.

### RL-23F

Some of the L-23Fs were modified to RL-23F configuration with battlefield surveillance radar systems for collection of combat intelligence information.

### Model 65-A90-1/U-21A

Design of the U-21A began in October 1966, and in the following month construction of the prototype started. This Model was a development of the NU-8F powered by two 550shp Pratt & Whitney PT6A-20 propeller-turbines, accommodating up to 10 combat troops plus a crew of two, able to be adapted quickly for air evacuation ambulance work or cargo carrying duties. The airframe of the U-21A was generally similar to that of the Model 65-B80, but a forward-hinged cargo door was installed, giving a 4ft 5½in x 4ft 3½in opening (1.36m by 1.31m). All-weather operation was made possible by a full set of electronics, navigation aids and de-icing equipment. In March 1967, only four months after design had started, the prototype made its initial flight, and the FAA Type Certificate was granted on 27 April 1967. An initial contract for 48 U-21As was placed by the US Army in October 1966, and follow-on contracts raised the number of U-21As on order to 129. The first of these was taken in charge on 16 May 1967 and deliveries continued until the spring of 1968. Two aircraft were eventually converted to JU-21As (66-18002 and 67-18065).

### RU-21A

The RU-21A was the basic U-21A fitted with Army Security Agency electronic warfare equipment.

* * *

The Excalibur modification of the Beech Queen Air carried out by Swearingen included installation of two 400hp Lycoming IO-720-A1Bs driving Hartzell HC-A3VK-2A three-blade propellers, as well as new engine mountings, exhaust system, low-drag engine nacelles and Excalibur fully-enclosed wheel-well doors. The modifications of the Beech Queen Air 65, A65 and 80 were designated Queenaire 800, while similar modifications of Queen Air A80/B80s had the designation Queenaire 8800. By early 1988 Excalibur had completed a total of 166 Queenaire conversions including 51 U-8Fs for the US Army and Queen Airs for the Venezuelan Air Force. In 1963, the French aircraft manufacturers SFERMA and Sud-Aviation initiated the design of a turbine-powered Queen Air. The selected powerplant was the 600shp Turboméca Astazou X, but this project was eventually abandoned.

## Military Operators

**US Army**: the U-8Fs were operated by units of the US Army such as 89th ARCOM, 97th ARCOM, 281st AvCo, 327th AvCo as well as units of the ARNG. Three of them (63-12902, -15360 and -15361) were converted to NU-8F. The U-21As were operated by 56th AvCo136th AvCo, TRADOC, 2nd MIB 15th MIB, 224th MIB, Forces

*A U-8F-BH (c/n LF-37, s/n 62-3840) belonging to the 44th Aviation Detachment, HQ ARADCOM, at Grand Forks, Montana in July 1973.* (D Slowiak)

Command, Signal Center 138th ASA, USAICS, etc. Aircraft s/ns 66-18002 and 67-18065 became JU-21A, and several other where modified to RU-21 configuration. (*see Appendix VII*).

**Argentina**: the Commando de Aviación del Ejército Argentino received two Model 65-B80s (AE-102, reserialled AE-256, and AE-199, c/n LD-461, reserialled AE-257) which were operated by Instituto Geográfico Militar. Comando de Aviación Naval Argentina (CANA) equipped its Escuadrilla Aeronaval Reconocimiento (EARec), stationed at Punta del Indio, with five Queen Air 65-B80s (c/n LD-447 serialled 0679 and coded 1-F-21, c/n LD-449/0687/3-G-81, c/n LD-450/0688/3-G-82, c/n LD-452/0689/3-G-83 and c/n LD-453/0690/1-G-84).

**Brazil**: eight aircraft are believed to have been delivered (with serials 2101/2108). Two of them (2101 and 2102) were EU-8 navaid checking aircraft which eventually were registered PT-KYG and PT-KYH.

**Burma**: People's Socialist Republic of the Union of Burma took delivery of a single Queen Air (serialled UB-380).

**Colombia**: three Model B80s were operated by Escuadrón de Transporte 412 of Grupo 41 based at Barranquilla.

**Ecuador**: one Queen Air (c/n LD-240, serialled IGM-240) is known to have been taken on charge by the Aviación de Ejército Ecuatoriano while another one (c/n LD-230, ex HC-AKI) served with Fuerza Aérea Ecuatoriana.

**Israel**: seven Model 65-B80s were delivered to IDF/AF with US temporary registrations (c/n LD-481 ex N7323R, LD-484/487 ex N7326R/7329R, LD-489/490 ex N7331R and N7324R).

**Japan**: the Nansei Shien Hikotai, stationed at Naha used five Queen Air A65s (c/ns LC-320/322 and 334/335 serialled 03-3091/3095) while JMSDF flew 19 Model 65s (serialled 6701/6719) and nine Model A65s (serialled 6720/6728). These were operated by 2 Kokutai at Hachinobe, 5 Kokutai at Naha and 202 Kyoiku Kokutai at Tokushima. In May 1980, five of these aircraft were transferred to the JASDF for radar support tasks.

**Nepal**: the Nepalese Air Force had one Model 65-80 rcgistered 9N-RF4 (c/n LD-113) which was eventually sold as VT-DYR.

**Pakistan**: one or two ex-US Army U-8Fs were reportedly in use (one was s/n 63-7975).

**Peru**: the Fuerza Aerea del Peru took delivery of 18 Model 65-A80s (c/ns LD-245, LD-251, LD-254,

*One of the Model 65s operated by the Japanese Self Defence Force. This one (c/n LC-151, s/n 6706) belongs to the 202nd Kyoiku Kokutai based at Tokushima.* (T Toda)

LD-247/248, LD-252/253, LD-258/262, LD-264/269, serialled 729 to 746) to equip the Grupo de Comunicaciones 8 stationed at Callao and the Servicio Aerofográfico National. One VIP aircraft was operated by the Peruvian Navy (c/n LC-233, serialled EP751). Two other Queen Airs serving with Servicio Aerofográfico were registered OB-F-790 and OB-F-791.

**Thailand**: at least two Model 65-A80s are known (c/n LD-199 ex-N6892Q and c/n LD-255 ex-N2018W).

**Uruguay**: eight Model A65 were delivered to Uruguay and were operated by the Grupo de Aviación 4 at Carrasco (serials-c/ns were T-540, T-541/LC-326, T-542/LC-317, T-543/LC-266, T-544/LC-279, T-545/LC-294, T-546 and T-547).

**Venezuela**: two Model 65s were delivered to the Venezuelan Air Force (c/ns LC-23 and LC-25, serialled 2345 and 4939 respectively) as well as seven Model 65-A80s (c/n LD-290, LD-444, LD-445, LD-293, LD-446, LD-389 and LD-294, serialled respectively 1864, 3168, 5702, 7662, 7815, 8215, 8888). In addition the Army Aviation had two aircraft serialled EV-7001

*One of the nine Model A65s operated by the Japanese Navy. This one (s/n 6726), belonging to the 202th Kyoiku Kokutai, is seen at Atsugi in August 1970.* (T Toda)

*One of the two Model 65s which were delivered to the Venezuelan Air Force. The Meaning of serial '4939' remains unknown.* (J Wegg collection)

and 7002, and the National Guard Air Detachment had one (GN-7427).

## Model 65

Two 340hp Lycoming IGSO-480-A1B6.
Span 45ft 10½in (13.98m); length 33ft 4in (10.16m); height 14ft 2in (4.32m); wing area 277.06sq ft (25.73sq m).
Empty weight 4.640lb (2,105kg); maximum take-off weight 7,700lb (3,493kg); wing loading 27.8lb/sq ft (135.7kg/sq m); power loading 11.32lb/hp (5.14kg/hp).
Maximum speed 239mph (385km/h) at 12,000ft (3,600m); maximum cruising speed (70% power) 214mph (344km/h) at 15,200ft (4,630m); rate of climb 1,300ft/min (396m/min) at sea level; service ceiling 31,300ft (9,540m); range at economic cruising speed with 45min reserves 1,200 miles (1,930km).

## Model A65

Two 340hp Lycoming IGSO-480-A1E6.
Dimensions as for Queen Air 65 except length 35ft 6in (10.82m).
Empty weight 4,890lb (2,218kg); maximum take-off weight 7,700lb (3,493kg); wing loading 27.8lb/sq ft (135.7kg/sq m); power loading 11.32lb/hp (5.14kg/hp).Performance as for Queen Air 65 except range at economic cruising speed with 45min reserves 1,660 miles (2,670km).

## Model 65-80

Two 380hp Lycoming IGSO-540-A1A.
Span 45ft 10½in (13.98m); length 35ft 3in (10.74m); height 14ft 8in (4.47m); wing area 277.06sq ft (25.73sq m).
Empty weight 4,800lb (2,177kg); maximum take-off weight 8,000lb (3,629kg); wing loading 28.9lb/sq ft (141.1kg/sq m); power loading 10.52lb/hp (4.77kg/hp.
Maximum speed 252mph (406km/h) at 11,500ft (3,505m); maximum cruising speed (70% power) 230mph (370km/h) at 15,000ft (4,570m); rate of climb 1,600ft/min (490m/min) at sea level; service ceiling 34,500ft (10,520m); range at economic cruising speed with 45min reserves 1,330 miles (2,140km).

## Model 70

Two 340hp Lycoming IGSO-480-A1E6.
Span 50ft 3in (15.32m); length 33ft 4in (10.16m); height 14ft 2in (4.32m); wing area 293.9sq ft (27.3sq m).
Empty weight 5,282lb (2,396kg); maximum take-off weight 8,200lb (3,720kg); wing loading 27.8lb/sq ft (135.7kg/sq m); power loading 12.06lb/hp (5.47kg/hp).
Maximum speed 239mph (385km/h) at 12,000ft (3,655m); cruising speed (70% power) 214mph (344km/h) at 15,200ft (4,630m); rate of climb 1,375ft/min (419m/min) at sea level; service ceiling 30,000ft (9,145m); maximum range with 45min reserves (70% power) 1,115 miles (1,794km).

## Model 65-A90-1/U-21A

Two 550shp Pratt & Whitney (UACL) PT6A-20.
Span: 45ft 10½in (13.98m); length 35ft 6in (10.82m); height 14ft 2½in (4.33m); wing area 279.7sq ft (25.98sq m).
Empty weight 5,434lb (2,464kg); maximum take-off weight 9,650lb (4,377kg); wing loading 34.48lb/sq ft (168.35kg/sq m); power loading 8.77lb/hp (3.98kg/hp).
Maximum speed 265mph (426km/h) at 10,000ft (3,050m); rate of climb 2,160ft/min (658m/min) at sea level; service ceiling 26,150ft (7,970m); maximum range with 30min reserves 1,676 miles (1,956km).

## Model B80

Two 380hp Lycoming IGSO-540-A1D.
Dimensions as for Queen Air A65 except span 50ft 3in (15.32m) and wing area 293.9sq ft (27.3sq m).
Empty weight 5,180lb (2,350kg); maximum take-off weight 8,800lb (3,992kg); wing loading 29.9lb/sq ft (146kg/sq m); power loading 11.58lb/hp (5.25kg/hp).
Maximum speed 248mph (400km/h) at 11,500ft (3,500m); maximum cruising speed (70% power) 229mph (368km/h) at 15,000ft (4,570m); rate of climb 1,485ft/min (453m/min) at sea level; service ceiling 28,900ft (8,800m); maximum range with 45min reserves 1,530 miles (2,460km).

## Model 88

Two 380hp Lycoming IGSO-540-A1D.
Dimensions and weights as for Queen Air B80.
Maximum speed 246mph (396km/h) at 11,500ft (3,500m); maximum cruising speed (70% power) 221mph (356km/h) at 15,000ft (4,570m); maximum range with 45min reserves 1,495 miles (2,405km).

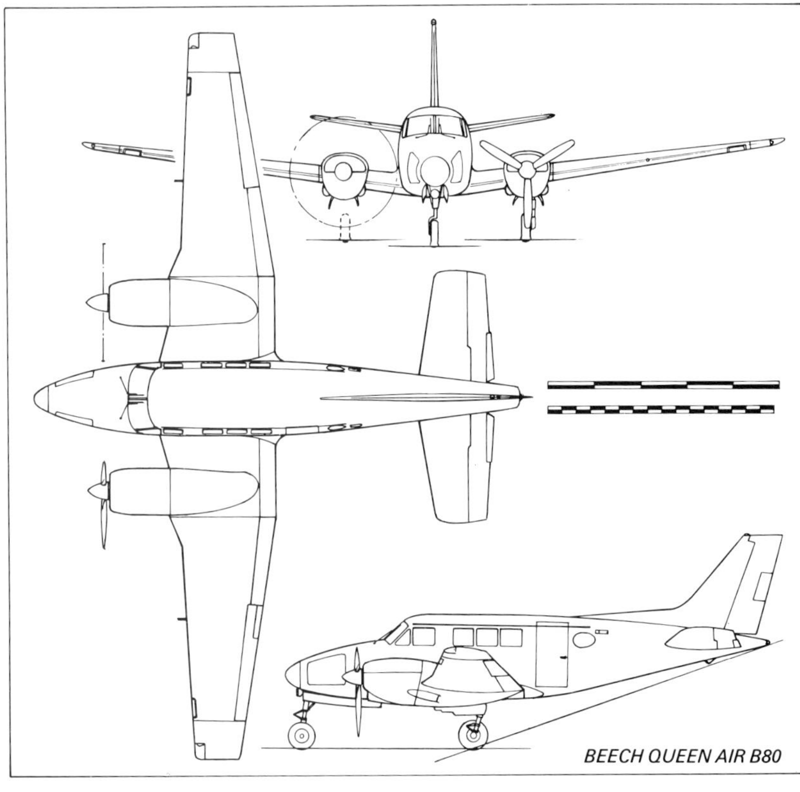

# Model 33 Debonair and Bonanza

With the appearance of the high-performance Cessna 182 and Piper Comanche, Beech developed the Debonair from the ubiquitous Bonanza. The Debonair was a four-seat single-engine executive aircraft with a general configuration similar to that of the Bonanza, except for the tail section, which was conventional with swept-back vertical surfaces. First flown on 14 September 1959, the prototype Debonair (c/n CD-1, N831R) had a very simplified interior.

A total of 1,195 Debonairs had been built by the end of 1966. Production models were known as the Debonair until 1967, when the name Bonanza was reused. Production totalled 1,462 by the end of 1968, 2,007 by 1 January 1976, 2,655 by 1 January 1988, and 3,105 Model 33s by 1 January 1991.

## Model 35-33 Debonair

The Model 35-33 was introduced in November 1959, and drew such customer interest that 233 aircraft were built in the first year. Nevertheless, salesmen soon found it hard to sell because the aircraft was found too basic (the aircraft was left unpainted and had only exterior trim paint, and the interior was spartan). The Model 35-33 was powered by a six-cylinder, fuel-injected 225hp Continental IO-470-J engine driving a two-blade, constant-speed Hartzell propeller. Production totalled 233 aircraft.

## Model 35-A33 Debonair

Introduced in 1961, the Model 35-A33 had several improvements to make it more appealing. New features included sun visors, seat padding, and chart box. Overall exterior paint was made standard. Production totalled 154 aircraft powered with two different engines: 50 aircraft (c/ns CD-251 to CD-300) had the 225hp Continental IO-470-J engine, and 104 aircraft (CD-301 and after) had the 225hp Continental IO-470-K engine.

## Model B33 Debonair

The Model B33 was introduced in late 1961 and had some additional refinements as found on the 35 Bonanza. These consisted of a new instrument panel, adjustable front seat backs, a small fairing to the fin, a stall-warning horn and Model N35 Bonanza-like leading-edge fuel tanks which provided 29 US gallons (109 litres) additional capacity as an option. The undercarriage extension speed was increased to 165mph (265km/h). The B33 retained the 225hp Continental IO-470-K six-cylinder air-cooled engine, with fuel injection, driving a two-blade metal constant-speed propeller. A total of 426 Model B33s were built (200 in 1962 137 in 1963, 87 in 1964, and 2 in 1965).

## Model C33 Debonair

The 1965 Model C33 had several new changes. The dorsal fin fairing was extended forward, the aft seats had adjustable backs, and a larger third cabin window was made optional. Gross weight was increased to 3,050lb (1,382kg), and the Model C33 was available with a

*The Model F33 Bonanza was a refinement of the E33. Note the 'Speed Sweep' windshield* (Beech)

four-colour exterior paint scheme. The engine was still the 225hp Continental IO-470-K, and standard fuel capacity in two wing tanks was 50 US gallons (189.5 litres). An 80 US-gallon (303 litres) capacity was available as an option. Standard equipment included Mark 12A nav/com, with VOA-4 conv/ind and Beechcraft B-11-1 antenna. Production totalled 304 aircraft (157 in 1965, 85 in 1966, and 62 in 1967).

*F33 Bonanza (N36641) operated by Lufthansa, at Goodyear, Arizona. It is white overall with dark red trim.*
(J G Handelman)

### Model C33A Debonair

Introduced in 1966, the Model C33A was powered by a 285hp Continental IO-520-B engine which was canted down two degrees and right two and a half degrees to reduce rudder force during take-off and climb. Externally distinguishable by its new exterior paint scheme, the C33A had a one-piece windshield. A total of 179 Model C33As were manufactured (102 in 1966, and 77 in 1967).

### Model D33

In 1965, at Eglin AFB, Florida, the US Air Force conducted tests with a Model S35 butterfly-tail Bonanza, (c/n D-7859, registered N5847K) modified as a light ground-attack aircraft. Designated Model D33, the aircraft was fitted with a conventional tail unit and six wing hardpoints, the inboard points stressed for 600lb and the outboard points stressed for 300lb. A variety of ordnance could be carried, such as 7.62mm miniguns, 250lb napalm bombs, 272lb general purpose bombs, and 2.75in FFAR rockets.

### Model PD 249

The Model PD 249 (PD standing for Preliminary Design) was an improved version of Model D33 which was evaluated by the US Air Force. While wing hardpoints remained unchanged, a 350hp Continental GIO-520 engine was installed, driving a three-blade propeller. Although tests seemed to be promising, the USAF cancelled the project in the early 1970s.

### Model E33 Bonanza

In 1968, the Model 33 was no more a Debonair, but a Bonanza. The Model E33 was fitted with a 225hp Continental IO-470-K engine, The aircraft carried 50 US gallons of fuel in standard tanks (80-US gallon tanks were optional), the third cabin window was made standard, and the new, larger Speed Sweep windshield was introduced. Production totalled 116 aircraft (81 in 1968, and 35 in 1969).

### Model E33A Bonanza

The Model E33A was similar to the Model E33 in every respect, except for the engine which was a 285hp Continental IO-520-B. Beech also included a Mark 12A nav/com radio as standard equipment, later changed to the solid-state Mark 16 unit. A total of 85 E33As were produced (56 in 1968, and 29 in 1969).

### Model 1074

During the Vietnam War, the Model 1074 was built at the request of the US Air Force for electronic surveillance missions. Designated Pave Eagle I, the Model 1074 led to the Model 1079 improved variant (*which see*).

### Model E33B Bonanza

On 18 June 1968 Beech announced the Model E33B, an aerobatics capable version. It differed from the standard Bonanza by structural changes that were necessary for FAA certification. These changes included new structural members in the rear fuselage and modifications to the ailerons (Queen Air aileron ribs), a tailplane using Travel Air front and rear spars, a fin with heavier gauge skin leading edge, etc. Standard equipment included shoulder harness for both front seats, a quick-release cabin door and a g meter. Permitted manoeuvres were rolls, inside loops, Immelmann turns, Cuban eights, split S turns, snap rolls, spinning and limited inverted flight. In fact, no E33B was produced.

### Model E33C Bonanza

The Model E33C was identical to the Model E33B except for the engine, which was a 285hp Continental IO-520-B. Deliveries began

*The first E33C Debonair (c/n CJ-1, N7629N) at Reading in June 1973.*
(W Steeneck/AAHS)

*Beech F33A Bonanza (N9133S) over Lake Powell.* (Beech)

in August 1968 and 25 aircraft were built.

### Model F33 Bonanza

The Model F33 introduced in 1970 had some refinements such as the restyled third cabin window of the Model V35B butterfly-tail Bonanza, Speed sweep windshield, three-undercarriage gear down annunciator lights, redesigned instrument panel, etc. The engine was still the 225hp Continental IO-470-K. Twenty Model F33s were built.

*The Beech F33A Bonanza was introduced in 1970 and is still in production.* (Beech)

### Model F33A Bonanza

Introduced in 1970, this Model was similar to the Model V35B, and powered by a 285hp Continental IO-520-BA engine. Two different versions of the F33A were produced, the short-fuselage model, of which 26 were produced in 1970, and the long-fuselage model, featuring a 19in-extension allowing a larger baggage door and six-seat accommodation. The 1985 model includes as standard equipment a large cargo door, measuring 3ft 2in by 1ft 10½in (0.96m by 0.57m), a three-blade propeller, and super soundproofing. The Model F33A is still in production.

### Model F33C Bonanza

This is the aerobatics capable variant which is produced to special order. Five F33Cs had the short fuselage, and from 1973 all F33Cs had the long fuselage. Powered by a 285hp Continental IO-520-BB engine driving a McCauley three-blade constant-speed propeller, the F-33C has the same structural features as the Model E33C.

### Model G33 Bonanza

The Model G33 appeared in 1972 and was created by installing a 260hp Continental IO-470-N engine in the Model F33 airframe. The Model G33 had the improved interior configuration of the Model V35B. Only fifty G33s were built (45 in 1972, and 5 in 1973), and the main operator was Pacific Southwest Airlines, which acquired ten Model G33s for airline crew training.

* * *

Colemill Enterprises Inc of Nashville, Tennessee, offered conversion of Models C33A, E33A, and F33A with new 300hp Teledyne Continental IO-550-B engine, driving Hartzell Sabre Blade four-blade Q-tip propellers, and Zip-tip winglets. Such modified aircraft, known as Colemill Starfire Bonanzas, have a cruising speed of 203mph (326km/h) and a maximum rate of climb of 1,210ft/min (369m/min).

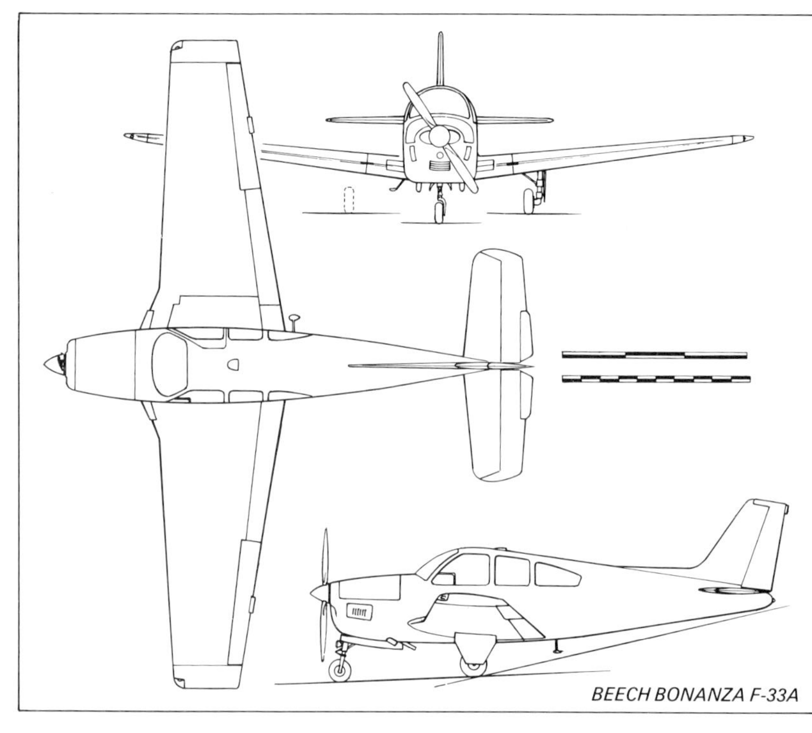


## Foreign Military Operators

**Haiti**: an unknown number of F33s were delivered.

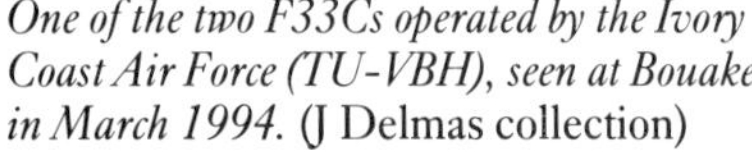

*One of the two F33Cs operated by the Ivory Coast Air Force (TU-VBH), seen at Bouake in March 1994.* (J Delmas collection)

**Iran**: the Iranian Islamic Revolutionary Air Force took delivery of 10 Model F33As (serialled 49601/9610) and 16 Model F33Cs.
**Ivory Coast**: the Force Aérienne de Côte d'Ivoire operated two Model F33Cs (c/n CJ154, registered TU-VBG and TU-VBH).
**Mexico**: 20 Model F33Cs (EBA-401/420) were delivered in 1974 to Fuerza Aérea Mexicana. The Escuadrón Basico de Aviación Naval received ten F33Cs in 1976, which replaced the ageing T34 Mentors.
**Netherlands**: the Government Flying School operates 16 F33Cs.
**Spain**: 54 F33As (E.24A in the Spanish designation system) and F33Cs (E.24B) were delivered to the Spanish Air Ministry and the Air Force. The E.24As were operated by Escuadrón 791 of the Academia General del Aire while E.24Bs were allotted to Escuela Nacional de Aeronautica. The aircraft were serialled E.24A1/29 and E.24B30/54.

*The Spanish Air Force took delivery of fifty-four F33As which were redesignated E.24A in the Spanish system. They are operated by Escuadrón 791.*

### Model B33

One 225hp Continental IO-470-K.

Span 32ft 10in (10.m); length 25ft 6in (7.77m); height 8ft 3in (2.51m); wing area 177.6sq ft (16.49sq m).

Empty weight 1,745lb (791kg); maximum take-off weight 3,000lb (1,360kg); wing loading 16.9lb/sq ft (82.5kg/sq m); power loading 13.33lb/hp (6.04kg/hp).

Maximum speed 195mph (314km/h); maximum cruising speed (75% power) 185mph (298km/h) at 7,000ft (2,135m); rate of climb 960ft/min (293m/min) at sea level; service ceiling 18,400ft (5,600m); range with maximum fuel at 180mph (290km/h) with 45min reserves 1,135 miles (1,825km).

### Model C33A

One 285hp Continental IO-520-B.

Dimensions as for Model B33.

Empty weight 1,780lb (807kg); maximum take-off weight 3,300lb (1,497kg); wing loading 18.58lb/sq ft (90.78kg/sq m); power loading 11.58lb/hp (5.25kg/hp).

Maximum speed 208mph (335km/h) at sea level; maximum cruising speed (75% power) 200mph (322km/h); rate of climb 1,200ft/min (365m/min) at sea level; service ceiling 18,300ft (5,575m); range at economic cruising speed with 45min reserves 1,080 miles (1,738km).

### Model E33B

One 225hp Continental IO-470-K.

Dimensions as for Model B33.

Empty weight 1,885lb (855kg); maximum take-off weight 2,800lb (1,270kg); wing loading 15.76lb/sq ft (76.97kg/sq m); power loading 12.44lb/hp (5.64kg/hp).

Maximum speed 195mph (314km/h) at sea level; maximum cruising speed (75%) power 185mph (298km/h) at 7,000ft (2,135m); rate of climb 930ft/min (283m/min) at sea level; range at economic cruising speed with 45min reserves 650 miles (1,045km).

### Model F33A

One 285hp Continental IO-520-BA.

Span 33ft 6in (10.21m); length 26ft 8in (8.13m); height 8ft 3in (2.51m); wing area 181sq ft (16.8sq m).

Empty weight 2,076lb (942kg); maximum take-off weight 3,400lb (1,542kg); wing loading 18.8lb/sq ft (91.8kg/sq m); power loading 11.93lb/hp (5.41kg/hp).

Maximum speed 208mph (335km/h) at sea level; maximum cruising speed (75% power) 200mph (322km/h) at 6,500ft (1,980m); rate of climb 1,136ft/min (346m/min) at sea level; service ceiling 17,500ft (5,335m); range at economic cruising speed with 45min reserves 976 miles (1,570km).

# Model 55 Baron, Model 56 Turbo Baron, T-42A Cochise

Introduced in November 1960, the Model 95-55 Baron was a development of the Travel Air. The wings were basically as for the Travel Air, with NACA 23016.5 wing section at the roots, and NACA 23010.5 at the tips. Power came from two 260hp Continental IO-470-L six-cylinder air-cooled engines, driving McCauley Type 2AF36C39 fully-feathering propellers. Fuel was housed in four tanks in the wings with total capacity of 112 US gallons (424 litres). Stand-d equipment included Mark 12A nav/com, with VOA-8 VOR/LOC conv/ind and Beechcraft B-11-1 antenna, as well as blind-flying instrumentation. Optional equipment included navigation radio, marker beacon and glideslope receivers, ADF, DME, rotating beacons, Bendix radar, etc. The prototype accomplished its maiden flight on 29 February 1960, and received its FAA Type Certificate on 9 October 1961. A total of 190 95-55 Barons were built in 1961 when production switched to the A55 model.

### Model 95-A55

The Model 95-A55 which appeared in 1962 offered an optional six-seat interior, and an udercarriage extension speed of 175mph with flaps extended to 15 degrees. Production totalled 309 (187 Model 95-A55s were built in 1962 and 122 in 1963). In 1963, at the request of the French manufacturer SFERMA, Beech built nineteen engineless Model A55s airframes (*which see*).

### Model 95-B55/T-42A Cochise

Beech introduced the Model 95-B55 in 1964. Among the most noticeable changes were a longer nose that increased baggage space by 50 per cent, a 120lb increase in gross weight, and new Beechcraft two-blade constant-speed propellers for improved rate of climb. This model received FAA Type Approval in September 1963, and export deliveries included 15 for the Spanish Air Ministry and six for the Civil Air Bureau of Japan. Production lasted until 1982 and totalled 1,956 aircraft, including the T-42As.

In February 1965, the US Army announced it had selected the Model 95-B55 Baron as winner of its competition for a twin-engined fixed-wing instrument trainer. Subsequently, 65 Model 95-B55Bs were ordered, under the designation T-42A Cochise, and the first five aircraft were delivered on 2 September 1965. During 1971, five more aircraft were taken on charge by the US Army, for redelivery to Turkey, under MAP agreement, and in 1972 seven Cochises were sold to the Spanish Air Force.

### Model 95-C55

This new member of the Baron family appeared in August 1965. It

*The Model B55 had a longer nose for increased baggage space.* (Beech)

*Introduced in 1960, the Baron was a development of the Travel Air. Seen here is the Model 95-A55 registered N9377Y.* (Beech)

had two 285hp Continental IO-520-C engines, and a longer fuselage. Other improvements were a one-piece windshield, a larger tailplane that spanned 15ft 11¼in, and minor refinements to the interior. 265 Model 95-C55s were produced in 1966 and 185 in 1967. The College of Air Training at Hamble, Southampton, in England purchased twelve C55s in 1967 for use as trainers for British airline companies.

*The Baron A55 c/n TC-459 was offered for sale at Toussus-le-Noble in September 1970.* (A J Pelletier)

## Model D55

The Model D55 followed the Model C55 on the production lines in 1968 and 1969. It was fitted with the same powerplant but had a new pneumatic pressure system in place of the vacuum system. Production totalled 316 (181 in 1968, and 135 in 1969) before production switched to the Model E55.

## Model E55

The Model E55, which was introduced in 1970, was powered by the same 285hp Continental IO-520-C engines. It had an improved interior as well as various refinements, and was licenced in the FAA Normal category on 12 November 1969. Production, which lasted until 1982, totalled 434 aircraft.

## Model 56TC Turbo Baron

The first example of this turbo-supercharged version of the Baron was flown on 25 May 1966 by engineering test pilot Bob Hagan, and received FAA Type Approval on 19 May 1967. The Turbo Baron was powered by two 380hp Lycoming TIO-541-E1B4 six-cylinder horizontally-opposed air-cooled turbo-supercharged engines, driving Hartzell three-blade metal constant-speed propellers. Standard fuel capacity was 142 US gallons (536 litres), with optional additional tankage raising total capacity to 178 US gallons (673.5 litres). Wing, tail surfaces and propeller de-icing equipment was made available as an option. Deliveries began in September 1967, and 82 Model 56TCs were produced from 1967 until 1969, when the improved Model A56TC was introduced on the production lines.

### Model A56TC Turbo Baron

Produced from 1970, the Model A56TC had the same Lycoming TIO-541-E1B4 engines as the Model 56TC but had its fuel capacity increased to 207 US gallons (784 litres). Only eleven Model A56TCs were produced (nine in 1970, and two in 1971).

* * *

Colemill Enterprises Inc of Nashville, Tennessee, offers conversion of Models C55, D55 and E55 with new 300hp Teledyne Continental IO-550-C engines, driving Hartzell Sabre Blade four-blade Q-tip propellers and Zip-Tip winglets. Such modified aircraft, known as Colemill Foxstar Barons, have a maximum cruising speed (75% power) of 236mph (380km/h) and a maximum rate of climb of 1,840ft/min (561m/min). The same enterprise offers conversions of A55 and B55 Barons with Continental IO-520-E engines (aircraft known as President 600), or with Continental IO-550-E engines (President II).

*A T-42A Cochise (s/n 62-12721) of the Minnesota Army Guard, in June 1990.* (R J Francillon)

### SFERMA-Beechcraft PD.146 Marquis

Development of the Marquis began when SFERMA (Société Française d'Entretien and de Réparation de Matériel Aéronautique) modified a Beechcraft Travel Air to take two 450hp Turboméca Astazou IIJ turbines driving Ratier-Figeac three-blade metal variable-pitch propellers, in place of the original 180hp Lycoming piston engines. The prototype of the re-engined aircraft (No.1, registered F-WJHC) flew for the first time on 12 July 1960 with Jacques Lecarme at the controls, and was then known as the Turbo-Travel Air. Subsequently it was fitted with completely new and larger tail surfaces, based on those of the Beechcraft Baron, and renamed the Marquis. SFERMA assembled Baron airframes supplied by Beechcraft and modified them to Marquis standard. Following receipt of a Certificate of Airworthiness, the first

*A 1978 Model Baron E55. Production of this variant ended in 1982.* (Beech)

production delivery (No.4, registration D-ILFA) was made to Travelair GmbH of Bremen on 23 July 1962, this aircraft being destroyed on 8 November 1962. Aircraft No.9 was sent to the United States, where Type Certification was granted on 6 March 1963. After a first batch of ten production aircraft, a second batch of 25 aircraft was ordered into production but due to a lack of customers and the emergence of the King Air, the production ceased with aircraft No.18 (No.19 remained unfinished). Two aircraft (No.2 and 10) were eventually equipped with 741shp Astazou XII and then 921shp Astazou XIVs. The last flying aircraft (No.10, F-BLLP) was withdrawn from use in 1987.

## Military Operators

**US Army**: the US Army operated 65 T-42A-BH Cochises at the Army Aviation School at Fort Rucker. Most of them were eventually delivered to the Army National Guard units. One of them (s/n 65-12707) was later used as JT-42A, and several went on to the civil market (65-12682/N97688; 65-12686/N89N; 65-12694/N9775Q; 65-12702/N5085Q; 65-12707/N7042R; 65-12714/N5069J; 65-12724/N9114S; 66-4300/N820M; 66-4301/N5150M), and three went to Turkey.
**Chile**: one Model 56TC, ex-Fuerza Aérea de Chile (c/n TG-61, serialled FAC471), was operated by the Dirección de Aeronáutica Civil (serialled A-2).
**Mexico**: the Cuarto Escuadrón Aeronaval stationed at NAS La Paz operated one Model B55 (serialled ME-051) which had been confiscated from drug smugglers. In 1976, several Model B55s joined the Escuela de Aviación Naval (EAN) and, in the early 1980s, the Sexto Escuadrón Aeronaval was formed with three former EAN Barons and based at Tapachula airport.
**Pakistan**: the 41st Flight of the Pakistan Air Force operated a single Model 55 serialled TC-1887 (c/n TC-1887, ex AP-AYL).
**Spain**: seven T-42As were sold by the US Army in 1972 under temporary registrations N1609W to N1615W. Twelve other Model 95-B55s were later added to the inventory, bringing the total to 19 aeroplanes (serialled E.20-1 to E.20-19). At first, these aircraft were briefly used by Escuadrón 912, then by Escuadrón 744 of the Escuela de Polimotores.
**Turkey**: five T-42As were delivered under MAP (71-21053/21057) and three ex-US Army aircraft (66-4307/4309) were later added to the inventory.
**Venezuela**: the Venezuelan National Guard Air Detachment received a single Model 55 serialled GN-7428.
**Zimbabwe**: a single Model 95-C55 (c/n TE-234) was operated with serial 7310. It was later sold as VP-WHF.

*The Turbo Baron benefited from two 380hp Lycoming T1O-541-E1B4 turbo-supercharged engines.*
(R F Besecker)

### Model 95-A55

Two 260hp Continental IO-470-L.
Span 37ft 10in (11.53m); length 26ft 8½in (8.14m); height 9ft 7in (2.92m); wing area 199.2sq ft (18.5sq m).
Empty weight 2,960lb (1,343kg); maximum take-off weight 4,880lb (2,213kg); wing loading 24.5lb/sq ft (119.6kg/sq m); power loading 9.38lb/hp (4.26kg/hp).
Maximum speed 236mph (380km/h); maximum cruising speed 225mph (362km/h); rate of climb 1,700ft/min (518m/min) at sea level; service ceiling 20,000ft (6,100m); maximum range with 45min reserves 1,225 miles (1,970km).

### Model 95-B55

Two 260hp Continental IO-520-C.
Span 37ft 9¾in (11.52m); length 27ft 3in (8.31m); height 9ft 7in (2.92m); wing area 199.2sq ft (18.5sq m).

*A Beech Baron registered in Mauritania seen wearing two registrations: 5T-TJR on the fuselage and 5T-CJR under the wings.*
(H B Adams/AAHS)

*On this Marquis, the tenth to be built, the Turbomeca Astazou XIVJs are well in evidence. Only two aircraft were so engined.* (L Sampité collection)

Empty weight 3,075lb (1,395kg); maximum take-off weight 5,100lb (2,313kg); wing loading 25.6lb/sq ft (125kg/sq m); power loading 9.81lb/hp (4.45kg/hp).

Maximum speed 236mph (380km/h) at sea level; maximum cruising speed (75%) power 225mph (362km/h) at 7,000ft (2,135m); rate of climb 1,670ft/min (510m/min) at sea level; service ceiling 19,700ft (6,000m); maximum range with 45min reserves 1,225 miles (1,970km).

## Model C55

Two 285hp Continental IO-520-C.

Dimensions as for Model 95-A55, except length 28ft 3in (8.61m).

Empty weight 3,025lb (1,372kg); maximum take-off weight 5,300lb (2,405kg); wing loading 26.6lb/sq ft (130kg/sq m); power loading 9.3lb/hp (4.22kg/hp).

Maximum speed 242mph (390km/h) at sea level; maximum cruising speed (75% power) 230mph (370km/h); rate of climb 1,670ft/min (510m/min) at sea level; service ceiling 20,900ft (6,370m); maximum range with 45min reserves 1,143 miles (1,840km).

## Model D55

Two 285hp Continental IO-520-C.

Dimensions as for Model B55 except length 29ft (8.84m) and height 9ft 3in (2.82m).

Empty weight 3,075lb (1,395kg); maximum take-off weight 5,300lb (2,405kg); wing loading 26.6lb/sq ft (130kg/sq m); power loading 9.3lb/hp (4.22kg/hp).

Maximum speed 242mph (390km/h) at sea level; maximum cruising speed (75% power) 230mph (370km/h); rate of climb 1,670ft/min (510m/min) at sea level; service ceiling 20,900ft (6,370m); maximum range with 45min reserves 1,143 miles (1,840km).

## Model E55

Two 285hp Continental IO-520-C.

Dimensions as for Model 95-A55, except length 29ft (8.84m) and height 9ft 2in (2.79m).

Empty weight 3,191lb (1,447kg); maximum take-off weight 5,300lb (2,405kg); wing loading 26.6lb/sq ft (130kg/sq m); power loading 9.30lb/hp (4.22kg/hp).

Maximum speed 242mph (390km/h) at sea level; maximum cruising speed (75% power) 230mph (370km/h); rate of climb 1,670ft/min (510m/min) at sea level; service ceiling 20,900ft (6,370m); range (65% power) with 45min reserves 960 miles (1,545km).

## Model 56TC

Two 380hp Lycoming TIO-541-E1B4.

Dimensions as for Model C55.

Empty weight 3,625lb (1,645kg); maximum take-off weight 5,990lb (2,717kg); wing loading 30.1lb/sq ft (146.9kg/sq m); power loading 7.88lb/hp (3.57kg/hp).

Maximum cruising speed 290mph (467km/h) at 25,000ft (7,620m); rate of climb 2,020ft/min (615m/min) at sea level; service ceiling 32,200ft (9,800m).

## SFERMA-Beechcraft PD.146 Marquis

Two 450shp Turboméca Astazou IIJ.

Dimensions as for Model 95-A55, except length 27ft 6in (8.39m) and height 10ft 8½in (3.26m).

Empty weight 4,762lb (2,160kg); maximum take-off weight 6,000lb (2,725kg); wing loading 30.11lb/sq ft (147kg/sq m); power loading 6.67lb/hp (3.03kg/hp).

Maximum speed 288mph (463km/h) at sea level; maximum cruising speed 286mph (460km/h); rate of climb 3,150ft/min (960m/min) at sea level; service ceiling 32,800ft (10,000m); maximum range 1,180 miles (1,900km).

*This Spanish Air Force E.20 is one of the seven T-42s delivered in 1972 to the Ejercito Del Aire.* (J A Cerdá)

# Model 23 and 24 Musketeer, Sundowner, Sport and Sierra

Beech made its entry into the light aircraft market in 1963 with the Model 23 Musketeer, which had been designed and developed under the leadership of John I Elliot. The Model 23 Musketeer was a low-cost four-seat cabin monoplane with a cantilever laminar-flow low wing with a NACA $63A_22415$ wing section, a 7.5 aspect ratio, and 6°30′ dihedral. Wing structure consisted of a single extruded main spar at 50 per cent chord with aluminium skin and stringers bonded to honeycomb Trussgrid ribs on the forward 50 per cent half of the wing. The Model 23 was powered by a 160hp Lycoming O-320-D2B four-cylinder horizontally-opposed air-cooled engine, driving a Sensenich two-blade fixed-pitch metal propeller. The undercarriage was of the non-retractable nosewheel type with Beech rubber-disc shock-absorbers. Standard equipment included a cabin heater, two rotating beacons, blind flying instrumentation and a Beechcraft VHF, nav/com radio package. Optional extras included a vacuum system, gyro horizon and directional gyro, Beechcraft autopilot, ADF, winterization kit, internal corrosion proofing and dual controls. The Model 23 Musketeer first flew in prototype form (N948B) on 23 October 1961, with S C Tuttle at the controls. But soon after the maiden flight the nosewheel unit was moved forward to improve ground handling characteristics. It received FAA certification on 20 February 1962 and first deliveries began during the autumn of 1962. Production of the Musketeer was centred at Beech's Liberal, Kansas, plant, and a total of 4,109 Model 23s and 24s were produced.

*An early production Beech Model 23 Musketeer (N2330Q).* (A J Pelletier collection)

## Model 23 Musketeer

Production Musketeers were similar to the production prototype expect for the nosewheel, which was moved further forward and made steerable through the rudder pedals. Fuel capacity totalled 60 US gallons (227 litres). Initial deliveries began in October 1962 from the Wichita factory and production totalled 553 aircraft.

## Model A23 Musketeer II

This improved Model was introduced in June 1964. It was powered by a 165hp fuel-injected Lycoming engine and benefited from several minor refinements. It was immediately recognisable by the third window added to the cabin. Production totalled 346 units all built in 1965.

## Model A23 Musketeer III

In October 1965, with the introduction of the Musketeer III, Beech introduced a range of three variants known as Custom, Sport and Super R which were given individual exterior paint schemes and renamed from their previous Musketeer designations. In 1974 these designations were changed to indicate the engine horsepower rating: Šierra 200 (formerly Model A24R Musketeer Super R), Sundowner 180 (Model C23, formerly Musketeer Custom) and Sport 150 (Model B19, formerly Musketeer Sport).

## Model A23A Custom III

This variant, which made its first flight on 15 October 1965, is a standard four-seat Musketeer III fitted with a 165hp Continental IO-346-A engine. In March 1967, a more powerful engine was introduced (180hp Lycoming O-360-A2G) on the six-seat Custom III. An aerobatic version is approved for rolls, Immelmann turns, loops, spins, chandelles, limited inverted flights and other manoeuvres, carrying only two people. Production of the Model A23A totalled 194 units (94 in 1966, 74 in 1967, and 26 in 1968).

## Sport III

This is a two-seat (optional four-seat) sporting and training version powered

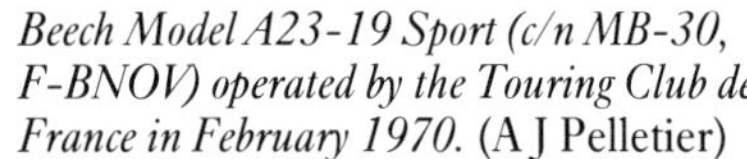

*Beech Model A23-19 Sport (c/n MB-30, F-BNOV) operated by the Touring Club de France in February 1970.* (A J Pelletier)

*A 1978 Model Beech Sport 150.* (Beech)

by a 150hp Lycoming O-320-E2C. The aerobatic version is approved for rolls, Immelmann turns, loops, spins, chandelles, limited inverted flight and other manoeuvres.

### Model A23-24 Super III

This model first flew on 19 November 1965 and is generally similar to the Custom III but powered by a 200hp Lycoming IO-360-A2B driving a two-blade fixed-pitch propeller. Production of the Model A23-24 totalled 363 aircraft.

### Model A23-19 Sport

In 1965, Beech introduced the two-seat Model A23-19 Sport as an economical variant of the A23-series powered by a 150hp Lycoming O-320-E2C. Only two cabin windows were installed. Production totalled 288 aircraft built in 1966 and 1967.

### Model B23 Musketeer Custom III

This variant was introduced in 1968 as a development of the A23A. Production totalled 190 aircraft.

### Model C23

Introduced in 1970, the Model C23 had a wider front to the cabin (4in added at the two front seats) and larger and reshaped windows. In 1972 the C23 was renamed Sundowner 180 and re-engined with a 180hp Lycoming O-360-A4G. A port side door became standard.

### Model 19A Musketeer Sport III

This aerobatic variant, introduced in 1968, was available with g-meter, quick-release starboard door and shoulder harnesses. Production lasted from 1968 till 1978, and totalled 596 aircraft.

### Model B19 Sport 150

Introduced in 1970, this two/four-seat sporting and training version was fitted with a 150hp Lycoming O-320-E3D, driving a Sensenich 74DM6S5-0-54 two-blade fixed-pitch metal propeller. It has a non-retractable undercarriage and is approved for rolls, Immelmann turns, loops, spins, chandelles and other manoeuvres. From 1978 the Model 19 became known as the Sport 150.

### Sundowner 180

This is the basic four-seat version

*The Beechcraft Sundowner 180 is the basic four-seat version.* (Beech)

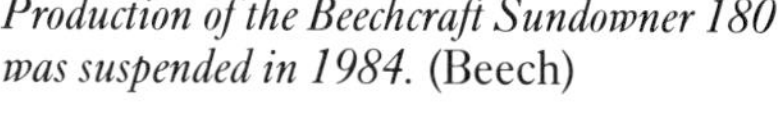

*Production of the Beechcraft Sundowner 180 was suspended in 1984.* (Beech)

*A Swiss Beechcraft Super R (HB-EWK) on display at Le Bourget Airshow in 1971.* (A J Pelletier)

powered by a 180hp Lycoming O-360-A4K engine, driving a Sensenich Type 76EM8S5-0-60 two-blade fixed-pitch metal propeller, and a non-retractable undercarriage. The aerobatic variant is approved for rolls, Immelmann turns, loops, spins, chandelles and other manoeuvres. In 1973 the instrument panel was lowered 1½in for improved forward visibility, and window height was increased in 1974. Production of the Sundowner 180 was suspended during 1984.

### Model A24R Super R

Designed in 1970, the Model A24R had an electro-hydraulic retractable undercarriage. The engine was a 200hp Lycoming IO-360-A1B and fuel capacity was 60 US gallons.

### Model B24R Sierra 200

The B24R was introduced in 1972, and 55 aircraft were manufactured that year. The Sierra 200 was generally similar to the Sundowner but had accommodation for four to six people, a 200hp Lycoming IO-360-A1B6 engine driving a Hartzell Type HC-M2YR-1BF/F7666A-2R two-blade metal constant-speed propeller, and a retractable tricycle undercarriage. It remained in production from 1973 to 1976, and 299 B24Rs were produced.

### Model C24R Sierra 200

The Sierra 200 entered production in 1977, and production totalled 345 aircraft. The C24R had fairings to reduce drag around main undercarriage, aileron gap seals and a new propeller that improved both speed and service ceiling.

## Foreign Military Operators

**Algeria**: eight Model C23s were procured by the Algerian Air Force (c/ns M-1871/1874, M-1876/1879), and at least seven Sierra B24Rs were taken on charge by the National Pilot Training School based in Tafaraoui (known c/n-registration tie-ups are MC-447/7T-WCD, MC-448/7T-WCE, MC-581/7T-WCF, MC-586/7T-WCG, MC-588/7T-WCH, MC-450 and MC-451).
**Canada**: the Canadian Armed Forces took delivery of 46 Model 23s. The first 25 aircraft were Model C23-19 Musketeers, also known as CT-134 Muskrats (serialled 134201/134225). The following 21 were delivered in late 1981 as C23 Sundowners with the designation CT-134A (serialled 134201/134246). All are operated by the 3rd CFFTS.
**Hong Kong**: the RHKAAF operated two Model B23-19s (serialled HKG4 and HKG5).
**Mexico**: in 1970, twenty Model 23s were delivered to the Fuerza Area Mexicana (serialled EBP-301/320).
**Morocco**: one Model 23 is known to have been delivered to the Moroccan Government (registered CN-AHN).

*The Beechcraft Sierra 200 had accommodation for four to six.* (Beech)

*Production of the Beechcraft Sierra 200 totalled 299 aircraft.* (A J Pelletier collection)

## Model 23

One 160hp Lycoming O-320-D2B.

Span 32ft 9in (9.98m); length 25ft (7.62m); height 8ft 3in (2.51m); wing area 146sq ft (13.57sq m).

Empty weight 1,300lb (590kg); maximum take-off weight 2,300lb (1,043kg); wing loading 15.86lb/sq ft (77.44kg/sq m); power loading 14.37lb/hp (6.52kg/hp).

Maximum speed 144mph (232km/h) at sea level; cruising speed (75% power) 135mph (217km/h) at 7,000ft (2,135m); rate of climb 710ft/min (216m/min) at sea level; service ceiling 13,500ft (4,110m); maximum range (75% power) 792 miles (1,275km).

## Custom

One 165hp Continental IO-346-A.

Dimensions as for Model 23.

Empty weight 1,375lb (624kg); maximum take-off weight 2,350lb (1,066kg); wing loading 16.10lb/sq ft (78.6kg/sq m); power loading 14.24lb/hp (6.46kg/hp).

Maximum speed 146mph (235km/h) at sea level; maximum cruising speed (75% power) 138mph (222km/h); rate of climb 728ft/min (222m/min) at sea level; service ceiling 11,870ft (3,620m); range (75% power) 778 miles (1,250km).

## Sport

One 150hp Lycoming O-320-E3D.

Span 32ft 9in (9.98m); length 25ft 8½in (7.84m); height 8ft 2½in (2.5m); wing area 146sq ft (13.57sq m).

Empty weight 1,433lb (650kg); maximum take-off weight 2,150lb (975kg); wing loading 14.73lb/sq ft (71.9kg/sq m); power loading 14.33lb/hp (6.5kg/hp).

Maximum speed 127mph (204km/h) at sea level; maximum cruising speed 125mph (201km/h); rate of climb 680ft/min (207m/min) at sea level; service ceiling 11,650ft (3,550m); maximum range (75% power) with 45min reserves 645 miles (1,038km).

## Sierra

One 200hp Lycoming IO-360-A1B6.

Span 32ft 9in (9.98m); length 25ft 8½in (7.84m); height 8ft 5in (2.57m); wing area 146sq ft (13.57sq m).

Empty weight 1,711lb (776kg); maximum take-off weight 2,750lb (1,247kg); wing loading 18.84lb/sq ft (91.9kg/sq m); power loading 13.75lb/hp (6.23kg/hp).

Maximum speed 161mph (259km/h) at sea level; maximum cruising speed 151mph (243km/h); rate of climb 891ft/min (272m/min) at sea level; service ceiling 14,340ft (4,370m); maximum range (75% power) with 45min reserves 646 miles (1,040km).

*The Canadian military Musketeers are also known as Muskrats. They are serialled in the 134201 range.* (J L Sherlock)

## Sundowner

One 180hp Lycoming O-360-A4K.

Span 32ft 9in (9.98m); height 8ft 2½in (2.5m); wing area 146sq ft (13.57sq m).

Empty weight 1,500lb (680kg); maximum take-off weight 2,450lb (1,111kg); wing loading 16.78lb/sq ft (81.9kg/sq m); power loading 13.61lb/hp (6.17kg/hp).

Maximum speed 138mph (222km/h) at sea level; maximum cruising speed 136mph (219km/h); rate of climb 792ft/min (241m/min) at sea level; service ceiling 14,400ft (4,390m); maximum range (75% power) with 45min reserves 585 miles (941km).

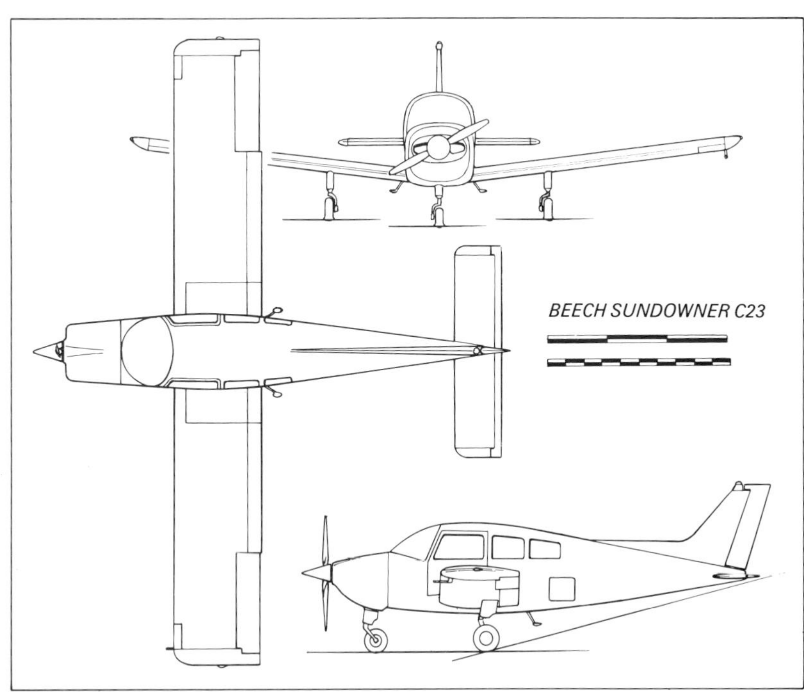

# Model 90 King Air VC-6, U-21, T-44

On 14 July 1963, Beech announced that a new pressurised six/eight-seat business aircraft powered by two United Aircraft of Canada PT6 propeller-turbines had been developed. In fact, the design had been initiated two years before, in 1961, as the Model 120. This aircraft was basically a Queen Air airframe fitted with propeller-turbine powerplants. A flying test-bed, converted from a Queen Air 65-80 (designed Model 87) and powered by PT6A-6 propeller-turbines, had been flown and had completed over 40 hours of flight testing by mid-August 1963. Construction of the prototype of the Model 65-90 King Air began during the summer of 1963, by which time Beech hoped to begin deliveries of production aircraft by the autumn of 1964. This prototype (registered N5690K) accomplished its inaugural flight on 24 January 1964. The Model 65-90 was a cantilever low-wing monoplane, using NACA 23014-1 (modified) wing section at the roots, NACA 23016-22 (modified) at the outer panel of the centre section, and NACA 23012 at the tips. It had a 7.51 aspect ratio, and 7deg dihedral. The structure comprised a two-spar aluminium alloy wing, fitted with single-slotted flaps, mated to an aluminium alloy semi-monocoque fuselage. Engines were two PT6A-6 rated at 550shp for take-off, 500shp continuous and driving three-blade constant-speed full-feathering non-reversible propellers. Total fuel capacity was 122 US gallons (462 litres) in nacelle tanks and 262 US gallons (991 litres) in wing tanks. The cabin pressurisation was provided by a single Roots-type supercharger mounted in the port nacelle. Normal pressurisation was limited to 3.4psi. The Model 65-90 King Air was in production from 1964 till 1966 and 112 of them were manufactured during that period (seven in 1964, 69 in 1965, and 36 in 1966). In 1966 production shifted to the Model 65-A90.

## Model 65-A90

This improved model was announced in February 1966. It had two 550shp Pratt & Whitney PT6A-20 propeller-turbines driving Hartzell three-blade constant-speed fully-feathering propellers; total fuel capacity was 384 US gallons (1,454 litres). A total of 221 King Airs had been delivered by the end of 1966. Standard avionics comprised a complete all-weather nav/com system, using Collins, Bendix, RCA, Sperry and Beechcraft equipment. The A90 also had an improved pressurisation system capable of operating at a maximum differential of 4.6psi. This Model made its maiden flight on 5 November 1965 and 206 of them were built in 1966/67 (72 in 1966, and 134 in 1967).

## Model A90

*See military variants.*

## Model B90

The Model B90 flew for the first time on 13 April 1967 and entered production in 1968. This variant was powered by two 550shp Pratt & Whitney (UACL) PT6A-20 propeller-turbines, and had improved systems. A total of 184 Model B90s were built (91 in 1968, 73 in 1969, and 20 in 1970).

## Model C90

The Model C90, which was introduced in September 1970, had an increased wingspan and 550shp PT6A-21 propeller-turbines, but a few early production C90s were powered by PT6A-6 engines that had been modified to PT6A-6/C20. In 1975 Beech delivered four King Air C90s to the Spanish Air Ministry's Civil Aviation School for instrument training and liaison, and on 17 April 1981 a Model C90 was the 3,000th King Air delivered by Beech (2,613 commercial plus 387 military

*Beech 65-A90 King Air (c/n LJ-136, F-BFRE) at Paris-Le Bourget in December 1970.* (A J Pelletier)

*Beech 65-A90 (c/n LJ-281, VH-DYN) as operated by the Swan Brewery Group. This aircraft was previously registered N5451U.* (M W Prime)

*This B90 (c/n LJ-353, PP-FOA) was operated by Inst Brasileiro do Café.* (D L de Camargo)

*Introduced in 1970, the Model C90 was powered by PT6A-21 propeller-turbines.* (Beech)

aircraft). This aircraft was taken in charge by Stroehmann Brothers Co. of Williamsport, Pennsylvania. Production of the Model C90 lasted until 1982, with a total of 507 machines built. That year this variant gave place to the improved Model C90-1.

## Model C90-1

Powered by two 550shp Pratt & Whitney (UACL) PT6A-21s, the Model C90-1 had a maximum take-off weight of 9,650lb, carried 384 US gallons of fuel, and pressurisation was increased to 5psi. The model C90-1 first flew on 29 September 1970 and production totalled 54.

## Model C90A

The Model C90A was the first variant to incorporate major changes. It had two 550shp Pratt & Whitney Canada PT6A-21s driving three-blade Hartzell propellers, faired into Pitot-type cowlings with improved air intake design and using tapered exhaust stacks. These cowlings improved engine efficiency and reduced drag. Other improvements included an hydraulically-actuated undercarriage and a rudder boost system for engine-out flight conditions. The first Model C90A (c/n LJ-1063) first flew on 1 September 1983 with Jim Dolbee as pilot, and deliveries began in 1984. In April 1987 Beech announced structural changes which resulted in a 450lb (204kg) increase in the MTOW, permitting two more passengers and additional baggage to be carried. The first such aircraft was c/n LJ-1138 and deliveries began by the end of 1987.

## Model C90B

The Model C90B made its public debut in 1991 at the 44th NBAA Convention at Houston, Texas. It had four-blade, fully reversible, dynamically balanced, McCauley propellers, which improved take-off and landing performance. Other improvements included an upgraded, more comfortable interior designed to reduce noise and vibration levels. When Beechcraft celebrated its 50,000th aircraft delivery at Wichita on 23 March 1992 the aircraft was a Model C90B for a US customer.

## Model E90

Beech announced the Model E90 on 1 May 1972. This variant, which had flown for the first time on 18 January 1972, retained the C90 airframe but was powered by the 680ehp (flat rated to 550ehp) Pratt & Whitney (UACL) PT6A-28 propeller-turbines that powered the Model A100. Standard fuel capacity was 474 US gallons (1,794 litres), and the avionics package include RCA AVC-111A main VHF transceiver

*Beech C90 King Air (N839K) at Fort Lauderdale in August 1971.* (M Cristescu)

*A Beech King Air (N104Z) operated by the US Forest Service from Klamath Falls, Oregon, in August 1992.* (R J Francillon)

with B3 antenna, RCA AVC-110A standby VHF transceiver, RCA AVN-220A manual omni with glideslope, marker beacon receiver, Collins 331A-3G indicator, etc. Twenty-two aircraft were produced during the first year, and production eventually totalled 347. The last six aircraft were built in 1981.

*The Model E90 made its maiden flight on 18 January 1972.* (Beech)

## Model F90

The Model F90, which was introduced in 1979, had an airframe combining a Model E90 fuselage and wings with Model 200 T-tail empennage. The F90 had two 750shp Pratt & Whitney PT6A-135 propeller-turbines driving four-blade, constant-speed, fully-feathering, reversible propellers that reduced noise level. Another interesting feature was its advanced multi-bus electrical system. Production totalled 203 aircraft including the prototype. The F90 prototype (c/n LA-1) was eventually converted to the experimental Model G90 (c/n LE-0).

## Model F90-1

First flown by Vaughn Gregg on 7

*The Model F90 combined the fuselage of the E90 with the tail unit of the Model 200.* (Beech)

*This silver and white RU-21B (s/n 67-18093) was eventually operated by the 138 ASA.* (R W Simpson)

December 1982, and officially announced by Beech on 13 June 1983, the Model F90-1 had PT6A-135A engines faired into Pitot-type engine cowlings, that improved performance. Fuel tanks in the wings contained 388 US gallons and the auxiliary tanks, located in the wing centre section, held up to 41 US gallons. A total of 33 aircraft were built from 1983 to 1985, which were allocated constructor's numbers in the F90 series.

### Model G90

The F90 prototype (c/n LA-1) was converted to the experimental Model G90 (c/n LE-0).

### Model C90SE

In 1994 Beechcraft introduced a new King Air variant known as the C90SE (SE standing for Special Edition). This variant has three-blade propellers and numerous cabin modifications in order to lower the purchase price. Performance remains identical to that of the Model C90B.

## Military Variants

### VC-6A

One aircraft (No. 66-7943) was delivered to the USAF's 1254th Special Air Missions Squadron, 89th MAW, based at Andrews AFB for VIP transport duties under the designation VC-6A. It was eventually modified to VC-6B configuration.

### U-21A (Model A90-1C)

The US Army ordered the 550shp Pratt & Whitney PT6A-20 (T74-CP-700) powered Model A90-1 for military duty as the U21A, and a total of 141 of them were built from 1966 to 1968. This non-pressurised variant had square windows and a large cargo door combined with the standard airstair door. Most of these aircraft eventually served with the US Air Force in Southeast Asia, operating primarily as transport and surveillance aircraft. Two aircraft (Nos.66-18004 and 67-18096) were eventually loaned to the US Navy.

### EU-21A

Three aircraft were modified for electronic reconnaissance missions (Nos.66-18000, 68-18013, and 68-18027).

### GU-21A

Two aircraft are used for ground instruction (Nos.66-18006 and 66-18012).

### JU-21A

Three aircraft are used for special development tasks (Nos.66-18008, 66-18009, and 66-18036).

### RU-21A (Model A90-1)

Designation given to four U-21As which had been converted for electronic warfare duty with the Army Security Agency (Nos.67-18112/18115).

### RU-21B (Model A90-2)

Three PT6A-29 engined aircraft built in 1967 for special military applications with the US Army and operated by 138th ASA (Nos.67-18077, 67-18087, and 67-18093).

### RU-21C (Model A90-3)

Designation given to two aircraft that were built in 1967 for special military applications with the US Army and were operated by 138th ASA (Nos.67-18085 and 67-18089). These were similar to the RU-21B but had different antenna array and mission equipment.

### RU-21D (Model A90-1)

Designation given to sixteen aircraft and eighteen U-21A conversions, with modified cockpit and control pedestal arrangement.

### JRU-21D

Designation given to a single RU-21D used for special tests (Nos.67-18125).

### RU-21E (Model A90-4)

Built in 1971, the PT6-A28 engined Model A90-4 was designated RU-21E by the US Army and used for

*A Beech RU-21D (s/n 67-18107) operated by the US Army. This aircraft eventually went to Michigan ARNG.* (C Waldenmaier)

electronic surveillance and related missions. Three U-21A/RU-21D were so modified (Nos.70-15877, 70-15881, and 70-15890).

### U-21G (Model A90-1)

Designed to accommodate sophisticated equipment for use in electronic countermeasures and communications, seventeen U-21Gs were manufactured by Beech in 1971 (c/n LM-125/141).

### RU-21H (Model A90-4)

Built in 1971, these aircraft, almost identical to RU-21E (except for new wingtips and new undercarriage doors), were used by the US Army (15th MIB) for electronic surveillance and related missions (Nos.67-18105, 67-18111, 67-18119, 70-15876, 70-15879, 70-15880, 70-15883/15887, 70-15889, 70-15891, 70-15893/15895, 70-15898/15899 and 70-15902/15904).

### T-44A (Model H90)

In 1976, the US Navy ordered fifteen PT6A-34B engined King Air H90s, with an option on 56 more, as T-44A advanced trainers to meet its VTAM(X) (multi-engine advanced training aircraft) requirement. Deliveries of the first 15 aircraft, which replaced obsolete TS-2As and TS-2Bs, were completed by October 1977. First deliveries occurred on 5 April 1977 and most of the T-44As were assigned to Training Wing Four (TW-4) at NAS Corpus Christi, Texas. On 19 January 1977 Beech was awarded a follow-on contract for 23 additional T-44As.

* * *

Raisbeck Engineering Inc, of Seattle, Washington, has developed conversion kits for the Model 90. The Raisbeck's Mark VII System comprises 12 kits which have been certificated individually. The first kit comprises fully enclosed main undercarriage speed doors and adds 7mph (11km/h) to the cruising speed. The second kit, certificated in September 1983, introduced new area-ruled wing lockers, aft of the engine nacelles, which decrease drag and increase cruising speed. Other kits include four-blade propellers, dual aft-fuselage ventral strakes, and an ice protection system. By March 1991, 67 Model 90s had been modified by Raisbeck. Swearingen Aircraft Corp of San Antonio, Texas, has developed an engine modification for the Model 90 series. Known as the Swearingen Taurus Modification, it consists of replacing existing engines with 700shp Pratt & Whitney Canada PT6A-135 engines under new low-drag cowlings, installing new integral nacelle fuel tanks and provision of a new flow control system to provide dual bleed air pressurisation.

*One of the Model 90s operated by the Venezuelan Air Force. Serial GN-7839 has no connection with the Beech c/n.* (J Wegg)

## Foreign Military Operators

**Algeria**: the Algerian Air Force operates three Model 90s registered 7T-WCF/WCH.

**Bolivia**: in 1973 the Fuerza Aérea Boliviana received one Model A90 (serialled FAB-001, then FAB-006 and destroyed on 26 April 1979), replaced in 1981 by a single Model F90 (serialled FAB-018). These were operated by the Escuadrilla Presidencial.

**Chile**: only one aircraft is known to serve with Fuerza Aérea de Chile (serialled 498).

**Colombia**: two Model C90s are operated by the Escuadrón de Enlace of the Comando Aéreo de Transporte Militar (CATAM), stationed near Bogotá.

**Ecuador**: the Fuerza Aérea Ecuatoriana has one Model E90 (c/n LW-178; registered HC-DAC).

**Israel**: a small number of ex-US Army RU-21s are in use.

**Japan**: the JMSDF took delivery of eighteen Model C90s which are operated by the 202 Kyoiku Kokutai based at Tokushima. These aircraft are serialled 6801 to 6818 (6801/6809 are c/n LJ-597/599, 642, 670, 778, 855, 916 and 917).

*A Beech RU-21H (s/n 70-15884) in its early configuration and a low-visibility grey camouflage.*

*Beechcraft T-44A (BuNo. 160983), operated by the US Navy from NAS North Island in April 1979.* (P M Bowers)

**Mexico**: the Fuerza Aérea Mexicana operates a single Model 90 serialled TP-0208 (registered XC-UTG).
**Peru**: five C90s serialled 730, 731, 747, 748 and 750 are operated by Grupo de Comunicaciones 8 at Callao.
**Spain**: nine C90s have been delivered and designated E.22 in the Spanish system. They are serialled E.22-1 to 9 (c/ns LJ-603, 605, 608, 621, 623, 624, 663, 664, 665). Six of them are operated by the Escuadrón 744 of the Escuela de Polimotores and the remaining three are operated by the Escuela Nacional de Aeronáutica.
**South Korea**: one U-21A has been delivered (serial 67-18086).
**Thailand**: a single E90 (c/n LW-26; ex-N1769W) has been delivered and wears serial 01769.
**Venezuela**: the Guardia Nacional took delivery of five Model 90s (serialled GN7583, GN7593, GN7839, GN8270 and GN8274), while the Naval aviation operates E90 c/n LW-264 (serialled TR-0201).

## Model A90

Two 550shp Pratt & Whitney (UACL) PT6A-20.

Span 45ft 10½in (13.98m); length 35ft 6in (10.82m); height 14ft 8in (4.47m); wing area 279.74sq ft (25.9sq m).

Empty weight 5,680lb (2,576kg); maximum take-off weight 9,300lb (4,218kg); wing loading 33.24lb/sq ft (162.3kg/sq m); power loading 8.45lb/hp (3.83kg/hp).

Maximum speed 252mph (405km/h) at 21,000ft (6,400m); maximum cruising speed 252mph (405km/h) at 16,000ft (4,875m); rate of climb 1,900ft/min (580m/min) at sea level; service ceiling 30,200ft (9,200m); maximum range with 45min reserves 1,374 miles (2,211km).

## Model B90

Two 550shp Pratt & Whitney (UACL) PT6A-20.

Dimensions as for Model A90 except span 50ft 3in (15.32m) and wing area 293.9sq ft (27.3sq m).

Empty weight 5,685lb (2,578kg); maximum take-off weight 9,650lb (4,377kg); wing

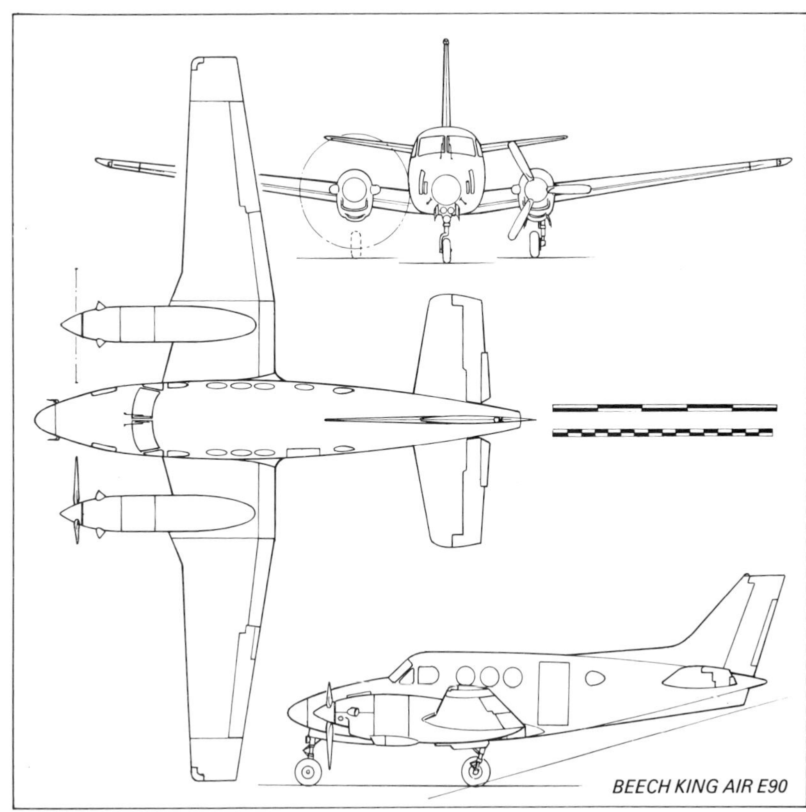

BEECH KING AIR E90

loading 32.8lb/sq ft (160.1kg/sq m); power loading 8.77lb/hp (3.98kg/hp).

Maximum speed 270mph (434km/h) at 21,000ft (6,400m); maximum cruising speed 253mph (407km/h) at 16,000ft (4,875m); rate of climb 2,595ft/min (790m/min) at sea level; service ceiling 30,200ft (9,200m); maximum range with 45min reserves 1,466 miles (2,359km).

### Model C90

Two 550shp Pratt & Whitney (UACL) PT6A-21.

Dimensions as for Model B90.

Empty weight 5,640lb (2,558kg); maximum take-off weight 9,650lb (4,377kg); wing loading 32.8lb/sq ft (160.1kg/sq m); power loading 8.77lb/hp (3.98kg/hp).

Maximum cruising speed 256mph (412km/h) at 12,000ft (3,660m); rate of climb 1,955ft/min (596m/min) at sea level; service ceiling 28,100ft (8,565m); maximum range at economic cruising speed with 45min reserves 1,475 miles (2,374km).

### Model C90A

Engines and dimensions as for Model C90.

Empty weight 5,765lb (2,615kg); maximum take-off weight 9,650lb (4,377kg); wing loading 32.8lb/sq ft (160.1kg/sq m); power loading 8.77lb/hp (3.98kg/hp).

Maximum cruising speed 278mph (448km/h) at 12,000ft (3,660m); rate of climb 2,155ft/min (656m/min) at sea level; service ceiling 28,100ft (8,565m); maximum range at economic cruising speed with 45min reserves 1,514 miles (2,437km) at 21,000ft (6,400m).

### Model E90

Two 680ehp Pratt & Whitney of Canada PT6A-28 flat rated to 550ehp.

Dimensions as for Model B90.

Empty weight 5,886lb (2,670kg); maximum take-off weight 10,100lb (4,581kg); wing loading 34.4lb/sq ft (168kg/sq m); power loading 7.4lb/hp (3.37kg/hp).

Maximum cruising speed 287mph (462km/h) at 12,000ft (3,660m); rate of climb 1,870ft/min (570m/min) at sea level; service ceiling 27,620ft (8,420m); cruising range at maximum cruise power 1,295 miles (2,084km) at 16,000ft (4,875m).

### Model F90-1

Two 750shp Pratt & Whitney Canada PT6A-135A.

Span 45ft 10½in (13.98m); length 39ft 9½in (12.13m); height 15ft 1¾in(4.62m); wing area 279.74sq ft (25.99sq m).

Empty weight 6,647lb (3,015kg); maximum take-off weight 10,950lb (4,966kg); wing loading 39.1lb/sq ft (190.8kg/sq m); power loading 7.3lb/hp (3.3kg/hp).

Maximum cruising speed 321mph (517km/h) at 12,000ft (3,660m); rate of climb 2,455ft/min (748m/min) at sea level; service ceiling 30,450ft (9,280m); range at maximum cruise power 1,106 miles (1,781km) at 12,000ft (3,660m).

## Model 60 Duke

Early in 1965, Beech began design work on an elegant four- to six-seat pressurised and turbo-supercharged transport aircraft, known within the house as the Model 60. Construction of the prototype (c/n P-1) of this aircraft, combining high comfort and very distinctive looks, began in January 1966, The maiden flight was made on 29 December 1966 with Beech test pilot Bob Hagan at the controls and its FAA Type Certificate was granted on 1 February 1968.

### Model 60

The Model 60 Duke was powered by two 380hp Lycoming TIO-541-E1A4 six-cylinder horizontally-opposed air-cooled turbo-supercharged engines, driving 6ft 2in-diameter (1.88m) Hartzell three-blade constant-speed and fully-feathering propellers. It had a cantilever low wing, with NACA 23010.5 wing section at the roots, and NACA 23012 at the tips. Aspect ratio was 7.243 and dihedral was 6 degrees. The wing had a two-spar semi-monocoque box-beam of conventional aluminium alloy construction and electrically-operated single-slotted aluminium alloy flaps. The fuselage has a semi-monocoque aluminium alloy structure too, using heavy-gauge chemically-milled skins. The undercarriage was of the electrically-retractable tricycle type. Standard fuel capacity was 142 US gallons (538 litres) but, optionally, four interconnected fuel cells in each wing, bringing total capacity to 204 US gallons (772 litres), were available. Using air from the engine's turbo-superchargers, the cabin could be pressurised to 4.6psi, providing sea level conditions up to 10,000ft (3,050m) and a 10,000ft cabin altitude at 24,800ft (7,560m). Standard accommodation comprised four individual seats arranged in pairs, with a centre aisle. Optional extras included 5th and 6th seats. Equipment and avionics included blind-flying instrumentation, a heated pitot-tube, electric fuel vent anti-icing, Narco Mark 24 VHF nav/com (360 channels) with VOA-9 VOR/ILS conv/ind and B6 com antenna, Bendix T-12C ADF, Narco MBT-24R marker beacon with B16 antenna, Narco UGR-2 glide slope. Between 1968 and 1970, a total of 122 Model 60s were built by Beech (15 in 1968, 91 in 1969, 16 in 1970).

### Model A60

In the latter half of 1970 Beech began delivering the improved Model A60. The turbo-superchargers weighed less and had internal changes that extended their life and permitted the TSIO-540-E1C4 to achieve full rated horsepower to a higher altitude. New interior fabrics and leathers were offered and the

*This Model 60, registered in Australia (c/n P-45, VH-ILI) to Baldwin Investments Ltd of Perth, was previously N7648N.* (M W Prime)

pressurisation control system was modified to allow a smoother overall operation and better cabin comfort. That year, Beech delivered 23 Model A60s, and production, which ended in 1973, totalled 121 aircraft.

### Model B60

In 1974 Beech offered the improved Model B60 which had two 380hp Lycoming TIO-541-E1C4 engines as well as a wider and longer cabin with redesigned seats for increased comfort. More improvements were added in 1975, when the Model B60 received a redesigned, lightweight AiResearch pressurization system with Lexan valves and a mini-sized controller unit that allows selection of cabin altitude before take-off or landing. Additional refinements were offered to Duke owners in 1976 with new, wet-cell wingtip fuel tanks that held 30 US gallons (113 litres), increasing the B60's range to 1,287 miles (2,070km) at 65 per cent power setting.

The Model B60 was produced until 1982, when the 350th B60 and 593rd Duke left Beech production line.

* * *

Certification process of an Allison 250-B17F/1 powered Duke has recently begun. Known as the Galaxy 300, this aircraft has been modified by Galaxy Group Inc., of Van Nuys, California. A 36-inch (0.91m) plug has been engineered for placement forward of the wing front beam to balance the aircraft properly and compensate for the lighter Allison engines. The Galaxy 300 has tip tanks that increase range and fuel capacity.

## Military Operators

**Angola**: the República Popular de Angola uses a single Duke, c/n P-375, registered D2-ELT.

**Jamaica**: in 1975 the Jamaican Air Force received a single Model 60 serialled JDFT-4 but its c/n is unknown.

### Model 60

Two 380hp Lycoming TIO-541-E1A4. Span 39ft 4in (11.99m); length 34ft (10.36m); height 12ft 4in (3.76m); wing area 213sq ft (19.79sq m).

*A 1978 Model B60 reveals its elegant silhouette.* (Beech)

*The Duke B60 was offered to customers in 1974.* (Beech)

*This early Duke (c/n P-9, N7034D) is fitted with winglets.* (J Wegg)

Empty weight 4,100lb (1,859kg); maximum take-off weight 6,725lb (3,050kg); wing loading 31.6lb/sq ft (154.2kg/sq m); power loading 8.85lb/hp (4.01kg/hp).

Maximum speed 286mph (460km/h) at 23,000ft (7,010m) ; maximum cruising speed (75% power) 271mph (436km/h) at 25,000ft (7,620m) ; rate of climb 1,615ft/min (492m/min) at sea level ; service ceiling 31,300ft (9,540m) ; maximum range with 45min reserves 1,660 miles (2,670km).

## Model B60

Two 380hp Lycoming TIO-541-E1C4.

Span 39ft 3¼in (11.97m); length 33ft 10in (10.31m); height 12ft 4in (3.76m); wing area 212.9sq ft (19.78sq m).

Empty weight 4,275lb (1,939kg); maximum take-off weight 6,775lb (3,073kg); wing loading 31.8lb/sq ft (155.3kg/sq m); power loading 8.91lb/hp (4.04kg/hp).

Maximum speed 270mph (434km/h) at 23,000ft (7,010m); maximum cruising speed (75% power) 272mph (438km/h) at 25,000ft (7,620m); rate of climb 1,601ft/min (488m/min) at sea level; service ceiling 30,000ft (9,145m); maximum range (45% power) with 45min reserves 1,413 miles (2,274km).

## Galaxy 300

Two 450shp Allison 250B17F/1.

Span 39ft ¼in (11.89m); length 36ft 10in (11.22m); height 12ft 4in (3.76m); wing area 212.9sq ft (19.78sq m).

Empty weight 3,889lb (1,762kg); maximum take-off weight 6,775lb (3,073kg); wing loading 31.8lb/sq ft (155.3kg/sq m); power loading 7.5lb/hp (3.39kg/hp).

Maximum cruising speed (75% power) 245kt (438km/h) at 20,000ft (6,100m); rate of climb 2,700ft/min (823m/min) at sea level; service ceiling 30,815ft (9,392m); maximum range with 45min reserves 1,703 miles (2,740km).

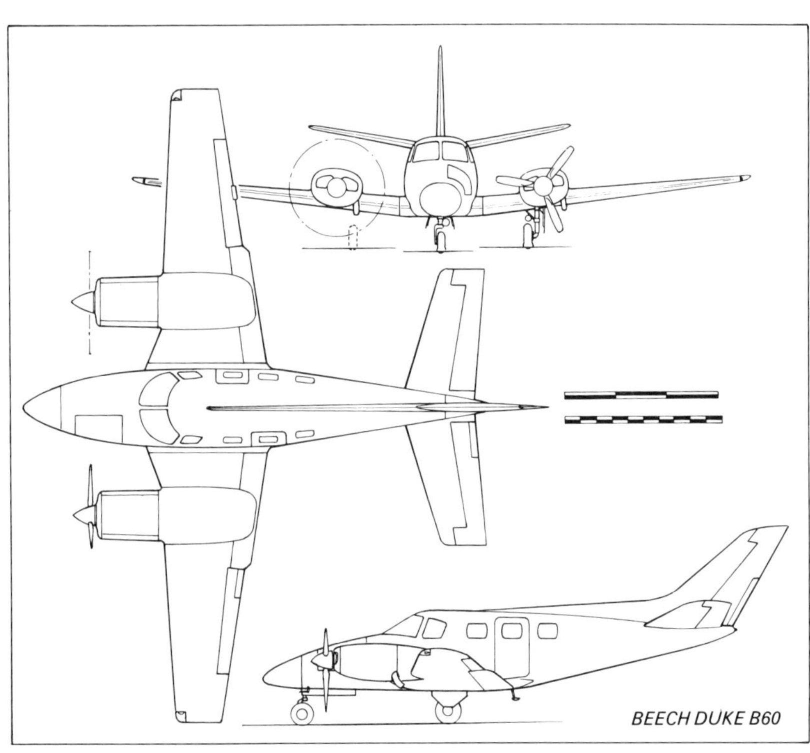

*BEECH DUKE B60*

# Model 99 Airliner

In 1967 Beech unveiled the largest aircraft yet to be marketed by the Wichita company, the 17-seat twin-propeller-turbine Model 99 Airliner. This aircraft was designed specifically for the scheduled airline and air taxi market. During the initial phase of its development, an extended-fuselage Queen Air had been used as a testbed to help airframe design before propeller-turbine powerplants were installed. The maiden flight of this stretched aircraft took place during December 1965 and the prototype (c/n U-1) flew for the first time in July 1966. The Model 99 has two 550shp Pratt & Whitney PT6A-20 propeller-turbines driving Hartzell three-blade, fully feathering and reversible pitch, constant-speed, 6ft 7½in (2.02m) diameter propellers. Rubber fuel tanks are located in the wings, providing a total capacity of 374 US gallons (1,415 litres). The wings have NACA 23018 modified aerofoil at the roots, NACA 23012 aerofoil at the tips, and dihedral is 7deg positive. In order to accommodate the wide centre of gravity range introduced by the longer fuselage, the entire tailplane can be electrically trimmed by the pilot, with elevators acting in the conventional manner for pitch control. As a safety feature a standby electrical trim system, geared to operated at one-third the speed of the main trim system, provides redundancy. Accommodation is provided for a crew of two seated side-by-side in the cockpit and 15 passengers in removable chairs, two abreast with a centre aisle in the cabin. For greater flexibility, installation of an optional cargo door fitted forward of the standard air-stair door permits the Model 99 Airliner to be used for all-cargo or cargo-passenger operations, with the installation of a movable bulkhead separating freight and passengers. Standard avionics include dual 360-channel nav/com systems, three-light marker beacon with Beechcraft B-16 antenna, dual VOR/ILS converter-indicators, ADF and DME.

*A Beech 99 of Cascade Airways (N2880A). The 17-seat Model 99 was introduced in 1967. It was then the largest aircraft in the Beech range.* (A J Pelletier collection)

## Model 99

Production of the Model 99 was expected to begin by the spring of 1966 with full production rate scheduled to attain 100 units a year by mid-1968 in order to meet the increasing world-wide orders which came from some fifteen US regional and commuter airlines, and from ten airlines spread over nine foreign countries. The first US deliveries

*Allegheny Airlines was among the first operators of the Beech Airliner.* (K M Sumney/AAHS)

*In France, the first operator of the Beech Airliner was Air Alpes. Here aircraft c/n U-62 (F-BSUJ) is seen leaving Paris Le Bourget in January 1972*

*Only a few Model B99s were produced, and several Model 99s and 99As were modified to this standard. This one, c/n U-110 (N4212A) of Air Michigan, is seen at Willow Run in 1971.* (W Steeneck/ AAHS)

were made to Commuter Airlines Inc on 2 May 1968 with initial foreign deliveries going to Australia, Canada and Mexico. By June 1969 a total of 91 of these aircraft were in service with 32 airlines. Production of the Model 99 totalled 101 units (44 built in 1968, 56 in 1969 and 1 in 1970) before it switched to the Model 99A.

## Model 99A Airliner

The Model 99A was introduced in 1968 while the initial Model 99 was still in production. A total of 43 units were built before production was discontinued in 1971 (one in 1968, 25 in 1969, 16 in 1970, and one in 1971). This variant used two derated 550shp UACL PT6A-27 propeller-turbines and had a higher maximum take-off weight as well as extended range.

## Model A99A

Only one Model A99A was built in 1970. This had reduced fuel capacity.

## Model B99 Airliner

Introduced in 1972, the Model B99 was the third standard model. It had its gross weight increased to 10,900lb (4,944kg) and was powered by two 680shp Pratt & Whitney Aircraft of Canada (UACL) PT6A-28s propeller-turbines. Unfortunately, the Model B99 failed to attract large orders and was produced during only four years at a low rate (four in 1972 one in 1973, eight in 1974 and five in 1975). However, some Model 99s and Model 99As were converted to B99 configuration.

## Model B99 Executive

This variant was basically the same as the standard Model B99, but offered optional seating arrangements for eight to seventeen and various executive interior stylings.

## C99 Airliner

On 7 May 1979 Beech announced its intention of re-entering the commuter aircraft market, initially with two aircraft designated Commuter C99 and Commuter 1900 (*which see*). In 1980 the Model 99 c/n U-50 (purchased from Allegheny Airlines and registered N41990) was rebuilt by Beech to become the Model C99 prototype. The aircraft was modified to accept two 715shp modular-concept Pratt & Whitney Canada

*The Model B99 had an increased gross weight. This one was operated by Allegheny Commuter.* (Beech)

PT6A-36 reverse-flow free-shaft propeller-turbines. Among many other improvements, this variant incorporated a redesigned two-bus electrical system with solid-state voltage regulation, an improved hydraulic undercarriage system and a stronger wing spar structure. The Model C99 also had alternative interior layouts for mixed passenger/cargo or all-cargo use. The maiden flight of this variant took place at Wichita on 20 June 1980 with Beech test pilot Jim Dolbee at the controls. Production of the Model C99 began in September 1980 and the first deliveries took place on 30 July 1981, following FAA type certification earlier in the same week. The first aircraft went to two commuter airlines, Christman Air Systems of Washington, Pennsylvania, and Sunbird Airlines of Charlotte, North Carolina. Model C99s were produced at Beech's Selma, Alabama, Division, and a total of 76 Model C99s were built from 1982 to 1986 when production ceased (40 in 1982, 13 in 1983, 11 in 1984, six in 1985, and six in 1986).

* * *

During 1975, Beech modified a Model 99 to test a system for increasing the stability. This system comprised separate electro-mechanically-powered control surfaces. Designated PD 280, the aircraft underwent testing by the University of Kansas Flight Research Laboratory, under a NASA-funded contract.

*A Beech B99 used as a demonstrator by the manufacturer. It is fitted with the ventral cargo pod.* (Beech)

## Military Operators

**Chile**: in July-August 1970, nine Beech Model 99As with derated UACL PT6A-27 engines were supplied to the Fuerza Aeréa de Chile for SAR and IFR navigation training, replacing a fleet of ageing Beech C-45s. The 99s are operated by the reactivated Grupo 11, stationed at Base Aeréa de Quintero, near Valparaiso. The Grupo 2, based at Cerrillos, flies modified electronic reconnaissance Model 99s which are known locally as Petrels. These are easily recognisable by their electronic pack fitted under centre fuselage. The Chilean Model 99s are c/ns U-137/U-145, serialled 300/308 and registered CC-EEO to CC-EEW.

*The Model C99 marked Beech's return to the commuter market. The aircraft shown is in fact the Model 99 c/n U-50 (N41990), which was remanufactured to Model C99 configuration and re-registered N4199C.* (Beech)

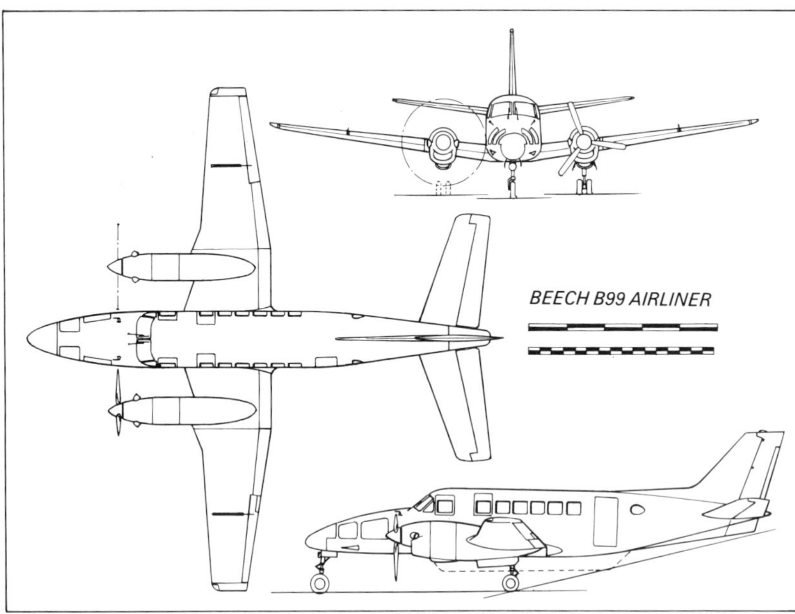


**Peru**: the Fuerza Aeréa Peruana is reported to operate two Model 99s bearing serials 747 and 748.
**Thailand**: the Royal Thai Army Aviation operates a single Model 99 (c/n U-120, ex N9018Q).

## Model 99

Two 550shp Pratt & Whitney (UACL) PT6A-20.

Span 45ft 10½in (14m) ; length 44ft 6¾in (13.58m) ; height 14ft 4¼in (4.38m) ; wing area 279.7sq ft (25.98sq m).

Empty weight 5,675lb (2,574kg); maximum take-off weight 10,200lb (4,627kg); wing loading 36.47lb/sq ft (178kg/sq m); power loading 9.27lb/hp (4.2kg/hp).

Maximum cruising speed 254mph (409km/h) at 10,000ft (3,050m); normal cruising speed 252mph (406km/h) at 12,000ft (3,650m); rate of climb 1,910ft/min (582m/min) at sea level; service ceiling 25,000ft (7,620m); range with 45min reserves 375 miles (603km).

## Model 99A

Two 550shp Pratt & Whitney (UACL) PT6A-27.

Dimensions as for Model 99.

Empty weight 5,749lb (2,607kg); maximum take-off weight 10,400lb (4,717kg); wing loading 37.18lb/sq ft (181.5kg/sq m); power loading 9.45lb/hp (4.29kg/hp).

Maximum cruising speed 280mph (451km/h) at 8,000ft (2,440m); rate of climb 1,700ft/min (518m/min) at sea level; service ceiling 26,200ft (7,986m); range at maximum cruising speed with 45min reserves 881 miles (1,417km).

## Model B99

Two 550shp Pratt & Whitney Canada PT6A-28.

Dimensions as for Model 99.

Empty weight 5,777lb (2,620kg); maximum take-off weight 10,900lb (4,944kg); wing loading 38.97lb/sq ft (190.3lb/sq m); power loading 9.91lb/hp (4.49kg/hp).

Maximum cruising speed 280mph (451km/h) at 8,000ft (2,440m); rate of climb 2,090ft/min (637m/min) at sea level; service ceiling 26,313ft (8,020m); range at maximum cruising speed with 45min reserves 832 miles (1,339km).

## Model C99

Two 715shp Pratt & Whitney Canada PT6A-36.

Dimensions as for Model 99.

Empty weight 6,494lb (2,946kg); maximum take-off weight 11,300lb (5,125kg); wing loading 40.4lb/sq ft (197.25kg/sq m); power loading 7.9lb/hp (3.58kg/hp).

Maximum speed 308mph (496km/h) at 8,000ft (2,440m); cruising speed 287mph (461km/h) at 8,000ft (2,440m); rate of climb 2,221ft/min (677m/min) at sea level; service ceiling 28,080ft 8,560m ; range 1,048 miles (1,686km).

*The Model A36 is still in production, with more than 2,800 aircraft produced to date.* (Beech)

# Model 36 Bonanza, QU-22

*The Model A36TC was the turbocharged variant. It is recognisable by the louvres on the engine cowling.* (Beech)

Introduced in June 1968, the Model 36 was a six-seat utility aircraft developed from the Bonanza Model V35A. It was generally similar to the V35A, but was distinguished by a conventional tail unit with sweptback vertical surfaces, similar to those of the E33 series. Powered by a 285hp Continental IO-520-B engine, the Model 36 was created by moving the E33A's aft cabin bulkhead back 19in (48cm) and adding a 10in (25cm) plug into the fuselage, thereby increasing the cabin area by 6cu ft (0.17cu m) compared with the V35A. The wing was relocated aft, increasing the centre of gravity range and thereby the stability of the aircraft. Two outward-opening doors were mounted on the starboard side of the fuselage for easier loading and unloading of bulky cargo when used in a utility role. Three interiors were offered: standard, utility and a deluxe design. The cabin seated six persons, and two removable seats and two folding seats permitted rapid conversion to utility configuration. Standard equipment included Narco Mark 12A nav/com, with VOA8 Omni conv/ind and Beechcraft antenna. Optional items included instrument flight equipment, autopilot, Beechcraft Constant co-pilot wing levelling device, Magic Hand undercarriage system, oxygen system, and various interior refinements.

Licenced in the FAA utility category at full gross weight, with no limitation of performance, the Model 36 was an immediate success, 105 being built in 1968, and 79 in 1969. The Model 36 is still in production in its A36 and B36TC variants, and some 3,400 of them have been built to date.

## Model A36

In 1970, Beech added the Model A36, fitted with a more luxurious interior similar to that of the V35B, three undercarriage-warning lights, Hartwell quick-release cowling latches, redesigned instrument subpanels, and new wingtips. In 1972, beginning with A36 c/n E-1111, electrically-operated, vertical-readout engine instruments were made standard, and in 1978 a 24-volt electrical system and four-second undercarriage retraction/extension time were incorporated. Another change occurred in October 1983 when Beech completely redesigned the instrument panel. The original engine was changed for a 300hp Continental IO-550-B, and small, wedge-like vortex generators were installed on the outboard wing leading edge for improved roll control at high angles of attack. Optional extras included the Magic hand automatic undercarriage control system, and refrigeration-type air-conditioning system. Avionics included King KX-170B 720-channel nav/com, with KI-201C VOR/LOC Omni conv/ind and Beechcraft antenna.

The Model A36 attracted orders from several airlines for pilot training. In April 1985 Saudi Arabian Airlines took delivery of four A36s for the carrier's pilot training academy at Jeddah; the Finnair Training Centre at Pori, Finland, took delivery of three A36s during 1987, and Japan Air Lines received five aircraft in 1990 with 23 more on order. In 1991 Lufthansa ordered 12 aircraft to replace existing F33As, then during the summer of 1991 the Civil Aviation College of Japan ordered 31 Model A36s to replace its fleet of Model F33s and Fuji FA-200s. Early in 1992 All Nippon Airways gave Beech an order worth $18 million for ten Model A36s to train pilots at the airline's flight training centre in California which

*A USAF Beech QU-22B (s/n 69-7702) in storage at MASDC in November 1978. The modified engine cowling and the wingtip tanks are noticeable.* (B Knowles)

opened in October 1992. At the time of writing, the Model A36 is still in production with more than 2,800 aircraft manufactured to date.

### Model A36AT (Airline Trainer)

In 1992 Beech introduced a trainer sub-variant of its Model A36, powered by a 290hp Continental IO-550B engine driving a three-blade Hartzell propeller of reduced diameter. This new version had a maximum take-off weight of 3,600lb (1,630kg). Customers include Lufthansa (twelve aircraft), RLS, a Dutch school that trains pilots for KLM (eight aircraft), Saudi Arabian Airlines (four aircraft), Finnair (three aircraft), Japan Air Lines (28 aircraft) and All Nippon Airways (20 aircraft).

### Model A36TC

In 1979, following FAA certification on 7 December 1978, Beech introduced the turbocharged Model A36TC powered by a 300hp Continental TSIO-520-UB flat-six engine, driving a three-blade metal propeller. Cowl flaps were replaced by louvres, and the standard Model A36 cabin heating system was modified to produce 20 per cent more heat. Beech manufactured 272 examples of this version before production was stopped to give place to the Model B36TC.

### Model B36TC

The improved Model B36TC was introduced in 1981. Numerous changes were then incorporated such as a completely redesigned instrument panel, an increased fuel capacity of 102 US gallons (386 litres), and a wing of greater span with NACA 23010.5 aerofoil section at the tips. Vortex generators were also installed on the wing leading edge to improve roll control at high angles of attack.

### Model T36TC

The Model T36TC was an unpressurised testbed powered by a 325hp Continental TSIO-520 engine with aft-mounted turbocharger, intended to investigate the feasibility of a pressurised Bonanza. It accomplished its maiden flight on 16 February 1979 and flew for the last time on 25 January 1980, after a total of 82hr 45min flying had been logged.

### Model 1079/QU-22B

The Beech Model 1079 was an improved version of the Model 1074 Pave Eagle I. Known as the QU-22B, this Model was basically a Model A36 fitted with wingtip tanks and a Continental IO-520-B engine with special reduction gearbox to turn the propeller at very low rpm for noise reduction. Modification of the basic commercial aircraft, by the Univac Division of Sperry Rand, included installation of remote control equipement and an electronic package. The QU-22Bs were procured for the USAF in 1969 for service over Vietnam as electronic intelligence-gathering drones in the Pave Eagle II project. They could be flown either manned or unmanned, on relay duties for the Igloo White surveillance system, the data being relayed either directly or with intermediate rebroadcasting by Lockheed EC-121Rs. These aircraft were deployed to Nakhon Phanom RTAFB in March 1969 and about ten of them were lost during the war (two in 1969, one in 1970, two in 1971, and five in 1972).

The six YQU-22A (PD 1079) prototypes were followed by 27 QU-22B production models. Some of these aircraft eventually found their way on to the civil market, as follows: 68-10534 became N83475, 68-10536/N94499, 69-7693/N75210, 69-7695/N90638, 69-7696/N40CA, 69-7698/N74TA, 69-7699/N90637, 69-7701/N73TA, 69-7702/N49893, 69-7703/N64285, 69-7704/N75208, and 70-1535/N22QU.

* * *

R/STOL Systems of Raleigh, North Carolina, modified a Model A36 with a full-span trailing-edge flap system and a full-span distributed-camber leading edge as well as vortex generators to improve low-speed performance and to permit safe STOL landings and take-offs. Take-off run was thereby reduced to 904ft (276m) and landing run to 550ft (168m).

In 1988 Allison Gas Turbine Division GMC, in conjunction with Soloy Conversions Ltd, obtained FAA certification of a propeller-turbine conversion of the Model A36, known as the Allison Turbine Bonanza. The conversion involved installation of an Allison 250 Turbine Pac rated at 420shp (or a 450shp Allison B17F/2), driving a three-blade Hartzell propeller. Two additional spars were added to the bottom of the fuselage for additional strength and the lighter Allison engine was installed 1ft 9in (0.53m) further forward to maintain the aircraft's centre of gravity. Other improvements included Osborne wingtip tanks, each with 20 US gallons (75.7 litres) capacity, incorporating a small sweptback winglet.The first flight of the 250-B17F/2 powered A36 (N7214D) was accomplished at Amarillo on 20 June 1991, and in October 1991 conversion work was

*A Bonanza A36 (N24158) was modified with a full-span trailing-edge flap system.* (Sierra)

*A Tradewind Prop-Jet Bonanza re-engined with an Allison 250 Turbine Pac by Tradewind of Amarillo, Texas.* (Tradewind)

passed to Tradewind Turbines Corp of Amarillo, Texas. This conversion is available for Model A36 and A36TC, but not for the Model F33. The converted aircraft are now known as Tradewind Prop-Jet Bonanzas, and a total of 24 had been converted by April 1991.

The Allison Prop-Jet Bonanza has set several speed records: Jack Schweibold, Harry Sutton and Larry Chambers flew from Tulsa to Indianapolis at 266.43mph; Jay Penner and Jack Schweibold flew from Indianapolis to Baltimore at 253.9mph, and the same crew flew from Baltimore to Atlantic City at 251.7mph.

Colemill Enterprises Inc of Nashville, Tennessee, offers conversion of the Model A36 with new 300hp Teledyne Continental IO-550-B engines, driving Hartzell Sabre Blade four-blade Q-tip propellers and Zip-Tip winglets. Such modified aircraft, known as Colemill Starfire Bonanzas, have a cruising speed of 203mph (326km/h) and a maximum rate of climb of 1,210ft/min (369m/min).

## Model 36

One 285hp Continental IO-520-B.

Span 32ft 10in (10.01m); length 26ft 4in (8.03m); height 8ft 5in (2.57m); wing area 177.6sq ft (16.5sq m).

Empty weight 1,980lb (898kg); maximum take-off weight 3,600lb (1,633kg); wing loading 20.2lb/sq ft (98.6kg/sq m); power loading 12.63lb/hp (5.73kg/hp).

Maximum speed 204mph (323km/h) at sea level; cruising speed (75% power) 195mph (314km/h) at 6,500ft (1,980m); rate of climb 1,015ft/min (309m/min) at sea level; service ceiling 16,000ft (4,875m); maximum range (75% power) with 45min reserves 875 miles (1,408km).

## Model A36

One 300hp Continental IO-550-BA.

Span 33ft 6in (10.21m); length 27ft 6in (8.38m); height 8ft 5in (2.57m); wing area 181sq ft (16.8sq m).

Empty weight 2,247lb (1,019kg); maximum take-off weight 3,650lb (1,655kg); wing loading 20.2lb/sq ft (98.6kg/sq m); power loading 12.17lb/hp (5.52kg/hp).

Maximum speed 212mph (340km/h) at sea level; maximum cruising speed (75% power) 202mph (326km/h) at 6,000ft (1,830m); rate of climb 1,210ft/min (368m/min) at sea level; service ceiling 16,000ft (4,875m); maximum range (75% power) with 45min reserves 800 miles (1,287km).

## Model B36TC

One 300hp Continental TSIO-520-UB.

Dimensions as for Model A36 except span 37ft 10in (11.53m); wing area 188.1sq ft (17.47sq m).

Empty weight 2,330lb (1,057kg); maximum take-off weight 3,850lb (1,746kg); wing loading 20.5lb/sq ft (100.1kg/sq m); power loading 12.83lb/hp (5.82kg/hp).

Maximum speed 245mph (394km/h) at 22,000ft (6,700m); cruising speed (75% power) 224mph (361km/h); rate of climb 1,049ft/min (319m/min) at sea level; service ceiling 25,000ft (7,620m); range (75% power) with 45min reserve 1,132 miles (1,822km).

## Allison Turbine Bonanza

One 420shp Allison 250-B17C Turbine Pac.

Span 33ft 5½in (10.2m); length 29ft 2in (8.89m); height 8ft 7in (2.62m); wing area 188.1sq ft (17.47sq m).

Empty weight 2,400lb (1,089kg); maximum take-off weight 3,833lb (1,739kg) ; wing loading 20.4lb/sq ft (100.1kg/sq m); power loading 9.13lb/hp (4.26kg/hp).

Maximum speed 242mph (389km/h); cruising speed 230mph (371km/h) at 15,000ft (4,570m); rate of climb 1,900ft/min (579m/min) at sea level; service ceiling 25,000ft (7,620m); range at maximum cruising power with 45min reserves 1,134 miles (1,825km) at 15,000ft (4,570m).

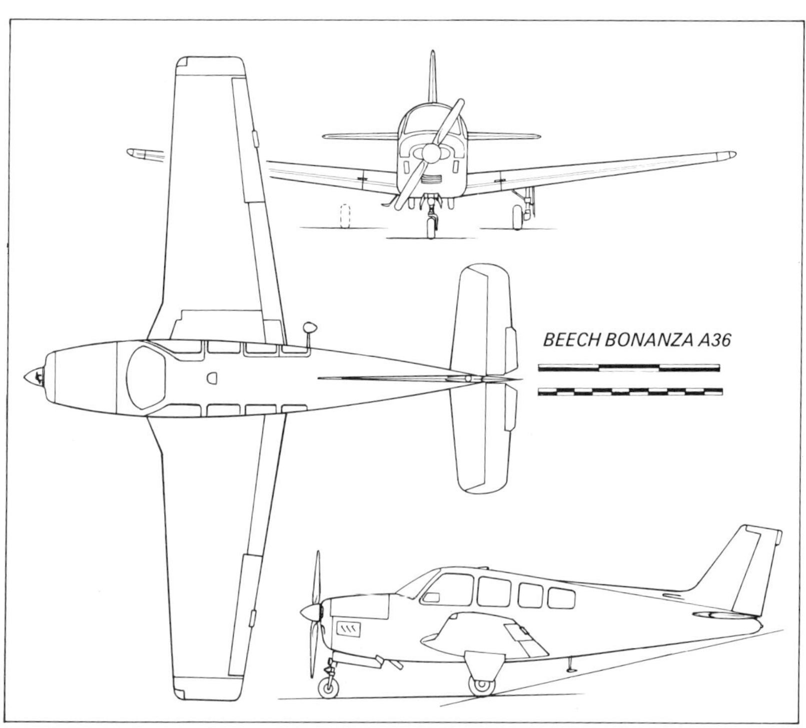

# Model 100 King Air, U-21F

After it had accomplished its maiden flight on 17 March 1969, the existence of the King Air 100 was announced by Beech on 26 May 1969 as a new variant of the successful King Air. The Model 100 was a pressurised transport with increased internal capacity and more powerful engines, enabling a greater useful load to be carried. Other salient features were a fuselage lengthened by 4ft 2in (1.27m), a reduced wing span, larger tail surfaces, fences on the wing upper surface, and dual-wheel main undercarriage. It had the same electrically-operated tailplane trim system as used in the Model 99. A variety of interior configurations were made available, including a 15-seat commuter layout. Other refinements comprised polarised cabin windows with rotatable interior panes, a revised control pedestal, and more avionics. Standard avionics comprise one Collins 618M-2B VHF com receiver, one Collins 51RV-2B Auto Omni with glideslope, 331-A-3G indicator, B-17 nav/GS antenna and voice filter, DME and ADF.

Engines were two 680shp Pratt & Whitney (UACL) PT6A-28 propeller-turbine engines driving Hartzell three-blade fully-feathering and reversible-pitch constant-speed propellers with 7ft 9½in (2.37m) diameter. The fuel system comprised rubber fuel cells in the wings, with a total capacity of 374 US gallons (1,415 litres), and new jet pumps replacing transfer pumps. The pressurisation system was limited to a maximum differential of 4.7psi. The King Air 100 was approved for Category 2 landing minima by the FAA, and initial deliveries occurred in August 1969. Production of the King Air 100 totalled 89 aircraft (seven in 1969, 60 in 1970, and 22 in 1971) before production switched to the Model A100.

## King Air A100

After it had made its first flight on 20 March 1970, the upgraded Model A100 replaced the Model 100 in 1971 on Beech's production lines. It had four-blade propellers and two additional fuel cells in each outer wing, providing a total fuel capacity of 470 US gallons (1,779 litres). Two aircraft were equipped with a Beech-developed UNACE package (Universal Aircraft Com/Nav Evaluation) and delivered to Belgium and Indonesia. Outside the USA, export deliveries included aircraft for Algeria, Canada, Chile, Jamaica, Malaysia, Mexico and Saudi Arabia. Production totalled 162 aircraft (including one prototype and two development aircraft) manufactured between 1971 and 1979.

## King Air B100

enerally similar to the Model A100, the Model B100 differed only in its power plant. It had two 715shp Garrett AiResearch TPE-331-6-251B/252 fixed-shaft propeller-turbines which gave a maximum cruising speed of 306mph. This variant made its first flight on 20 March 1975. Initiated in 1976, production of the Beech King Air B100 lasted until 1983, and totalled 137 machines.

* * *

*The Beech King Air A100 made its maiden flight on 20 March 1970. It had four-blade propellers and additional fuel cells. This one (N925B) is named* The Free Enterprise. (Beech)

*The King Air B100 benefited from more powerful engines developing 715shp each.* (Beech)

Raisbeck modification kits (*see under* Model 90) are available for the King Air 100, and a few aircraft have been modified.

## Military Variant

### U-21F (Model A100)

In 1971 the US Army purchased five Model A100s (Nos.70-15908/15912) to serve as pressurised transports under designation U-21F. All five were produced and delivered in 1971, and operated by the Military District Washington.

## Foreign Military Operators

**Argentina**: the Comando de Aviación del Ejercito Argentino took delivery of a single Model 100 (c/n B-82, serialled AE-100) which was damaged on 13 August 1971.
**Chile**: a single Model A100 (c/n B-219), equipped for photographic survey, is operated by the Servicio Aerofotogramétrico.
**Indonesia**: two Model 100s were delivered to Indonesia National Armed Forces-Air Force to be used as navigation trainers.
**Jamaica**: a single Model A100 was delivered (c/n B-216, serialled JDFT-3).
**Morocco**: six Model A100s were delivered and registered CN-ANA to CN-ANF (c/ns B-180/183 and B-186/187).
**Spain**: two Model A100s have been taken in charge and designated E.23 in accordance with the Spanish designation system (c/n B-193 is E.23-1/EC-CHD, and B-195 is E.23-2/EC-BHE). Both are operated by the Escuela Nacional de Aeronáutica.

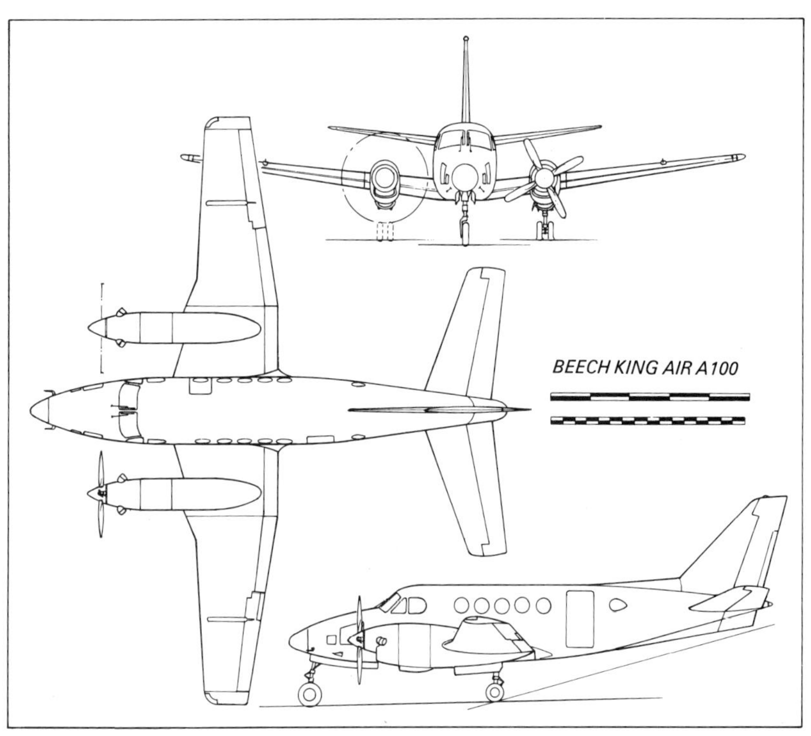

*A few King Air 100s were delivered to military customers. This A100 (c/n B-216) is operated by the Jamaican Air Force.* (J Wegg)

## King Air 100

Two 680shp Pratt & Whitney (UACL) PT6A-28.

Span 45ft 10½in (13.98m); length 39ft 11¼in (12.17m); height 15ft 4¼in (4.68m).

Empty weight 6,405lb (2,905kg); maximum take-off weight 10,600lb (4,808kg); power loading 7.79lb/shp (3.53kg/shp).Cruising speed 287mph (462km/h) at 12,000ft (3,660m); rate of climb 2,200ft/min (671m/min) at sea level; service ceiling 25,900ft (7,895m); range at high cruising power with 45min reserves 1,089 miles (1,752km) at 21,000ft (6,400m).

## King Air A100

Two 680shp Pratt & Whitney (UACL) PT6A-28.

Dimensions as for King Air 100.

Empty weight 6,759lb (3,065kg); maximum take-off weight 11,500lb (5,216kg); wing loading 40.8lb/sq ft (199kg/sq m); power loading 8.46lb/shp (3.83kg/shp).

Maximum cruising speed 285mph (459km/h) at 10,000ft (3,050m); rate of climb 1,963ft/min (598m/min) at sea level; service ceiling 24,850ft (7,575m); range at high cruising power with 45min reserves 1,384 miles (2,227km) at 21,000ft (6,400m).

## King Air B100

Two 715shp AiResearch TPE-331-6-252B.

Dimensions as for King Air 100.

Empty weight 7,127lb (3,232kg); maximum take-off weight 11,800lb (5,352kg); wing loading 42.2lb/sq ft (206.0kg/sq m); power loading 8.25lb/shp (3.74kg/shp).

Maximum speed 309mph (497km/h) at 12,000ft (3,660m); economic cruising speed 302mph (486km/h) at 20,000ft (6,100m); rate of climb 2,139ft/m (652m/min) at sea level; service ceiling 29,100ft (8,870m); range at economic cruising power with 45min reserves 1,501 miles (2,415km) at 20,000ft (6,100m).

# Model 58 Baron

In late 1969, Beech introduced a new version of the Baron designated Model 58. It retained the six-seat fuselage/cabin design of the Model 36 and the wing of the Model E55. The forward cabin section, extended by 10in (0.254m), allowed the windscreen, passenger door, instrument panel and front seats to be moved forward to provide a more spacious cabin. The Model 58 offered a cabin that could be easily loaded and unloaded through double doors installed on the starboard side of the fuselage. The aircraft had provision for club seating, with the centre two seats facing aft and the aft two seats facing forward. This improvement was made without affecting the wing main spar location, but the wheelbase had to be extended by moving the nosewheel undercarriage forward, in order to improve ground handling. Other new distinctive features included extended propeller hubs, redesigned engine nacelles to improve cooling and a fourth window on each side of the cabin.

*The Model 58 Baron flew for the first time in June 1969, and retained the fuselage of the Model 36, mated with the wing of the Model E55.* (Beech)

The Model 58 first flew on 23 June 1969 and received its FAA Type Certificate in the normal category on 19 November 1969. The Model 58 Baron was an immediate success, with 98 machines delivered during the first production year. By 1 May 1976 more than 700 of this Baron series had been delivered and 1,593 aircraft had been built by 1 January 1985. Significant deliveries included four for the Indonesian Civil Flying Academy in Java, and three for the Centre Multi-National Formation Aviation Civile of M'Vengue, Gabon; the US FAA staff pilot proficiency training programme received eight aircraft, Lufthansa pilot training 19; Air France three, and Japan Air Lines three, both for pilot training. By 1 January 1991 a total of 2,246 Model 58 Barons, including Model 58Ps and Model 58TCs had been delivered to customers around the world.

## Model 58

This is the main production model, powered by two 285hp Continental IO-520-C flat-six engines driving Hartzell two-blade metal propellers. The standard fuel system has a usable capacity of 136 US gallons (514 litres), with optional usable capacity of 166 US gallons (628 litres). From 1976, Beech offered wet wingtips on the Model 58 to give an increase in fuel capacity of 28 US gallons (108 litres). In 1984, several new improvements included double passenger/cargo doors on the starboard side, extended propeller hubs, redesigned engine nacelles to improve cooling and a fourth window each side of the cabin. The Model 58 Baron has been under constant production for more than 20 years, and at the time of writing the production totalled 1,677 aircraft.

## Model 58P

Design of this pressurised version of the Model 58 Baron started in June 1972, and this variant was first flown on 16 August 1973 and introduced on to the market in 1974. The Model 58P is powered by two 310hp Continental TSIO-520-LB1C engines and the pressurisation system provides an 8,000ft (2,440m) cabin environment to an altitude of 18,000ft (5,500m). On this variant the double doors are located on the port side of the fuselage while the pilot's entry door remains on the right side over the wing. As on the Model 58, six seats are standard. The first production aircraft was flown in late 1974 and Type Certification under FAR Part 23 was received in early 1975. From 1976, wet wing tips were made available giving an increase in fuel capacity of 24 US gallons (92 litres). The Model 58Ps were assembled at Beech's Salina, Kansas, facility and first deliveries began in late 1975, and a total of 21 Model 58Ps had been delivered by 1 January 1976.

Upgrades for the 1977 model year included the installation of new engines: 325hp Continental TSIO-520-WBs that increased cruising speed. Improved pressurisation differential provided a sea level cabin up to 8,350ft (2,545m) or a cabin altitude of 9,200ft (2,805m) at 21,000ft (6,400m). Other improvements included shoulder harnesses for the front seats, a three-position flap pre-select control switch, easier fuel tank selection to reduce pilot workload and a wide choice of custom-installed avionics. By 1 January 1985 a total of 469 Baron 58Ps had been delivered, 18 of which had been taken in charge by the US Department of Agriculture on 17 June 1982 for use by the US Forest Service as lead aircraft in directing water-bomber aircraft, as well as for reconnaissance, administration and cargo missions. Other operators include All Nippon Airways, the Indonesian Civil Flying Academy, the FAA, Lufthansa, Air France and Japan Air Lines. Production of the Model 58P ceased after a total of 495 examples had been built.

## Model 58TC

The design of this turbosupercharged version, generally similar to the Model 58P, originated in July 1974, and construction of a prototype to production aircraft standard began in February 1975. The maiden flight of this turbocharged variant was on 31 October 1975 and FAA Type Certification, in the normal category, was granted on 23 January 1976. The Model 58TC had two 310hp Continental TSIO-520 engines installed, and in 1976 the fuel management was simplified and wet cell fuel tanks were offered as an option for the first time. Shoulder harnesses became standard equipment on all forward-facing seats, and the flap system was revised with a three-position, pre-select-type control switch. In 1977 a Model 58TC was the 40,000th Beech aircraft built. The 1978 Model year saw another major change when 325hp Continental TSIO-520 engines were introduced. This version, of which 151 had been delivered by 1 January 1984 is no longer in production.

* * *

Several Model 58TCs and Model 58Ps were reworked in the field by Beech service engineering teams. Beech kit No.102-5010 was installed to increase the gross weight of both models from 6,100lb to 6,200lb. This kit also provided modifications that changed engine horsepower from 310hp to 325hp,

*The US Forest Service operates Baron 58Ps as lead planes for water bombers. This one (N132Z) is seen near Klamath Falls, Oregon, in August 1972.* (R J Francillon)

*A turbocharged variant was introduced in 1975. The Model 58TC was powered by two 310hp Continental TSIO-520 engines.* (Beech)

the powerplants being redesignated TSIO-520-LB1CWB1. These modified aircraft were Model 58TCs c/ns TK-85/91 and Model 58Ps c/n TJ-169/192.

Colemill Enterprises Inc of Nashville, Tennessee, offers conversion of the Model 58 with new 300hp Teledyne Continental IO-550-C engines, driving Hartzell Sabre Blade four-blade Q-tip propellers, Zip-tip winglets and a Shadin digital fuel computer. Such modified aircraft, known as Colemill Foxstar Barons, have a maximum cruising speed (at 75% power) of 236mph (380km/h) and a maximum rate of climb of 1,840ft/min (561m/min).

RAM Aircraft Corp of Waco, Texas, offers upgrades of Models 58P/TC which consist of the installation of 325hp TSIOL-520-WB engines with associated propellers.

Galaxy Group Inc, a company headed by former astronaut Gordon Cooper, has completed engineering for the modification and certification of a 450hp Allison 250-B17F/1 powered Model 58P driving an 80in-diameter three-blade Hartzell propeller. This variant is known as the Galaxy 400.

## Military operators

**Centrafrique**: the Force Aérienne Centrafricaine took delivery of a single Model 58 (c/n TH-903, ex F-ODHR) which was operated under registration TL-EBP.

**Haiti**: the Corps d'Aviation d'Haïti operates a single Model 58 (c/n TH-531, serialled 1251).

### Model 58

Two 285hp Continental IO-520-C.

Span 37ft 10in (11.53m); length 29ft 10in (9.09m); height 9ft 6in (2.9m); wing area 199.2sq ft (18.5sq m).

Empty weight 3,286lb (1,490kg); maximum take-off weight 5,400lb (2,449kg); wing loading 27.1lb/sq ft (132.3kg/sq m); power loading 9.47lb/hp (4.29kg/hp).

Maximum speed 242mph (390km/h) at sea level; maximum cruising speed (75% power) 230mph (370km/h) at 7,000ft (2,135m); rate of climb 1,694ft/min (516m/min) at sea level; service ceiling 17,800ft (5,425m); range (65% power) and 45min reserves 1,212 miles (1,950km).

### Model 58P

Two 310hp Continental TSIO-520-C.

Dimensions as for Model 58 except height 9ft 2in (2.79m).

Empty weight 3,985lb (1,808kg); maximum take-off weight 6,140lb (2,785kg); wing loading 32.4lb/sq ft (158.2kg/sq m); power loading 9.9lb/hp (4.49kg/hp).

Maximum speed 226mph (363km/h) at 16,000ft (4,875m); maximum cruising speed 226mph (363km/h) at 16,000ft (4,875m); rate of climb 1,424ft/min (434m/min) at sea level; service ceiling 25,000ft (7,620m); range (65% power) and 45min reserves 1,296 miles (2,086km).

### Model 58TC

Engines and dimensions as for Model 58P.

Empty weight 3,780lb (1,715kg); maximum take-off weight 6,100lb (2,767kg); wing loading 32.4lb/sq ft (158.2kg/sq m); power loading 9.84lb/hp (4.46kg/hp).

Maximum speed 287mph (461km/h); maximum cruising speed (81% power) 267mph (430km/h) at 20,000ft (6,100m); rate of climb 1,461ft/min (445m/min) at sea level; service ceiling 25,000ft (7,620m); range (81% power) with 45min reserves 1,025 miles (1,650km).

# Model 200 Super King Air, C-12 Huron and RU-21J

Project studies leading to the introduction of the Super King Air B200 began in mid-1969. After four years of research and development, Beech introduced the new model in 1973. Known as the Model 101 throughout the preliminary stages, the designation changed to Super King Air 200 when it was decided to market the aircraft. The aircraft's most salient feature was its large T-tail, the development of which consumed some 375 hours of wind tunnel testing. This new tail assembly procured better efficiency of the rudder and elevator, as well as reduced control loads. Construction of the first prototype and first pre-production aircraft started simultaneously in 1971. The first (c/n BB-1) flew on 27 October 1972 and the second (c/n BB-2) on 15 December 1972 with Beech test pilot Bud Francis making both maiden flights. While the flight-test programme was still under way, construction of the first production aircraft began in June 1973, and FAA certification under FAR Part 23 was awarded on 14 December 1973.

The Super King Air 200 had increased wingspan with extended tips, a new T-tail, additional fuel capacity, increased cabin pressurisation and a higher gross weight. The aerofoil section was a NACA 23018.5 (modified) at the roots, and NACA 23011.3 at the tips. The wing had 6 degree dihedral, a two-spar light alloy structure, and single-slotted trailing-edge flaps. The Super King Air was powered by two flat rated 850shp Pratt & Whitney Aircraft of Canada PT6A-41s, driving Hartzell three-blade constant-speed, fully-feathering and reversible-pitch propellers. Accommodation had been made for a crew of two and 13 passengers. A King Gold Crown electronics package included King KTR900A main and standby VHF transceivers, King KNR600A manual omni No.1 with Collins indicator,

*The most salient feature of the Model 200 was its new T-tail arrangement, which improved stability. N200KA was the demonstration aircraft and was named* The Free Enterprise. (Beech)

King KGM691 glideslope and RCA AVQ-47 radar.

Certificated in December 1973, initial deliveries of the Super King Air began in February 1974 when an aircraft was delivered to Arthur K Watson, a director of IBM. By 1 January 1976 Beech had delivered 100 Super King Airs to commercial and private operators. Over 830 Model 200s were built from 1974 to 1981.

## Model 200T

In 1976, Beech modified Model 200 c/n BB-186 for maritime patrol. The aircraft was fitted with 50 US gallon wingtip tanks for increased range, special bulged observation windows, a surveillance radar located under the fuselage and a lower-fuselage fairing housing various photographic equipment. Known as the Model 200T, this aircraft was able to remain on station for more than eight hours. A total of 23 aircraft were built from 1976 to 1987. Among these, two were delivered in February 1977 to France's Institut Géographique National. These had twin Wild RC10 Super-aviogon cameras, Doppler navigation systems and detachable wingtip fuel tanks, increasing total usable

*Two Model 200Ts are operated by France's Institut Géographique National for mapping. These have BT-1 and BT-2 c/ns and are registered respectively F-GALN and F-GALP.* (IGN)

*A Super King Air B200 operated by Hazelton Air Services (N3832E). Thanks to its new propeller-turbines, the B200 had better performance than the Super King Air 200.* (Beech)

capacity from 544 to 649 US gallons (2,059 to 2,456 litres). These aircraft were fitted with a high flotation main undercarriage, permitting the maximum take-off weight to be increased to 14,000lb (6,350kg). They are operated under a special French airworthiness certificate which allows maximum take-off and landing weights of 14,000lb (6,350kg) and 13,500lb (6,123kg) respectively.

## Model B200

Introduced in March 1981, the Model B200, which design had been begun in March 1980 on a modified Model 200 (c/n BB-343), was generally similar to the Super King Air 200, except for the installation of Pratt & Whitney PT6A-42 propeller-turbines which provide better cruise and altitude performance. In addition, maximum zero-fuel weight was increased by some 600lb (272kg) and cabin pressure differential was increased to 6.5psi. Many minor improvements were made to the interior, including a new double-wide cockpit pedestal. Several improvements were introduced through the years. In 1984, a 3,000psi hydraulic undercarriage system replaced the electro-mechanical installation and 98-in three-blade McCauley propellers were installed. An improved version was introduced at the 1992 NBAA Convention. Visually distinguishable from earlier versions of the Super King Air B200 by its 94-in four-blade McCauley propellers, it had numerous upgrades and systems improvements. These shorter propellers had reduced tip speed, generating less noise and vibration. Other refinements included a new flap actuator switch system that simplified flap operation, a lighter air conditioning compressor and new restyled cabin chairs. The Super King Air B200, of which 83 were built during the first year, is still under production.

## Model B200C

This variant is basically similar to the Super King Air B200 with the exception of the installation of a 52in by 52in (1.32m by 1.32m) cargo door. The first aircraft of this type was acquired by Vernair in April 1978.

## Model B200T Maritime Patrol

On 9 April 1979, Beech announced that it had begun to flight test a maritime patrol version of Super King Air B200. This special task

*A 1983 Model Beech Super King Air 200 (N83BA) was displayed at the 1983 Le Bourget airshow.* (A J Pelletier)

*The Model B200C has a large cargo door on the port side of the fuselage.* (Beech)

aircraft can be equipped for missions such as surface and sub-surface monitoring of exclusive economic zones (EEZs), detecting pollution, inspecting offshore installations, and conducting SAR flights. It can also be used for aerial photography, environmental and ecological research, airways and ground based equipment checks, target towing and ambulance duties. Modification included fitting new outboard wing assemblies, with 53-US gallon (200-litre) removable wingtip tanks, strengthened undercarriage, bubble observation windows, a hatch for dropping survival equipment, a VLF/Omega long-range navigation system, and a search radar with full 360deg scan in a radome beneath the fuselage (AIL AN/APS-128A or Litton AN/APS-504). Deliveries included 17 aircraft to Japan's Maritime Safety Agency, two for the Algerian Ministry of Defence, three to Australia, one to Chile, five to the Peruvian Navy, one to Puerto Rico, and one to the Uruguayan Navy.

### Model B200CT

Generally similar to the Super King Air B200T, this version is equipped with a cargo door and wingtip tanks as standard.

* * *

### PD 290

In 1975, Beech used the first Model 200 Super King Air as a testbed for Pratt & Whitney JT-15D-4 turbofan engines. So fitted, this aircraft (registered N38B) accomplished its maiden flight on 12 March 1975 with Beech test pilot Bud Francis at the controls. Designated PD 290, it logged 103 test flights, and last flew on 23 September 1977.

In February 1985, Raisbeck Engineering Inc of Seattle, Washington, certificated a four-blade propeller conversion kit for the Super King Air 200, which resulted in a considerably reduced flight deck and cabin noise level, a shorter take-off run and a rate of climb of 3,616ft/min (1,102m/min) compared to the standard 2,945ft/min (898m/min). The conversion, known as the Raisbeck-Western Mark VI system, used new advanced-technology lightweight 7ft 10in (2.39m) diameter turbofan propellers developed by Hartzell. First flight of such an equipped Super King Air B200 took place on 25 June 1984 and certification was completed in February 1985. In June 1987, Raisbeck announced FAA certification and first production deliveries of its Short-Field Enhancement System for Super King Air 200/B200. This modification also comprised new composite construction inboard wing leading edges, wing-to-fuselage fairings and flush mounted Goodrich de-icing boots. Another kit, the Raisbeck Ram Air Recovery System (RARS) provided improvements in cruising speeds and rates of climb. It included the installation of a more complete sealing of the engine nacelle air inlet section, a new fixed turning vane, the addition of a 'Coanda effect' curved surface on the rear portion of the movable inertial separator vane, and a new highly porous ice shedder screen. Deliveries of RARS equipped aircraft began on 15 June 1986. By March 1991, more than 300 Model 200s had been modified by Raisbeck.

*The Model B200T Maritime Patrol is equipped for surface and sub-surface missions. It was displayed at the 1985 Le Bourget airshow fitted with gun pods and Sea Skua missiles.* (A J Pelletier)

## Military Variants

### C-12A Huron (Model A200)

In August 1974, Beech received a first $20.6m contract for the delivery of 34 modified Super King Airs (20 for the US Army, and 14 for the US Air Force). The standard powerplant comprised two 750shp Pratt & Whitney Aircraft of Canada PT-6A-38 propeller-turbines, driving Hartzell three-blade fully-feathering and reversible-pitch constant-speed

*Beech B200 c/n BB-1367 (G-OBAA) was modified with a camera in the nose to be operated by BAA from London–Gatwick Airport.* (K Palmer)

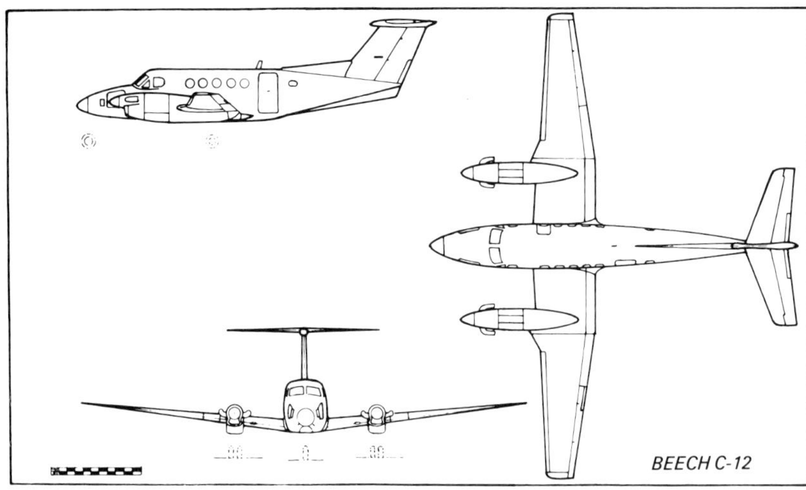


propellers. Usable fuel capacity was 348 US gallons (1,318 litres). The contract also included world-wide aircraft servicing, on-site personnel, facilities for inspection and maintenance. The first aircraft were accepted on 23 July 1975 and in August 1975 both the USAF and US Army exercised options to their contracts: the Air Force added 16 ($10.8m) and the Army 20 ($13.6m). Deliveries of these military Super King Airs extended into October 1977. On 27 December 1977, Beech received a US Army follow-on contract valued at $16m for a further 20 C-12As to be delivered through November 1978. US Army aircraft were later re-powered by PT6A-41s and 42s as C-12Cs and C-12Es. Production totalled 91, including one delivered to the Greek Air Force through Foreign Military Sales (FMS). The C-12As entered service at Fort Monroe, Virginia, in July 1975. They were operated by MAAGs, 58th MAS, 89th MAG and 7005th ABS. Two aircraft are flown by US Customs (73-22265 and 73-22266, registered N7068B and N7074G respectively).

## UC-12B (Model A200C)

The US Navy purchased nine Model A200Cs for use as personnel and utility transports. On 27 December 1978 Beech was awarded a $22.8m follow-on contract for 22 additional UC-12Bs for delivery between May 1980 and April 1981. Basically off-the-shelf aircraft, the UC-12Bs are powered by 850shp PT6A-41s and have a 52in by 52in (1.32m by 1.32m) cargo door and high-flotation undercarriage. A total of 66 (49 Navy 17 Marine Corps) were delivered by 31 May 1982. A further 12 aircraft were ordered in August 1985 for delivery beginning in 1986.

## C-12C

Basically similar to the C-12As, these aircraft are powered by PT6A-41 engines. The US Army took delivery of 14 of them, and re-engined its C-12A fleet. The C-12Cs are operated by 7th Corps, 6th, 56th, 62nd and 207th AvCo, 1st and 6th AvDet, and TRADOC.

## C-12D (Model A200CT)

Similar to the C-12Cs, the C-12D has cargo doors and provision for tip tanks. Wing span (over tip tanks) was increased to 55ft 6in (16.92m). A total of 33 aircraft, 27 for the US Army and six for the USAF, were initially procured (including thirteen modified RC-12Ds for the US Army, and five for Israel delivered through Foreign Military Sales), delivery of which was completed by March 1983. A further batch of twelve aircraft was ordered in August 1985 for delivery in 1986/87. C-12Ds are operated by US Embassies, ARNG and 163rd CavReg.

## JC-12C/D

Two aircraft (Nos.78-23133 and

*Beech C-12A-BH Huron (c/n BD-12, s/n 73-1216) operated by the 58th MAS, seen at Greenham Common in July 1983.* (A J Pelletier)

*Beech UC-12B BuNo. 161314 of the US Marine Corps Headquarters, at NAF Washington in July 1990. Trim is black and gold.* (J G Handelman)

78-23140) are used by US Army ATC for special tests.

## RC-12D Improved Guardrail V (Model A200CT)

This special mission version was procured by the US Army to supplement the unpressurised RU-21Hs (*see under Model 90*) for battlefield duties in Europe and South Korea. The RC-12D serves as the aerial platform for the AN/USD-9 Improved Guardrail V remotely controlled communications intercept and direction finding system, with direct reporting to tactical commanders at Corps level and below. It is fitted with an aircraft survivability equipment (ASE) suite, a Carousel IV-E inertial platform, and a Tacan set. Mission equipment includes a radio data link, AN/ARW-83(V)5 airborne relay facility, and ECM in wingtip pods which increase the span to 57ft 10in (17.63m). Prime system contractor is ESL Inc, with Beech as mission equipment integrator. Maximum take-off weight increased to 14,200lb (6,441kg). A first batch of thirteen RC-12Ds (included in total given for C-12D) were delivered from the summer of 1983. On 11 May 1983 a $15.3m Army follow-on contract was awarded for a further six aircraft for 1985 delivery. The RC-12Ds are operated by 1st, 2nd and 3rd MIBs.

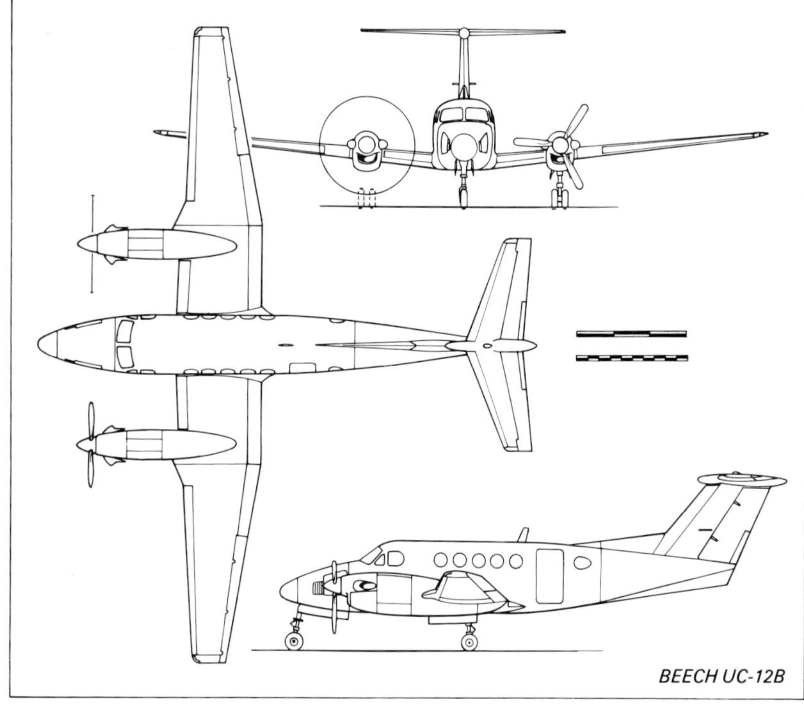

*BEECH UC-12B*

## UC-12D

This utility variant, basically similar to the C-12D, was ordered on 29 April 1983 when Beech received a $20.3m contract from the US Army for the delivery of 12 aircraft. Six found their way to the US Air Force, the other six to Army National Guard. Deliveries were completed by the first half of 1984.

## C-12E

Designation given to 29 C-12As re-powered by PT6A-42 engines for the US Air Force and assigned to various embassies.

## C-12F (Model B200C)

When the USAF selected the Beech Model B200C as an Operational Support Aircraft (OSA) to replace ageing CT-39 Sabreliners, Beech received a $86.6m contract for the lease of 40 aircraft (C-12F) for a five-year period, with an option on a further three-year lease and ultimate USAF purchase after eight years. Flight line, intermediate and depot total logistics and maintenance sup-

*Beech C-12C-BH Huron (s/n 78-23128) of the 207th AvCo.* (A J Pelletier collection)

*Beech C-12D (s/n 82-23784) operated by the US Army in an all-grey low-visibility colour scheme.* (C Waldenmaier)

*A Beech C-12F (s/n 84-0154) of the USAF's Military Airlift Command, in June 1989. This aircraft is operated by the 1401st MAS Det. 2.*

port for the C-12Fs were to be provided by Beech Aerospace Services Inc, and pilot training was to be given at the Beechcraft World-wide Customer Training Centre in Wichita. This variant is fitted with PT6A-42 engines, an hydraulically activated undercarriage, and a cargo door. The first C-12F was delivered in May 1984 to MAC at Scott AFB, Illinois. The US Army also procured 17 (delivered in 1986/87) and the Air National Guard six. On 9 May 1994 Beech announced it had been awarded a $9.3 million contract by the US Army for three C-12Fs, with follow-on options for up to 26 more. The C-12Fs are operated by 616th MAG, 13th, 1400th, 1401st, 1402nd, 1403rd MAS, 375th MAW and the Air National Guard.

### C-12L

Designation given to three Cefly Lancer modified RU-21Js (Nos.72-21058/21060).

### UC-12F

This is the US Navy equivalent of the C-12F with PT6A-42 propeller-turbines. The US Navy received the first out a batch of twelve in 1986.

### RC-12F

Designation given to two UC-12Fs modified as Range Surveillance Aircraft (RANSAC) for Pacific Missile Range facilities at Barking Sands, Hawaii.

### RC-12G

Special Mission US Army variant, converted from C-12D with MTOW increased to 15,000lb (6,804kg).

### RC-12H Improved Guardrail V

Special Mission US Army version, similar to RC12D but with MTOW of 15,000lb (6,804kg), and fitted with Improved Guardrail V combined airborne and ground communications intelligence system designed to intercept and locate enemy emitters. Six of them were delivered in 1985 to 3rd MIB stationed at Pyongtaek, in South Korea.

### RU-21J (Model 200)

During 1974, under an R&D contract, Beech had modified three aircraft for the US Army's Cefly Lancer programme. They were fitted with various types of electronic equipment and an array of antennae resembling those of the RC-12D. After serving as test beds for some years, these aircraft were stripped of the special mission avionics and reconfigured as VIP transports.

### RC-12K Guardrail Common Sensor

The RC-12K is an electronics special missions aircraft, nine of which were ordered by the US Army in October 1985. These converted C-12Ds were fitted with the Guardrail Common Sensor system which combined communications and electronic intelligence sensors. The RC-12K also had PT6A-67 engines, a large cargo door and oversized undercarriage. A further nine were ordered in 1989 for delivery starting in February 1992; three were ordered in 1991 for delivery starting in July 1993; six more were ordered during FY92 to be delivered in 1994. During May 1991, the first RC-12Ks to be based in Europe were delivered to the 1st MIB at Weisbaden, where they replaced the Grumman RV-1D Mohawks.

### UC-12M

US Navy equivalent of C-12F. Deliveries of twelve began in 1987. Two of them were eventually converted to RC-12Ms.

### RC-12M

Designation given to two UC-12Ms which were converted as RANSAC in 1988, and operated by PMTC at Point Mugu, California.

### RC-12N Guardrail Common Sensor

Electronic Intelligence variant. In 1993 Beech was awarded a $22.125m contract from the US Army for five aircraft to be delivered between September 1995 and June 1996, and a $10.6m sub-contract for the modification of seven RC-12Ns to RC-12Ps standard. The modified aircraft are to be delivered in 1994/95. The RC-12N are fitted with dual EFIS and aircraft survivability equipment and avionics control system (ASE/ACS). The prototype was converted from the ninth RC-12K.

### RC-12P Guardrail Common Sensor

Designation given to late RC-12Ns which are due to be modified with different equipment, lighter wing pods and increased MTOW (16,500lb). A first batch of seven is due to be delivered in 1994/95. A second batch of five aircraft will follow in 1995/96.

## Foreign Military Operators

**Algeria**: three Model 200s have been taken on charge by the Air force (c/ns BB-184, 175 and 171, registered 7T-WRG/I), while two Model 200Ts are government owned (c/ns BT-20/21, registered 7T-VRY/VRZ).

**Argentina**: two Model 200s were initially delivered as VIP transports (c/n BB-54 serialled 0697/5-T-31, and c/n BB-71 serialled 0698/5-T-32). Another six were ordered late 1978 to equip the 1a Escuadrilla

Aeronaval di Propósitos Generales of the Comando de Aviación Naval Argentina (CANA), and serialled 1-G-41, 1-G-42, 4-G-43, 4-G-44, 4-G-45, 2-G-46, 2-G-47, and 2-G-48.
**Bolivia**: in December 1974, the Fuerza Aérea Boliviana took delivery of Model 200 c/n BB-11 (ex N200MM, serialled FAB-001) and c/n BB-125 (serialled FAB-002). They were joined at a later date by Model 200C c/n BL-28 (serialled FAB-018). These aircraft are operated by the Escuadrilla Presidencial.
**Ecuador**: the single Model 200 was procured by the Air Force (c/n BB-723, registered HC-BHG) and was written off on 24 May 1981. Aviación del Ejercito Ecuatoriano received three aircraft (AEE-001, AEE-201, ANE-231) which are operated on surveillance duties.
**Greece**: two C-12Cs are operated by the Aeroporias Stratu on liaison and communication duties.
**Guatemala**: the Fuerza Aérea Guatemalteca has one Model 200 (c/n BB-125, serialled 001, delivered in 1976).
**Guyana**: the Guyana Defence Force Air Command has one Model 200 (c/n BB-82, registered 8R-GFB, delivered in September 1975).
**Hong Kong**: the RHK Auxiliary Air Force operates two Model B200Cs (c/ns BL-129/130, serialled HKG-8/9).

*The Beech RC-12N Guardrail Common Sensor is unmistakably recognisable by its antenna forest. The prototype shown here (s/n 85-1055) was converted from the ninth production RC-12K. Note additional fins under the tail.* (Beech)

**Ireland**: the training squadron of the Irish Air Corps in Mhic Easmuinn operated three Model 200s on maritime patrol missions (c/ns BB-208, 376 and 672; serialled 232, 234, 240 respectively). Two were eventually sold to private owners, and the last one (No.240) is used as a trainer by the Transport and Training Squadron of No.1 Support Wing at Baldonnel.
**Israel**: the IDFAF took delivery of four Model 200s during November and December 1990 as replacements for the Queen Airs that the IDFAF are keen to dispose of.
**Ivory Coast**: one Model 200 is operated by the Force Aérienne de Côte d'Ivoire under registration TU-VBB (c/n BB-295, delivered in 1977).
**Malaysia**: in May 1994, the Royal Malaysian Air Force took delivery of four Model 200Ts (c/ns BT-35/38, serialled M41-01/04) to equip No.16 Squadron at Subang Air Base.
**Mexico**: the Fuerza Aérea Mexicana has a single Model 200 (serialled TP-209 and registered XC-SLP).
**Saudi Arabia**: only one aircraft is known to have been delivered (c/n BB-76, serialled 025, ex N86DA).
**Sweden**: two Super King Air 200s have been operated by the Swedish Air Force since 1989 as Tp 101s.
**Thailand**: one aircraft is believed to have been delivered.
**Turkey**: in December 1991, three Model B200s were delivered through Keflavik and Mildenhall (c/ns BB-1409, 1411 and 1413, serialled 10010/11012). In May 1992 two more Super King Airs were delivered to Türk Kara Ucak Komutanligi (Army Aviation).
**Uruguay**: since October 1980, the Aviación Naval Uruguaya has operated a single Model 200T (c/n BT-4, serialled 871, ex N2067D) as part of the Escuadron Antisubmarino y Exploracion.
**Venezuela**: four Model 200/200Cs are known to have been delivered to the Air Force with serials FAV2540, 2840, 3150 and 3240, while Army Aviation took delivery of aircraft c/n BB-489 (serial EV-7910).

### Super King Air 200

Two 850shp Pratt & Whitney Aircraft of Canada PT6A-41.

Span 54ft 6in (16.61m); length 43ft 10in (13.36m); height 14ft 10in (4.52m); wing area 303sq ft (28.15sq m).

Empty weight 7,315lb (3,318kg); maximum take-off weight 12,500lb (5,670kg); wing loading 41.25lb/sq ft (201.4kg/sq m); power loading 7.35lb/hp (3.33kg/hp).

Maximum speed 333mph (536km/h) at 15,000ft (4,570m); maximum cruising speed 320mph (515km/h) at 25,000ft (7,620m); rate of climb 2,450ft/min (747m/min) at sea level; service ceiling 31,000ft (9,450m); range at maximum cruising power and with 45min reserves 1,710 miles (2,752km) at 25,000ft (7,620m).

### Super King Air B200

Two 850shp Pratt & Whitney Canada PT6A-42.

Dimensions as for Super King Air 200 except length 43ft 9in (13.34m); height 15ft (4.57m).

Empty weight 7,538lb (3,419kg); maximum take-off weight 12,500lb (5,670kg); wing loading 41.3lb/sq ft (201.6kg/sq m); power loading 7.35lb/hp (3.33kg/hp).

Maximum speed 339mph (545km/h) at 25,000ft (7,620m); econ cruising speed 325mph (523km/h) at 25,000ft (7,620m); rate of climb 2,450ft/min (747m/min) at sea level; service ceiling 35,000ft (10,670m); range at economic cruise power 2,075 miles (3,339km) at 25,000ft (7,620m).

# Model 76 Duchess

During late summer 1974 Beech flew the prototype of a new four-seat twin-engine cabin monoplane planned for use by Beech Aero Centers. Designated PD 289 and registered N289BA, this test-bed aircraft had a large T-tail and a low-mounted cantilever wing with NACA 632A415 wing section with 6° 30′ dihedral. Bonded honeycomb structural technology was employed extensively throughout the airframe. The aircraft was powered by two 180hp Lycoming O-360-A1G6D flat-four engines driving two-blade, constant-speed, counter-rotating Hartzell propellers. One fuel tank was located in each wing and capacity totalled 100 US gal (378.5 litres). The accommodation for the four people was two on front separate seats with reclining seat backs, and two on a rear bench. The aircraft underwent a comprehensive flight test programme before production was launched. The first production aircraft, redesignated Model 76 and named Duchess, made its initial flight on 24 May 1977 with company test pilot Vaughn Gregg. FAA certification was granted on 24 January 1978 under the normal category for day and night VFR and IFR. The Model 76 was built at Beech's Liberal factory, and first deliveries were made in May 1978. The Duchess was available with three optional equipment packages known as Weekender, Holiday, and Professional. Production lasted from 1978 until 1982, and totalled 437 aircraft (72 in 1978, 213 in 1979, 86 in 1980, 55 in 1981, and 11 in 1982).

In 1979, Beech installed two 180hp turbocharged Lycoming TO-360 engines on a Model 76 (N18776). Known unofficially as the Model 76TC, the prototype had modified engine cowlings to provide extra room for the aft-mounted turbocharger. The first flight was made on 31 January 1979 with Vaughn Gregg at the controls, but the programme was cancelled after a total of 43 flights had been made.

## Model 76

Two 180hp Lycoming O-360-A1G6D.

Span 38ft (11.58m); length 29ft 0½in (8.86m); height 9ft 6in (2.9m); wing area 181sq ft (16.81sq m).

Empty weight 2,466lb (1,119kg); maximum take-off weight 3,900lb (1,769kg); wing loading 21.5lb/sq ft (105.2kg/sq m); power loading 10.83lb/hp (4.91kg/hp).

Maximum speed 197mph (317km/h); economic cruising speed 174mph (280km/h); rate of climb 1,248ft/min (380m/min); service ceiling 19,650ft (5,990m); range with maximum fuel and 45min reserves 717 miles (1,155km).

*Production of the Model 76 Duchess totalled 437 aircraft. N6705T is illustrated here.* (Beech)

*The Model 76 was developed for use by Beech Aero Centers. Designated PD 289 (N289BA), the prototype flew for the first time during the summer of 1974.* (Beech)

# Model 77 Skipper

In late 1974 Beech Aircraft announced that the company was building the prototype of a new single-engine trainer with the designation PD 285. Designed primarily as a low-cost basic trainer for Beech Aero Center flying clubs, the PD 285 embodied new construction techniques and a new constant-chord cantilever low wing with a GA(W)-1 airofoil, which originated from NASA researches into high-speed supercritical aerofoils. Maiden flight of the 100hp Continental O-200 powered prototype (N285BA) was made on 6 February 1975 and a comprehensive test programme was completed which led in the installation of a T-tail empennage to give better pitch control at low speeds and positive recovery from intentional spins. First flight of the production model, known as Model 77 Skipper, was accomplished on 12 September 1978 by Vaughn Gregg. It was powered by a 115hp Avco Lycoming O-235-L2C flat-four engine driving a Sensenich two-blade propeller. Total fuel capacity was 29 US gallons (110 litres) and the aircraft had accommodation for two seated side-by-side in adjustable seats. FAA certification was granted in April 1979 in the Utility Category, and production aircraft began reaching Beech Aero Centers in May 1979. Some 211 Skippers had been delivered by 1 January 1981, and production eventually totalled 312 aircraft when, in July 1981, Beech announced a suspension of the production pending an improvement in market conditions.

## Model 77

One 115hp Lycoming O-235-L2C.

Span 30ft (9.14m); length 23ft 10¾in (7.28m); height 7ft 6½in (2.3m); wing area 129.8sq ft (12.06sq m).

Empty weight 1,103lb (501kg); maximum take-off weight 1,675lb (760kg); wing loading 12.9lb/sq ft (63kg/sq m); power loading 14.56lb/hp (6.6kg/hp).

Maximum speed 122mph (196km/h); maximum cruising speed 121mph (195km/h) at 4,500ft (1,370m); rate of climb 720ft/min (219m/min) at sea level; service ceiling 12,900ft (3,930m); range 376 miles (606km).

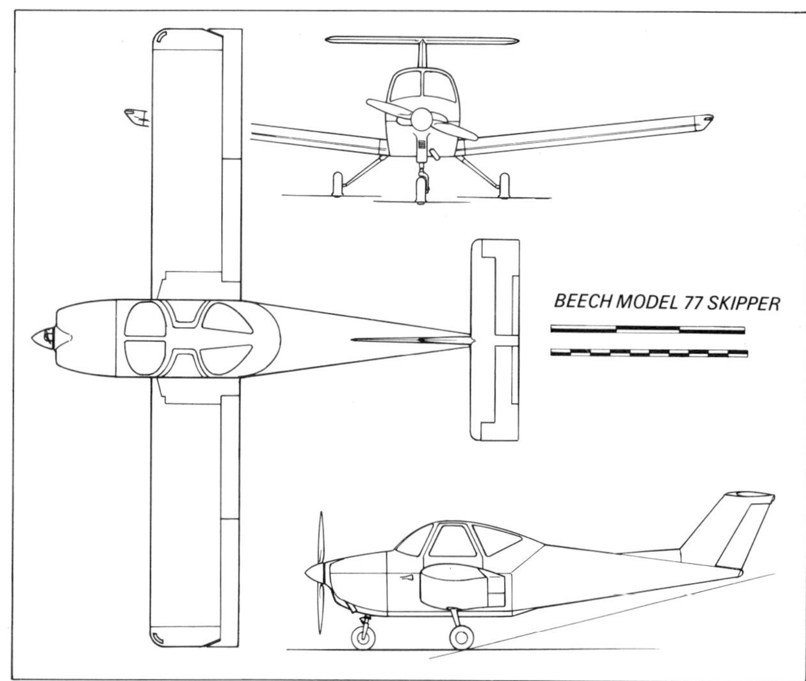

*The Beech Model 77 Skipper began its life as the Preliminary Design PD 285. Prototype N285BA is seen here during flight tests.* (Beech)

# Model 300 and 350 Super King Air

## Model 300

Design of this improved version of the Model B200 began in August 1980 using a Model 200 (c/n BB-343) fitted with two 1,050shp Pratt & Whitney Canada PT6A-60A engines as a development prototype. Other features of this variant included increased MTOW to FAA SFAR 41C standards, redesigned pitot-type engine cowlings, a 5in (12.7cm) forward extension of the leading edges, a 5.2in (13.2cm) forward extension of the propeller line, and hydraulically actuated undercarriage, etc. The maiden flight of this test-bed occurred on 6 October 1981 with Bud Francis and George Bromley at the controls, but the construction of the production prototype started a year later, in November 1982. This prototype accomplished its first flight in turn on 3 September 1983, piloted by Vaughn Gregg, and was awarded its FAA Type Certificate on 24 January 1984.

Customer deliveries of the Model 300 began by the spring of 1984 and by early 1985 a total of 50 had been delivered, and more than 230 units had been delivered by 1993 (including AT and LW Models). During the summer of 1986, the FAA ordered nineteen Super King Air 300s (c/ns FF-1/19) for airways calibration duties, equipped with automatic flight inspection system (AFIS). Delivery of these aircraft started on 4 April 1988. They are based at Atlanta, Georgia; Atlantic City, New Jersey; Battle Creek, Michigan; Oklahoma City, Oklahoma, and Sacramento, California.

## Model 300AT

This is an airline training variant of the Model 300 of which Finnair ordered two.

## Model 300LW

Announced in September 1988, this lightweight version (LW in the designation stands for lightweight) has been designed primarily for the European market, where its 12,500lb MTOW (5,670kg) allows it to qualify for reduced Eurocontrol fees. The Model 300LW is basically similar to the Model 300. A total of

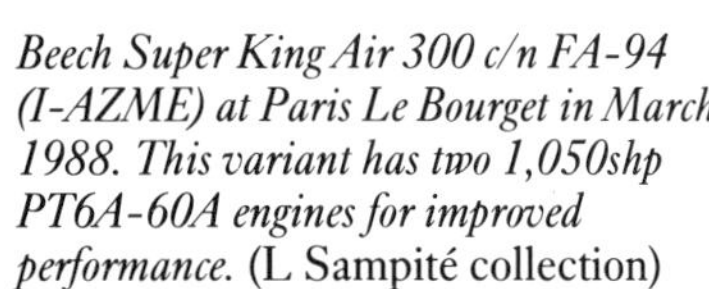

*Beech Super King Air 300 c/n FA-94 (I-AZME) at Paris Le Bourget in March 1988. This variant has two 1,050shp PT6A-60A engines for improved performance.* (L Sampité collection)

*Beech Super King Air 350 c/n FL-23 (N1543Q). This variant has a lengthened fuselage with an additional window. The aircraft illustrated is shown during the 1991 Le Bourget airshow.* (A Pelletier)

22 aircraft were delivered to customers by 1 January 1993.

### Model B300/350

Introduced at the 1989 NBAA Convention, this version is an alternative to the Super King Air 300. Compared to the Model 300, the Model 350 has a fuselage stretched by 2ft 10in (0.86m) and a wing span increased by 1ft 6in (0.61m). This wing is fitted with winglets that lower induced drag at high altitudes and, in combination with the wider-span wing, reduce stalling speed. It also has two additional windows each side, and double club seating for eight passengers with two more seats in the rear of the cabin as an option. The prototype (N120SK) accomplished its first flight in September 1988 and was certificated to FAR Part 23. The first delivery was made on 6 March 1990 and more than 100 units had been delivered by 1993.

### Model B300C/350C

This variant is fitted with a 52 by 52in (132 by 132cm) freight door with a built-in airstair passenger door. First delivery of a Model 350C was made in 1990 to Rossing Uranium in Namibia.

### Model RC-350 Guardian

Raytheon Electromagnetic Systems Division has developed an ELINT version of the Model 350 that incorporates a derivative of the company's AN/ALQ-142 electronic support measures set and other receivers to monitor and locate emitters in the 20MHz-18GHz frequency range. The aircraft, known as the RC-350 Guardian, flew for the first time from Raytheon's facility in 1991.

## Military Operators

**Switzerland**: from 1994, a Model 350 has been operated by the Swiss Air Force within the Flugswaffenbrigade 31 at Dübendorf.
**Paraguay**: the Paraguayan Air Force operates a single Model 350 serialled FAP-01.

* * *

Several aircraft have been upgraded using Raisbeck modification kits.

### Super King Air 300

Two 1,050shp Pratt & Whitney Canada PT6A-60A.

Span 54ft 6in (16.61m); length 43ft 9in (13.34m); height 15ft (4.57m); wing area 303sq ft (28.15sq m).

Empty weight 8,475lb (3,844kg); maximum take-off weight 14,000lb (6,350kg); wing loading 46.2lb/sq ft (225.6kg/sq m); power loading 6.66lb/hp (3.02kg/hp).

*The Beech Super King Air 350 prototype (appropriately registered N350KA). The winglets are clearly visible.* (Beech)

Maximum speed 365mph (587km/h); economic cruising speed 353mph (568km/h); rate of climb 2,844ft/min (867m/min) at sea level; service ceiling 35,000ft (10,670m); range at maximum cruise power with 45min reserves 1,428 miles (2,298km) at 24,000ft (7,315m).

*The US Forest Service operates a Beech Model 300 as lead plane for water bombers such as the C-130 Hercules visible in the background. This one (N107Z) is seen at Klamath Falls, Oregon, in August 1992.* (R J Francillon)

### Super King Air 350

Two 1,050shp Pratt & Whitney Canada PT6A-60A.

Span 57ft 11in (17.65m); length 46ft 8in (14.22m); height 14ft 4in (4.37m); wing area 310sq ft (28.8sq m).

Empty weight 9,051lb (4,105kg); maximum take-off weight 15,000lb (6,804kg); wing loading 48.4lb/sq ft (236.3kg/sq m); power loading 7.14lb/hp (3.24kg/hp).

Maximum speed 363mph (584km/h); maximum cruising speed 340mph (547km/h) at 35,000ft (10,670m); rate of climb 2,979ft/min (908m/min) at sea level; service ceiling 35,000ft (10,670m); range at maximum cruise power with 45min reserves 1,620 miles (2,607km) at 28,000ft (8,535m).

## Model 38 Lightning

During 1981, Beech modified a Model 58P as a proof-of-concept aircraft to investigate the feasibility of a pressurized single-engined propeller-turbine aircraft. The prototype (PD 336, c/n EJ-1, N336BA) was powered by a 550shp Garrett AiResearch TPE-331-9 engine and accomplished its maiden flight on 14 June 1982, piloted by Lou Johansen. A total of 133 flights were logged and the last flight of the Model 38P was made on 14 November 1983. The PD 336 prototype was also fitted with a 630shp UACL PT6A-40 powerplant and was flown by Lou Johansen on 9 March 1984. This aircraft logged 68 flights before the last flight was made on 8 August 1984. Three variants were expected to be offered to customers: the Model 38P powered by a PT6A-40, the Model 38P-1 powered by a PT6A-116 and the Model 38P-2 powered by a TPE-331-9. In spite of 75 letters of intent, Beech announced during the summer of 1984 that further development work on the Model 38P Lightning was being suspended because of poor market conditions.

### Model 38P

One 550shp UACL PT6A-40.

Span 37ft 10in (11.53m); length 29ft 10in (9.09m); height 9ft 2in (2.79m); wing area 188.1sq ft (17.48sq m).

Maximum take-off weight 5,800lb (2,361kg); wing loading 30.8lb/sq ft (135kg/sq m).

Maximum cruising speed 279mph (448km/h) at 20,000ft (6,100m); cruising speed 238mph (383km/h) at 25,000ft (7,620m); maximum range (maximum cruising power) with 45min reserves 1,075 miles (1,730km).

## Model 1900 Airliner and Exec-Liner

When Beech decided to re-enter the commuter airliner market, the first step was to put the Model 99 back into production, and the second step was to design a high-density derivative of the Model 200, the Model 1900. Using the Model 200 Super King Air cockpit, nose section, empennage and wings, Beech engineers designed a new semi-monocoque fail-safe wing structure using a completely new continuous main spar without bolts. This cantilever low-wing monoplane had a NACA 23000 wing section, 6 degrees dihedral, and single-slotted flaps. The fuselage was fitted with a small horizontal vortex generator on each side, immediately forward of the wing leading edge, hydraulically retractable. The undercarriage was of the nosewheel type with Beech oleo-pneumatic shock absorber. Avionics included duplicated King com/nav, glideslope receiver, transponder, ADF, DME, marker beacon receiver, Bendix RDR-160 weather radar, Sperry EFIS and Collins autopilot. The pressurised fuselage was much longer than that of the Super King Air and could seat up to 19 passengers. The original Model 1900 had two airstair doors, while the engines were two UACL PT6A-65B propeller-turbines, flat-rated to 1,100shp, driving four-blade, composite Hartzell propellers. Total fuel capacity was 430 US gallons (1,627 litres) contained in wing tanks.

Production of the basic model comprised three flying prototypes, a static test airframe and a fuselage pressure-cycle test airframe. The maiden flight of the performance prototype (c/n UA-1) was made on 3 September 1982, with Eric Griffin and Bryan Mee. It was followed by the system prototype (c/n UA-2) on 30 November 1982, while the third prototype (c/n UA-3) was used for function and reliability testing, equipment certification, and demonstration. FAA certification under SFAR Part 41C was granted on 22

November 1983 and included single-pilot approval under FAR 135 Appendix A.

## Model 1900C Airliner

This first production variant was fitted with a 52in by 52in (1.32 by 1.32m) cargo door. The initial aircraft was delivered in February 1984, and orders for this variant included six for Resort Air of St Louis, Missouri, and four for Business Express of Bridgeport, Connecticut. By the summer of 1988 Model 1900Cs were in service with eleven US and two European regional operators. Further orders included ten aircraft, with ten options, for Texas Air Corporation, to be operated by its Continental Express subsidiary, of which deliveries began in December 1987, and five for Conquest Airlines of Beaumont, Texas, delivery of which was completed in May 1988. Production of the Model 1900C was phased out in October 1991 when SFAR 41C expired, allowing small aircraft builders to manufacture certain aircraft with MTOW exceeding the 12,500lb (5,662kg) limit stipulated for Normal Category aircraft in Part 23 regulations. A total of 72 aircraft was produced by 1993.

## Model 1900 Exec-Liner

This is the corporate version, the first delivery of which was made to General Telephone Co of Illinois in the summer of 1985.

*Continental Express, a subsidiary of Texas Air Corp, is one of the numerous operators of the Model 1900C.* (Continental)

## Model 1900C-1

An advanced version of the Model 1900C entered production in 1987. It had a 'wet wing' providing a maximum fuel capacity of 685 US gallons (2,593 litres). Model 1900C-1s were delivered to commuter airlines such as Conquest Airlines, Commutair (12 aircraft), Continental Airlines, Stateswest Airlines, Frontier Air, Alpha Air, Skyway Airlines, Holiday Airlines, Mall Airways and L'Express Airlines. Production totalled 173 aircraft by 1993.

## Model 1900D

This variant was announced in March 1989 at the US Regional Airlines Association meeting. The cabin volume has been increased by 28.5 per cent, and winglets have been fitted for better hot and high performance, as well as twin ventral strakes to improve directional stability. Engines are two Pratt & Whitney Canada PT6A-67Ds flat rated at 1,279shp. The Model 1900D prototype (N5584B) made its first flight on 1 March 1990, and the type was certificated to FAR Part 23 Amendment 34 in March 1991. The launch

*The Model 1900D (c/n UE-7, N136MA) of the* Sydney Morning Herald *has since been re-registered appropriately VH-SMH. It is owned by Hamerst Pty Ltd.* (Beech)

*The first Model 1900D (c/n UE-1) was used by Beechcraft as a demonstrator aircraft.* (Beech)

customer was United Express partner Mesa Airlines, which ordered a total of 58 Model 1900Ds. On 22 December 1992 Mesa Airlines announced an order for a further 20 examples, and in November 1994 placed an order worth more than $160 million for yet another 40. Other operators are Autec Range Services (two), Commutair (Champlain Enterprises) (26), Mark Air Express (10), Hamerst Pty Ltd of Australia, and Skoda Auto. Production totalled 62 aircraft at the end of 1993, and 36 were delivered during the first nine months of 1994, when orders extended production to beyond 1997.

In November 1994 Mesa Airlines signed a contract for the purchase of 40 additional 1900s.

### Model 190D

In May 1994 the new Bucharest-based Roumanian carrier Air Antares took delivery of two Model 190Ds.

### UC-12J (Model 1900C)

In March 1986, the USAF ordered six Model 1900Cs (c/ns UD-1/6, Nos.86-0078/0083) for delivery beginning in September 1987. These aircraft serve as Air National Guard mission support aircraft, and replaced Convair C-131 Samaritans.

## Foreign Military Operators

**Egypt**: six Model 1900Cs have been ordered by the Egyptian Air Force, four of which are configured for electronic surveillance missions, and two as maritime patrol aircraft. For this latter role the aircraft are equipped with Litton search radar (SLAMMR) and Singer S-3075 ESM systems. These aircraft were delivered in the course of January 1990 (known c/ns are UC-10, 15, 16, 18, 21).
**Taiwan**: deliveries of twelve Model 1900Cs for the Taiwan Air Force began in January 1988 (known c/ns are UC-5, 7, 25, 27, 29).

### Model 1900C

Two 1,100shp Pratt & Whitney Canada PT6A-65B.

Span 54ft 5¾in (16.61m); length 57ft 10in (17.63m); height 14ft 10¾in (4.54m); wing area 303sq ft (28.15sq m).

*The second production aircraft (c/n UE-2) was the first to be delivered to Mesa Airlines, the largest operator of the type.* (Beech)

*One of the six Egyptian Air Force Model 1900Cs during its delivery flight. It wears Egyptian roundels as well as the ferry registration N7242U.* (J Delmas collection)

Empty weight 8,700lb (3,947kg); maximum take-off weight 16,600lb (7,530kg); wing loading 54.8lb/sq ft (267.5kg/sq m); power loading 7.54lb/hp (3.42kg/hp).

Maximum cruising speed 295mph (474km/h) at 8,000ft (2,440m); rate of climb 2,330ft/min (710m/min) at sea level; service ceiling 25,000ft (7,620m); range at maximum cruise power with 45min reserves 913 miles (1,469km) at 25,000ft (7,620m).

### Model 1900D

Two 1,279shp Pratt & Whitney Canada PT6A-67D.

Span 57ft 10¾in (17.65m); length 57ft 10in (17.63m); height 14ft 10¾in (4.54m); wing area 303sq ft (28.15sq m).

Empty weight 10,400lb (4,717kg); maximum take-off weight 16,950lb (7,688kg); wing loading 54.7lb/sq ft (267kg/sq m); power loading 6.62lb/hp (3kg/hp).

Maximum cruising speed 334mph (537km/h) at 13,000ft (3,960m); rate of climb 2,625ft/min (800m/min) at sea level; service ceiling 25,000ft (7,620m); range at high-speed cruise power with 45min reserves 794 miles (1,278km) at 25,000ft (7,620m).

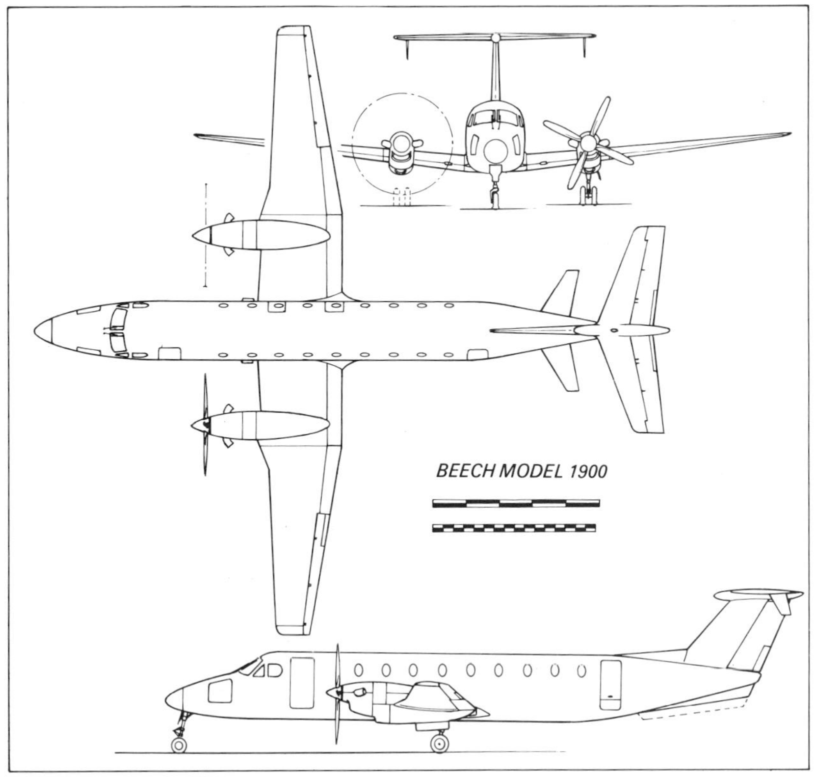


# Model 400 Beechjet and T-1A Jayhawk

In December 1985 Beech Aircraft Corporation acquired from Mitsubishi Heavy Industries and Mitsubishi Aircraft International the Diamond II business jet programme, the prototype of which (N181MA) had flown on 20 June 1984. Beech had worldwide marketing rights outside Japan and the aircraft was redesignated Model 400 Beechjet. Initially Mitsubishi supplied assemblies and sub-assemblies for final assembly by Beech, but Mitsubishi Aircraft International ceased all general aviation operations outside of Japan on 31 March 1986. In January 1988 Beech announced that all Beechjet manufacturing was being transferred to its facilities at Salina and Wichita, with total transfer scheduled for completion in June 1989.

The Beechjet is a cantilever low-wing monoplane using Mitsubishi MAC510 computer-designed wing sections and a pressurised, fail-safe fatigue resistant semi-monocoque structure. It is powered by two Pratt & Whitney Canada JT15D-5 turbofan engines, each rated at 12.9kN (2,900lb st) and fitted with Rohr thrust reversers. Beech has introduced as standard on the Beechjet an extended-range fuel tank, capacity 96 US gallons (363 litres) and a tail cone baggage compartment, both of which were optional on the Diamond II. Other improvements introduced by Beech include optional Bendix/King and Honeywell EFIS, and new interior styling and furnishings.

The first Beech assembled aircraft was rolled out on 19 May 1986 and deliveries began the following month. By 1 January 1988 a total of 25 Beechjets had been delivered. Beech has teamed with McDonnell Douglas and Flight Safety International to offer the Beechjet for the USAF's Tanker/Transport Training System (TTTS) requirement.

## Production History

### Model 400

Initial production version totalling 58 units. It has since been superseded by the improved Model 400A.

### Model 400A

Announced at the 1989 NBAA Convention, this new version has a MTOW of 16,100lb (7,293kg) and, beginning with the 24th production aircraft, a maximum landing weight of 15,700lb (7,112kg). First flight of the production 400A was made on 22 September 1989 and FAA Type Certification was granted on 20 June 1990. Deliveries began in November 1990, and 82 units had been delivered by the time of writing.

### T-1A Jayhawk (Model 400T)

On 21 February 1990 the US Air Force selected McDonnell Douglas, Beechcraft and a Quintron team to supply its new Tanker/Transport Training System (TTTS), this programme including the purchase of 211 Beech Model 400Ts designated T-1A Jayhawks. Prime contractor McDonnell Aircraft is providing the training system, and Quintron Corp is building flight simulators for the Jayhawk. The T-1A is a modified Model 400A with cabin-mounted avionics, a single-point refuelling system, greater fuel capacity and improved bird-strike protection for low-level operation. Deliveries were to begin in October 1991 and were to conform with the following schedule: 28 units in 1992, 36 in 1993, 48 in 1994, 39 in 1995, 43 in 1996, and 16 in 1997. The first T-1A (N2886B) made its maiden flight from Beech field on 5 July 1991, and for Jayhawk production Beech Plant IV at Wichita had to be extended by

*The Model 400 Beechjet came from the Mitsubishi Diamond II programme which was acquired by Beech Aircraft Corp. in 1985.* (Mitsubishi)

*A Model 400A Beechjet (N107BJ) over Dallas, Texas.* (Beech)

100,000sq ft (9,290sq m) by mid-1991. On 5 January 1993 the USAF exercised its fifth option on the T-1A contract for a further 35 aircraft to be delivered between July 1995 and June 1996.

### T-400

This is the JASDF version, which features thrust reversers, long-range inertial navigation and direction finding systems, as well as several interior changes.

## Service History

**USAF**: the first T-1A was handed over at the Wichita headquarters on 17 January 1992. In February 1992, the US Air Force took delivery of four additional T-1As for its Tanker/Transport Training System programme. The first unit to equip with the type was the 64th Flying Training Wing (52nd FTS) stationed at Reese AFB, Texas. Other units scheduled to receive T-1As are the 12th FTW (99th FTS) at Randolph AFB, Texas, the 14th FTW at Colombus AFB, Mississippi, the 47th FTW (86th FTS) at Laughlin AFB, Texas, the 71st FTW at Vance AFB, Oklahoma, and the 82nd FTW at Williams AFB, Arizona. The Jayhawks will be used to train crews for KC-10 Extenders, KC-135 Stratotankers, C-5 Galaxys and C-17 Globemaster IIIs. By the end of May 1992 fourteen T-1As had been delivered to the USAF and dedicated qualification operational tests and evaluation continued into July of the same year.

**Japan**: during the autumn of 1991 the Model 400T was selected by the JASDF to meet its TC-X requirement. This involves the purchase of nine Model 400Ts by 1995, with the first three funded in the FY92 defence budget. FY94 purchases included two Beechjet 400Ts.

### Model 400

Two 2,900lb st (12.9 kN) Pratt & Whitney Canada JT15D-5.

Span 43ft 6in (13.25m); length 48ft 5in (14.75m); height 13ft 9in (4.19m); wing area 241.4sq ft (22.43sq m).

Empty weight 10,115lb (4,588kg); maximum take-off weight 15,780lb (7,157kg); wing loading 65.37lb/sq ft (319.1kg/sq m).

Maximum speed 531mph (854km/h) at 29,000ft (8,840m); cruising speed 515mph (828km/h) at 39,000ft (11,890m); maximum operating altitude 45,000ft (13,715m); range 2,222 miles (3,575km).

### Model 400A

Engines and dimensions as for Model 400.

Empty weight 10,185lb (4,614kg); maximum take-off weight 16,100lb (7,293kg); wing loading 66.7lb/sq ft (325,1kg/sq m).

Maximum cruising speed 520mph (837km/h) at 35,000ft (10,670m); rate of climb 4,020ft/min (1,225m/min) at sea level; maximum operating altitude 45,000ft (13,715m); range 2,188miles (3,520km).

*The Beechjet is under procurement by the US Air Force as the T-1A Jayhawk. The aircraft shown is the 15th production example and wears s/n 90-0411.* (Beech)

# Model 2000 Starship 1

The design of the Beech Model 2000 was begun in 1979, when the Beech King Air series began to be faced with new potential competitors such as the innovative Learfan. A replacement for the successful King Air was then put on the drawing boards, but these plans were slowed when the company became a subsidiary of the Raytheon Company. In 1982 the project was given full pace, and arrangements were made with Burt Rutan for him to participate in the configuration study that led to finalisation of the advanced design in October 1982. This resulted in a rather unorthodox design and the building of an 85 per cent scale proof of concept (POC) prototype, the first flight of which took place on 29 August 1983 at Mojave, California. This scale version was built by Burt Rutan's Scale Composites Inc, a Beech subsidiary. More than 500 hours of flight test were completed, and proved that the configuration was viable. In addition, Beech completed a full-scale mock-up of the Starship 1 which was exhibited in October 1983 at the NBAA meeting at Dallas, Texas. At that time Beech announced that the full-scale prototype was to fly by the end of 1984, followed by FAA certification and first customer deliveries by the end of 1985. However, in June 1984 Beech revised this schedule, and certification was then expected in the last quarter of 1986 or in early 1987.

Six pre-production Starship 1s were built, three for flight testing and one each for static, damage tolerance and pressure cycle testing. The first full-scale prototype (c/n NC-1, N2000S) made its maiden flight, from Wichita, on 15 February 1986 with Bud Francis and Tom Carr as the pilots. This aircraft, which resembled closely the POC aircraft, was initially powered by two Pratt & Whitney Canada PT6A-65A-4 propeller-turbines pending

*The innovative Starship failed to find a sufficient market and production is due to be halted after the 53rd aircraft.* (Beech)

*The sixth production Starship (c/n NC-6, N1556S) served as a prototype for the Model 2000A configuration. This variant has improved performance.* (Beech)

delivery of the production PT6A-67A powerplants. Among several innovations, it had wing fences between the flaps and the elevons, underwing fences to reduce spanwise flow along the leading edges at high angles of attack, and an enlarged ventral rudder. The second prototype (c/n NC-2, N3042S), was fitted with the Collins advanced integrated avionics system specified for production Starships. It flew for the first time on 14 June 1986, with Lou Johansen and Tom Schaffstall as crew, and served as a flying testbed for the 3,000psi hydraulic

undercarriage system, multi-bus electrical system, fully automatic pressurisation system and the environmental system. On 5 January 1987 it was followed in the air by the third prototype (c/n NC-3, N3234S), which had a fully furnished cabin and performed function and reliability testing.

The Beech Model 2000 is a cantilever mid-low-wing monoplane designed with the help of CADAM (computer assisted design and manufacturing) and CATIA (computer aided three-dimensional interactive application). The wing has a specially developed wing section; dihedral angle is 1°18′36″, and sweep back is 24°24′ at quarter-chord. The wingtips are fitted with 7ft winglets which Beech referred to as 'tipsails', in order to eliminate the need for an additional vertical stabiliser, thus reducing weight and drag. The wing has a continuous tip-to-tip structure of honeycomb and graphite/epoxy monocoque, semi-monocoque and honeycomb sandwich with titanium used in high stress areas. The fuseage is of fail-safe construction using similar materials to the wings, and features a ventral fin for yaw trim/damping. At the forward end of fuselage, low-set, electrically-operated variable-geometry foreplanes with vortex generators are fitted (sweep range 4 degrees forward to 30 degrees back). The Model 2000 is powered by two Pratt & Whitney Canada PT6A-67 propeller-turbines, flat rated at 1,200shp, driving Hartzell five-blade, fully-feathering, reversing propellers of 8ft 8in (2.64m) diameter. Total fuel capacity is 508 US gallons (1,923 litres) contained in integral wing tanks, and accommodation is provided for a pilot and eight passengers. The cabin has an 8.4psi pressure differential, providing a cabin altitude of 8,000ft (2,440m) at a cruising altitude of 41,000ft (12,500m). Avionics consist of a Collins integrated package comprising 12-colour and two monochrome CRT displays in an 'all glass' cockpit. The autopilot is a digital passive system and the weather radar is Collins solid-state equipment.

By June 1988, the three Starship prototypes had completed more than 1,650 flights totalling more than 2,000 hours. In June 1987 the third prototype was flown to the Paris Air Show, where it made its public debut outside the USA. Basic certification for two-crew operation was granted by the FAA on 14 June 1988, with full certification for two-crew operation granted in December 1989. Single-pilot certification, requiring functioning autopilot and flight management systems, was granted in May 1990. The first full production aircraft (c/n NC-4, N2000S) made its maiden flight on 25 April 1989 and was used for demonstration flights. It was demonstrated at the Paris Air Show in 1989. This aircraft was intended to be the first to be delivered to a United States customer (Wayne Densch), but this was postponed because the FAA decided to apply new High Energy Radio Frequency regulations to the Model 2000. Deliveries began in 1989, and the first overseas delivery was made to a Danish customer in late 1990. In June 1988 Beech held orders for more than fifty Starships from customers in Canada, Europe, the United Kingdom and USA, but by the end of 1993 only 40 aircraft (Model 2000 and 2000A) had been produced and production is scheduled to be terminated with aircraft c/n NC-53.

## Model 2000A

In June 1992, Beechcraft announced the FAA certification of the improved performance Model 2000A. This model has a 400lb (181kg) increase in MTOW, a 490lb (222kg) increase in maximum payload, a 202lb (915kg) increase in maximum fuel capacity, a reduction in stalling speed, an increase in maximum range and a reduction in take-off distance. In addition, this variant offers a new simplified six-passenger interior which saves 90lb (41kg). The first aircraft of this type began operations early 1993.

## Model 2000

Two 1,200shp Pratt & Whitney Canada PT6A-67.

Span 54ft 4¾in (16.6m); length 46ft 1in (14.05m); height 12ft 11in (3.68m); wing area 280.9sq ft (26.09sq m).

Empty weight 8,916lb (4,044kg); maximum take-off weight 14,000lb (6,350kg); wing loading 49.84lb/sq ft (243.4kg/sq m); power loading 5.83lb/hp (2.64kg/hp).

Maximum speed 405mph (652km/h) at 25,000ft (7,620m); maximum cruising speed 389mph (626km/h) at 35,000ft (10,670m); rate of climb 3,380ft/min (1,030m/min) at sea level; service ceiling 41,000ft (12,495m); range at maximum cruise power, with 45min reserves 2,294 miles (3,691km).

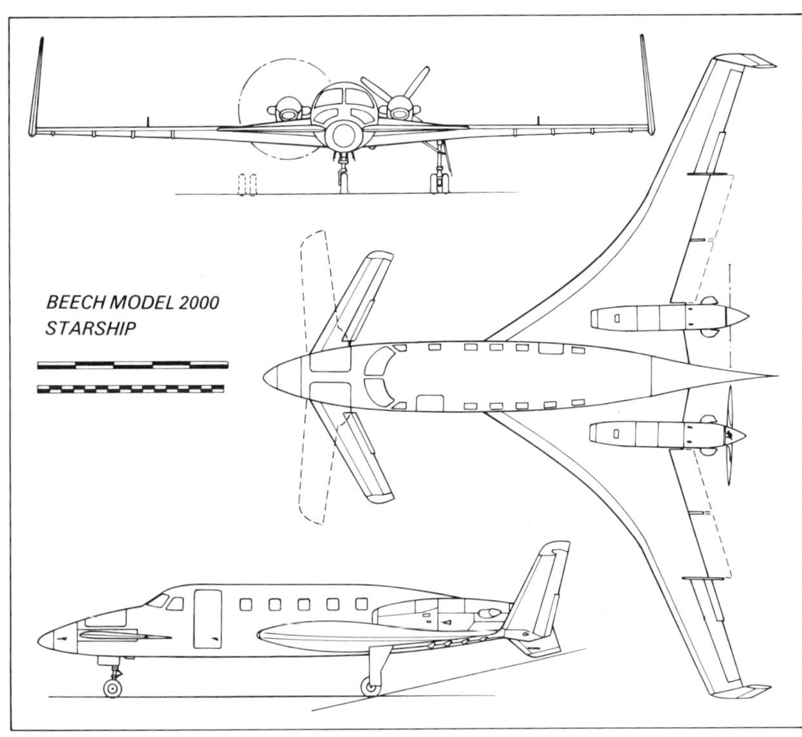

# Model 1300 Commuter

In January 1988 Beech announced the development of a regional airliner variant of its successful Super King Air B200. This new aircraft was designed for operations on long routes with light passenger loads, and, as its designation suggested (Model 1300), it provided accommodation for 13 passengers. The Model 1300 also had individual air, light and oxygen outlets at every seat, and dual overwing emergency exits. Dual outward-canted ventral fins were installed to increase stability at low speeds and high angles of attack. The adoption of panel-mounted avionics as standard enabled a baggage compartment to be provided in the aircraft's nose, capacity 13cu ft (0.37cu m), and the front-mounted instruments were interchangeable with those of the Model 99 Airliner. A belly cargo pod, capacity 44cu ft (1.25cu m), engine fire extinguishing system, and undercarriage and brake de-icing systems, were made available as options. Empty weight was 7,877lb (3,573kg) and the Model 1300 could cruise at 305mph (491km/h), maximum operating altitude being 25,000ft (7,620m).

Launch customer for the Model 1300 was Farmington based Mesa Airlines, New Mexico, which ordered five (with options on three additional aircraft), and the first production aircraft (N296YV) was handed over in late 1988. In all, production was limited to a total of 14 aircraft because the type was soon superseded by the larger Model 1900.

*One of the few Model 1300 Commuters to be built found its way to Burkina Faso as XT-MAX. The Model 1300 has dual ventral fins for increased stability at low speeds.* (J Brugaro)

# Miscellaneous Aircraft and Projects

## Model 17J

In the late thirties, design work was initiated on a single-seat military version of the Model 17. Intented to be powered with a 715hp Wright Cyclone, its cockpit was located aft of the wing trailing edge and a new upper gull-wing arrangement was designed to enhance pilot visibility.

## Model 20M

In 1937, Beech considered construction of a twin-engine derivative of the successful Model 17 to be powered by two Menasco C6S4 Super Buccaneer liquid-cooled six-cylinder piston engines each developing 260hp. With the emergence of the Model 18 development of the Model 20M came to a halt in 1938.

*In 1940, Beech engineers worked on a fighter aircraft evolved from the Model 17, to be powered by a 1,090hp Allison V-12 engine.* (Beech via Ed Phillips)

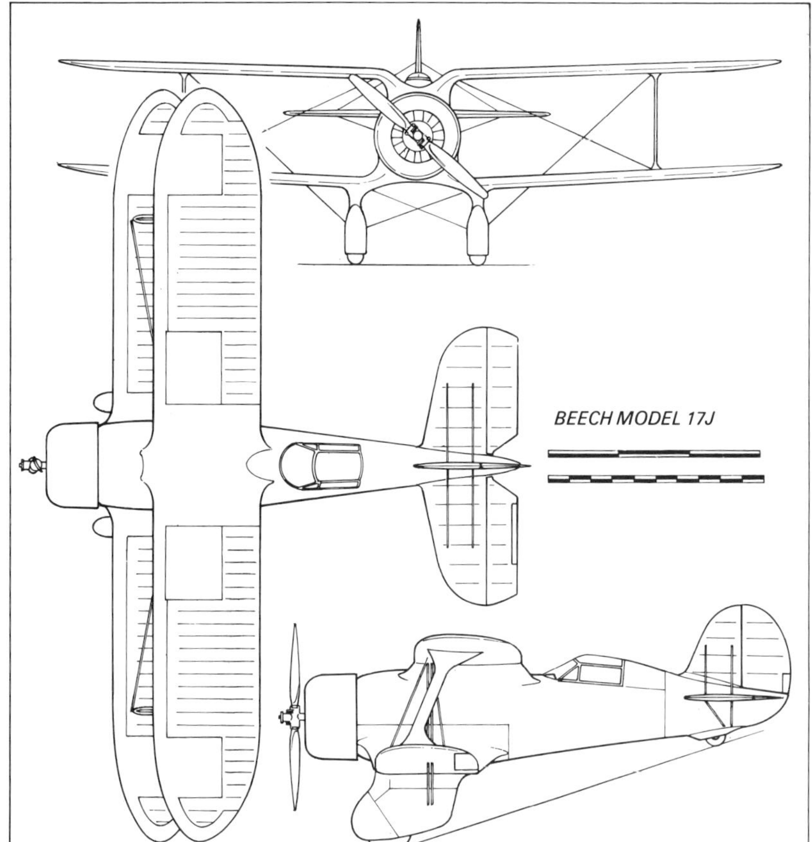


## Model 20M

Two 260hp Menasco C6S4.

Span 32ft (9.75m); length 26ft 9in (8.15m).

Calculated gross weight 4,850lb (2,197kg); power loading 9.32lb/hp (4.22kg/hp).

Expected maximum speed 240mph (386km/h); expected range 600 miles (965km).

## Beech/Morane-Saulnier MS 760 Paris Jet

On 28 April 1955 the French manufacturer Morane-Saulnier announced that an agreement had been signed with Beech Aircraft for the marketing of the MS 760 Paris four-seat twin-jet aircraft. The prototype Paris (No.1, F-BGVO) was shipped to New York by the following June and was presented throughout the United States to potential civil and military customers. The manufacture of fifty

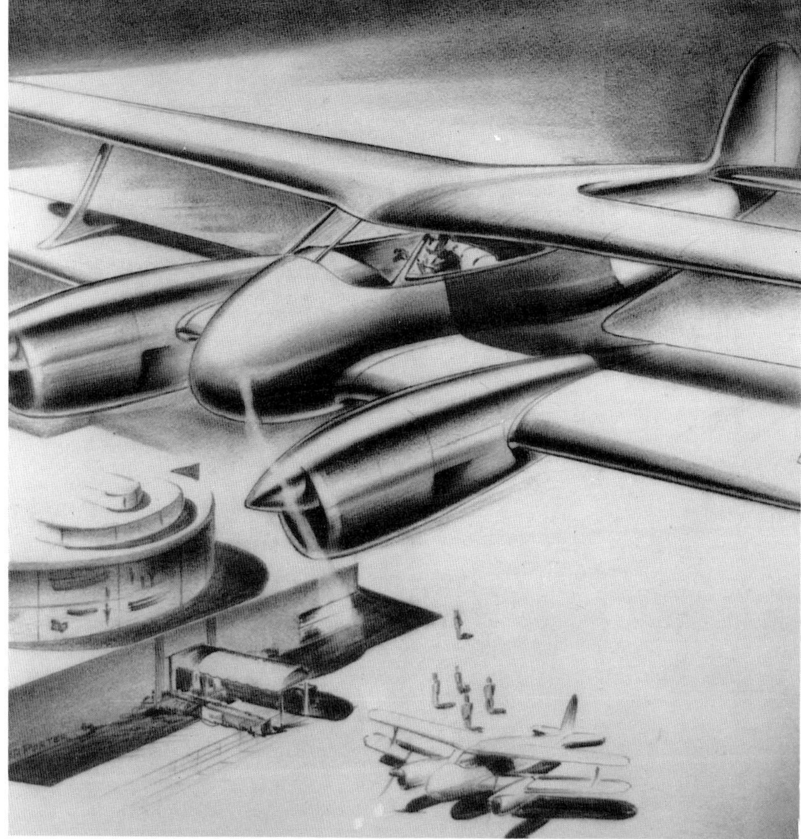

*The Beech Model 20M project.* (Beech via E Phillips)

*The French SNCASE Voltigeur was presented by Beech in the Army/Marines COIN programme.* (A J Pelletier collection)

MS 760s was then considered but eventually abandoned. The FAA Type Certificate was granted on 7 July 1958 and one production aircraft (No.6, N84J, ex-F-WJAB) was ordered by Beech on 29 October 1957 and delivered on 20 September 1958. It was used by Beech to test an air-refuelling system, and was eventually sold to John von Neumann of Geneva.

## Beechcraft PD 33/SNCASE Voltigeur

In mid-1963 Beech Aircraft and the French manufacturer SNCASE (Société Nationale de Constructions Aéronautique du Sud-Est) signed an agreement to compete for the Army/Marines COIN (Counter Insurgency) programme with the SE 117 Voltigeur twin-engined strike aircraft. The aircraft was then known as the Beech PD 33 but failed to attract the interest of the United States forces.

## Model 1080

Beech designed an air refuelling system which was flight tested using a Douglas B-26 (N7953C) and evaluated by the US Navy. Extension of the system was made through electrical release of the drogue which pulled out a 40ft-long flexible hose.

From this device, Beech evolved and produced a wingtip-mounted in-flight refuelling system for installation on the Boeing 707-3J9C tanker-transport aircraft operated by the Imperial Iranian Air Force. Designated the Beech Model 1080, this system is of the hose-and-drogue type, and was first displayed publicly at the Farnborough International airshow in September 1976. In 1984 Beech was awarded a $5.8m contract by Boeing for seventeen Model 1080s for installation on the eight KE-3A tankers ordered by the Royal Saudi Air Force. Other operators of the Model 1080 are Brazil (on its four KC-137s), Canada (on two CC-137s) and Morocco (on one Boeing 707-138B).

## Rutan Model 143 Triumph

During 1987 Beech announced that development projects were being undertaken by Burt Rutan and Beech-owned subsidiary Scaled Composites Inc. These concerned primarily a medium-sized pressurised twin-engined aircraft which drew on technology developed for the Starship I. It employed composite construction and had a three-surface configuration with a foreplane, a swept wing, a T-tail with rearward swept fin and forward swept tail unit, and a ventral fin. The airframe was designed to be readily adaptable to rotary, propeller-turbine or turbofan powerplants. A proof-of-concept prototype (N143SC), made its first flight on 14 July 1988 and was used until March 1990 as flight-test chase aircraft for the ARES programme and then stored.

*The Model 1080 air refuelling system as mounted on an Imperial Iranian Air Force Boeing 707-3J9C.* (Beech)

## Rutan Model 143

Two 1,800lb st (8,00kN) Williams International FJ44.

Span 48ft (14.63m); length 39ft (11.89m); height 10ft 10¾in (3.32m); wing area 199sq ft (18.49sq m).

Empty weight 5,000lb (2,268kg); maximum take-off weight 9,000lb (4,082kg); wing loading 45.1lb/sq ft (220.2kg/sq m).

Maximum speed 460mph (741km/h) at 35,000ft (10,670m); cruising speed 392mph (630km/h) at 35,000ft (10,670m); rate of climb 4,500ft/min (1,370m/min); service ceiling 41,000ft (12,500m); range 1,842 miles (2,965km).

## Rutan Model 81

This proof-of-concept aircraft, based on Rutan Design No.81, was built in 1987 to test engineering concepts for an all-composite single-engine aircraft to replace the Bonanza series. A five-seat aircraft, seating the pilot ahead of two rows of passengers, it was test flown during 1987 and, when the evaluation programme ended, no further development was undertaken by Beech. The powerplant was a 210hp Avco-Lycoming four-cylinder piston engine and cruising speed was 276mph (444km/h) at 25,000ft (7,620m).

## Advanced Technology Tactical Transport $AT^3$

Under a $2.5 million DARPA contract, Beech subsidiary Scaled Composites Inc (bought by Beech in June 1985 and sold back in November 1988) designed and built a 62 per cent scaled proof of concept (POC) version of an Advanced Technology Tactical Transport ($AT^3$), intended to fill the gap in military airlift capability between the Lockheed C-130 and large helicopters. The $AT^3$ prototype (N133SC) made its public début at Mojave Airport, California, on 20 January 1988, but it had flown for the first time on 29 December 1987. The airframe is of composite glass fibre/foam and carbon fibre, and, to achieve STOL performance, the aircraft has a unique 'trimaran' configuration with tandem high aspect ratio wings connected by long engine nacelles. Power is provided by a pair of 700shp Pratt & Whitney Canada PT6A-135 propeller-turbines. The forward wing has dihedral, the rear one anhedral. Eight fast-acting, electrically actuated flaps could be extended aft. For the start of take-off roll, they lowered rapidly in 1½ seconds to increase lift, enhancing STOL capability. All fuel is contained in the wings and engine nacelles. An in flight-openable rear loading ramp is incorporated for air dropping or paratroops.

## $AT^3$

Two 750shp Pratt & Whitney Canada PT6A-135A.

Span 53ft 2in (16.21m); length 44ft 10in (13.67m); 14ft 1in (4.29m); wing area (total) 297.56sq ft (27.64sq m ).

Maximum take-off weight 11,500lb (5,216kg); wing loading 43.7lb/sq ft (213.36kg/sq m); power loading 7.67lb/hp (3.48kg/hp).

Maximum speed 196mph (315km/h).

## JPATS/Beech PC-9 Mk.II

In August 1990 Beech and Pilatus Aircraft, of Switzerland, signed an agreement to compete for the US Navy and USAF Joint Primary Aircraft Training System (JPATS) programme, which calls for more than 700 new aircraft to replace ageing USAF Cessna T-37s and US Navy T-34s trainers. In addition, Beech Aircraft has signed a teaming agreement with British Aerospace,

*The tandem-wing configuration of the AT³ is well shown in this view of the prototype during a test flight.* (R Torres/Scaled Composites Inc)

which will be responsible for development of the ground based training system. The Beech/Pilatus proposal is a PC.9 variant known as the Beech PC-9 Mk.II, which uses an 1,707shp Pratt & Whitney PT6A-68 engine. The PC-9 Mk.II has an approximately 70 per cent redesigned airframe, including a strengthened fuselage, birdstrike proofing of the canopy, single-point refuelling, and a pressurised cockpit with zero-zero Martin-Baker Mk.16 ejection seats and new digital avionics including GPS, MLS, collision avoidance system and provision for a HUD (Head-up display).

A standard Pilatus PC-9 trainer (serialled 10421) was used by Beech as a proof-of-concept aircraft to develop the JPATS-configured PC-9 Mk.II, and the engineering test-bed aircraft (N26BA) flew for the first time during the autumn of 1992. By 16 June 1992 Beech JPATS demonstration pilots Erik Anderson and Robert Newsome had conducted more than 500 flights. The first Beech-built production prototype PC-9 Mk.II (N8284M), made its first flight, from Wichita, on 23 December 1992, followed by the second prototype on 29 July 1993.

## JPATS/Beech PC-9 Mk.II

One 1,707shp Pratt & Whitney PT6A-68.

Span 33ft 2in (10.124m); length 32ft 4in (10.175m); height 10ft 8in (3.26m), wing area 175.3sq ft (16.29sq m).

Empty weight 3,715lb (1,685kg); maximum take-off weight 4,960lb (2,250kg); wing loading 28.3lb/sq ft (138.1kg/sq m); power loading 2.9lb/hp (1.32kg/hp).

Maximum speed 310mph (500km/h) at sea level; climb rate 4,100ft/min (1,250m/min) at sea level; service ceiling 38,000ft (11,580m); range 75% power 1,020 miles (1,640km).

*Beech JPATS PC-9 Mk. II production prototype (N8284M) on its first flight, with the engineering testbed aircraft in the background.* (Beech)

# Pilotless Aircraft and Target Drones

Beech Aircraft also gained a solid reputation by designing and producing target drones which are operated by numerous nations throughout the world. Here is a selection of these special purpose systems.

## Model 997/BQM-126A

This system has been selected by the US Navy in its competition for a cost-effective recoverable replacement for the subsonic Ryan BQM-34 Firebee I. The most important feature of the BQM-126A is its ability to perform controlled high-g manoeuvres.

## Model 997/BQM-126A

One 899lb st (4kN) Microturbo TRI-60-2 Model 097; span 10ft (3.05m); length 18ft 1in (5.51m); empty weight 667lb (303kg); launching weight 1,398lb (634kg); maximum speed 667mph (1,073km/h); altitude range 20,000-40,000ft (6,000-12,200m); endurance 16½min to 1hr 36min.

## Model 999A

Variant of the MQM-107A Streaker supplied to Sweden and operated under RB06 Girun designation.

## Model 999E and H/MQM-107B

Models featuring system improvements tested and proven on MQM-107A. These include installation of a French Microturbo TRI-60 turbojet. Initial deliveries were made to the US Army and USAF. Under an April 1983 contract, the Army also ordered 139 production MQM-107Bs and the USAF 70. Deliveries began in 1984 and were completed in 1986. MQM-107Bs were also ordered by the United Arab Emirates, and delivered in 1983, which combine the shorter fuselage of the MQM-107A with a Microturbo TRI-60 turbojet.

## Model 999E

One 827lb st (3.68kN) Ames Industrial built Microturbo TRI-60-2 Model 074; dimensions as for MQM-107A except length 18ft 1in (5.51m); empty weight 540lb (245kg); launching weight 1,090lb (494kg); operating speed range 317-615mph (510-991km/h); operating height range 50,000-40,000ft (15,000-12,200m).

## Model 999D, F and L

These designations apply to various hybrid configurations of the MQM-107 system for delivery to international customers: Model 999D for South Korea, Model 999F for Taiwan, and Model 999L for Egypt.

## Model 1001/KDB-1/MQM-39A/ MQM-61A Cardinal 1025

The XKDB-1 pilotless remotely-controlled target, which won a US Navy design competition in 1955, was the first product of Beech's guided-missile division. Powered by a 125hp McCulloch six-cylinder opposed two-stroke turbo-supercharged air-cooled engine, it was intended as an out-of-sight target for surface-to-air and air-to-air gunnery practice. The US Navy placed two orders for substantial test quantities of XKDB-1s which were being built at Wichita, and the first free flights were accomplished at the USN Air Missile Test Center, Point Mugu, California, during the spring of 1957.

Production began in 1959 and more than 2,000 had been built by 1 March 1968. In various versions, the Model 1001 entered service with the US Navy and US Army as well as in Germany and Switzerland. The MQM-61A Cardinal version has been used to train the crews of Hawk, Redeye, Chaparral and other missiles and has supported US Army training in Canada, Alaska, Okinawa, Taiwan, Korea and Hawaii.

## Model 1001

One 125hp McCulloch TC6150-J-3; span 12ft 11½in (3.95m); length 15ft 1in (4.6m); height 3ft 4in (1.02m); wing area 24.4sq ft (2.27sq m); launching weight, with JATO 664lb (301kg); maximum speed over 350mph (560km/h); service ceiling over 43,000ft (13,100m); endurance at 25,000ft (7,600m) over one hour.

*Beech Model 997/BQM-126A.* (A J Pelletier)

### Model 1013

This Model was designed for photographic and television reconnaissance duties, carrying multiple cameras for battlefield surveillance by day and night, under remote control. Externally, it is almost identical to the Model 1001, but it is powered by a six-cylinder 110hp McCulloch engine. It has the alternative capability of delivering tactical supplies to isolated combat units.

#### Model 1013

One 110hp McCulloch; dimensions as for Model 1001; loaded weight 800lb (363kg); operational speed 260mph (418km/h); service ceiling 22,800ft (6,950m); endurance 75 minutes.

### Model 1019/KD2B-1/AQM-37A/Q-12

Developed in 1959, the AQM-37A has been in continuous use by the US forces since 1963. Winner of a joint Navy/Air Force design competition, the Model 1019 is a supersonic air-launched expendable high-altitude target drone, designed for air-to-air weapon systems evaluation and pilot training. The powerplant is a Rocketdyne twin-chamber liquid hypergolic bi-propellant rocket engine. The AQM-37A was launched successfully for the first time on 31 May 1961 at the PMTC, Point Mugu, California, and during tests it attained a height of more than 70,000ft (21,335m) and a speed of more than Mach 2, after being launched at 33,000ft (10,050m) from a McDonnell F-3B Demon. During weapon system training operations at Point Mugu in the spring of 1965, an AQM-37A, launched from a F-4B at a speed of Mach 1.3 at 47,000ft (14,300m), climbed to 91,000ft (27,750m) and maintained a speed of Mach 2.8. The AQM-37A has been operational since 1963 and a total of 1,470 had been delivered by 1 July 1967, including 15 to the United Kingdom.

In the spring of 1968, Beech received contracts to modify ten AQM-37As for the USAF and three for the US Army, making their electronics and destruct systems compatible with the current advanced weapons systems and range requirements of these Services. Beech was awarded a follow-on contract from the US Navy on 19 December 1972 for a further 202 AQM-37A targets, and production of these was completed in 1974. In late 1974 the US Naval Air Systems Command awarded Beech a contract to modify ten AQM-37A missile targets to perform low-altitude missions. This classified Navy programme, designated Sea Skipper (formerly Sea Skimmer), called for development and modification of missile targets capable of being air-launched over the sea at 1,200ft (365m) altitude and then flown as low as 50ft (15m) over predetermined points.

In early 1976 the US Army ordered 28 recoverable AQM-37As, fitted with a two-stage parachute system. Under this contract Beech produced two versions of the AQM-37A. One is a supersonic high-altitude target capable of operating at 70,000ft (21,335m); the other is a low-altitude modification which can be flown to within 180ft (55m) of the terrain. Deliveries began in November 1976. More recently, a modified version of the AQM-37A, known as the Challenger, was designed for expanded altitude and speed capability, and completed flight test and evaluation at the PMTC, Point Mugu, California, in 1980.

*Beech Model 1019/AQM-37A.* (Beech)

#### Model 1019

One 631lb st (286lkg st) Rocketdyne AMF LR64-P-4 rocket engine; span 3ft 3½in (1m); length 13ft 6½in (4,13m); height 1ft 8in (0.51m); wing area 9.35sq ft (0.87sq m); launching weight 565lb (256kg); operational speed Mach 0.4 to Mach 2.5; operational height 1,000-80,000ft (300-24,385m); endurance 15 minutes.

### Model 1025TJ

The Model 1025TJ is a turbojet-powered remote-controlled recoverable missile target, adapted from the MQM-39A. The basic Model 1025TJ accommodates multi-purpose equipment and can be converted for special missions.

#### Model 1025TJ

One 450lb st (204kg st) Continental Model 321-1; span 12ft 11in (3.94m); length 17ft (5.18m); height 3ft 9in (1.14m); launching weight 1,020lb (463kg); cruising speed over 460mph (740km/h); ceiling over 43,000ft (13,100m); endurance 1hr 12min at 25,000ft (7,600m).

### Model 1070 HAST

The HAST (High-Altitude Supersonic Target) is a continuation of the former Sandpiper project (*which see*), which concluded a successful flight test programme in 1968. The HAST is designed to be air-launched at speeds of Mach 1.2 to 2.5 and sustain manoeuvres with a 1.15 to 5g load factor. In 1971 Beech received authority to build twelve flight test units and thirteen refurbishment kits, deliveries of which began in 1972. By the end of 1975 the flight-test programme had been demonstrated successfully at up to Mach 3 at 80,000ft (24,385m). Subsequent missions in 1976 demonstrated flight at up to Mach 4 and 90,000ft (27,430m).

#### Model 1070

One 120 to 1,200lb st (0.53 to 5.34kN) UTC hybrid rocket engine; span 3ft 4in (1.02m); length 16ft 8in (5.08m); height 2ft 2in (0.66m); wing area 10.44sq ft (0.97sq m); launching weight 1,145lb (519kg); endurance at Mach 3 5min.

### Model 1072

This Model is the British version of the AQM-37A and designated Shorts SD.2 Stiletto. It has been re-engineered by Beech and Short Bros and Harland to meet British requirements, including virtually complete replacement of the radio and radar systems and control system changes. Principal modifications include incorporation of a British EMI T44/1 telemetry system, provision of additional 15V flight break-up system (WREBUS), installation of radioactive miss-distance indicator (RAMDI), modification to propulsion system to give Mach 2 performance at 60,000ft (18,300m), and changes in the radar augmentation system. Stiletto production totalled 190.

## Model 1088

Manufacturer's designation given to eleven targets supplied to Italy. Intended for air-launch from F-104S aircraft of the Italian Air Force.

## Model 1089 VSTT/MQM-107A Streaker

Beech took part, with Northrop Ventura, in a competition to design and develop a Variable-Speed Training Target (VSTT) for the US Army's Missile Command which was intended to serve as an aerial target for air defence systems such as Chaparral, Redeye, Hawk and Stinger. A total of 49 flights were completed in 1974, and on 4 April 1975 Beech announced the award of a $7.7 million initial contract for production of its winning design. These were built at Beech's Boulder, Colorado, Division. The first flight of a production MQM-107A was made in April 1976. In addition to its use by the US Army and other Department of Defence agencies, the MQM-107A system has been supplied by the US Army to Iran (MQM-107A) and Sweden and through Foreign Military Sales to Taiwan and South Korea.

## Model 1089

One 640lb st (2.85kN) Teledyne CAE 372-2 turbojet; span 9ft 10in (3m); length 16ft 10in (5.13m); height 4ft 10in (1.47m); wing area 27.16sq ft (2.52sq m); launching weight 1,014lb (460kg); operating speed range 285-575mph (459-925km/h); operating height range sea level to 40,000ft (12,200m); endurance 3hr plus.

## Model 1089E TEDS

In June 1975, Beech was awarded a $1.7-million contract to develop and produce flight demonstration examples of a new Tactical Expendable Drone System (TEDS). This contract covered a 21-month validation programme which included four months of flight testing and definition of the system in its tactical role. Basis of the Beech TEDS is the Model 1089E VSTT fitted with a Teledyne CAE turbojet and a payload developed by Sanders Associates.

## Model 1094/Matra Vanneau

In mid-1973 the French Armée de l'Air ordered a first batch of Model 1094s, deliveries of which began about a year later. A follow-on contract for 30 was announced in August 1974, and these were modified to Armée de l'Air requirements by Matra. The first target of this second batch was launched from Cazaux on 22 January 1975, and the

*The Beech/Shorts Model 1072 Stiletto was modified to meet British requirements.* (Shorts)

*A Beech Model 1094 Vanneau in position under a French Dassault Mirage III.* (Matra)

*A MQM-107A Streaker target drone.* (Beech)

first interception of a Vanneau by a Matra Super 530 missile was made on 28 May 1975.

### Model 1095

The British Ministry of Defence in August 1974 ordered ten Model 1095 targets. These were modified by Shorts to MoD specifications and were used for crew training exercises on the Hebrides range.

### Model 1098

Designation given to a batch of twenty AQM-37s for Israel.

*A US Navy Beech AQM-37C.* (Beech)

### Sandpiper

On 29 August 1967, Beech announced it was developing for the USAF's Armament Laboratory at Eglin AFB a high-performance rocket-powered target drone named Sandpiper. This system could simulate a wide variety of aircraft and missiles, and was powered by a hybrid engine that used both solid and liquid propellents. For development phase (Phase I), AQM-37A airframes were used as test vehicles, which were intended to develop and prove the proposed Sandpiper stability and control systems and programmed manoeuvre capabilities. Phase II covered development of the production model Sandpiper and established aircraft compatibility. The first flight test was completed successfully early in 1968 from a USAF F-4C Phantom II, and the test model reached a speed of Mach 2 at 49,000ft (15,000m) during a five-minute flight over the Gulf of Mexico. Subsequent flights progressed to Mach 2.5 at 77,000ft (23,500m).

### Sandpiper

Length 14ft 8in (4.47m); body diameter 13in (33cm); launching weight 633lb (287kg); maximum speed Mach 4; ceiling 90,000ft (22,500m).

### Model 1100/1101

Recoverable versions of AQM-37 (48 delivered to US Army).

### Model 1102

US Navy variant (415 delivered).

### Model 1104/AQM-37C

US Navy variant (56 delivered).

### Model 1105/AQM-37C

Variant version of AQM-37C designed for missions at Mach 4 and 100,000ft (30,480m). This variant features thermal protection of leading surfaces. Initially the US Navy funded eight vehicles for the development programme, and later funded development of 35 kits to modify AQM-37Cs to Variant configuration.

### Model 1107/AQM-37A

Current basic AQM-37A target, of which the US Navy ordered a further 205 in 1983, for delivery between February 1984 and September 1985.

### Model 1108

Training version of UK Model 1095, with single-chamber engine and modified performance. Total of 30 delivered to British MoD by late 1984.

### Raider

The Raider, which made its public debut at the 1985 Paris Air Show, is a tactical RPV making use of the airframe and powerplant of the MQM-107B. Ground-launched, it has both pre-programmed and ground-controlled capabilities, and is recoverable. Special missions payloads, housed in detachable pods, include passive and active ECM.

# Appendices

## Appendix I

# Milestones in Travel Air and Beech History

### 1891

Birth of Walter H Beech, at Pulaski, Tennessee (*30 January*).

### 1903

Birth of Olive Ann Mellor in Waverly (*25 September*).

### 1921

W H Beech, flying a Laird Swallow, wins the Aerial Tournament Triangular Race, at Nelson, Nebraska (*14-16 July*).

W H Beech, flying a Laird Swallow, wins the Aerobatic Contest at Liberal, Kansas (*7-9 November*).

### 1922

W H Beech, flying a Laird Swallow, wins the Aerobatic Contest of the Mid-West Flying Meet, at Monmouth, Illinois (*15-17 June*).

W H Beech, flying a Laird Swallow, wins the Tarkio Aero Meet Efficiency Contest and Free-For-All race (*27-29 July*).

W H Beech, flying a Laird Swallow, wins first prize in the On-to-Detroit race (*9 October*).

### 1923

W H Beech becomes a principal of the Swallow Airplane Manufacturing Company, in charge of all field work.

### 1924

W H Beech, flying a Laird Swallow, wins the Admiral Fullman Derby, at St Louis, Missouri.

W H Beech, flying a Laird Swallow, wins the Wichita Beacon Trophy Light Commercial Plane Handicap race, and the Walter Innes Trophy for two-seat, low-horsepower aircraft.

W H Beech, determined to prove advantage of the metal airframe, resigns from Swallow.

The Travel Air Manufacturing Company is founded by Walter H Beech, Lloyd Stearman and Clyde V Cessna.

### 1925

Travel Air Inc formed at Wichita, Kansas (*January*).

W H Beech, flying a Travel Air Model 2000, wins the Gliding Trophy at Tulsa Air Meet, and the Tulsa Daily World Trophy Speed Race.

First Ford Reliability Tour. Three Beech-designed Travel Air Model 3000s finish in first, second and third places.

### 1926

W H Beech, flying a Travel Air Model 2000, wins the J H Turner Trophy (*9 May*).

W H Beech, flying a Travel Air Model 4000, wins the Second Ford Reliability Tour (*8 August*).

Fred D Hoyt wins the Sesqui Rallye California to Philadelphia cross-country race (National Air Races) on a Travel Air 2000, in 146 hours (*4 September*).

W H Beech, flying a Travel Air Model 2000, wins the Flint Aero Association Trophy, at Flint Air Meet.

### 1927

A Travel Air Model 5000, piloted by Emory B Bronte and Ernest L Smith, is the first commercial aircraft to fly from California to Hawaii.

The Pacific Coast Air Derby is won by H C Lippiatt in a Travel Air Model 5000.

The Western Flying Trophy (National Air Races) is won by Eugene Detmer flying a Travel Air Model 2000.

The Dole Race, from Oakland, California, to Honolulu, Hawaii, is won by Arthur C Goebel and Lt W V Davis in the Travel Air *Woolaroc* (*16 August*).

### 1928

The Oakland to Los Angeles race is won by H C Lippiatt flying a Travel Air Model 6000.

Travel Airs entered by Doug Davis win first and second places in Atlantic Air Races.

D C Warren, flying a Travel Air Model 3000, wins the Civilian Free-For-All 50-mile race at National Air Races.

### 1929

The Portland to Cleveland Air Derby is won by Ted A Wells, flying a Travel Air D-4000, in 14hr 44min.

J O Donaldson wins the Rim of Ohio Derby flying a Travel Air B-4000.

The Toronto to Cleveland Race is won by Herbert St Martin, flying a Travel Air A-6000A.

Billy Parker wins the On-to-Tulsa 500-mile Derby with a Travel Air B-4000.

Louise Thaden wins the Santa Monica to Cleveland Women's Derby, flying a Travel Air B-4000.

Louise Thaden sets a new US altitude record for women, reaching more than 20,000ft in a Travel Air 4000.

Louise Thaden, in a Travel Air 2000, establishes a new endurance record for women of 22hr 3min 12sec (*16-17 March*).

The Mexico City of Kansas Air Derby is won by Art Goebel, flying a Travel Air 6000.

Doug Davis, flying the Travel Air Mystery Ship, wins the Experimental ship race at National Air Races at 113.38mph (182.43km/h); and the Thompson Trophy 50-mile closed course Free-for-All race at 194.9mph (305.54km/h).

Eric Wood, flying the Travel Air Mystery Ship, sets a New York to Boston speed record of 52min.

**1930**

A new Montreal to New York speed record is set at 115min by Dale Jackson, piloting the Travel Air Mystery Ship.

Florence L Barnes establishes a new speed record for women of 196.19mph (315.67km/h) in a Travel Air Mystery Ship at Los Angeles, California (*5 August*).

Capt Frank M Hawks, on a Travel Air Mystery Ship, flies from New York to Los Angeles in 14hr 50min 43sec, and sets a new east–west transcontinental record (*6 August*).

Capt Frank M Hawks flies a Travel Air Mystery Ship from Los Angeles to New York in 12hr 25min 3sec elapsed time (11hr 40min 30sec flying time), for a new west–east transcontinental record (*13 August*).

James Haizlip arrives second in the Thompson Trophy Race at the controls of a Travel Air Mystery Ship. Average speed: 199.8mph (321.47km/h). Paul Adams arrives in fourth place with a Travel Air Speedwing at 142.64mph (229.51km/h) (*September*).

Capt Frank M Hawks in a Travel Air Mystery Ship flies from New York to Havana, Cuba, in 9hr 21min elapsed time (*6 November*).

Capt Frank M Hawks in a Travel Air Mystery Ship flies from Havana to New York in 8hr 44min elapsed time (*9 November*).

Walter Beech marries Olive Ann Mellor.

**1932**

W Beech and his wife found the Beech Aircraft Company (*April*).

First flight of the Model 17R, with Pete Hill at the controls (*4 November*).

**1933**

The Texaco Trophy Race (Miami Air Races) is won by E H Wood flying the Beech Model 17 (*January*).

**1934**

Arlene Davis wins first place in the 50-mile Woman's Handicap in the National Air Races, flying Model B17L c/n 37.

**1936**

First, second and fourth places in Unlimited Race for Frank E Phillips Trophy at Denver Mile-High are won by Beech Model 17s (first place winner, Bill Ong).

New national speed record for women is set by Louise Thaden in a Model 17 at St Louis, Missouri, with 197.958mph (318.514km/h).

Louise Thaden and Blanche Noyes win first place in the Bendix Trophy race flying Beech Model C17R No.62 in 14hr 55min 1sec, at an average speed of 165.346mph (266.042km/h) (*4 September*).

**1937**

First flight of the Model 18A, with James N Peyton at the controls (*15 January*).

Jacqueline Cochran placed third in the Bendix Trophy Race flying Beech 17 No.13 in 10hr 29min 8sec, at an average speed of 194.74mph (313.337km/h) (*3 September*).

New US women's speed record is set by J Cochran flying a Model 17W at 203.895mph (328.067km/h).

Art Chester, flying a Model 17, wins the Unlimited Race for Frank E Phillips Trophy.

**1939**

Max Constant wins fourth place in the Bendix Trophy Race flying a Beech Model D17W in 8hr 49min 33sec at an average speed of 231.366mph (372.268km/h) (*2 September*).

Seattle to Alaska speed record is set by Kenneth Neese flying a Model 17 in 10hr 20min.

Jacqueline Cochran sets a new national women's altitude record, flying a Model 17, with 30,052.43ft (9,160m).

**1940**

T A Petras, flying a Beech Model D17, climbs to 21,500ft (6,553m) above Antarctica in order to measure cosmic radiation intensity (*9 March*).

W H Beech and H C Rankin, flying a Model 18, win the New York–Miami race (B MacFadden Trophy) in 4hr 37min at an average speed of 234mph (376km/h).

**1941**

First flight of Model 26/AT-10 Wichita, with H C Rankin at the controls (*19 July*).

**1944**

First flight of Model 28/XA-38 Grizzly, with Vern L Carstens at the controls (*7 May*).

**1945**

First flight of Model 35 Bonanza, with Vern L Carstens at the controls (*22 December*).

**1946**

Three Model D18s, flown by K G Clegg, D M McVicar and D Cunningham, fly from Wichita to Cairo, Egypt, via Terre–Neuve, Azores, Casablanca and Tripoli (*November*).

**1947**

First flight of Model 34 Twin-Quad (*October*).

**1948**

First flight of Model 45 Mentor, with Vern L Carstens at the controls (*2 December*).

**1949**

W Wodon, flying a Bonanza, sets a new distance record for light aircraft of 2,407.383 miles (3,873.479km) from Honolulu to Oakland, in 22hr 6min (*13 January*).

Capt William P Odom makes a nonstop flight of 4,957.24 miles (7,976km) in a Bonanza, between Hawaii and Teterboro, New Jersey (*7 and 8 March*).

First flight of Model 50 Twin Bonanza, with Vern L Carstens at the controls (*11 November*).

**1950**

Death of Walter H Beech, at Wichita, Kansas (*29 November*).

Beech Aircraft produces jettisonable fuel tanks for USAF F-80, F-86, F84E and F-94.

**1951**

Around-the-world flight by Congressman Peter F Mack Jr in the same Bonanza flown by Bill Odom. Mack covered 30 countries on his solo flight.

**1952**

First flight of the YL-23 Seminole (*30 January*).

World speed record for light aircraft set by Paul Burniat, of Brussels, Belgium, in a Bonanza, at 140.32mph (225.776km/h).

**1953**

Marion Hart, aged 61, accomplishes a solo flight across the Atlantic flying a Bonanza (*27 August*).

Bonanzas finish first, second, third and fourth in the first annual Jaycee Transcontinental Air Cruise, Philadelphia to Palm Desert, California. W H Hinselman wins first place and the O A Beech Trophy.

**1954**

Ann Waddell, flying a Bonanza, wins O A Beech Trophy for fastest speed in annual Skylady Derby, from Raton, New Mexico, to Kansas City.

Three Bonanzas win first, second and third places in the second annual Jaycee Transcontinental Air Cruise. W C Butler wins first place.

**1955**

Aerospace research and development operation is established at Boulder, Colorado.

Ann Waddell, flying a Bonanza, wins the Skylady Derby, from Little Rock, Arkansas, to Raton, New Mexico.

The Beech Model 73 Jet Mentor makes its first flight (*18 December*).

**1956**

First flight of Model 95 Travel Air (*6 August*).

Model E35 Bonanzas win first and second places in the Powder Puff Air Derby. Winning pilot is Frances Bera.

Beech Aircraft enters the field of missile targets with production of the KDB-1 for the US Navy.

**1957**

Alice Roberts, flying a C35 Bonanza, wins the Powder Puff Air Derby.

**1958**

Capt Pat Boling, in a J35 Bonanza, flies from Manilla to Pendelton, Oregon, (6,865.32 miles/11,031.82km) in 45hr 43min *(31 July*).

First flight of Model 65 Queen Air (*28 August*).

Frances Bera, flying an A35 Bonanza, wins first place in the Powder Puff Air Derby.

**1959**

First flight of Model 35-33 Debonair (*14 September*).

**1960**

James D Webber, flying a Queen Air, sets a new world altitude class record with 34,895ft (10,636m) (*8 February*).

First flight of Model 55 Baron (*29 February*).

**1961**

First flight of Model 80 Queen Air (*22 June*).

First flight of Model 23 Musketeer, with S C Tuttle at the controls (*23 October*).

Frances Bera, flying an E35 Bonanza, wins first place in the Powder Puff Air Derby.

First flight of the AQM-37A target missile.

**1962**

Frances Bera, flying an F35 Bonanza, wins first place in the Powder Puff Air Derby.

**1963**

First flight of Model 65-90 King Air (*24 January*).

**1965**

First flight of Model 88 Queen Air (*2 July*).

**1966**

First flight of Model A88 (*28 March*).

Robert L and Joan Wallick, flying a C55 Baron, fly around the world, covering 23,629 miles (38,019km) in 5 days 6hr 17min 10sec (*June*).

Beechcraft Turbo Baron 56TC and Model 99 are introduced.

Delivery of the 25,000th Beechcraft, a King Air A90 to Westinghouse Corporation.

First flight of Model 69 Duke, with Bob Hagan at the controls (*29 December*).

**1967**

R L Wallick, flying a C55 Baron, sets a new speed record around the world (in C.1 and C.1d categories) with 186.57mph (300.20km/h) (*1 June*).

Judy Wagner, flying a K35 Bonanza, wins first place in the Powder Puff Air Derby.

**1968**

Judy Wagner flying a K35 Bonanza, Janis Hobbs flying a Musketeer, and Pat McEwen flying an S35 Bonanza, win first, second and third places in the 18th Angel Derby (*22-25 April*).

Models E33B, E33C and Bonanza 36 are introduced.

AQM-37A supersonic missile target production is transferred from Wichita to Boulder Division.

FAA certification and first delivery of Model 99 Airliner.

**1969**

First flight of Model 100 King Air (*17 March*).

First flight of Model 58 Baron (*23 June*).

Beech Aircraft Corporation and Hawker Siddeley Aviation announce plans to co-operate on the development and marketing of a range of business jets, including the HS.125 (*18 December*).

**1971**

Louise Sacchi, flying an A36 Bonanza, sets a new speed record (C.1.d class) from New York to London, at an average speed of 198.8mph.

**1972**

First flight of Model 200 Super King Air (*27 October*).

**1975**

First flight of Model 77 Skipper (*6 February*).

**1976**

Delivery of 2,000th Model B55 Baron.

**1977**

Beech Aircraft Corporation completes production flight testing of the 10,000th Model 35 Bonanza (*17 February*).

The first Beechcraft T-44A advanced trainer is delivered to NAS Corpus Christi, Texas (*5 April*).

First flight of Model 76 Duchess (*24 May*).

A Model 58TC is the 40,000th Beechcraft built.

**1979**

Delivery of the 2,000th King Air (*September*).

**1980**

First flight of Model C99, marking the company's return to the commuter airliner market (*20 June*).

The Wright Brothers Memorial Trophy is presented to Olive Ann Beech (*12 December*).

**1981**

Beech Aircraft Corporation delivers the 3,000th King Air (*17 April*).

**1982**

Beech Aircraft Corporation celebrates the 35th anniversary of the start of Bonanza production. Almost 15,000 Bonanzas have been built, including some 10,400 of the V-tail Model 35 (*25 March*).

First flight of Model 38 Lightning (*14 June*).

First flight of Model 1900 (*3 September*).

**1983**

First flight of Model 300 (*3 September*).

**1985**

Model 400 Beechjet is introduced.

**1986**

First flight of Model 2000 Starship 1 (*15 February*).

**1987**

First flight of $AT^3$ Tactical Transport (*29 December*).

**1988**

First flight of Model 350 Super King Air (*September*).

**1989**

First flight of Model 400A Beechjet (*22 September*).

Model 1900D is introduced.

**1991**

First flight of Beechcraft T-1A Jayhawk (*5 July*).

Model C90B King Air is introduced.

**1992**

First delivery of a T-1A Jayhawk to the USAF (*17 January*).

Delivery of the 50,000th Beechcraft, a Model C90B King Air (*23 March*).

**1993**

Death of Olive Ann Beech, at her home in Wichita (*6 July*).

**1994**

Introduction of Model C90SE King Air (*April*).

# Appendix II

# Travel Air Model Designations

| Model | Year | ATC number | -2 number | Date approved | Engine and remarks |
|---|---|---|---|---|---|
| Travel Air No.1 | 1925 | – | – | – | Curtiss OX-5 |
| Model A | 1925 | – | – | – | Curtiss OX-5 or OXX-6 |
| B6 Special | 1925 | – | – | – | Curtiss C-6 |
| BH | 1926 | – | – | – | Wright-Hispano |
| BW | 1926 | – | – | – | Wright J-4 |
| CH | 1926 | – | – | – | Wright-Hispano A |
| 5000 | 1926 | – | – | – | Wright J-5-C |
| CW | 1927 | – | – | – | Wright J-4 |
| Model B | 1927 | – | – | – | Curtiss OX-5 or OXX-6 |
| 8000 | 1927 | 37 | – | 04.28 | Fairchild-Caminez |
| 9000 | 1927 | 38 | – | 04.28 | Siemens-Halske |
| 2000 | 1927 | 30 | – | 03.28 | Curtiss OX-5, OXX-6 |
| S-2000 | 1927 | 30 | – | 03.28 | Curtiss OX-5, OXX-6 |
| 3000 | 1928 | 31 | – | 03.28 | Wright-Hispano Model A or E |
| 4000 | 1928 | 32 | – | 03.28 | Wright J-5 |
| W-4000 | 1928 | 112 | – | 02.29 | Warner R-420 Scarab |
| DW-4000 | 1928 | 112 | – | 02.29 | Warner R-420 Scarab |
| A-4000 | 1928 | 148 | – | 05.29 | Axelson R-612 |
| C-4000 | 1928 | 149 | – | 05.29 | Curtiss Challenger |
| 6000 | 1928 | 100 | 2–28 | 01.29 | Wright J-5 |
| A-6000-A | 1928 | 116 | – | 02.29 | Pratt & Whitney R-1340 Wasp |
| SA-6000-A | 1928 | 175 | – | 07.29 | Pratt & Whitney R-1340 Wasp |
| 6000-B | 1928 | 130 | – | 07.29 | Wright J-6-9 |
| S-6000-B | 1928 | 130 | – | 03.29 | Wright J-6-9 |
| 7000 | 1928 | – | – | – | Wright J-4 or J-6 (category -3 licence) |
| D-2000 | 1928 | – | – | – | Curtiss OX-5, OXX-6 (experimental) |
| SD-2000 | 1928 | – | – | – | Aeromarine B (experimental) |
| 2000-T | 1928 | – | 2–368 | 20.07.31 | Milwaukee-Tank V-470 or V-502 |
| 10-B | 1929 | 278 | – | 02.12.29 | Wright J-6-8 |
| 10-D | 1929 | 278 | – | 02.12.29 | Wright J-6-7 |
| SC-2000 | 1929 | 111 | – | 02.29 | Curtiss C-6 |
| D-3000 | 1929 | – | – | – | Wright-Hispano (experimental) |
| B-4000 | 1929 | 146 | – | 06.29 | Wright J-5C |
| BC-4000 | 1929 | 189 | – | 07.29 | Curtiss Challenger |
| SBC-4000 | 1929 | – | 2–154 | 11.29 | Curtiss Challenger |
| BE-4000 | 1929 | 188 | – | 07.29 | Wright J-6 |
| J4-4000 | 1929 | – | 2–243 | 07.30 | Wright J-4 |
| BM-4000 | 1929 | 147 | – | 05.29 | Wright J-5C |
| B9-4000 | 1929 | – | 2–381 | 09.31 | Wright J-6 |
| D9-4000 | 1929 | – | – | – | Wright J-6-9 (restricted) |
| D-4000 | 1929 | – | 2–84 | 02.07.29 | Wright J-5 |
| E-4000 | 1929 | 188 | – | 07.29 | Wright J-6-5 |
| K-4000 | 1929 | 205 | – | 17.08.29 | Kinner K-5 |
| 4000-T | 1929 | – | – | – | Wright J-6-7 (experimental) |
| W-4000 | 1929 | 112 | – | 02.29 | Warner R-420 Scarab |
| SA-6000-A | 1929 | 175 | – | 07.29 | Pratt & Whitney R-1340 Wasp |
| 4-D | 1929 | 254 | – | 12.10.29 | Wright J-6-7 |
| Z4-D | – | – | – | – | Wright R-760 (restricted) |
| 4-P | 1929 | 280 | 2–60 | 12.12.29 | A.C.E. La-1 |

| Model | Year | ATC number | -2 number | Date approved | Engine and remarks |
|---|---|---|---|---|---|
| 4-S | 1929 | – | – | – | Powell Power Engine (experimental) |
| 4-U | 1929 | – | 2–432 | 28.12.32 | Comet (conversions) |
| D-4-D | 1929 | – | 2–178 | 02.30 | Wright J-6-7 |
| W-4-B | 1929 | – | – | – | Wright J-6-5 (previously experimental) |
| 6-B | 1930 | 352 | – | 13.08.30 | Wright J-6-7 |
| A-6-A | 1931 | 436 | – | 160.7.31 | Pratt & Whitney Wasp C1 |
| 12Q | 1931 | 401 | – | 12.02.31 | Wright L-320 Gipsy |
| 12K | 1931 | 406 | – | 23.03.31 | Kinner B-5 |
| 12W | 1931 | 407 | – | 23.03.31 | Warner R-420 Scarab |
| A14D | 1932 | 442 | – | 13.08.31 | Wright R-975E |
| B14B | 1932 | 485 | – | 01.06.32 | Wright R-975E |
| B14R | 1932 | – | 2–403 | 02.03.32 | Wright SR-975E |
| 14C | 1931 | – | 2–357 | 12.06.31 | Curtiss Challenger |
| C14B | 1932 | – | – | – | Wright R-975E |
| C14R | 1932 | – | – | – | Wright J-6-9 |
| B15B | 1932 | 485 | – | 01.06.32 | Wright R-975E |
| 15C | 1931 | 426 | – | – | Curtiss Challenger |
| 15D | 1931 | 444 | – | 22.08.31 | Wright R-760E |
| 15N | 1931 | 425 | – | 04.06.31 | Kinner C-5 |
| 16E | 1932 | 463 | – | 26.02.32 | Wright R-540 |
| 16K | 1932 | 411 | – | 07.04.31 | Kinner B-5 |
| 16W | 1932 | 429 | – | 18.06.31 | Warner R-420 Scarab |
| L4000 | 1941 | – | 2–560 | 08.41 | Lycoming R-680 |

Appendix III

# Surviving Travel Air Aircraft

| c/n | Type | Registration | c/n | Type | Registration | c/n | Type | Registration |
|---|---|---|---|---|---|---|---|---|
| 1 | 1000 | N241 | 539 | 4000 | N6010 | 884 | 6-B | NC8112 |
| A-1 | 4000 | N501V | 577 | 4000 | N6073 | 886 | D-4000 | N8114 |
| 3 | 2000 | N3027 | 589 | 4000 | N6085 | 887 | D-4000 | N8115 |
| 107 | 3000 | N1084 | 598 | 4000 | N6094 | 894 | 4000 | N8192 |
| 146 | 4000 | N510E | 603 | 2000 | N6105 | 895 | 4000 | N8134 |
| 164 | 4000 | N1499 | 604 | 4000 | N6106 | 902 | L-4000 | N8132 |
| 168 | 4000 | N2709Y | 614 | 4000 | N6116 | 913 | 4000 | N8877 |
| 181 | 4000 | N901 | 615 | 2000 | NC6117 | 914 | 4000 | N8140 |
| 185 | 2000 | N2937 | 628 | 2000 | N6130 | 926 | D-4000 | N8708 |
| 196 | 4000 | N1592 | 644 | 2000 | N6146 | 938 | D-4000 | N5140X |
| 203 | D-4000 | N1082 | 645 | 2000 | N6147 | 942 | D-4000 | N8175 |
| 214 | 4000 | N1339 | 655 | 4000 | N6203 | 944 | 4000 | N8715 |
| 222 | 4000 | N1473 | 669 | 2000 | N6217 | 948 | 2000 | N99X |
| 225 | 2000 | N1572 | 673 | 2000 | N6221 | 958 | 4000 | N9803 |
| 226 | 2000 | N3882 | 707 | 2000 | N6268 | 967 | 6000 | N8159 |
| 241 | 2000 | N1848 | 713 | 2000T | N6274 | 976 | 4000 | N8700 |
| 256 | 4000 | N3242 | 715 | 2000 | N6276 | 986 | S-6000-B | N8865 |
| 263 | 4000 | N3342 | 717 | 2000 | N6278 | 1001 | B9-4000 | NC8717 |
| 264 | 4000 | N4369P | 720 | 2000 | CF-AFG | 1003 | 4000 | N8719 |
| 288 | 4000 | N3670 | 721 | 2000 | NC6282 | 1006 | 4000 | N8842 |
| 289 | 2000 | N3677 | 730 | 4000 | N6263 | 1036 | S-6000-B | N9842 |
| 306 | 4000 | N3823 | 744 | 4000 | N6297 | 1044 | 4000 | N9824 |
| 319 | 4000 | N3945 | 745 | C-4000 | N6298 | 1047 | 4000 | N9826 |
| 321 | 3000 | N3947 | 756 | 3000 | N6415 | 1057 | 2000 | N9848 |
| 326 | 4000 | N3977 | 763 | 4000 | N6422 | 1059 | B-4000 | N9872 |
| 331 | 2000 | N4006 | 766 | 4000 | N6425 | 1064 | B-4000 | N9904 |
| 364 | 4000 | N4264 | 776 | 4000 | N6455 | 1067 | 4000 | N9923 |
| 370 | 2000 | N4317 | 785 | 4000 | N6464 | 1099 | ? | N9966 |
| 372 | 4000 | N4319 | 798 | D-4000 | N6478 | 1103 | B9-4000 | N9917 |
| 374 | 4000 | N4371 | 799 | 4000 | N6551C | 1104 | E-4000 | N9918 |
| 378 | 2000 | N4418 | 805 | 2000 | N9004 | 1117 | 4000 | N9907 |
| 381 | 4000 | N4421 | 806 | 4000 | N9005 | 1118 | 4000 | N9908 |
| 416 | 4000 | N1004 | 808 | 4000 | N4251N | 1122 | L-4000 | N9912 |
| 418 | 4000 | N4834 | 811 | 4000 | N9010 | 1127 | 4000 | N9943 |
| 441 | 4000 | N4910 | 821 | 4000 | N9021 | 1130 | 4000 | N9946H |
| 446 | 2000 | N4848 | 826 | 4000 | N9024 | 1150 | C-4000 | N9952 |
| 447 | 4000 | N4949 | 828 | D-4000 | N9027 | 1151 | E-4000 | CF-JNW |
| 450 | 2000 | N4952 | 831 | 2000 | N9030 | 1156 | L-4000 | N9958 |
| 475 | 4000 | N2709 | 832 | 4000 | N9031 | 1157 | B-4000 | N9954 |
| 482 | 4000 | N5282 | 833 | 4000 | N9032 | 1158 | L-4000 | N9188 |
| 483 | 4000 | N5283 | 839 | 6-B | N9038 | 1171 | B-4000 | N604H |
| 490 | 2000 | N5290 | 849 | E-4000 | N9048 | 1175 | D-2000 | N607H |
| 513 | 4000 | N5424 | 850 | 4000 | N9049 | 1177 | B-4000 | N681H |
| 515 | D-4-D | N434P | 861 | E-4000 | N9079 | 1180 | 4000 | N609H |
| 516 | 4000 | N5427 | 862 | 4000 | N9080 | 1182 | 4000 | N615H |
| 518 | L-4000 | N5429 | 865 | S-6000-B | N9084 | 1213 | 2000 | N666H |
| 519 | 3000 | N5432 | 867 | 4000 | N90539 | 1219 | 4000 | N674H |
| 522 | 4000 | N5433 | 868 | 4000 | N31439 | 1220 | E-4000 | N645H |
| 534 | 4000 | N6005 | 869 | E-4000 | N9088 | 1222 | B-4000 | N622H |
| 536 | 2000 | N6003 | 879 | 2000 | N8108 | 1224 | E-4000 | NC648H |

| c/n | Type | Registration | c/n | Type | Registration | c/n | Type | Registration |
|---|---|---|---|---|---|---|---|---|
| 1229 | 4000 | N653H | 1344 | C-4000 | N443N | RD2002 | R | N613K |
| 1232 | B-4000 | N675H | 1345 | E-4000 | N440N | 2003 | A-6-A | N377M |
| 1262 | B-4000 | N13906 | 1350 | D-4000 | N436N | 2003 | B-14-R | N12311 |
| 1264 | 4-D | N692H | 1353 | 4000 | N439N | R2004 | R | NR1313 |
| 1266 | D-4000 | N671H | 1355 | 4000 | N460N | 2004 | 16-K | N422W |
| 1271 | L-4000 | N359M | 1361 | D-4000 | N455N | 2005 | 12-Q | N439W |
| 1277 | 4000 | N691K | 1365 | B-4000 | N174V | 2005 | S-6000-B | N87B |
| 1282 | D-4-D | N606K | 1372 | D-4-D | N473N | 2008 | A-14-D | N12323 |
| 1291 | D-4000 | N625K | 1376 | D-4-D | N475N | 2009 | 12-W | N443W |
| 1295 | 4000 | N367M | 1378 | E-4000 | N471N | 2011 | 10-D | N418N |
| 1303 | E-4000 | N390N | 1379 | E-4000 | N477N | 2017 | 12-W | N413W |
| 1307 | E-4000 | N22466 | 1383 | 4000 | N469N | 2023 | 12-Q | N496W |
| 1309 | 4000 | N389M | 1387 | 4000 | N154V | 2024 | S-6000-B | N411N |
| 1310 | L-4000 | N390M | 1397 | 4000 | N158V | 2024 | 12-Q | N497W |
| 1317 | E-4000 | N397M | 1401 | 4000 | N166V | 2030 | 12-Q | N417W |
| 1319 | E-4000 | N390A | 1402 | 2000 | N167V | 2031 | 12-W | N418W |
| 1320 | 4-D | N697K | 1403 | 4000 | N168V | 2038 | 12-W | N11713 |
| 1323 | D-4000 | N688K | 1415 | L-4000 | N475W | 2040 | 6-B | N452N |
| 1326 | B-4000 | N13907 | 1416 | 4000 | N425W | 2040 | 12-W | N11715 |
| 1333 | E-4000 | N402N | 1417 | 4000 | N426W | 3504 | 16-E | N12337 |
| 1336 | E-4000 | N405N | 1418 | 4000 | N427P | 3508 | 16-E | N12352 |
| 1340 | D-4-D | N434N | 2002 | 12-W | N434W | 3520 | 16-E | N12380 |

# Appendix IV

# Beechcraft Model Designations

When Curtiss-Wright acquired the Travel Air Manufacturing Company, the continued Travel Air designs received CW model numbers (CW-6 to CW-11); new aircraft designed by former Travel Air engineers used the same new style designation numbers (CW-12, -14/-16) and, when Beech Aircraft Company was established, the Beech model designation system proceeded naturally with Model 17.
The 'year' column corresponds to the first flight date.

| Model | Year | Purpose, engine, variants and remarks |
|---|---|---|
| 1,2,3 | | Curtiss-Wright designs with no bearing on Travel Air designs. |
| 4 | | Curtiss-Wright CW-4, former Travel Air Model 4000/4 series. Also St Louis designation for Buffalo-designed T-32 Condor II. |
| 5 | | St Louis design, not built. |
| 6 | 1928 | Curtiss-Wright CW-6, former Travel Air Model 6000. |
| 7 | 1927 | Curtiss-Wright CW-7, former Travel Air Model 7000. |
| 8 | 1928 | Curtiss-Wright CW-8, former Travel Air Model 8000. |
| 9 | 1928 | Curtiss-Wright CW-9, former Travel Air Model 9000. |
| 10 | 1929 | Curtiss-Wright CW-10, former Travel Air Model 10. |
| 11 | 1929 | Curtiss-Wright CW-11, former Travel Air Model 11000/11. |
| 12 | 1930 | Curtiss-Wright CW-12 Sport Trainer, light two-seat biplane, 90hp Curtiss-Wright Gipsy or 110hp Warner Scarab, 41 aircraft built. |
| 13 | | Model number probably not allocated for commercial reasons. |
| 14 | 1931 | Curtiss-Wright CW-14 Sportsman, Speedwing and Osprey, three-seat biplane, development of the Travel Air 4000 series, 185hp Curtiss Challenger, 240hp Wright J-6-7 or 420hp Wright R-975E, approx. 15 aircraft built. |
| 15 | 1931 | Curtiss-Wright CW-15 Sedan, four-seat monoplane, 185hp Curtiss Challenger or 210hp Kinner C-5, 14 aircraft built. |
| 16 | 1931 | Curtiss-Wright CW-16 Light Sport, three-seat variant of CW-12, 165hp Wright J-6-5, 125hp Kinner B-5 or 110hp Warner Scarab. |
| 17 | 1932 | Staggerwing, five-seat cabin biplane, USAAF designation C-43 Traveler, US Navy designation GB and JB, various powerplants available. |
| 18 | 1937 | Light transport; two 450hp Pratt & Whitney. USAAF designations AT-7, AT-11 and C-45 Expeditor. US Navy designations JRB and SNB. |
| 19 | 1965 | Musketeer Sport, two/four-seat cabin monoplane; one 150hp Lycoming. |
| 20 | 1937 | Project of twin-engined derivative of Model 17; two 260hp Menasco. |
| 23 | 1961 | Musketeer, four-seat cabin monoplane; one 180hp Lycoming. |
| 24 | 1966 | Musketeer Super R, Sierra 200, four/six-seat cabin monoplane; one 200hp Lycoming. |
| 25 | 1941 | Wichita, light transport and trainer; two 295hp Lycoming; USAAF designation AT-10. |
| 26 | 1941 | Wichita, light transport and trainer; two 295hp Lycoming; USAAF designation AT-10. |
| 28 | 1945 | Grizzly, attack aircraft; two 2,300hp Wright Cyclone; USAAF designation XA-38; two aircraft built. |
| 33 | 1959 | Debonair and Bonanza, four-seat cabin monoplane; one 225hp Continental. |
| 34 | 1947 | Twin Quad; four 400hp Lycoming; one aircraft built. |
| 35 | 1945 | Bonanza, four-seat cabin monoplane; one 185hp Continental; 10,418 aircraft built. |
| 36 | 1968 | Bonanza, six-seat utility aircraft; one 285hp Continental. USAF designation QU-22. |
| 38 | 1982 | Lightning, experimental aircraft; one 550hp Garrett AiResearch; one aircraft built. |
| 40 | 1948 | Project of Bonanza modified with two 180hp Franklin engines. |
| 45 | 1948 | Mentor, two-seat primary trainer; one 225hp Continental or one 715shp Pratt & Whitney; 1,533 aircraft built. |
| 50 | 1949 | Twin Bonanza, six-seat cabin monoplane; two 260hp Lycoming. US Army designation L-23. 1,077 aircraft built. |
| 55 | 1960 | Baron, four/five-seat cabin monoplane; two 260hp Continental. US Army designation T-42. 3,726 aircraft built. |
| 56 | 1966 | Turbo Baron, four/five-seat cabin monoplane; two 380hp Lycoming; 93 aircraft built. |
| 58 | 1969 | Baron, four/six-seat cabin monoplane; two 285hp Continental. |

| Model | Year | Purpose, engine, variants and remarks |
|---|---|---|
| **60** | 1966 | Duke, seven/nine-seat business aircraft; two 340hp Lycoming; 593 aircraft built. |
| **65** | 1958 | Queen Air, seven/nine-seat business aircraft; two 340hp Lycoming. US Army designations L-23, U-8 and U-21. 412 aircraft built. |
| **70** | 1969 | Queen Air, seven/nine-seat business aircraft; two 340hp Lycoming; 35 aircraft built. |
| **73** | 1955 | Jet Mentor, two-seat jet trainer; one 920lb st Continental; one aircraft built. |
| **76** | 1977 | Duchess, four-seat cabin monoplane; two 180hp Lycoming; also known as PD 289; 437 aircraft built. |
| **77** | 1978 | Skipper, cabin monoplane; one 115hp Lycoming; also known as PD 285; 312 aircraft built. |
| **79** | 1965 | Queen Air A65; two 340hp Lycoming; 96 aircraft built. |
| **80** | 1961 | Queen Air, six/eleven-seat business aircraft; two 380hp Lycoming; 511 aircraft built. |
| **81** | 1987 | All-composite, proof of concept aircraft; Rutan design. |
| **87** | 1963 | Modified Queen Air with PT6A engines; one built. |
| **88** | 1964 | Queen Air; two 380hp Lycoming; 45 aircraft built. |
| **89** | 1965 | Queen Air variant, became Model 65-A80-8800. |
| **90** | 1965 | King Air, six/eight-seat business aircraft; two 550hp Pratt & Whitney. US Army/USAF designations VC-6 and U-21. US Navy designation T-44. |
| **95** | 1956 | Travel Air, four-seat cabin monoplane; one 180hp Lycoming; 720 aircraft built. |
| **99** | 1966 | Airliner, 17-seat passenger and freight transport; two 550shp Pratt & Whitney; 238 aircraft built. |
| **100** | 1969 | King Air, 15-seat commuter aircraft; two 680shp Pratt & Whitney. USAF designation U-21. 388 aircraft built. |
| **101** | 1969 | Project which led to Model 200. |
| **112** | | Project of executive aircraft; two Lycoming T53. |
| **120** | 1961 | Project of executive transport which led to King Air prototype. |
| **200** | 1972 | Super King Air, passenger/executive light transport; two 850shp Pratt & Whitney. USAF designations C-12 and U-21. |
| **300** | 1984 | Super King Air; two 1,050shp Pratt & Whitney Canada. |
| **316** | 1956 | Ground power unit for the US Navy. |
| **350** | 1988 | 12-seat business aircraft; two 1,050shp Pratt & Whitney Canada. |
| **385** | 1960 | Universal air refuelling store of the US Navy. |
| **400** | 1986 | Beechjet, business jet aircraft; two 2,900lb st Pratt & Whitney Canada. USAF designation T-1A Jayhawk. |
| **997** | | Target drone. US Navy designation BQM-126A. |
| **999** | 1983 | Target drone; one Microturbo TRI-60 turbojet; designations MQM-107A and MQM-107B. |
| **1001** | 1957 | Target drone; one 125hp McCulloch. US Army designations KDB-1 later MQM-39A Cardinal. |
| **1013** | | Target drone; one 110hp McCulloch. |
| **1019** | 1961 | Target drone; one Rocketdyne rocket engine. US Navy designations KD2B-1, later AQM-37A. USAF designation Q-12. |
| **1025** | 1961 | Target drone; one Continental turbojet. USAF designation MQM-61A. |
| **1070** | 1971 | Target drone, HAST. |
| **1072** | | SD.2 Stiletto, British variant of AQM-37. |
| **1074** | | Drone aircraft; one 375hp Continental. USAF designation QU-22A Pave Eagle I. |
| **1079** | 1969 | Drone aircraft; one 375hp Continental. USAF designation QU-22B Pave Eagle II. |
| **1080** | 1976 | Twin hose-and-drogue in-flight refuelling system. |
| **1088** | | Target drone; Italian variant of AQM-37A. |
| **1089** | | Target drone. Designation MQM-107A Streaker. |
| **1089E** | | Decoy; one Teledyne turbojet. Designation TEDS. |
| **1094** | 1973 | Target drone for France. Designation AQM-37A Vanneau. |
| **1095** | 1974 | Target drone for Great Britain. Designation AQM-37A. |
| **1098** | | Target drone for Israel. Designation AQM-37A. |
| **1100** | | Target drone for US Army. |
| **1101** | | Target drone for US Army. |
| **1102** | | Target drone for US Navy. |
| **1104** | 1984 | Target drone for US Navy. Designation AQM-37C. |
| **1105** | | Target drone. Designation Variant. |
| **1107** | 1983 | Target drone for US Navy. Designation AQM-37A. |
| **1108** | 1984 | Training variant of Model 1095 for Great Britain. |
| **1300** | 1988 | Commuter, 13-seat transport aircraft; two 850shp Pratt & Whitney Canada; 14 aircraft built. |
| **1900** | 1983 | Airline/Exec-Liner, 19-seat transport aircraft; two 1,110/1,279shp Pratt & Whitney Canada. |
| **2000** | 1983 | Starship, eight-seat business aircraft; two 1,200shp Pratt & Whitney Canada. |

# Appendix V

# Type Certificates Issued to Commercial Beechcraft Aeroplanes

The Type Certificate (TC, or Approved Type Certificate, ATC, as it was originally known) is issued to aircraft that meet full licensing requirements for unlimited commercial operation. Approval is usually granted as a result of the manufacturer's test programme before the first aircraft is delivered to the customer.

| Date issued or amended | TC No. | Beechcraft Model |
|---|---|---|
| 20 December 1932 | 496 | Model 17R |
| 8 August 1934 | 548 | Model A17F |
| 4 December 1934 | 560 | Model B17L |
| 9 May 1935 | 566 | Model B17E |
| 6 July 1935 | 577 | Model A17FS |
| 22 July 1935 | 579 | Model B17R |
| 1 November 1935 | 560 | Model SB17L |
| 16 April 1936 | 602 | Model C17L, C17B, SC17L and SC17B |
| 29 April 1936 | 560 | Model B17B |
| 6 May 1936 | 604 | Model C17R |
| 13 August 1936 | 615 | Model C17E |
| 4 March 1937 | 630 | Model 18A |
| 7 November 1937 | 713 | Model D17A |
| 20 May 1937 | 638 | Model D17R |
| 22 May 1937 | 641 | Model E17B |
| 16 July 1937 | 649 | Model D17S |
| 9 August 1937 | 641 | Model SE17B |
| 1 September 1937 | 649 | Model SD17S |
| 18 October 1937 | 641 | Model E17L |
| 29 October 1937 | 656 | Model 18B and S18B |
| 15 June 1938 | 684 | Model 18D and S18D |
| 26 August 1938 | 689 | Model F17D |
| 2 November 1939 | 710 | Model 18S |
| 7 November 1939 | 604 | Model SC17R |
| 17 April 1940 | 710 | Model B18S |
| 7 May 1940 | 684 | Model A18A, SA18A, A18D and SA18D |
| 10 June 1941 | 689 | Model SF17D |
| 13 October 1941 | 630 | Model S18A |
| 23 September 1944 | 757 | Model C18S (military models C-45, C-45A, UC-45B, UC-45F, AT-7, AT-7A, AT-7B, AT-7C, JRB-1, JRB-2, JRB-3, JRB-4, SNB-2, SNB-2C and AT-11 are eligible as Model C18S). |
| 26 April 1946 | 765 | Model D18S |
| 2 May 1946 | 2-582 | AT-11 and SNB-1 |
| 11 October 1946 | 779 | Model G17S |
| 25 March 1947 | 777 | Model 35 |
| 10 April 1947 | L-12 | AT-10, AT-10-BH and AT-10-BL |
| 3 June 1947 | 770 | Model D18C-T |
| 16 July 1947 | 765 | Model D18C |
| 15 July 1948 | 777 | Model A35 |
| 28 December 1949 | 777 | Model B35 |
| 17 July 1950 | 5A3 | Model 45 |
| 16 January 1951 | 777 | Model C35 |
| 25 May 1951 | 5A4 | Model 50 |
| 6 June 1951 | 777 | Model 35R |
| 5 January 1953 | 777 | Model D35 |

| Date issued or amended | TC No. | Beechcraft Model |
|---|---|---|
| 31 July 1953 | 5A4 | Model B50 |
| 21 September 1953 | 5A3 | Model A45 and B45 |
| 15 January 1954 | 777 | Model E35 |
| 19 July 1954 | 765 | Model E18S |
| 13 October 1954 | 5A4 | Model C50 |
| 5 January 1955 | 777 | Model F35 |
| 1 December 1955 | 777 | Model G35 |
| 6 December 1955 | 5A4 | Model D50 |
| 1 December 1956 | 3A15 | Model H35 |
| 1 December 1956 | 5A4 | Model E50 |
| 18 June 1957 | 3A16 | Model 95 |
| 29 October 1957 | 5A4 | Model D50A and F50 |
| 13 November 1957 | 3A15 | Model J35 |
| 3 March 1958 | 765 | C-45G, TC-45G, C-45H, TC-45H |
| 29 October 1958 | 3A15 | Model K35 |
| 10 November 1958 | 5A4 | Model D50B and G50 |
| 19 January 1959 | 765 | Model E18S-9700 |
| 4 February 1959 | 3A20 | Model 65 |
| 2 October 1959 | 3A15 | Model M35 |
| 8 October 1959 | 765 | Model G18S |
| 13 November 1959 | 3A15 | Model 35-33 |
| 13 November 1959 | 3A16 | Model B95 |
| 13 November 1959 | 5A4 | Model D50C, H50 |
| 9 March 1960 | 5A3 | Model D45 |
| 15 March 1960 | A1CE | Model 23 |
| 3 November 1960 | 3A15 | Model 35-A33 |
| 3 November 1960 | 3A16 | Model 95-55 |
| 10 November 1960 | 5A4 | Model D50E |
| 16 November 1960 | 5A4 | Model J50 |
| 9 March 1961 | 3A16 | Model B95A |
| 3 October 1961 | 3A15 | Model 35-B33 |
| 9 October 1961 | 3A16 | Model 95-A55 |
| 20 October 1961 | 3A15 | Model N35 and P35 |
| 20 February 1962 | 3A20 | Model 65-80 |
| 20 February 1962 | A1CE | Model 23 |
| 10 April 1962 | 765 | SNB-5, TC-45J, UC-45J |
| 11 July 1962 | 765 | Model H18 |
| 17 May 1963 | 3A16 | Model D95A |
| 7 June 1963 | A1CE | Model A23 |
| 30 August 1963 | 765 | JRB-6 |
| 9 September 1963 | 3A16 | Model 95-B55 |
| 3 January 1964 | 3A15 | Model S35 |
| 26 March 1964 | 3A20 | Model 65-A80 |
| 19 May 1964 | 3A20 | Model 65-90 |
| 26 August 1964 | 3A16 | Model 95-B55B |
| 2 December 1964 | 3A15 | Model 35-C33 |
| 18 August 1965 | 3A16 | Model 95-C55 |
| 21 September 1965 | 3A20 | Model 65-88 |
| 22 October 1965 | 3A15 | Model V35 |
| 22 October 1965 | 3A20 | Model 65-A80-8800 |
| 5 November 1965 | A1CE | Model A23A |
| 9 December 1965 | A1CE | Model A23-19 |
| 20 January 1966 | 3A15 | Model 35-C33A and C33A |
| 7 March 1966 | A1CE | Model A23-24 |
| 7 March 1966 | 3A20 | Model 65-A90 |
| 27 April 1966 | 3A20 | Model 65-A90-1 |
| 4 August 1966 | A1CE | Model D33 |
| 3 November 1966 | 3A20 | Model A65 |
| 19 May 1967 | 3A16 | Model 56TC |

| Date issued or amended | TC No. | Beechcraft Model |
|---|---|---|
| 31 August 1967 | A1CE | Model 19A |
| 6 October 1967 | 3A15 | Model V35A |
| 9 October 1967 | 3A20 | Model A65-8200 |
| 10 October 1967 | 3A15 | Model E33 and E33A |
| 17 October 1967 | 3A16 | Model D55 and E95 |
| 14 November 1967 | 3A20 | Model B90 |
| 13 December 1967 | A1CE | Model B23 |
| 31 January 1968 | 765 | 3N, 3NM and 3TM (Canada) |
| 1 February 1968 | A12CE | Model 60 |
| 12 March 1968 | A1CE | Model 19A (aerobatic) |
| 1 May 1968 | 3A15 | Model 36 |
| 2 May 1968 | A14CE | Model 99 |
| 9 September 1968 | 3A15 | Model E33C |
| 31 October 1968 | 3A16 | Model 95-B55A, 95-C55A and D95A |
| 22 November 1968 | A1CE | Model B23 (aerobatic) |
| 27 November 1968 | 3A20 | Model 70 |
| 14 January 1969 | 765 | RC-45J and SNB-5P |
| 10 February 1969 | A14CE | Model 99A |
| 20 March 1969 | 3A20 | Model 65-A90-2 and 65-A90-3 |
| 24 July 1969 | A14CE | Model 100 |
| 24 October 1969 | 3A15 | Model V35B |
| 24 October 1969 | 3A15 | Model F33, F33A, F33C and A36 |
| 12 November 1969 | 3A16 | Model E55 and A56TC |
| 19 November 1969 | 3A16 | Model 58 |
| 9 December 1969 | A1CE | Model M19A |
| 23 December 1969 | A1CE | Model A24R |
| 30 January 1970 | A12CE | Model A60 |
| 5 February 1970 | A1CE | Model A24 |
| 13 February 1970 | A1CE | Model B19 and C23 |
| 10 June 1970 | A14CE | Model 99A |
| 16 June 1970 | 3A16 | Model E55A |
| 23 October 1970 | 3A20 | Model C90 and C90-1 |
| 10 November 1970 | 3A16 | Model 58A |
| 19 February 1971 | A14CE | Model A99 and A99A |
| 17 March 1971 | 3A15 | Model G33 |
| 7 May 1971 | A14CE | Model A100 |
| 10 December 1971 | 3A20 | Model 65-A90-4 |
| 27 March 1972 | A14CE | Model B99 |
| 13 April 1972 | 3A20 | Model E90 |
| 1 November 1972 | A14CE | Model A100A |
| 18 June 1973 | A1CE | Model B24R |
| 5 October 1973 | A12CE | Model B60 |
| 14 December 1973 | A14CE | Model A100C |
| 14 December 1973 | A24CE | Model 200 |
| 21 March 1974 | 5A4 | Model D50E-5990 |
| 21 May 1974 | A23CE | Model 58P |
| 21 May 1974 | A24CE | Model A100-1 |
| 20 June 1975 | A24CE | Model A200 |
| 1 December 1975 | A14CE | Model B100 |
| 24 January 1976 | A23CE | Model 58TC |
| 12 May 1976 | A23CE | Model 58PA and 58TCA |
| 1 October 1976 | A1CE | Model C24R |
| 15 December 1976 | A24CE | Model 200T |
| 17 December 1976 | A26CE | T-34C and T-34C-1 |
| 23 March 1977 | 3A20 | Model H90 |
| 24 January 1978 | A29CE | Model 76 |
| 25 August 1978 | A26CE | T-34C |
| 7 December 1978 | 3A15 | Model A36TC |
| 21 February 1979 | A24CE | Model 200C, 200CT and A200C |

| Date issued or amended | TC No. | Beechcraft Model |
|---|---|---|
| 19 March 1979 | A30CE | Model 77 |
| 18 May 1979 | A31CE | Model F90 |
| 17 April 1980 | A24CE | Model A200CT |
| 31 February 1981 | A24CE | Model B200, B200C, B200T and B200CT |
| 27 July 1981 | A14CE | Model C99 |
| 15 January 1982 | 3A15 | Model B36TC |
| 22 November 1983 | A24CE | Model 1900 |
| 1 December 1983 | 3A20 | Model C90A |
| 24 January 1984 | A24CE | Model 300 |
| 1 April 1986 | A16SW | Model 400 |
| 30 September 1988 | A24CE | Model 300LW |
| 28 March 1989 | A24CE | Model A200CT (restricted category) |
| 14 June 1990 | A38CE | Model 2000 |
| 20 June 1990 | A16SW | Model 400A |
| 19 March 1991 | A24CE | Model 1900D |
| 20 November 1991 | A16SW | Model 400T |

## Appendix VI

# Beechcraft Production Details

**Note**: figures given in italics refer to Models still under production and are the latest known at the time of writing.

| Model | Quantity | Constructor's numbers (c/n) | Remarks |
|---|---|---|---|
| **Model 17** | | | |
| 17R | 2 | 1 and 2 | |
| A17F | 1 | 5 | |
| A17FS | 1 | 11 | |
| B17B | 1 | 20 | |
| B17E | 3 | 22, 49 and 51 | |
| B17L | 46 | 3/4, 6/10, 12/21, 23/49 and 58/61 | |
| B17R | 16 | 38, 50, 52/56, 63/66 and 68/72 | Three aircraft impressed in USAAC. |
| C17B | 38 | 67, 84/89, 101/104, 106, 108, 110/112, 121, 123 and 125/135 | 11 aircraft impressed in USAAC. |
| SC17B | 1 | 99 | |
| C17E | 2 | 78 and 117 | sold to Tokyo Hikoki Seisaku-Jo and assembled in Japan. |
| C17L | 7 | 83/84, 100, 105, 107, 109 and 124 | Two aircraft impressed in USAAC. |
| C17R | 17 | 73/77, 79/82, 113/116, 118/120 and 122. | Five aircraft impressed in USAAC. |
| SC17R | 1 | 113 | |
| D17A | 8 | 305, 356/361 and 363. | One aircraft impressed in USAAC. |
| D17R | 26 | 137, 148, 166/167, 180/182, 184, 188, 214/215, 217/218, 235/237, 253, 278, 289, 313, 325/326, 328/329, 397 and 405. | 14 aircraft impressed in USAAC. |
| D17S | 68 | 147, 165, 168, 179, 183, 185/187, 199/203, 216/217, 238/239, 254, 263/264, 279, 284/288, 295/304, 306, 314, 327, 354/355, 362, 385/387, 395/396, 398/404, 406/408, 415/424. | 16 aircraft impressed in USAAC. |
| SD17S | 1 | 279 | |
| D17W | 2 | 136 and 164 | c/n 136 delivered as C17R, c/n 164 impressed in USAAC. |
| E17B | 54 | 138/145, 149/160, 162/163, 189/198, 204/210, 212/213, 219, 227/228, 231/234, 251, 274, 280, 336, 388. | 31 aircraft impressed in USAAC. |
| SE17B | 4 | 160, 210, 227 and 280. | |
| E17L | 1 | 161 | |
| F17D | 59 | 211, 225/226, 229, 240/250, 252, 255, 256/262, 270/273, 275/277, 281/283, 307/312, 330/335, 337/339, 389/394, 410, 412/413. | 38 aircraft impressed in USAAC. |
| SF17D | 1 | 414 | |
| **Model 18** | | | |
| 18A | 2 | 62 and 291 | |
| S18A | 1 | 172 | |
| 18B | 3 | 170/171 and 174 | |
| S18B | 1 | 173 | |
| 18D | 9 | 175/176, 220/221, 223/224, 265 and 267/268 | |
| S18D | 2 | 177/178 | |
| 18R | 6 | 321 and 376/380 | |
| 18S | 10 | 266, 269, 290, 292, 294, 316, 430/431, 433/434 | Two aircraft impressed in USAAC. |

| Model | Quantity | Constructor's numbers (c/n) | Remarks |
|---|---|---|---|
| C18S | 2 | 432 and 445 | |
| D18S | 1,035 | A-1/1035 | A-601/700 became Expeditor Mk.3Ns with c/ns CA-1/100; A-702/715, A-736/755, A-767/769, A-780, A-782, A-784, A-786, A-788, A-790/800 and A-851/930 became Expeditor Mk.3NMs with c/ns CA-102/115, CA-136/155, CA-176/194, CA-201/ 280; A-701, A-716/735, A-756/766, A-770/779, A-781, A-783, A-785, A-787, A-789 and A-931 became Expeditor Mk.3TMs with c/ns CA-101, CA-116/135, CA-156/175, CA-195/200 and CA-281. |
| E18S | 407 | BA-1/402, BA-497 | |
| E18S-9700 | 57 | BA-403/433, BA-435/460 | |
| G18S | 156 | BA-434, BA-461/562, BA-564/579, BA-581/617 | |
| H18 | 149 | BA-580, BA-618, BA-650/765 | |
| **Model 19** | | | |
| **Model 23** | | | |
| **Model 24** | | | |
| 23 | 553 | M-1/2, M-4/554 | |
| A23 | 346 | M-3, M-555/900 | |
| A23A | 194 | M-901/1094 | |
| B23 | 190 | M-1095/1284 | |
| C23 | 1,107 | M-1285/2392 | |
| A23-19 | 288 | MB-1/288 | |
| 19A | 172 | MB-289/460 | |
| M19A | 20 | MB-461/480 | |
| B19 | 423 | MB-481/905 | c/n MB-723 not built |
| A23-24 | 363 | MA-1/363 | 86 aircraft equipped with 200hp Lycoming engine. |
| A24 | 5 | MA-364/368 | c/n MA-366 equipped with 200hp Lycoming engine. |
| A24R | 149 | MC-2/150 | |
| B24R | 299 | MC-152/795 | |
| **Model 25** | 1 | ? | USAAC, destroyed. |
| **Model 26** | 1,771 | ? | USAAC AT-10. |
| **Model 28** | 2 | ? | USAAF XA-38. |
| **Model 33** | | | |
| 35-33 | 233 | CD-1/224, CD-233/234, CD-236, CD-241, CD-246/250 | |
| 35A33 | 154 | CD-225/232, CD-235, CD-237/240, CD-242, CD-245, CD-251/387. | |
| 35-B33 | 426 | CD-388/813 | |
| 35-C33 | 304 | CD-814/981, CD-983/1118 | |
| 35-C33A | 179 | CE-1/179 | |
| E33 | 116 | CD-1119/1234 | |
| E33A | 85 | CE-180/235, CE-249/250, CE-260, CE-264/ 268, CE-270/289. | c/n CE-236/248, CE-251/255, CE-257/259, CE-261/263 and CE-269 modified to E33C at factory with c/n CJ-1/25. |
| E33C | 51 | CJ-1/51 | CJ-1/25 are ex-E33As, CJ-31/51 are ex-G33s. |
| F33 | 20 | CD-1235/1254 | |
| F33A | *1,487* | CE-290/1011, CE-1014/*1788* | in production |
| F33C | *127* | CJ-52/*178* | in production |
| G33 | 50 | CD-1255/1304 | c/n CD-1305/1325 modified to F33C at factory with c/n CJ-31/51; sold to Iran. |

| Model | Quantity | Constructor's numbers (c/n) | Remarks |
|---|---|---|---|
| **Model 35** | | | |
| 35 | 1,499 | D-1/1500 | 13 aircraft changed as Model 35R with new c/n R-1/12 and 14 (respectively D-25, D-3, D-721, D-838, D-588, D-535, D-532, D-1424, D-944, D-1186, D-927, D-329 and D-122) |
| 35R | 13 | R-1/12 and 14 | modified Model 35s |
| A35 | 701 | D-1501/2200, D-15001 | c/n D-15001 used as engineering prototype. |
| B35 | 480 | D-2201/2680 | |
| C35 | 719 | D-2681/3292, D-3294/3400 | |
| D35 | 298 | D-3401/3698 | |
| E35 | 301 | D-3293, D-3699/3998 | |
| F35 | 392 | D-3999/4375, D-4377/4391 | |
| G35 | 476 | D-4392/4865, D-4376, D-15002 | c/n D-15002 used as engineering prototype. |
| H35 | 464 | D-4866/5061, D-5063/5330 | |
| J35 | 396 | D-5062, D-5331/5725 | |
| K35 | 436 | D-5726/6161 | |
| M35 | 400 | D-6162/6561 | |
| N35 | 280 | D-6562/6841 | |
| O35 | 1 | ? | |
| P35 | 467 | D-6842/7139, D-7141/7309 | |
| S35 | 668 | D-7140, D-7310/7976 | |
| V35 | 622 | D-7977/8598 | including 79 V35TCs turbo-charged models |
| V35A | 470 | D-8599/9068 | including 46 V35A-TCs turbo-charged models |
| V35V | 1,335 | D-9069/10403 | including 7 V35B-TCs turbo-charged models |
| **Model 36** | | | |
| 36 | 184 | E-1/184 | |
| | 6 | CED-1/6 | YQU-22A |
| | 27 | EB-1/27 | QU-22B |
| A36 | *2,705* | E-185/*2889* | in production |
| A36TC | 271 | EA-1/241, E-243/272 | |
| B36TC | *287* | EA-242, EA-271, EA-273/*566* | in production |
| T36TC | 1 | EC-1 | |
| **Model 45** | | | |
| A45T | 3 | | |
| B45 | 318 | | |
| T-34A | 348 | G-7/156, G-257/306, G-697/846 | |
| T-34B | 423 | BG-1/423 | |
| T-34C | 350 | GP-1/51, GL-1/184, GL-231/353 | GP-1/6 originally numbered GM-72/77 |
| T-34C-1 | 91 | GM-1/71, GM-78/89 | |
| **Model 50** | | | |
| 50 | 11 | H-1/11 | |
| 50 | 4 | ? | YL-23 |
| 50 | 55 | LH-1/55 | L-23A |
| B50 | 99 | CH-12/110 | |
| B50 | 1 | LH-9 | L-23A |
| B50 | 40 | LH-56/95 | L-23B |
| C50 | 250 | CH-111/360 | |
| D50 | 154 | DH-1/154 | DH-88/91 became L-23Es. |
| D50A | 44 | DH-155/198 | |
| D50B | 38 | DH-199/236 | |
| D50C | 64 | DH-237/300 | |
| D50E | 47 | DH-301/347 | |
| E50 | 70 | EH-1/70 | |
| F50 | 25 | FH-71/93, FH-95 and FH-96 | |
| G50 | 24 | GH-94, GH-97/119 | |
| H50 | 30 | HH-12/149 | |
| J50 | 37 | JH-150/176 | |
| E50 | 56 | LH-96/151 | U-8D |

| Model | Quantity | Constructor's numbers (c/n) | Remarks |
|---|---|---|---|
| E50 | 93 | RLH-1/93 | RU-8D |
| E50 | 29 | LH-152/180 | U-8D |
| E50 | 8 | LHC-3/10 | RU-8D |
| E50 | 4 | LH-192/195 | RU-8D |
| E50 | 11 | LHE-6/16 | U-8G |
| **Models 95-55 and 55** | | | |
| 95-55 | 190 | TC-1/190 | |
| 95-A55 | 309 | TC-191/349, TC-351/370, TC-372/501 | |
| 95-B55 | 1,956 | TC-371, TC-502/2456 | |
| 95-C55 | 451 | TC-350, TE-1/49, TE-51/451 | |
| D55 | 316 | TE-425/767 | |
| E55 | 434 | TE-768/1201 | |
| B55B | 70 | TF-1/70 | T-42A |
| **Model 56** | | | |
| 56TC | 82 | TG-2/83 | |
| A56TC | 11 | TG-84/94 | |
| **Model 58** | | | |
| 58 | *1,728* | TH-1/*1728* | in production |
| 58P | 495 | TJ-3/497 | |
| 58TC | 151 | TK-1/151 | |
| **Model 60** | | | |
| 60 | 122 | P-4/122, P-124/126 | |
| A60 | 121 | P-123, P-127/246 | |
| B60 | 350 | P-247/596 | |
| **Model 65** | | | |
| 65 | 478 | L-1/6, LF-7/76, LC-1/239 | U-8F |
| A65 | 44 | LC-240/272, LC-325/335 | |
| A65-8200 | 52 | LC-273/324 | |
| **Model 65-80** | | | |
| 65-80 | 148 | LD-1/33, LD-35/45, LD-47/150 | |
| 65-A80 | 121 | LD-34, LD-46, LD-151/269 | |
| 65-B80 | 242 | LD-270/511 | |
| **Model 65-88** | 45 | LP-1/26, LP-28, LP-30/47 | |
| **Model 65-90** | | | |
| 65-90 | 112 | LJ-1/75, LJ-77/113 | |
| 65-A90 | 206 | LJ-76, LJ-114/317, LJ178A | |
| 65-A90-2 | 3 | LS-1/3 | |
| 65-A90-3 | 2 | LT-1/2 | |
| 65-A90-4 | 16 | LU-1/16 | |
| **Model 70** | 35 | LB-1/35 | |
| **Model 73** | 1 | ? | |
| **Model 76** | 437 | ME-1/437 | |
| **Model 77** | 312 | WA-1/312 | |
| **Model 87** | 1 | LG-1 | NU-8F/YU-21A |
| **Model 90** | | | |
| A90-1 | 140 | LM-1/141 | U-21A |
| A90-2 | 3 | LS-1/3 | (R)U-21B |
| A90-3 | 2 | LT-1/2 | (R)U-21C |
| A90-4 | 16 | LU-1/16 | (R)U-21E/H |
| B90 | 184 | LJ-318/501 | |
| C90 | 507 | LJ-502/985, LJ-987/995, LJ-997/1010 | |
| C90-1 | 54 | LJ-986, LJ-996, LJ-1011/1062 | |

| Model | Quantity | Constructor's numbers (c/n) | Remarks |
|---|---|---|---|
| C90A | *313* | LJ-1063/*1375* | in production |
| D90 | 0 | LK- | none built |
| E90 | 347 | LW-1/347 | |
| F90 | 203 | LA-2/201, LA-203/204, LE-01 | |
| F90-1 | 34 | LA-202, LA-205/237 | |
| H90 | 61 | LL-1/61 | T-44A |
| **Model 95** | | | |
| 95 | 301 | TD-2/302 | |
| B95 | 150 | TD-303/452 | |
| B95A | 81 | TD-453/533 | |
| D95A | 175 | TD-534/707 | |
| E95 | 14 | TD-708/721 | |
| **Model 99** | | | |
| 99 | 101 | U-1/35, U-37/49, U-51/79, U-86/88, U-90/92, U-94/95, U-98/100, U-102/103, U-106/109, U-114, U-119/122, U-124, U-136. | |
| 99A | 42 | U-36, U-80/85, U-89, U-93, U-96/97, U-101, U-104/105, U-110/113, U-115/118, U-123, U-125/131, U-133/135, U-137/145, U-147. | |
| A99A | 1 | U-132 | |
| B99 | 18 | U-146, U-148/164 | |
| C99 | 76 | U-50, U-165/239 | |
| **Model 100** | | | |
| 100 | 89 | B-2/89, B-93 | |
| A100 | 162 | B-1, B-90/92, B-94/204, B-206/247 | |
| B100 | 137 | BE-1/137 | |
| **Model 200** | | | |
| A100-1 | 3 | BB-3/5 | RU-21J |
| 200 | 815 | BB-1/202, BB-264/269, BB-271/407, BB-409/468, BB-470/488, BB-490/509, BB-511/529, BB-531/550, BB-552/562, BB-564/572, BB-574/590, BB-592/608, BB-610/626, BB-628/646, BB-648/664, BB-666/694, BB-696/792, BB-794/797, BB-799/822, BB-824/828, BB-830/853, BB-872/873, BB-892/893, BB-912. | |
| A200 | 75 | BC-1/75 | C-12A |
| A200 | 30 | BD-1/30 | C-12A |
| A200C | 66 | BJ-1/66 | |
| A200CT | 19 | GR-1/19 | RC-12K |
| A200CT | 3 | FC-1/3 | RC-12D, ex-BP-20/21/13 |
| A200CT | 69 | BP-1/69 | RC-12D/F |
| A200CT | 31 | FE-1/31 | RC-12K |
| B200 | *625* | BB-793, BB-829, BB-854/870, BB-874/891, BB-894, BB-896/911, BB-913/990, BB-992/1051, BB-1053/1092, BB-1094/1095, BB-1099/1104, BB-1106/1116, BB-1118/*1491* | in production |
| B200 | 2 | FG-1/2 | RC-12K for Israel |
| 200C | 36 | BL-1/36 | |
| B200C | 12 | BU-1/12 | UC-12F |
| B200C | 12 | BV-1/12 | UC-12M |
| B200C | *101* | BL-37/57, BL-61/*140* | in production; C-12F; BL-113/117 not built. |
| 200CT | 1 | BN-1 | ex-BL-24 |
| B200CT | 3 | BN-2/4 | ex-BL-58/60 |

| Model | Quantity | Constructor's numbers (c/n) | Remarks |
|---|---|---|---|
| 200T | 23 | BT-1/22, BT-28 | ex-BB-186, BB-203, BB-270, BB-408, BB-469, BB-489, BB-510, BB-530, BB-551, BB-563, BB-573, BB-591, BB-609, BB-627, BB-647, BB-665, BB-687, BB-695, BB-823, BB-871, BB-895, BB-991 and BB-1117 respectively. |
| B200T | 8 | BT-23/27, BT-29/31 | ex-BB-1052, BB-1093, BB-1096, BB-1098, BB-1105, BB-1097, BB-1185 and BB-1264 respectively |
| **Model 300** | | | |
| 300/300LW | *230* | FA-1/*230* | in production |
| 300 | 19 | FF-1/19 | to FAA |
| B300(350) | *122* | FL-1/*122* | in production |
| B300C(350C) | *8* | FM-1/*8* | in production |
| **Model 400** | | | |
| 400 | *54* | RJ-3, RJ-9/*61* | in production |
| 400A | *94* | RK-1/*94* | in production |
| 400T | *97* | TT-1/*97* | T-1A; in production |
| 400T | *6* | TT-1/*6* | in production; for JASDF |
| **Model 1900** | | | |
| 1900 | 3 | UA-1/3 | |
| 1900C | *72* | UB-1/*72* | in production |
| 1900C-1 | *173* | UC-1/*173* | in production |
| 1900C-1 | 6 | UD-1/6 | C-12J |
| 1900D | *116* | UE-1/*116* | in production |
| **Model 2000** | *53* | NC-1/*53* | in production |
| PC-9 Mk.II | 3 | PT-1/3 | |

# Appendix VII

# Serial Numbers of US Army and Air Force Aircraft Designed by Beechcraft

| Serial No. | Type | Quantity | Remarks |
|---|---|---|---|
| 39-139/141 | YC-43 Traveler | 3 | c/ns 295/297; Nos.39-139 impressed in RAF as DR628 |
| 39-142/155 | F-2-BH Expeditor | 14 | cancelled and re-ordered with s/ns 40-682/695 |
| 40-180/190 | C-45-BH Expeditor | 11 | c/ns 364/374; became UC-45-BH |
| 40-682/695 | F-2-BH Expeditor | 14 | |
| 41-1143/1209 | AT-7-BH Navigator | 67 | redesignated T-7-BH in 1948 |
| 41-1711/1860 | AT-10-BH | 150 | |
| 41-1861/1880 | C-45A-BH Expeditor | 8 | became UC-45A-BH |
| 41-9246/9436 | AT-10-BH | 191 | |
| 41-9437/9586 | AT-11-BH Kansan | 150 | conversions to AT-11A-BH; many rebuilt as C-45G/H; redesignated T-11-BH in 1948. |
| 41-21042/21155 | AT-7-BH Navigator | 114 | redesignated T-7-BH in 1948 |
| 41-21156/21161 | AT-7A-BH Navigator | 6 | |
| 41-26252/27331 | AT-10-BH | 80 | |
| 41-27332/27681 | AT-11-BH Kansan | 250 | conversions to AT-11A-BH; many rebuilt as C-45G/H; redesignated T-11-BH in 1948. |
| 42-2064/2413 | AT-10-BH | 350 | |
| 42-2414 | AT-7B-BH Navigator | 1 | |
| 42-2415/2513 | AT-7-BH Navigator | 99 | redesignated T-7-BH in 1948. |
| 42-3057/3080 | AT-11-BH Kansan | 24 | ex-RNEIAF aircraft impressed in USAAC; c/ns 3057/3080. |
| 42-22246 | UC-43C-BH Traveler | 1 | undetermined origin |
| 42-22247 | UC-45C-BH | 1 | impressed Model B18S c/n 316. |
| 42-34584/35183 | AT-10-GF | 600 | |
| 42-36825 | UC-43C-BH Traveler | 1 | impressed Model F17D c/n 250 ex-NC2585 |
| 42-36826/37713 | AT-11-BH Kansan | 888 | conversions to AT-11A-BH; many rebuilt as C-45G/H; redesignated T-11-BH in 1948. |
| 42-38226/38231 | UC-43A-BH | 6 | impressed Model 17R: 42-38226 c/n 214 ex-NC18789; 42-38227 c/n 215 ex-NC18790; 42-38228 c/n 313 ex-NC20776; 42-38229 c/n 289 ex-NC20752; 42-38230 c/n 405 ex-NC21919; 42-38231 c/n 167 ex-NC18565. |
| 42-3823/38236 | UC-43B-BH Traveler | 5 | impressed Model D17S: 42-38232 c/n 146 ex-NC18027; 42-38233 c/n 396 ex-NC129M; 42-38234 c/n 199 ex-NC18776; 42-38235 c/n 186 ex-NC18582; 42-38236 c/n 416 ex-NC1244. |
| 42-38237/38241 | UC-43C-BH Traveler | 5 | impressed Model F17D: 42-38237 c/n 391 ex-NC21921; 42-38238 c/n 333 ex-NC20798; 42-38239 c/n 275 ex-NC20789; 42-38240 c/n 394 ex-NC20786; 42-38241 c/n 310 ex-NC20772. |
| 42-38242 | UC-43C-BH Traveler | – | serial reserved for impressment but not taken up. |
| 42-38243/38244 | UC-43C-BH Traveler | 2 | impressed Model F17D: 42-38243 c/n 393 ex-NC21922; 42-38244 c/n 312 ex-NC20774. |
| 42-38245 | UC-43A-BH Traveler | 1 | impressed Model D17R c/n 278 ex-NC203W. |
| 42-38246/38248 | UC-43C-BH Traveler | | impressed Model F17D: 42-38246 c/n 242 ex-NC19454; 42-38247 c/n 390 ex-NC303W; 42-38248 c/n 276 ex-NC20790. |
| 42-38249 | UC-43C-BH Traveler | – | serial reserved for impressement but not taken up. |
| 42-38281 | UC-43B-BH Traveler | 1 | impressed Model D17S c/n 422 ex-NC1600. |
| 42-38282 | UC-43A-BH Traveler | 1 | impressed Model D17R c/n 166 ex-NC900. |

| Serial No. | Type | Quantity | Remarks |
|---|---|---|---|
| 42-38283/38284 | UC-43C-BH Traveler | 2 | impressed Model F-17D: 42-38283 c/n 331 ex-NC19451; 42-38284 c/n 259 ex-NC289Y. |
| 42-38357/38358 | UC-43A-BH Traveler | 2 | impressed Model D17R: 42-38357 c/n 148 ex-NC18029; 42-38358 c/n 180 ex-NC18576. |
| 42-38359 | UC-43B-BH Traveler | 1 | impressed Model D17S c/n 362 ex-NC900. |
| 42-38360 | UC-43B-BH Traveler | 1 | serial reserved for impressement but not taken up. |
| 42-38361/38363 | UC-43C-BH Traveler | 3 | impressed Model F17D: 42-38361 c/n 272 ex-NC238Y; 42-38362 c/n 241 ex-NC18783; 42-38363 c/n 273 x-NC292Y. |
| 42-38665/38670 | UC-43-BH Traveler | 6 | ex-US Navy BuNos. 12348/12353. |
| 42-38671/38691 | UC-43-BH Traveler | 21 | 42-38674/38691 to RAF as Traveller I c/ns FL653/670. |
| 42-43461/43477 | AT-7-BH Navigator | 17 | redesignated T-7-BH in 1948. |
| 42-43478/43483 | AT-7B-BH Navigator | 6 | |
| 42-43484 | UC-45E-BH Expeditor | 1 | on AT-7B-BH contract. |
| 42-43485 | AT-7B-BH Navigator | 1 | |
| 42-43486 | UC-45E-BH Expeditor | 1 | on AT-7B-BH contract. |
| 42-43487 | AT-7B-BH Navigator | 1 | |
| 42-43488/43510 | AT-7-BH Navigator | 23 | redesignated T-7-BH in 1948. |
| 42-43517 | UC-43C-BH Traveler | 1 | impressed Model F17D c/n 335 ex-NC20754. |
| 42-43485 | UC-43D-BH Traveler | 1 | impressed Model E17B c/n 153 ex-NC18042. |
| 42-46635 | UC-43C-BH Traveler | 1 | impressed Model F17D c/n 211 ex-NC18786. |
| 42-46636 | UC-43D-BH Traveler | 1 | impressed Model E17B c/n 193 ex-NC18559. |
| 42-46905 | UC-43B-BH Traveler | 1 | impressed Model D17S c/n 355 ex-NC239Y. |
| 42-46906/46908 | UC-43C-BH Traveler | 3 | impressed Model F17D: 42-46906 c/n 240 ex-NC18782; 42-46907 c/n 255 ex-NC18568; 42-46908 c/n 413 ex-NC21935. |
| 42-46909/46910 | UC-43D-BH Traveler | 2 | impressed Model E17B: 42-46909 c/n 190 ex-NC18043; 42-46910 c/n 158 ex-NC18556. |
| 42-46914 | UC-43C-BH Traveler | 1 | impressed Model F17B c/n 412 ex-NC21932. |
| 42-46915 | UC-43D-BH Traveler | 1 | impressed Model E17B c/n 195 ex-NC18587. |
| 42-46916 | UC-43C-BH Traveler | 1 | impressed Model F17D c/n 410 ex-NC248Y. |
| 42-47383 | UC-43A-BH Traveler | 1 | impressed Model D17R c/n 218 ex-NC18793. |
| 42-47384 | UC-43B-BH Traveler | 1 | impressed Model D17S c/n 415 ex-NC18793. |
| 42-47385/47388 | UC-43C-BH Traveler | 4 | impressed Model F17D: 42-47385 c/n 243 ex-NC19471; 42-47386 c/n 389 ex-NC3048; 42-47387 c/n 277 ex-NC20791; 42-47388 c/n 381 ex-NC2627. |
| 42-47389 | UC-43E-BH Traveler | 1 | impressed Model C17R c/n 82 ex-NC16434. |
| 42-47442/47448 | UC-43D-BH Traveler | 7 | impressed Model E17B: 42-47442 c/n 156 ex-NC17071; 42-47443 c/n 191 ex-NC18044; 42-47444 c/n 142 ex-NC17091; 42-47445 c/n 162 ex-NC18560; 42-47446 c/n 189 ex-NC18585; 42-47447 c/n 138 ex-NC17083; 42-47448 c/n 145 ex-NC18026. |
| 42-47449/47450 | UC-43C-BH Traveler | 2 | impressed Model F17D: 42-47449 c/n 337 ex-NC20771; 42-47450 c/n 256 ex-NC18573. |
| 42-49070 | UC-43D-BH Traveler | 1 | impressed Model E17B c/n 152 ex-NC18041. |
| 42-49071 | UC-43F-BH Traveler | 1 | impressed Model D17A c/n 305 ex-NC19453. |
| 42-52999 | UC-43A-BH Traveler | 1 | impressed Model D17R c/n 72 ex-NC15817. |
| 42-53000/53001 | UC-43D-BH Traveler | 2 | impressed Model E17B: 42-53000 c/n 212 ex-NC18787; 42-53001 c/n 192 ex-NC18558. |
| 42-53002 | UC-43B-BH Traveler | 1 | impressed Model D17S c/n 287 ex-NC20750. |
| 42-53005 | UC-43D-BH Traveler | 1 | impressed Model E17B c/n 208 ex-NC18785. |
| 42-53006 | UC-43G-BH Traveler | 1 | impressed Model C17B c/n 143 ex-NC17092. |
| 42-53007/53008 | UC-43D-BH Traveler | 2 | impressed Model E17B: 42-53007 c/n 197 ex-NC18588; 42-53008 c/n 411 ex-NC21900. |
| 42-53013 | UC-43D-BH Traveler | 1 | impressed Model E17B c/n 251 ex-NC19479. |
| 42-53021 | UC-43D-BH Traveler | 1 | impressed Model E17B c/n 155 ex-NC17069. |
| 42-53508/53509 | UC-43D-BH Traveler | 2 | impressed Model E17B: 42-53508 c/n 141 ex-NC16449; 42-53509 c/n 207 ex-NC18784. |
| 42-53510 | UC-45C-BH Expeditor | 1 | impressed Model B18S c/n 292 ex-NC20756. |
| 42-53511 | UC-43D-BH Traveler | 1 | impressed Model E17B c/n 231 ex-NC19467. |

| Serial No. | Type | Quantity | Remarks |
|---|---|---|---|
| 42-53516/53517 | UC-43D-BH Traveler | 2 | impressed Model E17B: 42-53516 c/n 159 ex-NC18557; 42-53517 c/n 205 ex-NC903. |
| 42-53522 | AT-7A-BH Navigator | 1 | |
| 42-56085 | UC-43B-BH Traveler | 1 | impressed Model D17S c/n 183 ex-NC18579. |
| 42-56087 | UC-43D-BH Traveler | 1 | impressed Model E17B c/n 140 ex-NC17085. |
| 42-56703/56784 | AT-7-BH Navigator | 82 | redesignated T-7-BH in 1948. |
| 42-56785 | UC-45D-BH Expeditor | 1 | converted AT-7-BH. |
| 42-56786/56851 | AT-7-BH Navigator | 66 | redesignated T-7-BH in 1948. |
| 42-56582 | C-45B-BH Expeditor | 1 | on AT-7-BH contract. |
| 42-61092/61093 | UC-43D-BH Traveler | 2 | impressed Model E17B: 42-61092 c/n 163 ex-NC2388; 42-61093 c/n 198 ex-NC18775. |
| 42-61097 | UC-43B-BH Traveler | 1 | impressed Model D17S c/n 216 ex-NC18791. |
| 42-68337 | UC-43C-BH Traveler | 1 | impressed Model F17D c/n 252 ex-NC19480. |
| 42-68339 | UC-43A-BH Traveler | 1 | impressed Model D17R c/n 137 ex-NC17082. |
| 42-68340 | UC-43B-BH Traveler | 1 | impressed Model D17S c/n 279 ex-NC20793. |
| 42-68359/68360 | UC-43D-BH Traveler | 2 | impressed Model E17B: 42-68359 c/n 144 ex-NC18025; 42-68360 c/n 154 ex-NC17066. |
| 42-68855 | UC-43G-BH Traveler | 1 | impressed Model C17B c/n 67 ex-NC15812. |
| 42-68856 | UC-43H-BH Traveler | 1 | impressed Model B17R c/n 53 ex-NC15414. |
| 42-78019 | UC-43H-BH Traveler | 1 | impressed Model B17R c/n 69 ex-NC15814. |
| 42-78039 | UC-43E-BH Traveler | 1 | impressed Model C17R c/n 76 ex-NC15834. |
| 42-88620 | UC-43G-BH Traveler | 1 | impressed Model C17B c/n 125 ex-NC17063. |
| 42-88628/88629 | UC-43G-BH Traveler | 2 | impressed Model C17B: 42-88628 c/n 99 ex-NC16440; 42-88629 c/n 102 ex-NC16443. |
| 42-88634 | UC-43G-BH Traveler | 1 | impressed Model C17B c/n 88 ex-NC15845. |
| 42-88636 | UC-43C-BH Traveler | 1 | impressed Model F17D c/n 283 ex-NC2626. |
| 42-94124 | UC-43D-BH Traveler | 1 | impressed Model E17B c/n 149 ex-NC18038. |
| 42-94133 | UC-43J-BH Traveler | 1 | impressed Model C17L c/n 105 ex-NC16446. |
| 42-94137 | UC-43H-BH Traveler | 1 | impressed Model B17R c/n 54 ex-NC15411. |
| 42-97048/97050 | UC-43C-BH Traveler | 3 | impressed Model F17D: 42-97048 c/n 338 ex-NC294Y; 42-97049 c/n 261 ex-NC291Y; 42-97050 c/n 392 ex-NC2801. |
| 42-97411 | UC-43C-BH Traveler | 1 | impressed Model F17D c/n 260 ex-NC19469. |
| 42-97413 | UC-43J-BH Traveler | 1 | impressed Model C17L c/n 83 ex-NC15813. |
| 42-97415 | UC-43G-BH Traveler | 1 | impressed Model C17B c/n 134 ex-NC17079. |
| 42-97417 | UC-43E-BH Traveler | 1 | impressed Model C17R c/n 116 ex-NC2000. |
| 42-97420 | UC-43J-BH Traveler | 1 | impressed Model C17B c/n 78 ex-NC15836. |
| 42-97424 | UC-43E-BH Traveler | 1 | impressed Model C17R c/n 117 ex-NC1600. |
| 42-97426/97428 | UC-43G-BH Traveler | 3 | impressed Model C17B: 42-97426 c/n 98 ex-NC16439; 42-97427 c/n 101 ex-NC16442; 42-97428 c/n 95 ex-NC16436. |
| 42-97431 | UC-43E-BH Traveler | 1 | impressed Model C17R c/n 80 ex-NC2166. |
| 42-107277 | UC-43K-BH Traveler | 1 | impressed Model D17W c/n 164 ex-NX18562. |
| 42-107411 | UC-43C-BH Traveler | 1 | impressed Model F17D c/n 332 ex-NC20797. |
| 42-107414 | UC-43C-BH Traveler | 1 | impressed Model F17D c/n 245 ex-NC19473. |
| 43-10318/10489 | AT-11-BH Kansan | 172 | conversions to AT-11A-BH; many rebuilt as C-45G/H; redesignated T-11-BH in 1948. |
| 43-10818/10892 | UC-43-BH Traveler | 75 | c/ns 4866/4940; 43-10870/10877, 10884/10887, 10874/10875 to UK as Traveller I with serials FZ428/435, FZ436/439 and FZ442/443. |
| 43-14406/14407 | XA-38-BH Grizzly | 2 | |
| 43-32765/33280 | AT-7-BH Navigator | 516 | redesignated T-7-BH in 1948; 7 delivered to Dutch AF. |
| 43-33281 | UC-45D-BH Expeditor | 1 | on AT-7-BH contract. |
| 43-33282/33285 | UC-45E-BH Expeditor | 4 | on AT-7B-BH contract. |
| 43-33286/33378 | AT-7-BH Navigator | 93 | redesignated T-7-BH in 1948; 21 delivered to Dutch AF. |
| 43-33379/33664 | AT-7C-BH Navigator | 286 | |
| 43-35446/35667 | C-45B-BH Expeditor | 222 | one aircraft transferred to US Navy: 43-35601 reserialled BuNo. 86294. |
| 43-35668/35945 | UC-45F-BH Expeditor | 278 | 20 aircraft transferred to US Navy as JRB-4 (43-35733, -35735/35737, 35739, 35773/35774, 35776, 35778, 35823/35824, 35826/35828, 35871/35872, 35874/35875 |

| Serial No. | Type | Quantity | Remarks |
|---|---|---|---|
| 43-35668/35945 *continued*: | UC-45F-BH Expeditor | | reserialled BuNo. 76760/76777; 43-35868 reserialled BuNo. 86293; 43-35867 reserialled BuNo. 86296); conversions to RC-45F-BH (43-35937). |
| 43-49963/50223 | AT-7C-BH Navigator | 261 | |
| 43-52226/52227 | AT-7C-BH Navigator | 2 | |
| 44-47049/47748 | UC-45F-BH Expeditor | 700 | transfers to US Navy as JRB-3 and JRB4; 25 aircraft converted to F-2B-BH: 44-47317/47318, 47363, 47393, 47435, 47449, 47457, 47465, 47473, 47481, 47489, 47497, 47513, 47529, 47545, 47561, 47577, 47593, 47609, 47661, 47706, 47715, 47729, 47742, 44747. |
| 44-67700/67804 | UC-43-BH Traveler | ·105 | ex-US Navy: 44-67700 ex-BuNo. 23657; 44-67701/67705 ex-BuNo. 23661/23665; 44-67706/67713 ex-BuNo. 23671/23678; 44-67715 ex-BuNo. 23680; 44-67717/67723 ex-BuNo. 23682/23688; 44-67765/67766 ex-BuNo. 23679 and 23681; 44-67767/67774 ex-BuNo. 23689/23696; 44-67800/67804 ex-BuNo. 23697/23701. Two aircraft transferred to US Navy: 44-47100/47101, reserialled BuNo. 76778/76779. |
| 44-72005/72026 | AT-11-BH Kansan | 22 | c/ns 3057/3066, 3069/3080, ex-RNEIAF aircraft. |
| 44-76029/76091 | UC-43-BH Traveler | 63 | to US Navy as GB-1. |
| 44-86898/87441 | UC-45F-BH Expeditor | 644 | 78 to US Navy as JRB-4 (4487304/87306, 87308, 87310/87315, 87351/87363, 87377/87385, 87388/87389, 87392/87406, 87409/87412, 87415/87434 and 87438/87441 reserialled BuNo. 66395/66471; 44-87137 reserialled BuNo. 86295); 17 aircraft converted to F-2B-BH: 44-86902, 86914, 86920, 86926, 86938, 86950, 86962, 86974, 86986, 86998, 87022, 87034, 87091, 87226, 87256, 87257 and 87341. |
| 50-735/737 | YT-34-BH Mentor | 3 | |
| 51-11444/11503 | C-45G-BH Expeditor | 60 | c/n AF-1/60; rebuilt RC-45A, C-45F, AT-7 and AT-11. |
| 51-11504/11599 | TC-45G-BH Expeditor | 86 | c/ns AF-61/156; rebuilt aircraft. |
| 51-11600/11911 | C-45G-BH Expeditor | 312 | c/ns AF-157/468; rebuilt RC-45A, C-45F, AT-7 and AT-11. |
| 52-1800/1803 | YL-23-BH Seminole | 4 | 52-1801 (c/n LH-9) later brought up to L-23A-BH standards. |
| 52-6162/6216 | L-23A-BH Seminole | 55 | c/ns LH-1/55; most rebuilt as L-23D-BH. |
| 52-7626/7685 | T-34A-BH Mentor | 60 | c/ns G-7/66. |
| 52-8253/8286 | T-34A-CCF Mentor | 34 | c/ns CCF34-26/59; built in Canada. |
| 52-10539/10970 | C-45H-BH Expeditor | 432 | c/ns AF-469/900; rebuilt aircraft; 52-10748 transferred to US Army. |
| 53-3306/3395 | T-34A-BH Mentor | 90 | c/ns G-67/156 |
| 53-4091/4156 | T-34A-CCF Mentor | 66 | c/ns CCF34-60/125; built in Canada. |
| 53-4157/4206 | T-34A-BH Mentor | 50 | c/ns G-257/306. |
| 53-6153/6192 | M-23B-BH Seminole | 40 | c/ns LH-56/95; most rebuilt as L-23D-BH; redesignated U-8D-BH in 1962. |
| 55-140/289 | T-34A-BH Mentor | 150 | c/ns G-697/846. |
| 55-3465 | XL-23C-BH Seminole | 1 | to U-8G-BH. |
| 56-3695/3718 | L-23D-BH Seminole | 24 | c/ns LH-96/119; redesignated U-8D-BH in 1962; 56-3712 converted to RU-8D-BH. 56-3710 to U-8G-LH c/n LHE-6. |
| 56-4039/4044 | L-23E-BH Seminole | 6 | redesignated U-8E-BH in 1962; 564039/4041 and 4044 converted to U-8G-BH; 56-4039 c/n DH-88; 564041 c/n DH-89; 56-4043 c/n DH-90; 564044 c/n DH-91. |
| 57-3084/3101 | L-23D-BH Seminole | 18 | c/ns LH-120/137; redesignated U-8D-BH in 1962; 57-3092 converted to U-8G-BH. |

| Serial No. | Type | Quantity | Remarks |
|---|---|---|---|
| 57-6029/6076 | L-23D-BH Seminole | 48 | c/ns RLH-1/48; rebuilt L-23As and L-23Bs; redesignated U-8D-BH in 1962; 576030, 6044, 6046, 6049, 6051, 6060, 6063 and 6075 converted to RU-8D-BH. |
| 57-6077/6094 | L-23D-BH Seminole | 18 | c/ns LH-138/155; redesignated U-8D-BH in 1962. |
| 58-1329/1353 | L-23D-BH Seminole | 25 | c/ns LH-156/180; redesignated U-8D-BH in 1962; 58-1331 and 1340 converted to RU-8D-BH. |
| 58-1354/1356 | L-23F-BH Seminole | 3 | c/ns L-3/5; redesignated U-8F-BH in 1962. |
| 58-1357/1364 | RL-23D-BH Seminole | 8 | c/ns LHC-3/10; redesignated RU-8D-BH in 1962; 58-1357, 1363 and 1364 converted to U-8G-BH; 58-1358/1360 and 1362 converted to RU-8D-BH; 58-1361 converted to NU-8D-BH. |
| 58-3048/3092 | L-23D-BH Seminole | 45 | c/ns RLH-49/93; rebuilt L-23As and L-23Bs; redesignated U-8D-BH in 1962; 58-3060 converted to RL-23D-BH; 58-3055, 3056, 3061 converted to U-8G-BH; 58-3050, 3058, 3059 and 3089 converted to RU-8D-BH. |
| 59-2535/2543 | RL-23D-BH Seminole | 90 | redesignated RU-8D-BH in 1962; 59-2536/2538 converted to U-8G-BH. 59-2535/2538 c/ns LH-192/195. |
| 59-4990/4992 | RL-23D-BH Seminole | 30 | redesignated RU-8D-BH in 1962; 59-4990 converted to U-8G-BH. |
| 60-3453/3470 | L-23F-BH Seminole | 18 | redesignated U-8F-BH in 1962; 60-3453/3463 c/ns LF-9/19. |
| 60-5386/5390 | L-23F-BH Seminole | 5 | c/ns LF-20/24; redesignated U-8F-BH in 1962. |
| 61-2426/2430 | L-23F-BH Seminole | 5 | c/ns LF-25/29; redesignated U-8F-BH in 1962. |
| 62-3832/3875 | L-23F-BH Seminole | 44 | c/ns LF-30/73; redesignated U-8F-BH in 1962. |
| 63-7975 | L-23F-BH Seminole | 1 | c/n LF-74; redesignated U-8F-BH in 1962. |
| 63-12902 | NU-8F-BH Seminole | 1 | c/n LG-1; rebuilt from U-8G-BH c/n LD-75. |
| 63-13636/13637 | L-23F-BH Seminole | 2 | c/ns LF-75 and 76; redesignated U-8F-BH in 1962. |
| 65-12679/12733 | T-42A-BH Cochise | 55 | c/ns TF-1/55. |
| 66-4300/4309 | T-42A-BH Cochise | 10 | c/ns TF-56/65. |
| 66-7943 | VC-6A-BH King Air | 1 | c/n LJ-91. |
| 66-15360/15361 | NU-8F-BH Seminole | 2 | |
| 66-15365 | U-8F-BH Seminole | 1 | c/n LF-8, to VU-8FX. |
| 66-18000/18048 | U-21A-BH King Air | 49 | c/ns LM-1/48; 66-18000, -18013, -18027 converted to EU-21A-BH; 66-18002 converted to JU-21A-BH. |
| 67-18049/18076 | U-21A-BH King Air | 28 | c/ns LM-49/77; 67-18057 converted to EU-21A-BH; 67-18065 converted to JU-21A-BH. |
| 67-18077 | RU-21A-BH King Air | 1 | c/n LS-1. |
| 67-18078/18084 | U-21A-BH King Air | 7 | c/ns LM-78/84. |
| 67-18085 | RU-21C-BH King Air | 1 | c/n LT-1. |
| 67-18086 | U-21A-BH King Air | 1 | c/n LM-85. |
| 67-18087 | RU-21B-BH King Air | 1 | c/n LS-2. |
| 67-18088 | U-21A-BH King Air | 1 | c/n LM-86. |
| 67-18089 | RU-21C-BH King Air | 1 | c/n LT-2. |
| 67-18090/18092 | U-21A-BH King Air | 3 | c/ns LM-87/89. |
| 67-18093 | RU-21B-BH King Air | 1 | c/n LS-3. |
| 67-18094/18128 | U-21A-BH King Air | 35 | c/ns LM-90/124; 67-18112/18115 converted to RU-21A-BH; 67-18104, 18106/18110, 18121 and 18124/18128 converted to RU-21D-BH; 67-18105, 18111 and 18119 converted to RU-21H-BH; 67-18125 converted to JTU-21D. |
| 68-10531/10536 | YQU-22A-BH | 6 | c/ns CED-1/6. |

| Serial No. | Type | Quantity | Remarks |
|---|---|---|---|
| 69-7693/7705 | QU-22B-BH | 13 | c/ns EB-1/13. |
| 70-1535/1548 | QU-22B-BH | 4 | c/ns EB-14/27. |
| 70-7859 | YAU-22A-BH | 1 | ex-N5847K. |
| 70-15875/15890 | RU-21D-BH King Air | 16 | c/ns LU-1/16; converted to RU-21E-BH; 70-15876, 15879/15881, 15883/15887 and 15889 converted to RU-21H-BH; 70-15877 and 15882 converted to U-21H-BH. |
| 70-15891/15907 | U-21A-BH King Air | 17 | c/ns LM-125/141; 70-15896, 15897 and 15901 converted to U-21G-BH; 70-15891, 15893/15895, 15898, 15899 and 15902/15904 converted to RU-21H-BH; 70-15892 converted to U-21H-BH. |
| 70-15908/15912 | U-21F-BH King Air | 5 | |
| 71-21053/21057 | T-42A-BH Cochise | 5 | c/ns TF-66/70; for Turkish Army. |
| 72-21058/21060 | RU-21J-BH King Air | 3 | c/ns BB-3/5. |
| 73-1205/1219 | C-12A-BH Huron | 15 | c/ns BD-1/15. |
| 73-21058/21060 | C-12L-BH Huron | 3 | |
| 73-22250/22269 | C-12A-BH Huron | 20 | 73-22250/22257 c/ns BC-1/8; 73-22258/22260 c/ns BC-9/20; conversions to C-12C-BH. |
| 75-0001/0016 | C-12A-BH Huron | 16 | |
| 76-0158/0173 | C-12A-BH Huron | 16 | 76-0158/0169 c/ns BD-15/26; 760170 c/n BD-30; 760171 c/n BD-28; 760172 c/n BD-29; 760173 c/n BD-27. |
| 76-3239 | C-12A-BH Huron | 1 | |
| 76-22545/22564 | C-12A-BH Huron | 20 | 76-22545/22557 c/ns BC-21/33; 76-22558/22564 c/ns BC-35/41; conversions to C-12C-BH. |
| 76-22951 | C-12A-BH Huron | 1 | c/n BC-34. |
| 77-22931/22950 | C-12A-BH Huron | 20 | c/ns BC-42/61; conversions to C-12C-BH |
| 78-23126/23139 | C-12C-BH Huron | 14 | c/ns BC-62/75. |
| 78-23140/23145 | RC-12D-BH Huron | 6 | c/ns BP-1/6; 78-23141/23145 renumbered with c/ns GR-6/10. |
| 80-23371/23380 | RC-12D-BH Huron | 10 | c/ns BP-12/21; 80-23371 c/n GR-2; 80-23372 c/n FC-3; 80-23373 c/n GR-4; 80-23374 c/n GR-12; 80-23375 c/n GR-5; 80-23376 c/n GR-11; 80-23377 c/n GR-3; 80-23378 c/n GR-13; 80-23379 c/n FC-1; and 80-23380 c/n FC-2. |
| 80-23525 | Queen Air 65 | 1 | |
| 81-23541/23546 | C-12D-BH Huron | 6 | c/ns BP-22/27; 81-23542 converted to RC-12D with c/n GR-1. |
| 81-23638/23642 | RC-12D-BH Huron | 5 | c/ns BP-7/11; to Israel. |
| 81-23658 | Queen Air 65 | 1 | |
| 82-23659 | Queen Air 65 | 1 | |
| 82-23781/23785 | C-12D-BH Huron | 5 | c/ns BP-28/32. |
| 82-24029 | Queen Air 65 | 1 | |
| 82-24054 | Queen Air 65 | 1 | |
| 82-24370 | Queen Air 65 | 1 | |
| 83-0494/0499 | C-12D-BH Huron | 6 | c/ns BP-40/45. |
| 83-1286/1310 | MQM-107B | 25 | |
| 83-24128 | Baron B55 | 1 | |
| 83-24145/24150 | C-12D-BH Huron | 6 | c/ns BP-34/39. |
| 83-24188 | Queen Air 65 | 1 | |
| 83-24313/24318 | RC-12D-BH Huron | 6 | c/ns GR-14/19. |
| 84-0143/0182 | C-12F-BH Huron | 40 | c/ns BL-73/112. |

| Serial No. | Type | Quantity | Remarks |
|---|---|---|---|
| 84-0484/0489 | C-12F-BH Huron | 6 | |
| 84-0495/0539 | MQM-107 | 45 | |
| 84-24320 | Queen Air 65 | 1 | |
| 84-24377/24380 | C-12F-BH Huron | 4 | c/ns BP-48/51. |
| 85-0147/0155 | RC-12K-BH Huron | 9 | c/ns FE-1/5. |
| 85-0261/0296 | MQM-107 | 36 | |
| 85-1261/1272 | C-12F-BH Huron | 12 | c/ns BP-52/63. |
| 85-1800/1807 | MQM-107 | 8 | |
| 85-23525 | Queen Air 65 | 1 | |
| 85-24370 | Queen Air 65 | 1 | |
| 85-24373/24374 | Queen Air 65 | 2 | |
| 85-25349 | Queen Air 65 | 1 | to N51694. |
| 86-0078/0083 | C-12J-BH Huron | 6 | c/ns UD-1/6. |
| 86-0084/0089 | C-12F-BH Huron | 6 | c/ns BP-64/69. |
| 86-0092 | King Air 90 | 1 | |
| 86-1683 | King Air 90 | 1 | |
| 87-0142 | Queen Air 65 | 1 | |
| 87-0160/0161 | C-12F-BH Huron | 2 | c/ns BP-70/71. |
| 88-0325/0327 | RC-12K-BH Huron | 3 | |
| 90-0400/0413 | T-1A Jayhawk | 14 | c/ns TT-3, TT-7/9, TT-6, TT-4, TT-11, TT-10, TT-12/15, TT-2 and TT-16 respectively. |
| 91-0075/0102 | T-1A Jayhawk | 28 | c/ns TT-18, TT-17, TT-1 and TT-19/43 respectively. |
| 92-0330/0363 | T-1A Jayhawk | 34 | c/ns TT-44/77. |
| 93-0626/0640 | T-1A Jayhawk | 15 | c/ns TT-83/97. |

# Appendix VIII

# Bureau of Aeronautics Numbers of US Navy Aircraft Designed by Beechcraft

## Second serial series (Nos. 0001/7303)

| BuNos. | Type | Quantity | Remarks |
|---|---|---|---|
| 0801 | JB-1 Traveler | 1 | impressed Model C-17R c/n 115 |
| 1589/1595 | GB-1 Traveler | 7 | |
| 1898/1900 | GB-1 Traveler | 3 | |
| 2543/2547 | JRB-1 Expeditor | 5 | |
| 4709/4710 | JRB-1 Expeditor | 2 | |
| 4711/4725 | JRB-2 Expeditor | 15 | 4711/4716, 4718/4721 and 4725 converted to SNB-5; redesignated TC-45J/UC-45J in 1962. |
| 4726/4729 | JRB-1 Expeditor | 4 | |

## Third serial series (from No.0001)

| BuNos. | Type | Quantity | Remarks |
|---|---|---|---|
| 01624/01646 | GB-2 Traveler | 23 | 0645 transferred to USAAF; 6 delivered to Brazil. |
| 03553/03562 | SNB-2 Navigator | 10 | 03554/03555 converted to SNB-2P; 03554, 03555, 03557, 03558 and 03561 converted to SNB-5; redesignated TC-45J/UC-45J in 1962. |
| 09765 | GB-2 Traveler | 1 | impressed Model D17S c/n 400 ex-NC20755. |
| 09766 | GB-1 Traveler | 1 | impressed Model D17S c/n 421 ex-NC21933. |
| 09771 | JRB-2 Expeditor | 1 | impressed Model 18 ex-NC1040; remanufactured to RC-45J. |
| 09772 | GB-1 Traveler | 1 | impressed Model D17S c/n 401 ex-NC21917. |
| 09773 | GB-2 Traveler | 1 | impressed Model D17S c/n 407 ex-NC21920. |
| 09774 | GB-2 Traveler | 1 | impressed Model D17S c/n 398 ex-NC20779. |
| 09776/09778 | GB-1 Traveler | 3 | impressed Model D17W and D17S: 09776 c/n 136 ex-NC17081; 09777 c/n 165 ex-NC18563; 09778 c/n 168 ex-NC18566. |
| 09780 | GB-1 Traveler | 1 | impressed Model D17S c/n 185 ex-NC18581. |
| 09800 | GB-1 Traveler | 1 | impressed Model D17. |
| 12330/12353 | GB-2 Traveler | 24 | 12348/12353 to USAAF as UC-43-BH and supplied to China. |
| 12354/12389 | SNB-2 Navigator | 36 | some delivered as SNB-2C; others modified to SNB-2D/AH and 2P. 12355/12364, 12366/12367, 12370/12372, 12374, 12376/12379, 12381/12383, 12386, 12388/12389 remanufactured in 1951 to SNB-5/5P; redesignated TC-45J/UC-45J in 1962. 12354, 12373, 12375 and 12385 remanufactured to RC-45J. 12375 and 12385 transferred to USAAF. |
| 23657/23756 | GB-2 Traveler | 100 | 37 to USAAF as UC-43-BH: 23657, 23661/23665 and 23671/23678 to 44-67700/67713; 23679 to 44-67765; 23680 to 44-67715; 23681 to 44-67766; 23682/23688 to 44-67717/67723; 23689/23696 to 44-67767/67774; 23697/23701 to 44-67800/67804. |
| 23757/23856 | SNB-2C Navigator | 100 | 23759/23763, 23768, 23770, 23772/23774, 23776, 23779, 23783, 23786, 23788, 23790/23791, 23795, 23797/23798, 23800, 23802, 23804, 23806, 23811, 23815/23816, 23818/23825, 23827/23829, 23831, 23833/23837, 23839/23847, 23849, 23851/23854 and 23856 remanufactured in 1951 to SNB-5/5P; redesignated TC-45J/UC-45J in 1962. 23789, 23793, 23801 and 23813 remanufactured to RC-45J; |

| BuNos. | Type | Quantity | Remarks |
|---|---|---|---|
| 23757/23856 *continued*: | SNB-2C Navigator | | 23783 to USAAF as VC-45J; 23822 to USAAF as C-45J; 23829 to USAAF as NC-45J. |
| 29551/29668 | SNB-2/2C/3/3N Navigator | 118 | 29665/29668 cancelled and reassigned. 29551, 29553/29559, 29561, 29564/29565, 29568/29572, 29575/29576, 29578/29579, 29581/29582, 29584, 29587/29588, 29590/29595, 29597, 29599, 29602/29603, 29608/29609, 29613, 29617, 29619/29623, 29625/29627, 29629/29633, 29635/29642, 29644, 29646/29652, 29655, 29657, 29659/29664 remanufactured in 1951 to SNB-5/5P; redesignated TC-45J/UC-45J in 1962. 29566, 29580, 29583, 29585, 29604, 29618 and 29645 remanufactured to RC-45J. |
| 32867/32936 | GB-2 Traveler | 70 | first 49 allotted to Return Lend-Lease aircraft from UK; remaining 21 cancelled. |
| 32992/33066 | GB-2 Traveler | 75 | 12 supplied to Brazil: 33044/33045, 33052/33053, 33055/33057 and 33061/33065. |
| 39192/39291 | SNB-2 Navigator | 100 | 39195, 39197, 39202, 39205/39206, 39208, 39212/39213, 39219, 39224/39230, 39232/39233, 39235, 39237, 39239/39241, 39243/39257, 39260, 39262/39267, 39269, 39272/39278, 39280/39282, 39284, 39286/39287, 39289/39290 remanufactured in 1951 to SNB-5/5P; redesignated TC-45J/UC-45J in 1962. 39196, 39203, 39210, 39217, 39231, 39234 and 39258 remanufactured to RC-45J. |
| 39749/39998 | SNB-1 Kansan | 250 | 39749/39750, 39752, 39754, 39758/39762, 39765, 39767/39768, 39772/39773, 39775/39778, 39782, 39788/39789, 39793, 39797, 39799, 39801, 39803/39804, 39806/39807, 39810, 39812/39813, 39815/39816, 39822, 39827, 39829, 39838, 39840/39842, 39847, 39850/39851, 39853/39854, 39856, 39862/39863, 39865/39867, 39869/39870, 39875, 39877, 39881/39883, 39885/39887, 39889, 39898/39899, 39902, 39904, 39906, 39908/39910, 39915/39916, 39920, 39922/39923, 39927/39928, 39930/39931, 39934/39939, 39941/39943, 39945, 39947/39948, 39951, 39956, 39958/39959, 39961, 39963, 39965/39966, 39968/39970, 39973, 39976/39977, 39980, 39982/39983, 39988, 39990 and 39994 remanufactured in 1951 to SNB-5/5P; redesignated TC-45J/UC-45J in 1962. 39763, 39769, 39771, 39779/39781, 39783, 39787, 39795/39796, 39814, 39817, 39820, 39823, 39830, 39832/39833, 39845/39846, 39852, 39857/39859, 39871, 39879, 39884, 39901, 39903, 39921, 39932, 39940, 39952/39953, 39962, 39964, 39974, 39976, 39985/39987, 39991/39993, 39995/39997 remanufactured to JRB-6. |
| 44315 | JRB-4 Expeditor | 1 | ex-USAAF UC-45F-BH 44-47103. |
| 44555/44684 | JRB-4 Expeditor | 130 | ex-USAAF UC-45F-BH. 44564, 44605 and 44633 to USCG. 44555, 44560, 44566, 44576, 44578/44581, 44583, 44588/44589, 44605, 44607, 44610, 44617, 44624, 44655, 44658, 44662 and 44677 remanufactured in 1951 to SNB-5/5P; redesignated TC-45J/UC-45J in 1962. |
| 44685/44704 | JRB-4 Expeditor | 20 | cancelled. |
| 48243/48251 | JRB-4 Expeditor | 6 | 48246/48251: ex-USAAF UC-45F-BH; 48247 remanufactured in 1951 to SNB-5; some modified to JRB-6 standard. |
| 51023/51094 | SNB-1 Kansan | 72 | 51026/51029, 51031/51032, 51034, 51036, 51038/51039, 51041, 51045/51047, 51053/51057, 51061, 51064/51066, 51068/51079, 51081, 51083/51086, 51089/51092 and 51094 remanufactured in 1951 to SNB-5/5P; redesignated TC-45J/UC-45J in 1962. 51035, 51037, 51048, 51060, 51067, 51080 and 51082 remanufactured to JRB-6. |
| 51095/51199 | SNB-2C Navigator | 105 | 51096, 51098, 51100/51101, 51104/51105, 51107/51110, 51112, 51114/51122, 51124/51126, 51128, 51130/51132, 51135, 51137/51141, 51143/51152, 51154/51158, |

| BuNos. | Type | Quantity | Remarks |
|---|---|---|---|
| 51095/51199 *continued*: | SNB-2C Navigator | | 51160/51161, 51163/51173, 51176, 51178, 51180/51183, 51185/51189, 51191/51192, 51194/51198 remanufactured to SNB-5/5P; redesignated TC-45J/UC-45J in 1962. 51129 and 51190 remanufactured to RC-45J. |
| 51200/51293 | SNB-2 Navigator | 94 | 51200/51201, 51204, 51206/51211, 51213, 51216, 51219/51220, 51224/51226, 51228/51230, 51232, 51235/51236, 51238/51242, 51244/51249, 51253/51257, 51259/51263, 51268, 51270/51275, 51277/51281, 51284/51285, 51287/51291 and 51293 remanufactured to SNB-5/5P; redesignated TC-45J/UC-45J in 1962. 51214, 51218, 51233, 51251, 51267 and 51269 remanufactured to RC-45J. 51288 to USAAF. 51269 to USCG. |
| 51294/51349 | SNB-2C Navigator | 56 | 51294/51300, 51302/51303, 51307/51308, 51311/51312, 51314/51315, 51317/51319, 51323, 51327, 51330, 51333/51335, 51338/51339, 51342/51345 and 51349 remanufactured to TC-45J/UC-45J in 1962. 51329 remanufactured to RC-45J. 51312 to USAAF as C-45J. |
| 66395/66594 | JRB-4 Expeditor | 200 | last 123 cancelled (66472/66594); remaining 77 diverted from USAAF C-45F-BH contracts as follows: 66395/66397: ex-44-87304/87306; 66398: ex-44-87308; 66399/66404: ex-44-87310/87315; 66405/66417: ex-44-87351/87363; 66418/66426: ex-44-87377/87385; 66427/66428: ex-44-87388/87389; 66429/66443: ex-44-87392/87406; 66444/66447: ex-44-87409/87412; 66448/66467: ex-44-87415/87434; 66468/66471: ex-44-87438/87441. 66429, 66431, 66443, 66448, 66464 and 66470 remanufactured to SNB-5/5P; redesignated TC-45J/UC-45J in 1962. 66459 remanufactured to RC-45J. 66440 and 66469 to USCG. |
| 66472/66594 | JRB-4 Expeditor | 123 | cancelled. |
| 67100/67383 | SNB-2 Navigator | 284 | 67130/67154 cancelled. 67103, 67105, 67107, 67111/67112, 67114/67120, 67122/67123, 67126, 67128/67129, 67158/67159, 67161/67163, 67165/67168, 67170, 67174/67177, 67179, 67181/67185, 67187/67188, 67190/67191, 67193/67194, 67197/67198, 67200/67214, 67218/67224, 67227/67228, 67230, 67234/67236, 67256, 67261/67263, 67265, 67267/67269, 67271, 67274/67275, 67277/67281, 67285, 67287/67288, 67293/67294, 67296/67298, 67300, 67302/67303, 67305, 67311/67314, 67316/67317, 67319/67326, 67329, 67335, 67337, 67344/67347, 67349, 67355, 67361, 67363, 67382/67383 remanufactured to SNB-5/5P; redesignated TC-45J/UC-45J in 1962. 67108, 67124, 67127, 67217, 67232 and 67233 remanufactured to RC-45J. 67248, 67276, 67282/67284, 67286, 67328, 67332/67336, 67338/67340, 67343, 67348, 67350, 67352, 67357/67358, 67360, 67366, 67374, 67376, 67378/67381 remanufactured to JRB-6. |
| 76740/76759 | JRB-3 Expeditor | 20 | transferred USAAF UC-45B-BH. 76740/76742, 76745/76746, 76750, 76753, 76755/76758 remanufactured to SNB-5/5P; redesignated TC-45J/UC-45J in 1962. |
| 76760/76779 | JRB-4 Expeditor | 20 | diverted from USAAF UC-45F-BH contracts as follows: 76760 ex-43-35733; 76761/76763 ex-43-35735/35737; 76764 ex-43-35739; 76765/76766 ex-43-35773/35774; 76767/76768 ex-43-35776/35777; 76769/76770 ex-43-35823/35824; 76771/76773 ex-43-35826/35828; 76774/76775 ex-43-35871/35872; 76776/76777 ex-43-35874/35875; 76778/76779 ex-44-47100/47101; 76762, 76764/76765, 76771, 76773/76774 and 76776 remanufactured to SNB-5/5P; redesignated TC-45J/UC-45J in 1962. |
| 84032 | JRB-3 Expeditor | 1 | transferred USAAF C-45B-BH. |

| BuNos. | Type | Quantity | Remarks |
|---|---|---|---|
| 85096/85135 | JRB-4 Expeditor | 40 | transferred USAAF UC-45F-BH. 85100, 85106, 85110, 85115, 85121 and 85135 remanufactured to SNB-5/5P; redesignated TC-45J/UC-45J in 1962. |
| 85391/85458 | GB-2 Traveler | 68 | contract cancelled. |
| 86293 | JRB-4 Expeditor | 1 | ex-USAAF C-45F-BH 43-35868. |
| 86294 | JRB-3 Expeditor | 1 | ex-USAAF C-45B-BH 43-35601. |
| 86295/86296 | JRB-4 Expeditor | 2 | ex-USAAF C-45F-BH 44-87137 and 43-35867. |
| 87752 | JRB-3 Expeditor | 1 | ex-USAAF C-45B-BH. |
| 87753 | JRB-4 Expeditor | 1 | ex-USAAF C-45F-BH. |
| 89466/89494 | SNB-5 Navigator | 29 | reassigned BuNos. allotted to ex-USAAF C-45s transferred post-war to US Navy. 89466/89471, 89473/89475, 89477/89479, 89481/89485, 89487/89488, 89491, 89493/89494 remanufactured to SNB-5/5P; redesignated TC-45J/UC-45J in 1962. |
| 90522/90523 | JRB-2 Expeditor | 2 | presumably ex-USAAF transfers. 90522, 90536, 90549, 90569, 90574 and 90581 remanufactured to SNB-5/5P; redesignated TC-45J/UC-45J in 1962. |
| 90532/90581 | JRB-4 Expeditor | 50 | ex-USAAF C-45F-BH. 90564 and 90580 to USCG. |
| 134004 | JRB-4 Expeditor | 1 | reassigned BuNo. |
| 134692/134697 | SNB-5 Navigator | 6 | supplied under MDAP to Netherlands Navy as 21-41 to 21-46 (later reserialled 080/085). |
| 134698/134717 | SNB-5 Navigator | 20 | supplied under MDAP to French navy. |
| 140667/140956 | T-34B Mentor | 290 | c/ns BG-1/290. |
| 140987/140992 | SNB-5 Navigator | 6 | transferred from USAAF; redesignated TC-45J in 1962, later UC-45J. |
| 143984/144116 | T-34B Mentor | 133 | c/ns BG-291/423. |
| 147543/147547 | T-34 Mentor | 5 | supplied under MAP. |
| 147548 | E-18S Expeditor | 1 | supplied under MAP. |
| 160265/160282 | T-34C Turbo Mentor | 18 | 160266 converted to NT-34C. |
| 160462/160536 | T-34C Turbo Mentor | 75 | 160482 to NASA. |
| 160629/160651 | T-34C Turbo Mentor | 223 | |
| 160839/160856 | T-44A King Air | 18 | |
| 160931/160963 | T-34C Turbo Mentor | 33 | |
| 160967/160986 | T-44A King Air | 20 | |
| 161023/161056 | T-34C Turbo Mentor | 34 | |
| 161057/161079 | T-44A King Air | 23 | |
| 161185/161206 | UC-12B | 22 | |
| 161306/161327 | UC-12B | 22 | |
| 161497/161518 | UC-12B | 22 | |
| 161627 | U-8F | 1 | |
| 161790/161849 | T-34C Turbo Mentor | 60 | |
| 162247/162306 | T-34C Turbo Mentor | 60 | |
| 162620/162649 | T-34C Turbo Mentor | 30 | |
| 163553/163562 | UC-12F | 10 | |
| 163836/163847 | UC-12M | 12 | |
| 163563/163564 | UC-12F | 2 | |
| 164155/164173 | T-34C Turbo Mentor | 19 | |
| 164579/164583 | T-44B King Air | 5 | |

# Appendix IX

# Serial Numbers of British Commonwealth Military Aircraft Designed by Beechcraft

| Serial | Type | Quantity | Remarks |
|---|---|---|---|
| DR628 | Model C17R | 1 | c/n 295, ex-39-139, allotted for personal use of Prince Bernhardt; returned to USAAF circa July 1945. |
| DS180 | Model C17R | 1 | c/n 118, ex G-AESJ, impressed in May 1941; struck off charge 7 January 1944. |
| EB279/280 | Model C17 | 2 | EB280 ex-NC21094, sold 3.11.43 and reverted to NC21094. |
| FL653/670 | Traveller I | 18 | ex-USAAF 42-38674/38691, delivered from March 1943 to Middle East (Suez).<br>FL653: Aden Communication Flight, struck off charge 25.7.46;<br>FL654: No.205 Group Communication Flight, struck off charge 26.9.46;<br>FL655: No.210 Group Communication Flight, sold 6.12.46;<br>FL656: No.8 squadron; struck off charge 26.4.45;<br>FL657: to Middle East; sold 22.11.46;<br>FL658: No.205 Group Communication Flight, ditched at Bari 25.7.45;<br>FL659/670: lost at sea in ss *Agurmonte* on 10.6.43, en route to Middle East. |
| FR879/883 | Navigator | 5 | FR879: BOAC; returned to US 31.12.45;<br>FR880: BOAC; used by Netherlands Government and numbered PB-2 (Prince Bernhardt No.2);<br>FR881/882: to India;<br>FR883: to Middle East. |
| FR940/948 | Expeditor I | 9 | all to No.32 OTU in Canada. |
| FT461/535 | Traveller I | 75 | ex-US Navy GB-2s and USAAF UC-43s; all to Royal Navy. |
| FT975/979 | Expeditor I | 5 | all to Royal Navy. |
| FT980/996 | Expeditor II | 17 | all to Royal Navy. |
| FZ428/439 | Traveller I | 12 | ex-USAAF 43-10870/10877; delivered from October 1944:<br>FZ428: Aden Communication Flight, forced landing 4.4.45;<br>FZ429: crashed in the US before delivery;<br>FZ430: to Middle East, sold 23.9.46;<br>FZ431: to Middle East, sold 22.11.46;<br>FZ432: to Middle East, sold 22.11.46;<br>FZ433: No.201 Group Communication Flight, sold 22.11.46;<br>FZ434: to Middle East, struck off charge 21.6.45;<br>FZ435: to Middle East, sold 22.11.46;<br>FZ436: Communication Flight Lydda, belly-landed 10.5.45;<br>FZ437: to Middle East, struck off charge 27.3.47;<br>FZ438: Aircraft Delivery Flight; wrecked at Wilhelma on 9.10.44;<br>FZ439: Aden Communication Flight, sold 22.11.46. |
| HB100/206 | Expeditor I | 107 | 6 converted to Mk.III for RCAF (HB127, HB131, HB146, HB148, HB151 and HB189); 26 returned to the US in 1946. |
| HB207/299 | Expeditor II | 93 | 9 converted to Mk.III for RCAF (HB207, HB213, HB215, HB219, HB228, HB232, HB237, HB238 and HB269); 42 returned to the US in 1946. |
| HB759 | Expeditor | 1 | delivered to Admiralty. |
| HD752/776 | Expeditor II | 25 | main deliveries to Royal Navy. |
| KJ468/560 | Expeditor II | 93 | deliveries to Middle East. |
| KN100/149 | Expeditor II | 50 | deliveries to India for the RAF (February to July 1945). |
| KP100/124 | Expeditor II | 25 | to FAA communications. |

# Appendix X
# NACA/NASA Aircraft

| Type | Registration | c/n | s/n | From | Until | Remarks |
|---|---|---|---|---|---|---|
| Model F17D | NC20780<br>NACA 150 | 339 | | 6.6.40 | 12.6.40 | Acquired from factory at Wichita for vibration testing at Langley. |
| Model D17S | NC19494<br>NACA 151 | 264 | | 17.6.40 | 20.6.40 | Owned by Texaco Oil Company. Used for vibration tests. |
| UC-45 Expeditor | ? | ? | 44-47264 | 9.3.45 | 8.1.54 | Utility and programme support, Langley. |
| UC-45 Expeditor | NACA 105 | ? | 44-47110 | 11.1.46 | 5.47 | Utility and programme support. Transferred from Langley to NACA Muroc High Speed Research station. |
| EUC-45F Expeditor | NACA 125 | ? | 43-35906 | 22.8.49 | 18.3.59 | Used at Langley for gust alleviation research. Nose modified to a point with a test boom installed. |
| C-45F Expeditor | NACA 106 | ? | 44-47106 | 24.3.55 | 17.3.59 | Utility and programme support at Langley. |
| C-45H Expeditor | N650NA<br>NASA 650 | AF-534 | 51-11534 | 28.5.72 | 9.10.79 | R&D/Environmental at Marshall. Acquired from Marshal Space Flight Center (7.76). Utility and programme support at Wallops. Disposed to MASDC. |
| C-45H Expeditor | N6NA<br>NASA 6 | AF-817 | 52-10887 | 17.10.60 | 04.82 | ex-N925Z. Administrative and utility at JPL, Pasadena, California. Had the No.3 Volpar Tri-gear conversion. Transferred to Kennedy Space Center, Florida, (5.66) for R&D and programme support. |
| AT-11 Kansan | ? | ? | ? | 7.47 | 8.47 | At Langley. No further information. |
| AT-11 Kansan | ? | ? | 42-37209 | 7.2.47 | 2.9.47 | Utility and programme support at Ames. |
| AT-11 Kansan | NACA 119 | ? | 42-36941 | 1.46 | 7.53 | Utility and R&D at Lewis Research Center. Development of icing and cloud measurement instrumentation. |
| Bonanza B35 | N5094C | ? | – | 24.8.50 | 28.11.50 | Evaluation of butterfly tail, Langley. |
| Bonanza A36 | N440SU | E-1115 | – | circa 79 | | Test of winglets on small aircraft, Langley. |
| T-34B Mentor | N614NA<br>NASA 614 | BG-329 | 144022 | 18.1.89 | current | R&D at Lewis for Educational Service Experiments. |
| T-34C Mentor | N510NA<br>NASA 510 | GL-108 | 160482 | 1.6.78 | current | R&D and photo chase at Langley. |
| Sundowner C23 | N504NA<br>NASA 504 | M-1608 | – | 14.1.75 | 23.2.90 | ex-N6624R. R&D at Langley for spins in light aircraft and GAW-2 aerofoils. |
| Duke 60 | ? | ? | – | circa 76 | ? | R&D sponsored by JPL for hydrogen enrichment engine tests at Beech factory. |
| Queen Air 65-80 | N9NA<br>NASA 9 | LD-49 | – | 29.5.65 | 3.11.82 | Administrative and utility at Marshall Space Flight Center. |
| Queen Air 65-80 | N7NA<br>NASA 7 | LD-77 | – | 1.7.65 | 19.1.82 | Administrative and utility at JPL. |
| Queen Air 65-80 | N8NA<br>NASA 8 | LD-79 | – | 3.68 | 10.10.81 | Administrative and utility at JPL. Transferred to Wallops Flight Facility, Virginia (8.7.68). |
| Queen Air 65-80 | N506NA<br>NASA 506 | LD-507 | – | 1.6.77 | current | ex-N1530L. Utility and programme support at Langley. |
| Super King Air 200 | N8NA<br>NASA 8 | BB-950 | – | 10.10.81 | current | Administrative aircraft for Wallops. Replaced Queen Air. |

| Type | Registration | c/n | s/n | From | Until | Remarks |
|---|---|---|---|---|---|---|
| Super King Air 200 | N7NA<br>NASA 7 | BB-997 | – | 19.1.82 | current | Administrative and utility aircraft at JPL. Replaced Queen Air. |
| Super King Air 200 | N9NA<br>NASA 9 | BB-1092 | - | 03.10.82 | current | Administrative and utility aircraft at Marshall. Replaced Queen Air. |
| Super King Air 200 | N701NA<br>NASA 701 | BB-1164 | – | 5.8.83 | current | Utility and programme support at Ames. |

# US Coast Guards Beech Model 18s

| BuNos. | Type | Remarks |
|---|---|---|
| 44564 | JRB-4 Expeditor | sold 26.3.59 (total time 4,579.2 hours) |
| 44605 | JRB-4 Expeditor | Coast Guard Reserve |
| 44633 | JRB-4 Expeditor | sold 26.3.59 (total time 4,567 hours), to N5552A |
| 51269 | SNB-2P Navigator | |
| 66440 | JRB-4 Expeditor | sold 26.3.59 (total time 4,499.5 hours), to N6569D |
| 66469 | JRB-4 Expeditor | |
| 90564 | JRB-4 Expeditor | stationed at Elizabeth City (NC) |
| 90580 | JRB-4 Expeditor | sold 26.3.59 (total time 3,520 hours) |

# FAA Beech Model 18s

| Registration | Type | c/n | Registration | Type | c/n | Registration | Type | c/n |
|---|---|---|---|---|---|---|---|---|
| N4 | C-45H | AF-701 | N73 | C18S | 6273 | N132 | C-45H | AF-799 |
| N7 | C-45H | AF-626 | N78 | C18S | ? | N134 | C-45H | AF-480 |
| N20 | C18S | 4185 | N81 | C-45H | AF-725 | N135 | C-45H | AF-755 |
| N51 | C18S | ? | N86 | C18S | 5666 | N136 | C-45H | AF-666 |
| N59 | C18S | 6799 | N91 | C18S | 6947 | N137 | C-45H | AF-779 |
| N60 | C18S | ? | N93 | C18S | ? | N138 | C-45H | AF-777 |
| N62 | C18S | ? | N95 | C18S | 6029 | N140 | C-45H | AF-700 |
| N63 | C18S | ? | N104 | C18S | 6273 | N141 | C-45H | AF-478 |
| N68 | C18S | 4321 | N116 | C18S | ? | | | |
| N72 | C18S | 5668 | N131 | C-45H | AF-703 | | | |

# Abbreviations and Acronyms

ABS Air Base Squadron
ADF Automatic Direction Finder
AFB Air Force Base
AFIS Automatic Flight-Inspection System
AFRES Air Force Reserve
AirDet Air Detachment
ANG Air National Guard
AOA Angle of Attack
ARNG Army National Guard
ASE Aircraft Survivability-Equipment
AUW All-Up Weight
AvCo Aviation Company
BAD Base Air Detachment
BASI Beech Aerospace Service Inc
CAA Civil Aviation Authority
CADAM Computer Assisted Design and Manufacturing
CAR Civil Aviation Regulations
CATIA Computer Aided Three-Dimensional Inter-active Application
CavReg Cavalry Regiment
CG Centre of Gravity
COIN Counter-Insurgency
conv/ind Converter/indicator
CRT Cathodic-Ray Tube
DARPA Defense Advanced Research Projects Agency
DF Direction Finder
DME Distance Measuring Equipment
DoD Department of Defence
EFIS Electronic Flight Instrumentation System
FAA Federal Aviation Administration Agency
FAC Forward Air Control
FAF Fly Away Factory
FAI Fédération Aéronautique Internationale
FAR Federal Aviation Regulations
FAR Part 23 Defines airworthiness of private aircraft up to 12,500lb (5,670kg)
FAR Part 25 Defines airworthiness of private aircraft exceeding 12,500lb (5,670kg)
FBO Fixed Based Operations
FTW Flight Training Wing
FY Fiscal Year (1 July to 30 June)
GINA General Inspector of Naval Aircraft
GSE Ground Support Equipment
HAST High Altitude Supersonic Target
HF High Frequency
IFR Instrument Flight Rules
ILS Instrument Landing System
InfDiv Infantry Division
ITT Interstage Turbine Temperature
JASDF Japan Air Self-Defence Force
JATO Jet-Assisted Take-Off
JCAB Japan Civil Airworthiness Board
JGSDF Japan Ground Self-Defence Force
JMSDF Japanese Maritime Self-Defence Force
JPATS Joint Primary Aircraft Training System
LOC Localiser
LRPTS Long Range Pilot Training School
MAAG Military Assistance Advisory Group
MAC Military Airlift Command
MAG Military Airlift Group
MAP Military Assistance Program
MAS Military Airlift Squadron
MAW Military Air Wing
MIB Military Intelligence Battalion
MTOW Maximum Take-Off Weight
NACA National Advisory Com-mittee for Aeronautics
NAF Naval Aircraft Factory
NAS Naval Air Station
NASA National Aeronautics and Space Administration
NAT National Air Transport
NATC Naval Air Training Command
Navairdet Naval Air Detachment
nav/com navigation/communication
NBAA US National Business Aircraft Association
NRAB Naval Reserve Air Base
OMI Omni-bearing Magnetic Indicator
OPEVAL Operational Evaluation
OSA Operational Support Aircraft
POC Proof of Concept
RANSAC Range Surveillance Aircraft
RCAF Royal Canadian Air Forces
R&D Research & Development
RPV Remotely Piloted Vehicle
SAR Search and Rescue
SFAR Special Federal Aviation Regulations
SFERMA Société Française d'Entretien et de Réparation de Matériel Aéronautique
SLAR Side-Looking Airborne Radar
STARC State Area Command
STOL Short Take-Off and Landing
TAC Tactical Air Command
TACAN Tactical Air Navigation
TAS True Air Speed
TEDS Tactical Expendable Drone System
TRADOC Training and Doctrine Command
TTTS Tanker Transport Training System
UACL United Aircraft of Canada Ltd
UHF Ultra High Frequency
UNACE Universal Aircraft Com/nav Evaluation
USAAC United States Army Air Corps
USAAF United States Army Air Forces
USAF United States Air Force
USCG United States Coast Guards
USMC United States Marine Corps
USMTM US Military Training Mission
USN United States Navy
VHF Very High Frequency
VOR VHF Omni-directional Range
VSTT Variable-Speed Training Target

# Index of Aircraft Types

Page numbers in italics refer to illustrations only.

# Index of People

Page numbers in italics refer to illustrations only.